Chaucer

Blackwell Guides to Criticism
Editor Michael O'Neill

'I very much like the way this general approach to the specific volumes has been formulated. The *Critical Heritage* volumes were so good, so useful. But I think your idea to thicken the editorial commentary is important.' JEROME J. McGANN.

The aim of this new series is to provide undergraduates pursuing literary studies with collections of key critical work from an historical perspective. At the same time emphasis is placed upon recent and current work. In general, historic responses of importance are described and represented by short excerpts in an introductory narrative chapter. Thereafter landmark pieces and cutting edge contemporary work are extracted or provided in their entirety according to their potential value to the student. Each volume seeks to enhance enjoyment of literature and to widen the individual student's critical repertoire. Critical approaches are treated as 'tools', rather than articles of faith, to enhance the pursuit of reading and study. At a time when critical bibliographies seem to swell by the hour and library holdings to wither year by year, Blackwell's *Guides to Criticism* series offers students privileged access to and careful guidance through those writings that have most conditioned the historic current of discussion and debate as it now informs contemporary scholarship.

Forthcoming volumes

Roger Dalrymple:	*Middle English*
Uttara Natarajan:	*Romantic Poetry*
John Niles:	*Anglo-Saxon*
Francis O'Gorman:	*The Victorian Novel*
Michael O'Neill:	*Twentieth-century British and Irish Poetry*
Gareth Reeves:	*American Poetry from Whitman to the Present*
Emma Smith:	*Shakespeare's Comedies*
Emma Smith:	*Shakespeare's Histories*
Emma Smith:	*Shakespeare's Tragedies*
Michael Whitworth:	*Modernism*

Chaucer

Edited by Corinne Saunders

BLACKWELL
Publishers

Copyright © Blackwell Publishers Ltd 2001
Editorial matter, selection and arrangement copyright © Corinne Saunders 2001

First published 2001

2 4 6 8 10 9 7 5 3 1

Blackwell Publishers Ltd
108 Cowley Road
Oxford OX4 1JF
UK

Blackwell Publishers Inc.
350 Main Street
Malden, Massachusetts 02148
USA

All rights reserved. Except for the quotation of short passages for the purposes of criticism and review, no part of this publication may be reproduced, stored in a retrieval system, or transmitted, in any form or by any means, electronic, mechanical, photocopying, recording or otherwise, without the prior permission of the publisher.

Except in the United States of America, this book is sold subject to the condition that it shall not, by way of trade or otherwise, be lent, resold, hired out, or otherwise circulated without the publisher's prior consent in any form of binding or cover other than that in which it is published and without a similar condition including this condition being imposed on the subsequent purchaser.

British Library Cataloguing in Publication Data

A CIP catalogue record for this book is available from the British Library.

Library of Congress Cataloging-in-Publication Data

Chaucer / edited by Corinne Saunders.
    p. cm.—(Blackwell guides to criticism)
  Includes bibliographical references (p.) and index.
  ISBN 0–631–21711–8 (alk. paper)—ISBN 0–631–21712–6 (pb.: alk. paper)
  1. Chaucer, Geoffrey, d. 1400—Criticism and interpretation—Handbooks, manuals, etc.
  I. Saunders, Corinne J., 1963–II. Series.

PR1924 .C37 2001
821'.1–dc21

2001025673

Typeset in 10 on 12.5 pt ACaslon
by Kolam Information Services Pvt. Ltd, Pondicherry, India
Printed in Great Britain by TJ International, Padstow, Cornwall
This book is printed on acid-free paper

Contents

Preface		viii
Acknowledgements		x
Introduction		1
1	**The Development of Chaucer Criticism**	**5**
2	**Chaucer's Reading and Audience: Critical Extracts**	**22**
	The English and European Literary Traditions *Derek Brewer*	22
	Chaucer: The Teller and the Tale *Gabriel Josipovici*	32
	The Audience *Paul Strohm*	43
3	**Dream Vision Poetry: An Overview**	**57**
4	**Dream Vision Poetry: Critical Extracts**	**68**
	The Lady White and the White Tablet: *The Book of the Duchess* *Judith Ferster*	68
	'The Dido Episode' in *The House of Fame* *Wolfgang Clemen*	76
	Chaucer's Fame and Her World: The Poem *Piero Boitani*	83
	Park of Paradise and Garden of Love *J. A. W. Bennett*	96

Contents

	The Parliament of Fowls A. C. Spearing	101
	The Narrator as Translator Donald W. Rowe	115
	Chaucer's Classical Legendary Lisa J. Kiser	121
5	*Troilus and Criseyde*: An Overview	**129**
6	*Troilus and Criseyde*: Critical Extracts	**139**
	The Ending of 'Troilus' E. Talbot Donaldson	139
	The Heart and the Chain John Leyerle	150
	Criseyde: Woman in Medieval Society David Aers	161
	Coda: The Narrator C. David Benson	171
	History versus Romance Lee Patterson	177
7	The *Canterbury Tales*: An Overview	**189**
8	The *Canterbury Tales*: Critical Extracts	**201**
	The Unity of the *Canterbury Tales* Robert M. Jordan	201
	The Esthetics of this Form Donald R. Howard	212
	An Encyclopedia of Kinds Helen Cooper	218
	The Knight's Tale and Its Settings V. A. Kolve	239
	Fabliau, Confession, Satire W. A. Davenport	250
	Gems of Chastity Ian Bishop	269
	Anti-feminism Jill Mann	283

The Franklin's Tale *Angela Jane Weisl*	299
'Glose/Bele chose': The Wife of Bath and Her Glossators Eunuch Hermeneutics *Carolyn Dinshaw*	307
Epilogue	325
Bibliography	327
Index	350

Preface

This volume, the first in the series, offers a critical introduction to the most influential of medieval English writers, Geoffrey Chaucer. Chaucer's work, brilliant in its own right, has played a formative role in the history of English literature, and has attracted a vast, sometimes bewildering, range of scholarship. This study combines consideration of Chaucer's writing with an examination of the development of Chaucer criticism: various critical perspectives are represented through a series of extracts from some of the most influential and thought-provoking scholarship on Chaucer. Chapter 1 summarizes Chaucer's life and works, and traces the history of Chaucer criticism, with particular emphasis on the formative period of the early twentieth century; in chapter 2, critical extracts consider Chaucer's reading and readership. Chapters 3–8 focus on the main divisions of Chaucer's writing: the dream vision poetry, *Troilus and Criseyde*, and the *Canterbury Tales*. Overviews are provided of the main themes of the works in question, followed by discussion of the critical approaches to them. These are then selectively exemplified by a series of critical extracts, preceded by discussion. Glosses (indicated by asterisks in the verse) are given for those less familiar with Middle English; these are largely based on the *Riverside Chaucer*, essential for any reader. Other explanatory notes are given in square brackets in the text. Brief bibliographical details are offered in the text; full information will be found in the bibliography, along with further reading and details of audio and electronic material. This kind of study cannot but be highly selective, and I regret the necessity of excluding so much excellent and interesting criticism. I hope that the book will serve as a *point de repère* for the study of Chaucer and as a way into the polyphony of voices surrounding one of the greatest of all English writers.

My first debt is to Chaucer and his critics, who have provided a constant intellectual stimulus and pleasure. I owe many thanks to Blackwell Publishers,

Preface

in particular to Andrew McNeillie for inviting me to write this first volume in the series, and for his enthusiasm for the project, as well as to Alison Dunnett for her care and patience in seeing the book through its various stages, Jack Messenger for his careful copy-editing, and Leanda Shrimpton for her picture research. My General Editor, Michael O'Neill, could not have been more encouraging and helpful. I am very grateful to the University of Durham for a Research Award that released me from teaching, funded my research in other libraries, and defrayed the photography costs, and for the support of my colleagues in the Department of English Studies.

A particular debt is owed to David Fuller for his consistent interest in and willingness to discuss Chaucer, and his careful reading of all parts of the book, which owes much to his thoughtful comments and sharp eye. Thanks are due as well to Tom Craik, for his excellent proofreading, and to Helen Cooper, with whom I have had so many valuable discussions of Chaucer and related topics, and whose work could not provide a better exemplar. I am most grateful, too, for the constant encouragement of my parents and friends.

Acknowledgements

The editor and publisher gratefully acknowledge the following for permission to reproduce copyright material:

David Aers, from 'Criseyde: Woman in Medieval Society', *Chaucer Review* 13 (1978–9), 177–200, reproduced by permission; J. A. W. Bennett, 'Park of Paradise and Garden of Love' in *'The Parlement of Foules': An Interpretation*, Clarendon Press, 1957, reproduced by permission; C. David Benson, 'Coda: The Narrator' from 'Character' in *Chaucer's Troilus and Criseyde*, Routledge (Allen and Unwin), 1990; Ian Bishop, 'Gems of Chastity' in *The Narrative Art of the 'Canterbury Tales': A Critical Study of the Major Poems*, Dent, 1988, used by permission; Piero Boitani, 'Chaucer's Fame and Her World: The Poem' in *Chaucer and the Imaginary World of Fame*, Chaucer Studies 10, 1984, by permission of Boydell and Brewer Ltd; Derek Brewer, 'The English and European Literary Traditions' in *A New Introduction to Chaucer*, 2nd edn, Longman, 1998, reproduced by permission; Wolfgang Clemen, '"The Dido Episode," in *The House of Fame*' in *Chaucer's Early Poetry*, trans. C. A. M. Sym, Routledge (Methuen), 1963; Helen Cooper, 'An Encyclopedia of Kinds' in *The Structure of the 'Canterbury Tales'*, Duckworth, 1983, reproduced by permission; W. A. Davenport, '*Fabliau*, Confession, Satire' in *Chaucer and His English Contemporaries: Prologue and Tale in 'The Canterbury Tales'*, Macmillan, 1998, reproduced by permission; Carolyn Dinshaw, from '"Glose/Bele chose": The Wife of Bath and Her Glossators' and 'Eunuch Hermeneutics' in *Chaucer's Sexual Poetics*, University of Wisconsin Press, 1989, reproduced by permission; E. Talbot Donaldson, from 'The Ending of "Troilus"' in *Speaking of Chaucer*, Athlone Press, 1970, reproduced by permission; Judith Ferster, 'The Lady White and the White Tablet: *The Book of the Duchess*' in *Chaucer on Interpretation*, Cambridge University Press, 1985, used by permission; Donald R. Howard, 'The Esthetics of this Form' from 'Memory and Form' in *The Idea of the 'Canterbury Tales'*, University of California Press, Berkeley, copyright ©

Acknowledgements

1976 the Regents of the University of California; Robert M. Jordan, from 'The Unity of the *Canterbury Tales*' in *Chaucer and the Shape of Creation: The Aesthetic Possibilities of Inorganic Structure*, Harvard University Press, Cambridge, MA, 1967, by permission of the author; Gabriel Josipovici, from 'Chaucer: The Teller and the Tale' in *The World and the Book: A Study of Modern Fiction*, 2nd edn, Macmillan 1979, by permission of Macmillan Ltd; Lisa J. Kiser, from 'Chaucer's Classical Legendary' in *Telling Classical Tales: Chaucer and the 'Legend of Good Women'*, copyright © 1983 by Cornell University Press, used by permission of the publisher, Cornell University Press; V. A. Kolve, from 'The Knight's Tale and Its Settings' in *Chaucer and the Imagery of Narrative: The First Five Canterbury Tales*, by permission of Stanford University Press; John Leyerle, from 'The Heart and the Chain' in Larry D. Benson, ed., *The Learned and the Lewed*, Harvard English Studies 5 (1974), 113–45, used by permission; Jill Mann, from 'Anti-feminism' in *Geoffrey Chaucer*, Harvester Wheatsheaf, 1991, reproduced by permission; Lee Patterson, 'History versus Romance' from 'Troilus and Criseyde and the Subject of History' in *Chaucer and the Subject of History*, Routledge, 1991, reproduced by permission; Donald W. Rowe, 'The Narrator as Translator' in *Through Nature to Eternity: Chaucer's 'Legend of Good Women'*, University of Nebraska Press, 1988, reproduced by permission; A. C. Spearing, 'The Parliament of Fowls' in *Medieval Dream Poetry*, Cambridge University Press, 1976; Paul Strohm, from 'The Audience' in *Social Chaucer*, Harvard University Press, 1989, reproduced by permission; Angela Jane Weisl, from 'The Franklin's Tale' in 'Public Authority and Private Power' in *Conquering the Reign of Femeny: Gender and Genre in Chaucer's Romance*, D. S. Brewer, 1995, by permission of Boydell and Brewer Ltd.

The publishers apologize for any errors or omissions in the above list and would be grateful to be notified of any corrections that should be incorporated in the next edition or reprint of this book.

Introduction

The writings of Geoffrey Chaucer more than most, medieval or modern, create a vibrant and memorable sense of authorial voice. The unfamiliarity of medieval language and thought does not negate its extraordinary vividness and dramatic quality: the *Miller's Tale* retains its comedy, *Troilus and Criseyde* its high tragedy. In his time, Chaucer was viewed as one of the great 'makars', in whose footsteps writers such as Lydgate, Henryson and Dunbar followed, and later, Shakespeare and Spenser. Although only a few medieval references to Chaucer are known, these celebrate his poetry: the French courtly poet Deschamps refers to him as 'grant translateur, noble Geffroy Chaucier' ('Ballade to Chaucer,' *c*. 1386); his English contemporary John Gower writes of England as full of his songs of love, 'of ditees and of songes glade' (*Confessio Amantis* VIII, *c*. 1390); and his friend Thomas Usk styles him 'the noble philosophical poete in Englissh' (*Testament of Love* III, *c*. 1387).[1] His popularity is attested too by the evidence for swift and wide circulation of his writing: there remain some fifty manuscripts of his complete works, a very large number for this period. Chaucer's poetry is full of mocking yet self-conscious references to the fame that he was evidently gaining as a poet, in particular of love, but also as a translator and philosopher. To these labels could be added comedian and tragedian, moral writer and satirist, lyric and narrative poet, rhetorician and voice of experience, idealist and realist, master of all styles. This polyvalent quality underlies Chaucer's enduring fame: his writing, perhaps more than that of any other writer except Shakespeare, can signify in dramatically different ways to different individuals and cultures. It is as if the centuries have produced one Chaucer after another according to the *Zeitgeist* of each particular age.

Whereas many of the writers of the medieval period were anonymous, Chaucer was not only known by name but also shaped a clear literary identity for himself. This strong sense of the Chaucerian voice has played a significant

Introduction

role in the shaping of Chaucer's fame and, indeed, in the focus of Chaucerian criticism. The celebrated quality of Chaucerian irony is often rooted in the gap between the voice of the narrator – detached, self-deprecating, bookish and naive – and the story he tells. In the *Book of the Duchess* and the *Parliament of Fowls* he presents himself as a disappointed lover; in *Troilus and Criseyde* his stance is that of the servant of lovers, not daring to be one himself; in the *House of Fame* the plump and bookish 'Geoffroi', when he is caught up in the claws of the giant eagle which offers to teach him the secrets of the universe, insists that he prefers to read about them instead. In the *Canterbury Tales* Chaucer the pilgrim is a naively trusting observer figure, whose

Plate 1 Chaucer, from *The Ellesmere Chaucer*. The Art Archive/Victoria and Albert Museum, London.

contributions to the story-telling competition leave much to be desired – his first attempt, the tale of *Sir Thopas*, is so doggerel-like that he is eventually cut off by the Host, 'Namoore of this', 'Thy drasty rymyng is nat worth a toord'; his second, the *Tale of Melabye*, is an immensely long, prose moral treatise.[2]

These vignettes of the failed story-teller cannot but have amused those who knew the real Geoffrey Chaucer, a widely read scholar, courtier and diplomat leading a sophisticated, public life. Born in the early 1340s, Chaucer belonged to a new upper-middle class: his father was a successful vintner in London, who had served as deputy chief butler to Edward III; the young Chaucer probably attended a grammar school in London, and his writings reflect a knowledge not only of Latin literature, but also of history, theology, natural philosophy, astrology and law. His public career began in the noble household of Elizabeth, Countess of Ulster (1357), in whose employ he travelled and served in the military campaign in France (1359–60), when he was captured and ransomed. Chaucer's links with the court were both public and personal: in 1366 he married a knight's daughter and lady-in-waiting, Philippa de Roet, whose sister was to become the third wife of one of the king's sons, John of Gaunt; the next year, Chaucer became a member of the royal household of Edward III. As one of perhaps forty men in the king's service, his duties would have ranged from household tasks to diplomatic missions, and his numerous journeys to the Continent provided access to the literatures that were to be so formative in his writing. While Chaucer's early dream vision poems, particularly *The Book of the Duchess* (1368–72), reflect the influence of French poetry, and he translated part of *Le Roman de la Rose* before 1372, the later dream vision poems, *The House of Fame* (1378–80), *The Parliament of Fowls* (1380–2) and *The Legend of Good Women* (1380–7), draw on Italian writing, in particular the poetry of Dante, Petrarch and Boccaccio: *Troilus and Criseyde* (1382–6) translates Boccaccio's *Il Filostrato* (*c.* 1335).[3]

In 1374 Chaucer was given the important public office of comptroller of the customhouse, and made responsible for the collection of an export tax and other taxes. His diplomatic missions also continued. Eventually he left London for Kent, where he was made a justice of the peace and member of parliament; he then became clerk of the king's works, responsible for the construction and repair of all the royal residences and the king's holdings; finally he became overseer of the royal forest in Somerset. It was during this later period that he undertook the *Canterbury Tales* (*c.* 1387 onwards). Chaucer's numerous appointments suggest his rare success as diplomat and civil servant in a turbulent political world; his friend Thomas Usk, by contrast, was beheaded for treason. A royal protection issued for Chaucer describes him as 'our beloved esquire going about divers parts of England on the king's arduous and pressing business' (1398).[4] Despite our considerable knowledge of Chaucer's life, however, there are many gaps, such as the mysterious record of his

Introduction

release from *raptus*, a charge that can mean either rape or abduction, by one Cecily Chaumpaigne: the record is connected with other legal accusations brought against Chaucer by two London citizens, so may well have been part of a financial dispute of some sort. Chaucer appears to have had two sons, 'little Lewis,' to whom his *Treatise of the Astrolabe* (*c.* 1391) is dedicated, but about whom we know nothing, and Thomas, who like his father led a highly successful public life, and one of whose daughters married the powerful Duke of Suffolk. For the Middle Ages, Chaucer's life was relatively long: his tomb records the date of his death as 25 October 1400. In the last year of his life Chaucer had leased a house in the parish of Westminster Abbey, and thus was buried there – the beginning of Poets' Corner.

Notes

1 For these and other early references (up to 1930), see J. A. Burrow's anthology, *Geoffrey Chaucer: A Critical Anthology* (Penguin, Harmondsworth, 1969). This chapter is generally indebted to Burrow's invaluable collection. See also Caroline F. E. Spurgeon's three volumes, *Five Hundred Years of Chaucer Criticism and Allusion, 1537–1900* (Russell and Russell, New York, 1960, [1914–22]) and Derek S. Brewer, *Chaucer: The Critical Heritage* (Routledge, London, 1978).
2 Geoffrey Chaucer, *The Canterbury Tales* in *The Riverside Chaucer*, 3rd edn, ed. Larry D. Benson (Oxford University Press, Oxford, 1988 [1987] lines 919, 930. All subsequent references to Chaucer's works will be from this edition and cited by line number.
3 In general, Chaucer's works cannot be dated precisely, and there has been much debate about chronology; these are the approximate dates adopted in *The Riverside Chaucer*, the notes of which include full discussion.
4 Quoted in *The Riverside Chaucer*, xxi; documents pertaining to Chaucer's life may be found in Martin M. Crow and Clair C. Olson, *Chaucer Life-Records* (Clarendon Press, Oxford, 1966).

1

The Development of Chaucer Criticism

In Chaucer's own age, as references that term him 'translator' suggest, he was viewed as the inheritor of a great tradition as well as the inventor of a new one, and his writing makes clear his desire to follow in the footsteps of the great ancient writers, in particular Ovid and Virgil. It is only with Chaucer and his contemporaries that English becomes a sophisticated literary language, and it is striking that Chaucer consistently places himself in the context of classical writers, referring to them as his authorities even when they are filtered through Continental writers. In subsequent centuries, however, Chaucer came to be seen instead as the great innovator, the 'father of English literature'.

In the period immediately following his death, he was most commonly viewed as a skilled courtly poet: he would be seen as inspiring a line of courtly poets down to Wyatt. It was often his 'eloquence' that was praised, but also his learning. Thomas Hoccleve's lament for Chaucer in his *Regement of Princes* (1412), for example, refers to Chaucer as 'flour of eloquence' but also 'universel fadir in science', renowned for his 'excellent prudence' and 'philosophie' to rival Aristotle: for Hoccleve, Chaucer follows in the footsteps of Virgil. Lydgate, also writing in the early fifteenth century, similarly praises 'excellence / In rethorike and in eloquence' and 'sentence', but refers as well to the variety and humour of Chaucer's writing. A little later, Dunbar admires him as 'rose of rethoris all' (*The Golden Targe*, 1503), and Caxton, who printed the *Canterbury Tales* (Proem, 1484), places him as 'laureate poete' because he has 'by hys labour enbelysshyd, ornated and made faire our Englisshe'. Gavin Douglas, referring to Chaucer's defence of Dido in his translation of the *Aeneid* (Prologue, 1513), offers a description that critics return to again and again: 'he was evir (God wait) all womanis frend.' These views of Chaucer as great learned poet and 'rhetor', father of English literature, are sustained across the sixteenth century: Sir Brian Tuke, in the preface to William Thynne's

1532 edition, again refers to Chaucer's 'excellent learning in all kinds of doctrines and sciences' and his 'fruitfulness in words'; Gabriel Harvey praises him for his treatise on the astrolabe (*c*.1574); George Puttenham places him 'as the most renowned of them all' for his translation, wit and metre in the 'first age' of English writing, which was to be followed by a second 'company of courtly makers', Wyatt and Surrey (*The Art of English Poesy* I, 1589). Spenser's *Faerie Queene* (1596) emulates the 'heroick' language of 'Dan Chaucer, well of English undefyled' (IV, ii), and Francis Beaumont defends him from 'incivility' (1597), praising his art of description and his eloquence.[1]

In the course of the seventeenth century, however, doubts arise regarding Chaucer's status, as his language becomes less familiar and new learning replaces that of the Middle Ages. Edward Phillips, like Beaumont, places Chaucer as, despite his 'uncouth' terms, 'by some few admired for his real worth' (1675); Addison, however, describes him as 'a merry bard,' but one with whom 'age has rusted what the poet writ, / Worn out his language and obscur'd his wit' (1694). Dryden in his *Fables* (1700) translates a collection of the *Canterbury Tales* – avoiding the profane ones. In his preface he particularly admires Chaucer's realism:

> He must have been a man of a most wonderful comprehensive nature, because, as it has been truly observed of him, he has taken into the compass of his *Canterbury Tales* the various manners and humours (as we now call them) of the whole English nation, in his age. Not a single character has escaped him. All his pilgrims are severally distinguished from each other; and not only in their inclinations, but in their very physiognomies and persons.... there is such a variety of game springing up before me, that I am distracted in my choice, and know not which to follow. 'Tis sufficient to say according to the proverb, that here is God's plenty. We have our forefathers and great-grand-dames all before us, as they were in Chaucer's days; their general characters are still remaining in mankind, and even in England, though they are called by other names than those of Monks, and Friars, and Canons, and Lady Abbesses, and Nuns; for mankind is ever the same, and nothing lost out of Nature, though everything is altered.[2]

Dryden compares him favourably to Ovid, 'Chaucer writ with more simplicity, and followed Nature more closely', and praises too his 'philosophy and philology', his description and translation; he places Chaucer as 'the father of English poetry', but remarks, however, that because of his imperfect metre, 'though he must always be thought a great poet, he is no longer esteemed a good writer.' For Dryden, Chaucer is defensible because he writes 'in the infancy of our poetry', and his work needs to be revived in modern English, in order to be understood – but also to be perfected.

The Development of Chaucer Criticism

Eighteenth-century views reflect both Dryden's praise and his concerns: Pope (1730) praises Chaucer as 'master of manners and of description' in the art of tale-telling, and also offers a translation; Johnson (*Dictionary*, 1755) criticizes Dryden for excessive praise of 'the illustrious Geoffrey Chaucer', but also those who censure Chaucer excessively for adding 'whole cartloads of foreign words'. Chaucer's realism and ability to inspire emotion, in particular to convey a sense of the pathetic, were singled out by late eighteenth-century writers such as Richard Hurd, Thomas Warton and Joseph Warton.

One of the most memorable Romantic considerations of Chaucer is that of William Blake, who discusses at length the Canterbury pilgrims in the context of his own painting of the subject (*A Descriptive Catalogue*, 1809). Blake explores the significances of the characters, who come to represent 'the eternall Principles that exist in all ages':

> The characters of Chaucer's Pilgrims are the characters which compose all ages and nations: as one age falls, another rises, different to mortal sight, but to immortals only the same; for we see the same characters repeated again and again, in animals, vegetables, minerals, and in men; nothing new occurs in identical existence; Accident ever varies, Substance can never suffer change nor decay.
>
> Of Chaucer's characters, as described in his *Canterbury Tales*, some of the names or titles are altered by time, but the characters themselves for ever remain unaltered, and consequently they are the physiognomies or lineaments of universal human life, beyond which Nature never steps. Names alter, things never alter.[3]

For example, the Pardoner, like the Summoner, represents the Devil, who plays a crucial role in the shaping of man's destiny: 'This man is sent in every age for a rod and scourge, and for a blight, for a trial of men, to divide the classes of men; he is in the most holy sanctuary, and he is suffered by Providence for wise ends, and has also his great use, and his grand leading destiny.' Blake places Chaucer as 'the great poetical observer of men, who in every age is born to record and eternize its acts.'

In the nineteenth century, realism and the power to inspire sentiment were seen as Chaucer's great qualities: Crabbe (*Tales*, preface, 1812) writes of Chaucer's 'powerful appeals to the heart and affections'; Hazlitt (*Lectures on the English Poets*, 1818) of the 'severe activity of mind' that leads to Chaucer's reality of sentiment, particularly pathos; Coleridge (1834) of 'How exquisitely tender he is' – and how knowable by contrast to Shakespeare; Leigh Hunt of how his images are 'copied from the life' (1844). Englishness was crucial to understandings of Chaucer: for Ruskin (*Lectures on Art*, 1870), Chaucer's was 'the most perfect type of a true English mind in its best possible temper',

7

The Development of Chaucer Criticism

combining beauty, jest and the danger of degenerate humour! Arnold ('The Study of Poetry,' 1880) offered a learned discussion of Chaucer in terms of his French and Italian, and placed him as 'a genuine source of joy and strength, which is flowing still for us and will flow always'; he admired his humanity, his plenty, his 'truth of substance' and especially his fluidity. For Arnold, praise of Chaucer needed to be qualified: 'he lacks the high seriousness of the great classics, and therewith an important part of their virtue', yet 'He has poetic truth of substance, though he has not high poetic seriousness, and corresponding to his truth of substance he has an exquisite virtue of style and manner. With him is born our real poetry.'[4]

By the early twentieth century, then, a collection of critical commonplaces about Chaucer had been established. Notions of Chaucer as rhetorician and learned philosopher had largely been displaced by notions of Chaucer as realist, master of pathos, comic writer. Difficulties of supposed unevenness of language and metre, and bawdiness, were viewed with more and less emphasis as the flaws in Chaucer's writing. What was sustained from his own time and even through the more critical Augustan period, when his metre was deprecated, was the strong sense of Chaucer as father of English poetry. Criticism emphasized his timelessness, his continued appeal, his humanism, his realism – although there was also a new sense that the medieval period had been one of great artistic sophistication and poetic innovation. For W. P. Ker, who wrote a celebrated study of the medieval genres of epic and romance (1896), Chaucer's writing, far from being rooted in a dark Middle Ages, demonstrated many of the qualities later associated with the Renaissance, but retained too an extraordinary immediacy:

> The art of Chaucer has nothing to fear by comparison with anything in modern fiction, and, over and above the strength of what one may call its prose imagination, it is also poetry.
> Chaucer has come down with both feet on the real world.
> What has this to do with the Renaissance?[5]

Alongside the development of Chaucer criticism, a more technical emphasis was maintained in Chaucer studies. Early admiration of Chaucer's writing was accompanied by an antiquarian and scholarly interest in editing and publishing his collected works, culminating in the collected edition of William Thynne (1532), which included various Middle English texts not in fact written by Chaucer. Although this was often reprinted, sometimes with additions, no new edition based on the manuscripts appeared until John Urry's in 1721, which included many 'corrections'; this was followed by the more reliable edition of Thomas Tyrwhitt (1775–8).[6] The obscurity of Chaucer's writing by the Romantic period led to translations of his work by a series of

English writers: Wordsworth, Leigh Hunt and Elizabeth Barrett Browning. A revived interest in the nineteenth century in antiquarianism, philology, the origins of the English language and early English writing, however, inspired great new scholarly projects, in particular the Oxford English Dictionary (first volume, 1884) and the Early English Text Society (1864), responsible for the editing and publication of early works. It was natural that scholars should also turn to the writings of Chaucer, to invest them with a new authority. Work on editing continued, while a number of essential strands of international Chaucer scholarship were established: E. G. Sandras produced a critical study of Chaucer's sources (1859), the American Francis J. Child completed a consideration of Chaucer's language (1862), and the German Bernhard ten Brink published a study of authorship and date in Chaucer's works (1865). Alongside these initiatives, F. J. Furnivall had founded a Chaucer Society 'to do honour to Chaucer and let lovers and students of him see how far the best unprinted manuscripts of his works differ from the printed texts';[7] Furnivall undertook a new, six-text edition of the *Canterbury Tales* (first volume, 1867) and the Society published the Chaucer manuscripts.[8] From this point on, a good deal of attention was devoted to questions of editing and authorship – the establishment of the 'Chaucer canon'. Further manuscript studies led to Walter W. Skeat's six-volume scholarly edition (1894–7), which removed apocryphal texts, and his study *The Chaucer Canon* (1900). J. M. Manly and Edith Rickert published a vast, eight-volume edition of the *Canterbury Tales* (1940), which collated all known manuscripts, around ninety in total; R. K. Root studied the manuscripts of *Troilus and Criseyde* to produce a similarly detailed edition (1914). Such scholarship was the basis for F. N. Robinson's standard edition (1933, revised 1957), and L. D. Benson's revision of this in *The Riverside Chaucer* (1987), the current student edition, which draws on a range of new technical and critical work. Manuscript studies continue, with the gradual publication of a *Variorum Chaucer* (first volume, 1979) and hypertext editions that take advantage of new computer technology.

Alongside the editing of Chaucer, related and influential studies of the dating of his works and the order of the *Canterbury Tales* appeared, as did works on his language and versification.[9] Current criticism often takes for granted aspects such as Chaucer's romance vocabulary, first examined by Joseph Mersand, who gives a highly technical analysis, yet writes memorably of Chaucer's poetry, 'Chaucer was a Merlin of language. In his poetry he has locked up beauties of sound, of sense, and of rhythm which seem incapable of disenchantment at the hands of misguided modernizers and over-zealous text-emenders';[10] his views would be echoed, for instance, by A. E. Housman, who compared Dryden's translation negatively with Chaucer's own language (*The Name and Nature of Poetry*, 1933). Chaucer's stylistics, language structure, usage, versification and prosody remained for some time central critical issues, as in the work of Ruth Crosby and Dorothy Everett. The biographical trend continued in various directions, perhaps most importantly in Martin Crow and Clair C. Olson's collection of the *Chaucer Life-Records* (1966), and studies of Chaucer's times, such as those of Edith Rickert, Roger Sherman Loomis and Maurice Hussey. Scholars took special account of Chaucer's own learning and medieval learning more generally, and this has been an interest sustained in contemporary cultural studies.[11] Source studies have also played a crucial role in Chaucer criticism, although interest has shifted from attempting to trace the origin of popular stories, for example, by looking at Eastern analogues, to analysing Chaucer's use of more direct sources and analogues: Chaucer critics rely on works such as W. F. Bryan and Germaine Dempster's *Sources and Analogues of Chaucer's 'Canterbury Tales'* (1958).

What kind of literary criticism accompanied these ground-breaking historical studies? It was certainly not the case that Chaucer was seen exclusively in historical terms, although criticism often drew on contemporaneous literary and historical archeology. But as well, early criticism relied on and developed the Victorian admiration for Chaucer's realism and humanism. At the end of the nineteenth century Thomas R. Lounsbury's three-volume study (1892) developed the notion of Chaucer as father of English literature and hence as essential to the study of English. For Lounsbury, Chaucer was second only to Shakespeare, and he praised in particular the 'transcendent' quality of his poetry: 'he brought a lightness, a grace, a delicacy of fancy, a refined sportiveness even upon the most unrefined themes'; 'There is no other English author so absolutely free, not merely from effort, but from the remotest suggestion of effort'.[12] Early twentieth-century critics like G. L. Kittredge and his near-contemporary J. M. Manly pursued this notion of a new ease and injection of life in English writing, placing particular emphasis on how Chaucer learned to move away from medieval literary conventions into a new mode of realism. In a famous series of lectures on Chaucer, Kittredge explores in detail the ways such realism is effected, developing the notion of the *Canterbury Tales* as 'roadside drama': 'The Canterbury Pilgrimage is ... a Human Comedy, and the Knight and the Miller and the Pardoner and the Wife of Bath and the rest are the *dramatis personae*'.[13] He urges the need to explore the tales in this context:

> The story of any pilgrim may be affected or determined, – in its contents, or in the manner of the telling, or in both, – not only by his character in general, but also by the circumstances, by the situation, by his momentary relations to the others in the company, or even by something in a tale that has come before.[14]

Kittredge vividly imagines the pilgrims, their lives and relations, linking them to Chaucer's life and world, and to other literary texts. He is, however, best known now for his analysis of the 'marriage group' of *Canterbury Tales*, in which he argues that the tales treating marriage function as a dialogue between their narrators. The Wife of Bath's lively defence of female sexuality and power is redressed by the Clerk's sober and doctrinal tale of the patient wife Griselda; the Merchant's mock-romance is an embittered reflection on his own unhappy marriage; and the Franklin's tale is Chaucer's own response, an elegant, sincere depiction of honourable and equal marriage: 'the whole debate has been brought to a satisfactory conclusion, and the Marriage Act of the Human Comedy ends with the conclusion of the Franklin's Tale.'[15] Kittredge's emphasis on realism and dramatic interplay is often now seen as naive and limited, yet his animated discussion retains relevance, for it is informed both by an easy and perceptive familiarity with English literature, and an enduring engagement with Chaucer as a great English writer. As well, the identification of a central thematic pattern in the tales was to inspire and underpin an enormous amount of critical writing on the issues of love, marriage and gender.

Kittredge was by no means alone in his views: Virginia Woolf, in *The Common Reader* (1925), had described Chaucer as 'little given to abstract contemplation'; 'Chaucer fixed his eyes upon the road before him' – though she remarks too his questioning mind, and places his moral perspective as that of the novel rather than poetry. The editor J. M. Manly similarly admired most the realism of the tales, the move away from 'the thin prettiness of the *Book of the Duchess*' to 'methods of composition based upon close observation of life and the exercise of the creative imagination', which he attributed to the stimulating effect of Italian literature (*Chaucer and the Rhetoricians*, 1926). For G. K. Chesterton, Chaucer was a 'great humorist', 'a humorist in the grand style; a humorist whose broad outlook embraced the world as a whole, and saw even great humanity against a background of greater things'.[16] Interestingly, Chesterton emphasizes the large 'design' of Chaucer's writing and the entirety of his cosmos, anticipating a later critical notion of the Gothic design of the *Canterbury Tales*; he applauds, too, Chaucer's irony. John Livingston Lowes's 1932 series of lectures offers a classic, humane study of Chaucer in terms of 'human comedy': Lowes places his writing as 'modern' in its realism – and disagrees with the notion of J. M. Manly (*Some New Light on Chaucer*, 1926) that the Canterbury pilgrims were based on actual people.[17] The debate, now peculiarly dated, points to the new directions in which Chaucer criticism was moving, and the growing recognition of Chaucer as experimental writer. For Lowes, like Kittredge, it is drama that is central to Chaucer's originality: 'The *Canterbury Tales*, even though their plan remains a splendid torso only, are an organic whole, and that whole is essentially dramatic'.[18] The powerful sense of Chaucer as modern, dramatic and vibrantly realistic underlies the amazing success of Coghill's translation of Chaucer's *Canterbury Tales*, which attracted more than 2 million listeners when first read in 1946 on the BBC, and played an important role in popularizing Chaucer, though the *Miller's Tale* was considered too shocking to be included in the broadcast reading (Coghill's translation was later used in Martin Starkey's successful 1968 musical of the *Canterbury Tales*).[19] The 1944 Powell and Pressburger film *A Canterbury Tale* alludes to Chaucer's work in order to evoke an enduring notion of Englishness.

While the sense of Chaucer's genial realism and Englishness was sustained, successive generations of critics began to realize the limitations of this perspective, in particular, in considering Chaucer's other writings. A shift in critical opinion was most of all influenced by the work of C. S. Lewis. In Lewis's study *The Allegory of Love* (1936) he turned away from (and indeed rather dismissed) Chaucerian comedy as a distraction from Chaucer's poetic achievements, to focus on the early poems and their use of the French love allegory, *Le Roman de la Rose*. Lewis thus created a new critical perspective on Chaucer as 'poet of courtly love', whose writing employed to new effect the French conventions of 'radical allegory' and revealed the 'delicate threads' of a poetry 'written for a scholastic and aristocratic age'.[20] The French scholar Gaston Paris (1883) had already identified a distinctive attitude to love in medieval literature, which he termed *amour courtois*, and the English critic W. G. Dodd had written on this phenomenon in English writing in *Courtly Love in Chaucer and Gower* (1913). C. S. Lewis took up this notion with special reference to the thirteenth-century treatise of Andreas Capellanus on the art of loving, *De arte amandi*, to argue compellingly that medieval literature depicted 'love of a highly specialized sort, whose characteristics may be enumerated as Humility, Courtesy, Adultery, and the Religion of Love' – though in its ideal form, this love would not be consummated, as Dante's sublime love for the celestial Beatrice.[21] For Lewis, the great medieval examples are Lancelot and Guinevere, Tristan and Isolde, Troilus and Criseyde, but the celebration of such love is always shadowed by a sense of transience and human frailty: it is 'never...more than a temporary truancy. It may be solemn, but its solemnity is only for the moment. It may be touching, but it never forgets that there are sorrows and dangers before which those of love must be ready, when the moment comes, to give way.'[22] Lewis's incomparable prose captures the way such transience is often signalled at the end of medieval works, as in *Troilus and Criseyde*: 'We hear the bell clang; and the children, suddenly hushed and grave, and a little frightened, troop back to their master.'[23]

Lewis's role in illuminating the complexities and delicacies of medieval writing cannot be overestimated. There are, however, difficulties with his theory, in particular his absolute insistence on love as a fixed religion, despite the fact Andreas Capellanus's rules of love were not well known in the medieval period, and his insistence on adultery, which means that the many depictions of married love in medieval literature must be dismissed as poor shadows of the real thing. Critical debate over 'courtly love' has been extensive. E. Talbot Donaldson writes sceptically: 'courtly love provides so attractive a setting from which to study an age much preoccupied with love that if it had not existed scholars would have found it convenient to construct it – which, as a matter of fact, they have, at least partially, done.'[24] Donaldson emphasizes the idiosyncrasy of Andreas Capellanus and the fact that *amour courtois* was not a current medieval term, and remarks the 'spell' that Lewis's definition has cast on readers, obscuring the truth that 'there is very little adultery' in medieval literature.[25] The term *fin'amors* is now usually preferred, in that it implies a set of courtly conventions without the fixity of Lewis's definition and with the possibility of marriage.[26] It was, however, the power of Lewis's argument, and even more, his vibrant, acutely knowledgeable and imaginative engagement with the thought world of medieval literature, that effected a shift away from the sometimes desiccated historical approach of early scholars to a new recognition of the literary richness and sophistication of medieval writing, to a critical engagement with the interplay of convention and originality, and to the wealth of possibilities offered by the allegorical mode. Lewis's special interest was the rarefied fictional world of Chaucer's *Troilus and Criseyde*, and he wrote eloquently too on the 'process of *medievalisation*' of a classical text.[27]

The impact of Lewis's work was by no means immediate or absolute: it was not until Charles Muscatine's study, *Chaucer and the French Tradition* (1957), that the ideas presented by Lewis were developed as part of a New Critical approach that emphasized Chaucer's use of two literary modes, the courtly and the realist. Muscatine's book played an essential role in revitalizing traditional source study as cultural contextualization, and also represented the New Criticism advocated by such critics as F. R. Leavis, I. A. Richards and William Empson in its emphasis on the poem as verbal object and hence on analysis of structures such as irony and ambiguity, in particular through close reading of the text. Empson, considering Chaucer's language in *The Structure of Complex Words* (1951), writes of his 'sustained and always double irony'.[28] Critics of the 1950s, such as Kemp Malone, John Speirs and Raymond Preston, tended to reflect these new interests in their focus on Chaucer's language, while W. K. Wimsatt considered the nature of Chaucer's poetry in his study *The Verbal Icon* (1954). These studies emphasize technical aspects of Chaucer's poetry, often in relation to the French and Italian poetry that informed it. Typical of this period in its immensely scholarly attention to language and literary context is J. A. W. Bennett's monumental study of the *Parliament of Fowls* (1957; see p. 96), which reflects too the shift in critical interest to Chaucer's early dream vision poetry. By the later 1950s and 1960s, however, critical interest had shifted further to the topics of ambiguity and irony central to New Criticism: Muscatine contextualizes his own approach, writing, 'Our own generation has necessarily its peculiar sensibility. To use such terms as "irony", "ambiguity", "tension", and "paradox" in describing Chaucer's poetry is to bring to the subject our typical mid-century feeling for an unresolved dialectic.'[29] Although the difficulty of Chaucer's language made him a less popular subject for writers like Leavis, his evident love of irony, questioning tone and frequently unresolved texts rendered him a promising candidate for medievalists interested in the New Criticism. The widespread and radical shift within English and American critical tradition thus inspired a range of New Critical studies, which emphasized the exposition of poetic complexities – irony, ambiguity, organic unity.

This challenge to the positivist historicist emphasis of earlier critics resulted in a critical backlash, for while Chaucerians such as Muscatine, James I. Wimsatt, who published an influential study of *Chaucer and the French Love Poets* (1968), and Donaldson were deeply scholarly in their approach and most interested in the intertextuality of Chaucer's writing, other critics could seem to remove Chaucer from his historical context into a world governed only by the nuances of language and effects of ambiguity and irony. The New Criticism was thus opposed by the critic D. W. Robertson, Jr, who espoused a 'new historicism' of a specifically exegetical kind; Robertson and his followers offered exceedingly scholarly but exclusively allegorical interpretations in search of a 'medieval aesthetic' centred on the divine.[30] Robertson's approach could not be further from that of Kittredge or his predecessors, with their love of Chaucer's genial realism. For Robertson, 'all medieval literature is, like the Bible, designed to promote Charity (*caritas*) and condemn Cupidity (*cupiditas*)';[31] all medieval works are didactic and allegorical, aiming to expose the 'kernel' of truth, to separate the wheat from the chaff. Robertson employed examples from both classical and medieval literature and iconography to justify his approach, offering a new perspective on medieval aesthetics and the medieval imagination. He argues powerfully for the historical approach: writing of the *Book of the Duchess*, for instance, he states, 'What does Chaucer's poem, then, mean to us? It means nothing at all in so far as "emotional profundity" or "serious thought" are concerned unless we can place ourselves by an act of the historical imagination in Chaucer's audience, allowing ourselves, as best we can, to think as they thought and to feel as they felt.'[32] Yet his approach leads to some awkward and unpersuasive readings: it is difficult, for example, to subscribe to his moral reading of *Troilus and Criseyde* as 'the tragedy of every mortal sinner'. Robertson writes of Troilus, 'His fall is an echo of the fall of Adam. When his senses are moved, he proceeds to indulge in "pleasurable thought," allowing his lower reason to be corrupted as he cooperates with Pandarus in deceits and lies.'[33] Not only does Robertson portray Troilus as seemingly unaware of his manipulation by Pandarus, but also it is precisely his love for Criseyde that moves him to a sublime state, in which he composes hymns in celebration of divine love – the reverse of corruption. Robertson's disciple Bernard F. Huppé presents a similarly rigid moral reading of the *Canterbury Tales*: 'it is the end "for oure doctrine" toward which all the tales have been moving'. Huppé argues explicitly against the traditional view of Chaucer as genial, humane realist: 'To realize the pilgrims only for their warm humanity is to realize only a fraction of their reality, for they are seen in Chaucer's vision of humanity as human souls on a perilous journey, in which each action and each word have consequences terrifyingly absolute.'[34] This exegetical reading of the *Canterbury Tales* seems as limited as that which it opposes, the tales as 'roadside drama'. The dangers of the Robertsonian mode are memorably captured in E. T. Donaldson's essay, 'Designing a Camel: Or, Generalizing the Middle Ages': 'the image of the Middle Ages now current looks like a camel achieved by a Committee on Medieval Studies trying to design a horse'.[35] Donaldson demonstrates the need for a sophisticated critical engagement that allows for exceptions and originality, so that Chaucer may be seen as questioning and creating rather than simply preaching.

Reactions against the ahistoricism of the New Criticism also produced less radical, more fruitful, approaches, which followed in the footsteps of scholars such as Lewis, Bennett, Muscatine and Wimsatt, but often took a more questioning perspective. In the 1960s the study of Chaucer's poetics was reformulated: Robert Jordan in his influential book *Chaucer and the Shape of Creation* (1967), for example, aimed to contextualize Chaucer as both writing within and responding to the literary and aesthetic assumptions of his time. The 1970s brought a revival of interest in literary and cultural history: Chaucer was once again placed in his own social context, though often in ways radically different from the earlier historical studies of Manly or Lewis. Over the next few decades this 'new historicism' produced a large number of influential works which treated Chaucer's writings in light of other medieval literature and theories of rhetoric and poetics, but also examined related discourses and topics such as natural philosophy (medieval science), astronomy, law, theology and epistemology.[36] Biographical studies were reformed to produce more ideologically engaged contextual studies of Chaucer and his age, such as the various works of Derek Brewer, Donald R. Howard's comprehensive *Chaucer and the Medieval World* (1987) and Derek Pearsall's excellent, questioning *Life of Chaucer* (1992). Traditional source studies were replaced by more wide-ranging works on intertextuality (literary and intellectual), such as those of Robert P. Miller on the *Canterbury Tales* (1977), N. R. Havely on *Troilus* (1980), and B. A. Windeatt on Chaucer's dream poetry (1982). Miller powerfully argues for the need to see Chaucer, like other medieval writers, 'as part of a tradition of "authority" reaching back through their immediate literary predecessors to the great "clerks" of classical antiquity, and, indeed, to the six days of Creation'.[37] At the same time, interesting new writing was produced on the relation of literature to music, art and iconography.[38] New scholarship on Chaucer's language also continued to be undertaken.[39]

With the increasing popularity of critical theory in the 1980s, Chaucer studies were opened out still further.[40] Most influential of all were the Marxist and sociological approaches of the 'new historicism' advocated by Stephen Greenblatt. The notion of all social phenomena as historically determined, and hence, as products of the ruling ideologies of any given time, offered a new way of placing Chaucer's writing; this approach also opened up possibilities of revisionist readings for feminist critics.[41] Contemporary Chaucer criticism has also taken account of a range of other branches of critical theory: reception theory, reader response theory, semiotics and linguistic philosophy, deconstruction and psychoanalytic theory, gender theory and speech act theory. The tradition of serious, historically informed scholarship has always been sustained, as, for example, in works such as David Burnley's *The Language of Chaucer* (1983) and J. Kerkhof's *Studies in the Language of Geoffrey Chaucer* (1982). A great deal more has been written on the literary contexts of Chaucer's writing, from classical to medieval.[42] The best of recent Chaucer criticism combines the scholarship of traditional approaches with the questioning self-consciousness of postmodern theory. Recent incisive contextual studies include that of Peter Brown and Andrew Butcher, *The Age of Saturn* (1991), and Lillian M. Bisson's *Chaucer and the Late Medieval World* (1998).[43] Christopher Cannon's *The Making of Chaucer's English* (1998) uses speech act theory to examine the development, originality and reception of Chaucer's language, and challenge the notion that Chaucer created English as a literary language. Perhaps it is not surprising that the writings of Chaucer, himself a literary critic who questions and undercuts his own writings through his self-conscious use of form, genre and text, lend themselves extraordinarily well to the interests of postmodernism even while they remain rich with possibility for the historian.

Yet it should not be forgotten that much postmodern criticism takes for granted and builds upon the work of earlier critics and scholars even while dismissing their approaches as outdated: in their ways, men like C. S. Lewis and G. L. Kittredge are the giants on whose shoulders Chaucer criticism has been raised. For instance, although Lewis's discussion of 'courtly love' is problematic, the recognition of medieval notions of *fin 'amors* is essential to any study of romance writing, and it is to Lewis, too, that the influential notion of Criseyde's fear and vulnerability may be traced.[44] Similarly, while Kittredge can often seem patronizing and simplistic in his character study and humane praise of Chaucer, no study of the *Canterbury Tales* fails to engage in some way with his notion of a 'marriage group' of tales. Even D. W. Robertson's allegorical readings, though frequently constrictive, provide a salutary reminder of medieval scholarship and the religious world in which medieval literature is necessarily grounded. In one way or another, contemporary criticism inevitably rests upon, remakes and responds to that of the great Chaucerians of the early twentieth century.

There is such a plethora of criticism on Chaucer that selection is extremely difficult. The following chapters offer discussion of central aspects of Chaucer's major writings (the dream vision poems, *Troilus and Criseyde* and the *Canterbury Tales*), a summary of critical approaches to each, and discussion of and extracts from a range of critical works. Brief references are given to related reading. The bibliography gives full details of all works cited and some further reading, including useful journal articles, as well as essential reference tools, such as bibliographical guides, journals and websites. Particularly useful are John Leyerle and Anne Quick's *Chaucer: A Bibliographical Introduction* (1986), the *Chaucer Bibliographies* series, and the bibliography contained in yearly issues of *Studies in the Age of Chaucer*. Anne Rooney offers a helpful *Guide Through the Critical Maze* (1989). The *Oxford Guides to Chaucer* series provides invaluable introductions to the *Shorter Poems* (Alistair Minnis, 1995), *Troilus and Criseyde* (Barry Windeatt, 1992) and the *Canterbury Tales* (Helen Cooper, 1989). The *Oxford Companion to Chaucer Studies* (Beryl Rowland, 1979) and the *Cambridge Chaucer Companion* (Piero Boitani and Jill Mann, 1986) offer useful collections of introductory essays on texts and contexts. Christian K. Zacher and Paul E. Szarmach are currently editing a new series, *Basic Readings in Chaucer and his Time*, which combines influential critical essays with some new studies.[45] The anthologies of Burrow, Schoeck and Taylor, cited above, contain helpful collections of earlier criticism, as does that of George Economou (1975); the *Casebook* (J. J. Anderson, 1974) and *New Casebook* series (Valerie Allen and Ares Axiotis, 1997) comprise critical essays on the *Canterbury Tales*.[46] Derek Brewer's *A New Introduction to Chaucer* (1998), discussed below, provides an approachable way into Chaucer.[47]

Notes

1 See also Alice S. Miskimin's study of the reception of Chaucer in this period, *The Renaissance Chaucer* (Yale University Press, New Haven, CT, 1975).
2 J. A. Burrow, *Geoffrey Chaucer: A Critical Anthology* (Penguin, Harmondsworth, 1969). 66–7.
3 Ibid., 77.
4 Ibid., 101.

The Development of Chaucer Criticism

5   'Chaucer and the Renaissance' (1912) in Burrow, *Geoffrey Chaucer*, 111.
6   The first editions are by Caxton (1476 and 1482), Wynkyn de Worde, Caxton's assistant (1498), and Pynson (1492 and 1526). Thynne's edition is the basis for those of John Stow (1561) and Thomas Speght (1598, revised 1602 and 1687), who adds a glossary, biography, notes and 'arguments'. Material from these later editions is included in D. S. Brewer's facsimile of Thynne's edition, Geoffrey Chaucer, *The Works, 1532...* (Scolar Press, London, 1969).
7   L. D. Benson, 'A Reader's Guide to Writings on Chaucer' in Derek Brewer, ed., *Geoffrey Chaucer* (London, Bell, 1974), 326.
8   Further editions had been produced by Thomas Wright and the Percy Society (1847–51).
9   For early studies of dating and order, see, for example, the editions of Skeat and Robinson; Skeat, *The Chaucer Canon* (Clarendon Press, Oxford, 1900); and John S. P. Tatlock, *The Development and Chronology of Chaucer's Works* (Kegan Paul, Trench and Trübner, London, 1907); on language, see, for example, Joseph Mersand, *Chaucer's Romance Vocabulary* (Comet Press, New York, 1937).
10 Ibid., 2.
11 See, for example, Morton W. Bloomfield, 'Chaucer's Sense of History' (1952) in *Essays and Exploration: Studies in Ideas, Language and Literature* (Harvard University Press, Cambridge, MA, 1970); Walter Clyde Curry, *Chaucer and the Mediaeval Sciences* (Barnes and Noble, New York, 1960 [1926]); A. C. Cawley, ed., *Chaucer's Mind and Art* (Oliver and Boyd, Edinburgh, 1969); Chauncey A. Wood, *Chaucer and the Country of the Stars* (Princeton University Press, Princeton, NJ, 1970); Beryl Rowland, *Blind Beasts: Chaucer's Animal World* (Kent State University Press, Kent, OH, 1971); J. D. North, *Chaucer's Universe*, revd edn (Clarendon Press, Oxford, 1988); see also the various essays on medieval learning in Brewer, *Geoffrey Chaucer*, and Beryl Rowland, *Companion to Chaucer Studies* (Oxford University Press, New York, 1979).
12 Thomas R. Lounsbury, *Studies in Chaucer: His Life and Writings* (James R. Osgood, McIlvaine, London, 1892 [1891]), III, 444–5.
13 George Lyman Kittredge, *Chaucer and His Poetry* (Harvard University Press, Cambridge, MA, 1970 [1915]), 154–5.
14 Ibid., 156.
15 Kittredge, 'Chaucer's Discussion of Marriage' (1911–12) in Richard J. Schoeck and Jerome Taylor, *Chaucer Criticism*, 2 vols (University of Notre Dame Press, Notre Dame, IN, 1960–1), I, 157.
16 G. K. Chesterton, *Chaucer*. 2nd edn (Faber and Faber, London, 1948), 20.
17 John Livingston Lowes, *Geoffrey Chaucer and the Development of his Genius* (Houghton Mifflin, Boston; Clarendon Press, Oxford, 1934, 1944), 160, 162.
18 Ibid., 164.
19 See also Coghill's study, *The Poet Chaucer* (Oxford University Press, Oxford, 1949).
20 C. S. Lewis, *The Allegory of Love: A Study in Medieval Tradition* (Oxford University Press, Oxford, 1936), 161, 174. See also Lewis's study of medieval and Renaissance literature, *The Discarded Image: An Introduction to Medieval and Renaissance Literature* (Cambridge University Press, Cambridge, 1964).

21 Lewis, *The Allegory of Love*, 2.
22 Ibid., 42–43.
23 Ibid., 43.
24 E. Talbot Donaldson, 'The Myth of Courtly Love' (1965) in *Speaking of Chaucer* (Athlone Press, London, 1970), 155.
25 Ibid., 155–6.
26 For a sensitive treatment of 'the social and emotional dimensions' (p. 1) of medieval marriage, which argues against the predominant association of love with adultery in the literature of the period, see Neil Cartlidge, *Medieval Marriage: Literary Approaches, 1100–1300* (D. S. Brewer, Cambridge, 1997), in particular 1–32.
27 C. S. Lewis, 'What Chaucer Really Did to *Il Filostrato*' (1932) in Schoeck and Taylor, *Chaucer Criticism*, II, 17.
28 William Empson, *The Structure of Complex Words* (Chatto and Windus, London, 1951): Burrow, *Geoffrey Chaucer*, 160. See also Germaine Dempster's full-length study of *Dramatic Irony in Chaucer* (Humanities Press, New York, 1959).
29 Charles Muscatine, *Chaucer and the French Tradition: A Study in Style and Meaning* (University of California Press, Berkeley), 9–10; also quoted by Burrow, *Geoffrey Chaucer*, 116.
30 See, for example, D. W. Robertson, Jr, *A Preface to Chaucer: Studies in Medieval Perspectives* (Princeton University Press, Princeton, NJ, 1969 [1962]); see also Robertson's historical study, *Chaucer's London* (John Wiley and Sons, New York, 1968).
31 L. D. Benson, 'A Reader's Guide to Writings on Chaucer' in Brewer, *Geoffrey Chaucer*, 349.
32 D. W. Robertson, Jr, 'The Historical Setting of Chaucer's Book of the Duchess', *Essays in Medieval Culture* (Princeton University Press, Princeton, NJ, 1980), 255–6.
33 D. W. Robertson, Jr, 'Chaucerian Tragedy' (1952) in Schoeck and Taylor, *Chaucer Criticism*, II, 118.
34 Bernard F. Huppé, *A Reading of the 'Canterbury Tales'* (State University of New York, Albany, 1964), 239, 241.
35 E. Talbot Donaldson, 'Designing a Camel: Or, Generalizing the Middle Ages', *Tennessee Studies in Literature* 22 (1977), 1–16: 1.
36 Influential works on rhetoric and poetics include Joerg O. Fichte, *Chaucer's 'Art Poetical': A Study in Chaucerian Poetics* (Gunter Narr, Tübingen, 1980); Earle Birney, *Essays on Chaucerian Irony* (University of Toronto Press, Toronto, 1985).
37 Robert P. Miller, ed., *Chaucer: Sources and Backgrounds* (Oxford University Press, New York, 1977), 3. Studies of the influence of classical writing on Chaucer include John M. Fyler, *Chaucer and Ovid* (Yale University Press, New Haven, CT 1979) and Bernard L. Jefferson, *Chaucer and the 'Consolation of Philosophy' of Boethius* (Gordion Press, New York, 1968 [1917]); studies of the Italian influence include Piero Boitani, *Chaucer and Boccaccio* (Society for the Study of Medieval Languages and Literature, Oxford, 1977).

38 See, for example, on music, John Stevens, *Music and Poetry in the Early Tudor Court* (Cambridge University Press, Cambridge, 1979) and Nigel Wilkins, *Music in the Age of Chaucer* (D. S. Brewer, Cambridge 1995); on art and iconography, V. A. Kolve, 'Chaucer and the Visual Arts' in Brewer, *Geoffrey Chaucer* and *Chaucer and the Imagery of Narrative: The First Five Canterbury Tales*' (Edward Arnold, London, 1984).

39 See, for example, Paull F. Baum, *Chaucer's Verse* (Duke University Press, Durham, NC, 1961), Ian Robinson, *Chaucer's Prosody: A Study of the Middle English Verse Tradition* (Cambridge University Press, Cambridge, 1971), Ralph W. V. Elliott, *Chaucer's English* (André Deutsch, London, 1974), Helge Kökeritz, *A Guide to Chaucer's Pronunciation* (University of Toronto Press, Toronto, 1978 [1961]), Norman Davis, *A Chaucer Glossary* (Clarendon Press, Oxford, 1979), G. H. Roscow, *Syntax and Style in Chaucer's Poetry* (Rowman and Littlefield, Totowa, NJ, 1981), and Stephen Knight's study of language and meaning, *Rymymg Craftily: Meaning in Chaucer's Poetry* (Angus and Robertson, Sydney, 1973).

40 See Donald M. Rose's early collection of essays addressing the possibilities raised for Chaucer scholars by new theoretical strategies, *New Perspectives in Chaucer Criticism* (Pilgrim Books, Norman, OK, 1981).

41 Different approaches will be discussed at more length in subsequent sections. New historical approaches include: David Aers, *Chaucer* (Harvester, Brighton, 1986) and *Community, Gender and Individual Identity* (Routledge, London, 1988), Paul Strohm, *Social Chaucer* (Harvard University Press, Cambridge, MA, 1989), Lee C. Patterson, *Chaucer and the Subject of History* (Routledge, London, 1991); studies of rhetoric and poetics: Rita Copeland, *Rhetoric, Hermeneutics and Translation in the Middle Ages* (Cambridge University Press, Cambridge, 1991) and Leonard Michael Koff, *Chaucer and the Art of Storytelling* (University of California Press, Berkeley, 1988); feminist approaches: Carolyn Dinshaw, *Chaucer's Sexual Poetics* (University of Wisconsin Press, Madison, 1989), Priscilla Martin, *Chaucer's Women: Nuns, Wives and Amazons* (University of Iowa Press, Iowa City, 1990), Jill Mann, *Geoffrey Chaucer* (Harvester Wheatsheaf, New York, 1991), Elaine Tuttle Hansen, *Chaucer and the Fictions of Gender* (University of California Press, Berkeley, 1992); psychoanalytical and deconstructionist studies: Judith Ferster, *Chaucer on Interpretation* (Cambridge University Press, Cambridge, 1985), H. Marshall Leicester, Jr, *The Disenchanted Self: Representing the Subject in the Canterbury Tales* (University of California Press, Berkeley, 1990); and the various recent articles of Louise Fradenburg and R. A. Shoaf.

42 On classical influences, see A. J. Minnis, *Chaucer's 'Boece' and the Medieval Tradition of Boethius* (D. S. Brewer, Cambridge, 1993) and Michael A. Calabrese, *Chaucer's Ovidian Arts of Love* (University Press of Florida, Gainesville, 1994); on Italian influences, Howard H. Schless, *Chaucer and Dante* (Pilgrim Books, Norman, OK, 1984), David Wallace, *Chaucer and the Early Writings of Boccaccio* (D. S. Brewer, Woodbridge, 1985), Carla Taylor, *Chaucer Reads the 'Divine Comedy'* (Stanford University Press, Stanford, CA, 1989), Piero Boitani, *The European Tragedy of Troilus* (Clarendon Press, Oxford, 1989), Michael G. Hanly, *Boccaccio, Beauvau, Chaucer: 'Troilus and Criseyde'* (Pilgrim Books, Norman, OK, 1990) and

The Development of Chaucer Criticism

Richard Neuse, *Chaucer's Dante* (University of California Press, Berkeley, 1991); on French influences, Barbara Nolan, *Chaucer and the Tradition of the Roman Antique* (Cambridge University Press, Cambridge, 1992); on the Bible, David Lyle Jeffrey, *Chaucer and Scriptural Tradition* (University of Ottawa Press, Ottawa, 1984); on clerical tradition, Ann Astell, *Chaucer and the Universe of Learning* (Cornell University Press, Ithaca, NY, 1996); on theology and natural philosophy, Norm Klassen, *Chaucer on Love, Knowledge and Sight* (D. S. Brewer, Cambridge, 1995); and on medieval reception, Seth Lerer, *Chaucer and His Readers* (Princeton University Press, Princeton, NJ, 1993).

43 See also Brown's *Chaucer at Work: The Making of the Cantabury Tales* (Longman, London, 1994) and S. H. Rigby, *Chaucer in Context: Society, Allegory and Gender* (Manchester University Press, Manchester, 1996).

44 See Lewis's discussion, *The Allegory of Love*, 182–90.

45 Two volumes in this series have been published: Daniel J. Pinti, ed., *Writing After Chaucer: Essential Readings in Chaucer and the Fifteenth Century* (Garland, New York, 1998), and William A. Quinn, ed., *Chaucer's Dream Visions and Shorter Poems* (Garland, New York, 1999); see also Thomas Hahn, ed., *Chaucer's Readership in the Twentieth Century* (Garland, New York, 2000) and G. A. Rudd, ed., *A Complete Critical Guide to Chaucer* (Garland, New York, 2001).

46 For discussion of the numerous other introductory works and anthologies of criticism on the *Canterbury Tales*, see chapter 8, p. 193.

47 See also Brewer's useful collection of essays, *Tradition and Innovation in Chaucer* (Macmillan, London, 1982).

2

Chaucer's Reading and Audience: Critical Extracts

The English and European Literary Traditions

Derek Brewer

Derek Brewer has written extensively on medieval literature, and in particular on Chaucer; the following extract is drawn from his New Introduction to Chaucer, *aimed chiefly at students beginning their Chaucer studies. The book usefully sets Chaucer's writing in context, and offers as well a series of introductory readings. Brewer takes a traditional, humanist approach, but one that is by no means unquestioning, to summarize lucidly and accurately the various influences, literary and otherwise, on Chaucer. He draws on literary criticism and research into Chaucer's sources, and animates these through his own biographical work, suggesting, for instance, Chaucer's experience of the excitement of travel, but also his profound sense of loss. At its best, such imaginative revisiting of writers can provide a welcome antidote to the abstractions of more consciously theoretical approaches.*

This extract summarizes the chief literary influences on the young Geoffrey Chaucer – English, French and classical – and despite its apparent simplicity, introduces a number of issues central to any study of Chaucer's writing: literary sources and authority, convention and originality, courtly tradition and fin'amors, *idealism and realism, love and reason, the secular and the sacred, the notion of the Gothic, the use of a narrator-persona, the various literary genres of the medieval period. As we shall see, it is typical of Chaucer's writings that so many of his concerns may be formulated in terms of oppositions.*

Brewer grounds Chaucer in both English and French culture and imaginatively considers the possibility that Chaucer saw some of the most celebrated medieval manuscripts. His reading in youth would have included English romances, which his later writing satirizes but in which he found a range of formative literary conventions: the romance poet who speaks directly to his audience in the guise of the minstrel, for instance, provides the seeds of Chaucer's self-conscious narrator.

Traditional English lyrics also served as models in their treatment of secular and sacred love and use of the imagery of landscape and seasons, as well as the courtly imagery of love. In French courtly tradition, so familiar to an Anglo-French court, such conventions are more sophisticated, looking back to the troubadour poetry in which the lady was idolized from afar, and to the elegant romances of writers such as Chrétien de Troyes or Marie de France, who wrote of refined emotion for elevated courtly circles. Chaucer may have written in French and certainly translated French writing, most notably in his Romaunt of the Rose, *but also in his early narrative poem,* The Book of the Duchess. *While his French contemporaries, Guillaume de Machaut, Jean Froissart and Eustache Deschamps were important influences, especially in their use of the conventions of* fin'amors *(Brewer notes the problematic nature of the term 'courtly love'), the* Roman de la Rose *was probably Chaucer's single most important resource, both in terms of its combination of idealism and realism, and its irony.*

Alongside English and French influences Chaucer had available too a wide range of classical texts, and a wider range of names, which he does not hesitate to wield as his 'auctorite'. It is to these works – and especially those of Ovid – that Chaucer looks, in particular, for his legends of suffering and tragic women. Other inspiration is drawn from the popular devotional works of the time, such as saints' lives and moral treatises, as well as from the Bible itself. As Brewer discusses in later chapters, Chaucer's travels to Italy would render that country's literature another significant influence, while philosophical writings, especially Boethius's Consolation of Philosophy, *also played a formative role.*

For Brewer, the term 'Gothic' is crucial, and it is one to which a number of Chaucer critics return. It captures the contrastive, light and dark quality of Chaucer's writing, the desire to create a grand edifice of many parts, the encyclopedic aspect, but also the minute attention to detail. Important, too, is the innovative quality of Chaucer's poetry. He, like all writers of his time, comprehends writing in terms of its relation to the past: the ideal is less to invent new stories than to retell old ones in new ways, not to ignore but to wield skilfully the conventions and tropes of familiar texts, and to situate himself in the great literary tradition stretching back to 'Omer, Virgile...'. Yet in many ways he could not be more original: he challenges the archaism of romance and the naïveté *of traditional lyrics, yet uses some of their spontaneity and immediacy to infuse new life into what could be empty courtly conventions; he marries the idealism and cynical realism of the* Romance of the Rose, *and fuses too the traditions of London and Paris; he extends the notion of the 'Gothic frame-breaking narrator' and opens out the possibilities of literary ventriloquism in his use of women's voices.*

Derek Brewer, 'The English and European Literary Traditions' in *A New Introduction to Chaucer* 2nd edn, Longman Medieval and Renaissance Library. Longman, London and New York, 1998.

Early Reading

What had Chaucer been reading as a boy and young man? Youthful reading is the seedsowing time of the mind and Chaucer was obviously an avid reader. The reading which made the deepest impression on him, most attracted his imagination, and formed his intellectual habits, can be traced partly from its effects and partly from his own references. Everywhere he seems driven on by continuous curiosity, intellectual seeking, imaginative enjoyment. He had a powerful yet unstrained vitality, a wonderful sense of participation, and also a sharply critical response. He was always going beyond what he received. Without animus or reforming zeal, he both accepted and left behind what he experienced. There is no rebellious bitterness, yet no complacent conservatism.

The English Romances

The earliest impression was that made by English romances. We can detect their influence in Chaucer's earliest datable poem, *The Book of the Duchess*, at the least conscious level, the minor points of style. The first 15 lines of that poem are translated from a poem by Froissart. The style is that of oral delivery, real or imitated. It button-holes the reader with its direct, informal intimacy, its conversational, personal ease. At once a relationship is created between poet and audience or reader. It is in one sense a climax of the earlier minstrel style, but here the minstrel is the poet himself.

It is notable that these poems, and the lyrics to be mentioned in a moment, were in English. The establishment of the English language as that of the whole people at all cultural levels is proved by Chaucer's own poetry, but clearly took place independent of him earlier in the fourteenth century. English is his mother tongue, and the mother tongue of Court and City.

We may imagine Chaucer listening when younger to narrative poems, perhaps read to the family at home from such a book as the large Auchinleck manuscript (now in the National Library of Scotland), which among over 50 separate items, almost all in English, contains 18 romances. These account for three-quarters of the surviving bulk of the manuscript (and what has been lost is mostly texts of romance). This big book, produced around 1330–40 by a London bookshop, for just such an audience as wealthy merchants, contains many other items of a kind which influenced Chaucer; the four saints' lives, the 15 varied religious and didactic pieces, and the five humorous or satiric pieces. It has been argued that Chaucer knew this very volume. Whether he did or not, it is a true 'Gothic' miscellany of the very type of *The Canterbury Tales*.

The English romances are usually written in tail-rhyme: that is, of stanzas of around 12 four-stress, eight-syllabled lines, rhyming, and each stanza concluding with a two-syllable, one-stress phrase, the tail-rhyme itself. They tell stirring stories of virtuous, often patriotic, heroes who fight evil and win a bride and a kingdom. The stories are essentially folktales, to be associated with fairytales. The clear favourite is *Guy of Warwick*, which has versions in short couplets (like *The Book of the Duchess*) as well as in tail-rhyme. A very typical shorter example is the tale of *Sir Degaré*, where the hero, abandoned in childhood, almost marries his unknown mother, and has to discover his father.[1] Romances such as these were popular until the seventeenth century. Shakespeare knew *Guy of Warwick*.

These archetypal stories, often slackly written, came to seem as ridiculous to Chaucer as they do to most moderns. As usual he was avant-garde for his age and untypical in some of his tastes. He mocked them cruelly in *The Canterbury Tales* by the comic parody *Sir Thopas*, but it is quite significant that he attributes *Sir Thopas* to himself as one of the pilgrims. The self-mockery has a real basis in his actual origins, as well as in his poetic character.

English Lyrics

At the same time we may be sure that Chaucer knew a large number of English lyrics. Many such lyrics survive from the thirteenth century onwards and are of great charm. There is a great anthology of them recorded in what is now British Library Harley 2253. This manuscript of the early fourteenth century is a miscellany of French, medieval Latin and English poetry which thus illustrates not only English writing but the trilingual culture of the time. It was probably written somewhere in the West Midlands but the poems have place-names which refer as far afield as Lincoln. The famous lyric 'Blow Northern Wind' is among them. All England is represented in these English poems now known as 'The Harley Lyrics'. Many are love-songs, influenced by the French tradition and written in a variety of iambic metres, though with some alliteration.

Bytuene Mersh and Aueril	
When spray biginneth to spring	*leaves: grow*
The lutel foul hath hire wyl	*little bird*
On hyre lud to synge.	*song*
Ich libbe in loue-longinge	*I live*
For semlokest of alle thynge;	*loveliest*

He may me blisse bringe	*She*
Icham in hire baundone	*I am: power*
An hendy hap ichabbe yhent	*a gracious fortune I have received*
Ichot from heune it is me sent	*I know: heaven*
And lyht on Alysoun	
From alle wimmen my love is lent	

All the notes of spring and aching young love are here, the song of birds, the pain of the lover, the bliss he hopes for, the beauty of the lady, the sense that love is divine. It will all be repeated in a different style in *The Book of the Duchess*, as it had already a thousand times before, and will be millions of times later, down to the latest pop-songs, different as their tone is. Chaucer's Chantecleer sings a snatch of one of them, not otherwise recorded, 'My lief is faren in londe' (*CT*, VII, 2879) 'My love has gone away'. In Gower's poem *Confessio Amantis* written about 1390, he causes Venus, goddess of love, to say to himself in the poem:

And gret wel Chaucer when ye mete	*greet*
As mi disciple and mi poete,	
For in the floures of his youthe	*flower*
In sondri wise, as he wel couthe	*knew*
Of dities and of songes glade	*ditties*
The whiche he for mi sake made	
The lond fulfild is oueral.	

(Confessio Amantis (first version), VIII, 2941–7)

Chaucer explored the feelings of love more deeply than any previous English poet, continuing the line of the romances and lyrics, but just as he developed from the style of the romances, so he did even further from that of the lyrics. The style of the Harley Lyrics is provincial and old-fashioned by Chaucer's standards. He never seeks their fresh and unsophisticated response to spring and love, and in *The Miller's Tale* mocks such old-fashioned words as 'hende' (courteous) and provincial low-class names like 'Alison', which is also the name of the Wife of Bath. Chaucer, like his Monk, 'holds with the newe world the space'. His lyrics become philosophical, or witty in a courtly style. Yet the English lyric, whose beauties and variety cannot be explored here, and which also had a rich religious content, is where he started from. Of other earlier English verse, equal in wit and feeling to his own, he shows no knowledge.[2] It would perhaps be too much to say that Chaucer rebelled against his earliest English origins, or was ashamed of them, but he developed beyond them and mocked them, very much the English courtier who enriched English court culture by grounding the International Gothic Style in English life. Chaucer grew and developed from the English romances and lyrics under other powerful influences. At some depth was the complex of underlying new sensibilities like those related to the study of arithmetic, as already described, but more obvious, and more immediately useful, was his knowledge of French poetry – poetry of Paris.

There are two main sources which strike us particularly when considering Chaucer's early reading. The first is *Le Roman de la Rose*, and the second is the poems by Machaut. Other poems and poets there were, like the love-visions which derive from *Le Roman de la Rose*, and the poems of his contemporaries Froissart and Deschamps, who followed Machaut. There were manuscript anthologies of French poetry which must have been known to him. It has been argued that his own earliest poems were written in French, and there is a collection of poems in French by 'Ch' which could be attributed to him. Other English courtiers and Gower, as already noted, wrote poetry in French. But the only early poems which are certainly by Chaucer are imitations of the French, like *The Complaint unto Pity*, and such translations as *The Romaunt of the Rose* and *An ABC*.

Le Roman de la Rose

The English *Romaunt of the Rose*, which survives in only one manuscript, is a fragment of some 7,500 octosyllabic lines, of which probably only the first 1,705 lines are Chaucer's. This English *Romaunt* is a translation of parts of the French *Le Roman de la Rose*, one of the great formative books of the Middle Ages. More than 200 French manuscripts of the *Roman*, besides translations into other European languages, and 21 early printed editions, bear witness to its enormous popularity. It was at the well-head of the tradition in which Machaut, Deschamps and Froissart wrote. And although Chaucer actually translated very little of its more than 20,000 lines, he knew the whole poem extremely well. It permeated his thought so deeply that his later works reveal its influence even more profoundly than his early poems.

The *Roman* was written by two authors as different as chalk from cheese. Guillaume de Lorris wrote the delightful first part of some 4,000 lines, about the year 1225. The poem tells how the narrator fell asleep and dreamed it was the sweetest of May mornings. Wandering by a clear river, he came to a beautiful Garden 'from whose walls sorrow flies far', whose gate was kept by Idleness, and whose lord was Mirth, and from which everything old, ugly, poor and vicious was excluded. Within this garden of youthful delights the Dreamer eventually saw the Rose, and as he looked, the arrows of Cupid, the god of love, struck him again and again. But the Rose (a lady's love) was defended by thorns, by guardians such as Modesty and Rebuff (*Daunger*). Furthermore, the Lady Reason, who had been created in Paradise by God himself, attempted to dissuade the Dreamer from trying to win the Rose at all.

Guillaume did not finish his poem. It was finished some 50 years later by Jean de Meun, whose nickname, 'Le Clopinel', the Hobbler, not unaptly suggests his difference from Guillaume. Jean took over the machinery of the poem to convey a great quantity of very various matter: philosophy, science, nature poetry, controversy and satire of all kinds, but especially of women. It was this huge addition of Jean's that caused the *Roman* to be sometimes cited in the fourteenth century as a satire against love, notwithstanding its beginning.

The whole poem is a Gothic poetic encyclopedia. It set or reinforced the fashion for several important literary traditions. The device of the dream, the artificially bright May morning, the lovely Garden representing the youthful view of the joyous world, the allegorical framework, as well as many individual types and comments, from Guillaume's first part, all appear again and again in later poetry. Guillaume's poem sets out the 'law of love'. His god of love is the medieval Cupid: no fat, blind, naked infant, but a princely youth who hunts men. The lover receives his code from the god and learns that nobility must derive from virtue, not from lineage; that he must always be faithful; always fashionable though not extravagant in dress; accomplished in both manly and artistic exercises. In a word, he must be a gentleman in every respect, with his teeth as unstained as his honour. For the practice of these virtues the lover is promised the highest joys and bitterest sorrows that life can offer.

Even in Guillaume, however, love has an antagonist, the Lady Reason, who descends from her tower to defend Chastity and to argue against the dictates of Cupid. Guillaume makes her arguments seem cold and merely prudential, and we sympathize with the lover's rejection of them. But the conflict is deep at the heart of love as seen by the medieval poets, and it is by no means certain that Guillaume himself would have been finally on Cupid's side. The antithesis between the service of love and the service of God was clear, and always profoundly felt. There is no doubt that Chaucer also felt it.

Jean de Meun's addition, swollen and inconsistent as it is, contributed as much or more to the poem's reputation as Guillaume's beginning. In both parts the ideal of love is less intense than the feudal aristocratic tradition of Provence from which it derives, in which the lady was worshipped almost as a goddess. But it was perhaps largely due to Jean that later poets felt there was nothing strange in using the device of a love story to treat all kinds of philosophical and scientific matter in poetry. The habit of mind by which all subjects may be gathered in under one heading of love is aptly summed up in the words of Thomas Middleton as late as 1623:

> Love has an intellect that runs through all
> The scrutinous sciences, and like a cunning poet
> Catches a quantity of every knowledge

> Yet brings all home into one mystery,
> Into one secret, that he proceeds in.
> *(The Changeling,* Act III, Sc.3)

The scientific and philosophical aspects of Jean's addition were well calculated to stimulate Chaucer's already awakened interest and new sensibility towards intellectual questions. The new urban spirit breathes through this work from Paris.

Jean's work includes much more in its Gothic miscellaneity, some of it highly traditional. There is the clerical satire of women, which goes back for many centuries, and also the more rollicking rough derision of women found in popular folktale, which probably goes back to the beginning of the human race.

Parts of Boethius's *Consolation of Philosophy,* and Ovid's story of Pygmalion, are translated in the *Roman.* Jean also partly translates the twelfth-century Latin *Complaint of Nature* to create an image of fecund Nature, a goddess who urges both sexes to vigorous promiscuity in order to people the world. She has something of the power of myth. Jean's bold sophistry brings the whole poem to a remarkable ending in which he allegorically portrays, with a touch of humour, and without much concealment, the climax of sexual intercourse.

Machaut

The tradition of European love-poetry became exceedingly rich and varied by the fourteenth century. It was not so much a river as a whole series of rivers flowing in the same direction but each with a somewhat different course and character. Medieval romantic love certainly cannot be summed up as always adulterous, courteous, parodic of religion, joyous. It was all these things at times. It was also tender, pious, violent, tragic. Much of its charm lies in the different forms of story and song that it takes at different periods with different authors. It should not be called 'courtly love', a term invented by nineteenth-century scholars. We should rather call it romantic love, or use the term often mentioned in its own day, *fine amour,* 'refined love', which hits off its essential element and distinguishes it from simple sexual passion.

Machaut (*c.* 1300–77), who was the leading musician of his day, was also the leading poet of France (which was at that time made up of several kingdoms) and a major influence on Chaucer. He was nominally a cleric, yet he led the adventurous, amorous, much-travelled life of a courtier, indebted to various kings for patronage and for the conferment of well-paid benefices of which he was an absentee incumbent. He wrote many poems developing the tradition of love, and two debate-poems, the *Jugement du Roi de Behaigne* and the *Jugement du Roi de Navarre* which much influenced Chaucer. *Behaigne* presents a debate between a sorrowful knight and an equally sorrowful lady, who meet by accident in a forest. The lady's own knight is dead; while the lady of the knight in the forest has betrayed him. They debate as to whose plight is worse, and go to Jean of Luxembourg, King of Bohemia (Machaut's current patron) for a decision. He decides that the knight suffers more. Although the situation is set up artificially, the human problems are real and painful. The artificiality distances but does not trivialize them. Machaut has some delicacy of perception and an extraordinarily copious style. This may make him seem tedious now; it must have been a wonderful stimulus to the imagination of one brought up on the much barer style of English lyrics, or the colloquial clichés of the English romances. Close but not slavish imitation of *Behaigne* gave Chaucer the basic structure and much of the very phraseology for his much subtler *Book of the Duchess*. Both poems indicate by their fictional characters real people without being allegorical in any strict sense.

The other poem by Machaut, *Le Jugement du Roi de Navarre*, is notable for its prologue of 458 lines in which the poet tells of the horror he felt, shut up for safety in his own room, during the plague at Rheims, where he was a canon, and where he resided during Edward III's siege of 1359–60, when Chaucer was outside the walls. Most fourteenth-century European poets introduce themselves into some of their own poems. Guillaume virtually does so in *Le Roman de la Rose*; Dante is the most famous example; Machaut, Deschamps, Froissart follow suit, and all the major English poets, Langland, Gower, the *Pearl*-poet, and some minor poets, like Lydgate and Hoccleve, do the same. The poet-in-the-poem may be said to be a characteristically Gothic frame-breaking device, for he is both in and out of the picture. In the poem he is not quite literally his entire 'real' self, yet he is not entirely fictional. Such a personage is sometimes called the 'Narrator', and so he is, but the term is misleading if it implies a character entirely 'inside' the poem, unrelated to a genuine autobiographical 'outside' reality. Machaut illustrates this in *Navarre*. He was really in Rheims, as he writes in the poem, but when he describes himself going into the forest and having a dispute with a lady called 'Happiness' (*Bonneurté*), he slides into fiction. Yet the fiction was probably based on real situations and debates, for the lady in the poem accuses the judgement in the previous poem, *Behaigne*, of being unfair to woman. She probably represents actual criticisms made to Machaut in real life. Chaucer was influenced by this characteristically Gothic shifting viewpoint created by the poet's variable *persona* in the poem. He developed the device of the *persona* in his own way very elaborately and fluidly.

Other Reading and Influences

Chaucer's earliest work might almost be described in horse-breeding terms as by Machaut out of the English romances, but that would weaken the sense of other greatly varied resources acquired and poured into the prepared mould of English language and literature. We have so far concentrated on those literary influences which came to him through living how and when he did, in an English upper-class family and in an Anglo-French court culture. Not to be forgotten are the formally learned Latin school-texts, which made him not only an educated man but a poet. Virgil may have given him some sense of the dignity and gravity which great poetry could aspire to, and which he mentions at the end of *Troilus*, where he places himself quite consciously in the great line of

> Virgile, Ovide, Omer, Lucan and Stace.
> (V, 1792)

Of the poets mentioned besides Virgil, he could only have read Homer in a brief poor Latin summary, and he was relying rather on his great reputation, than on direct knowledge. Lucan and Statius were well-known Silver Latin poets of elaborately rich style with valuable material. Ovid was the favourite, as he was of almost everybody, read at school and cherished throughout life. Ovid, though a classical writer, enshrines a very medieval ideal of writing. He is full of matter, mythological, historical, amorous, personal, comic, pathetic. His style is richly rhetorical. He can be ironical, and in his *Ars Amatoria* is sexually very explicit. He also condemns love in his *Remedia Amoris*. Lively and various, he provides something for everyone. In his *Heroides*, a series of poems purporting to be letters from ladies betrayed by their lovers, wittily written but full of genuine pathos and sympathy for women, he touched a note which Chaucer responded to in various ways from *The Book of the Duchess* through *Troilus* to *The Legend of Good Women*, many of whose heroines are based on Ovid's poems. The sadness of betrayal in personal relationships, and of death, which is the greatest betrayal, imaged in these stories, corresponds to some deep sense of loss in Chaucer himself, which he managed at last to express and purge only in middle life.

Finally, we must recall the devotionally religious element in the early influences on Chaucer. On the basis of all those prayers learned at school and home was built a series of devotional works, saints' lives and sermons, which found incidental expression in many poems, and more explicitly in such major Canterbury tales as *The Man of Law's Tale of Constance, The Clerk's Tale of Patient Griselda, The Second Nun's Tale of Cecilia, The Prioress's Tale*, and the moralizing prose tracts *Melibeus* and *The Parson's Tale*. At this early stage in Chaucer's life the vein of devotion is represented by the translation from French, *An ABC*, a devout poem to the Virgin Mary, elaborate, pious, sentimental, metrically very adept. Probably he also tried his hand at prose, but no early prose survives. It would have been practical utilitarian devotional or scientific prose. English prose was becoming an instrument for fictional entertainment during Chaucer's own lifetime in the *Travels* of Sir John Mandeville, but this was an historical spoof of a kind which somehow seems quite alien to Chaucer. Chaucer's own prose is all serious, and at this point we may note that Chaucer shows, for a layman, such unusually wide knowledge of the Bible, which he would have taken as literal, historical, as well as divinely inspired, truth, that he must have had a copy of his own, read in private. It would have been in Latin.

While all this reading was going on, Chaucer was also living a full life as a young courtier and, for a brief interlude, a sort of soldier. He was travelling a great deal, in England, France and Spain. All this activity must have stimulated his extraordinarily vital imagination. Physically, intellectually and spiritually he was experiencing, exploring, seeking.

Notes

1 For a discussion of these related tales, and Chaucer's reaction, see Derek Brewer, *Symbolic Stories* (Cambridge, 1980).
2 For an introductory essay see Derek Brewer, *English Gothic Literature* (London, 1983), 30–69. For an account of the romances in rhyme, see ibid., 70–88.

Chaucer: The Teller and the Tale

Gabriel Josipovici

In the following extract, Gabriel Josipovici addresses some of the issues raised by Derek Brewer at more length; in particular, the questions of sources and literary authority. Like Brewer's, Josipovici's approach is intertextual: he places Chaucer's writings in the context of both other medieval works and fiction more generally. Josipovici's subject is the creation of fictional 'realities' and to such a topic the issue of authorial distance is especially relevant. His chapter on Chaucer will continue with a consideration of the Chaucerian narrator and of the relation of fiction and game. In this opening section the focus is on Chaucer's attitudes to 'olde bokes' (Legend of Good Women, Prologue, 25) and the authority that readers and later writers place on them. As Brewer's chapter makes clear, the use of literary sources was essential to any medieval theory of writing; Chaucer is no exception, but his use of sources is extraordinary in its fluidity. He can faithfully render the abstract philosophy of Boethius; he can also rewrite and subvert his sources, invent them, claim sources he has never used, or conceal those he has used. In the passage preceding this extract, Josipovici looks briefly at two contrastive texts, Dante's Divine Comedy *and* Langland's Piers Plowman. *Both these works employ a guide figure, who leads the narrator-dreamer through the dark wood of worldly confusion to the heavenly light of truth; both play on the notion too that books, if read correctly, can lead to the truth.*

Chaucer, however, in many ways overturns the certainty both of books and of truth itself. Josipovici instances Chaucer's early dream vision poem the House of Fame: *the narrator, 'Geoffroi', is taken up to the heavens not by a didactic authority such as Virgil, as in Dante's* Inferno, *or Lady Holy Church, as in Langland's* Piers Plowman, *but by a garrulous eagle. Swept up against his will, he refuses instruction and states that he prefers to learn from books. Experience and authority are set up in comic opposition to each other. This tension between books and human experience pervades Chaucer's works: books both lend authority and are inevitably distanced from the immediate. Josipovici compares Chaucer's questioning use of books to his treatment of dream theory: are dreams, as thinkers like Macrobius argued, prophetic or more immediately reflective of the dreamer's physical state? How far do we trust authorities? And which ones? How do we reconcile our experience with the authority of the past? For Josipovici, the tension between experience and authority renders the early poetry flawed, yet it may also be seen as lending intensity and the radical quality of experimentation noted by Brewer.*

Chaucer uses yet questions the doctrine of 'olde approved stories', often telling familiar tales in far from familiar ways: the treatment of Dido in the House of Fame *is a good example. This work, indeed, addresses the issue of which authors, and hence which version of a story, are remembered, to suggest that fame is arbitrary. If this is the case, which books should we trust; which provide the key to the truth? Josipovici's reference to the variety of critical readings of the* Legend of Good Women, *which commends 'old approved stories' (F Prologue, 21) so credulously as to be suspicious, draws attention to the difficulty of assessing Chaucer's ironic tone. The question of which story we believe becomes a central theme of the* Canterbury Tales, *where the idea of interpretation is shown to be crucial. There are not simply true and false books but, rather, books may be read in true and false, fleshly and spiritual ways. This opposition between secular and sacred is typical of medieval thought, according to which all worldly things were seen as possessing spiritual counterparts. Josipovici's examples demonstrate the subjectivity of interpretation: fleshly and spiritual readings can arise from the same book. Chaucer's fictional characters reflect changeable and subjective interpretation of sources, while the overt use of narrator figures illuminates authorial subjectivity. As readers, we are aware too of the varying attitudes and interpretations of critics: Josipovici notes, for instance, the difficulty of accepting an allegorical reading such as that of D. W. Robertson Jr. We are left with the notion of book as literal object, its writing waiting to be read and interpreted – and with the question of what the criteria of interpretation should be. In criticism perhaps the only possibility of truth is in the attempt to make those criteria transparent. Chaucer's fictional games, however, often rely on the inverse – the revelation of how subjective any criteria, including his own, are.*

Gabriel Josipovici, from 'Chaucer: The Teller and the Tale' in *The World and the Book: A Study of Modern Fiction* 2nd edn. Macmillan, London and Basingstoke, 1979.

The contrast with Chaucer is absolute and startling. There is a passage in *The House of Fame* which is worth bearing in mind as we explore Chaucer's vast and varied output. The Eagle, so reminiscent of Beatrice, has seized the dreamer despite his protestations that he is no Enoch or Ganymede, and borne him up into the sky towards the Palace of Rumour. Like many guides the Eagle is an inveterate talker and a tremendous bore, and he delivers a running commentary on all they see and are about to see. Eventually, however, his monologue comes to an end and the dreamer-poet is able to take stock of the situation:

> Tho gan y loken under me
> And beheld the ayerissh* bestes,　　　　　　　　　　　　*aerial
> Cloudes, mystes, and tempestes,
> Snowes, hayles, reynes, wyndes,
> And th' engendrynge in hir kyndes,*　　　　　　　　　　*natures
> All the wey thrugh which I cam.
> 'O God!' quod y, 'that made Adam,
> Moche ys thy myght and thy noblesse!'
> And thoo thoughte y upon Boece,*　　　　　　　　　　　*Boethius
> That writ 'a thought may flee so hye
> Wyth fetheres of Philosophye...'
>
> And than thoughte y on Marcian,*　*Martianus Capella, who wrote on astronomy
> And eke on Anteclaudian,*　　　　　*Alain de Lille's treatise on nature
> That sooth was her descripsion
> Of alle the hevenes region,
> As fer as that y sey the preve;
> Therfore y kan hem now beleve.
> 　With that this egle gan to crye,
> 'Lat be,' quod he, 'thy fantasye!
> Wilt thou lere of sterres aught?'

'Nay, certeynly,' quod y, 'ryght naught.'
'And why?' 'For y am now to old.'
'Elles I wolde the have told,'
Quod he, 'the sterres names, lo,
And al the hevenes sygnes therto,
And which they ben.' 'No fors,' quod y.
'Yis, pardee!' quod he; 'wostow why?
For when thou redest poetrie,
How goddes gonne stellifye*   *turn into a constellation
Bridd, fissh, best, or him or here,
As the Raven,* or eyther Bere,   *this and the following are names of constellations
Or Arionis harpe fyn,
Castor, Pollux, or Delphyn,
Or Athalantes daughtres sevene,
How alle these arn set in hevene;
For though thou have hem ofte on honde,
Yet nostow not wher that they stonde.'
'No fors,' quod y, 'hyt is no nede.
I leve as wel, so God me spede,
Hem that write of this matere,
As though I knew her places here;
And eke they shynen here so bryghte,
Hit shulde shenden al my syghte,
To loke on hem.' 'That may well be,'
Quod he.

(*HF* 964–1018)

This is an extraordinary passage. It is not enough to say that it is a parody of Dante. It is partly that, but this is no explanation. The dreamer-poet, asked by the eagle to look at the stars he and other poets have so often written about, refuses – their brightness hurts his eyes, he says, and, besides, he is too old for any fresh experience! But of course the feeling we get is that he has not had *any* experience in his life; what he has written about has only come from books. And, as the eagle tells him in an earlier passage, his continuous poring over old books has made him 'mased', unable to respond to the world around him.

Why does the poet present himself in this way? The *persona* of the bookish dreamer of no experience is one that we meet with again and again in these early dream vision poems, and that undergoes only slight modifications in the depiction of the narrator of *Troilus* and of *The Canterbury Tales*. Instead of making experience reinforce what old books say Chaucer seems to be at pains to pull the two apart. The perpetual concern with dreams is just another aspect of this problem, since the question whether dreams are prophetic or not is really the question of how far God impinges on this world and how far we can tell what kinds of relation exist between this world and God's providence. In Dante and Langland, we saw, there was an answer to these questions, an answer that had to be sought for, but which was connected with the public facts of the Incarnation and the sacraments of the Church. But Chaucer's poems make no mention of this. Instead they merely raise the question and leave us more puzzled than before. The prologue to the *Legend of Good Women* provides a good example of the method:

> A thousand sythes have I herd men telle
> That there is joye in hevene and peyne in helle,
> And I accorde wel that it be so;
> But natheless, this wot I wel also,
> That there ne is non that dwelleth in this contre,
> That eyther hath in helle or hevene ybe,
> Ne may of it non other weyes witen,
> But as he hath herd seyd or founde it written;
> For by assay there may no man it preve*.   *test, experience
> But Goddes forbode, but* men shulde leve   *God forbid but that
> Wel more thyng than men han seyn with ye!
> Men shal nat wenen every thyng a lye,
> For that he say it nat of yore ago.
> God wot, a thyng is nevere the lesse so,
> Thow every wyght ne may it nat yse.
> Bernard* the monk ne say nat al, parde!   *probably Bernard of Clairaux
>   Thanne mote we to bokes that we fynde,
> Thourgh whiche that olde thynges ben in mynde,
> And to the doctryne of these olde wyse,*   *wise writers
> Yeven credence, in every skylful wyse,
> And trowen on these olde approved storyes,
> Of holynesse, of regnes, of victoryes,
> Of love, of hate, of othere sondry thynges,
> Of whiche I may nat make rehersynges.
> And if that olde bokes were awaye,
> Yloren* were of remembrance the keye.   *lost
> Wel oughte us thanne on olde bokes leve,
> There as there is non other assay by preve.
> And as for me, though that my wit be lite,
> On bokes for to rede I me delyte,
> And in myn herte have them in reverence,
> And to hem yeve swich lust and swich credence....
>   (*LGW* G 1–32)

I think it would be wrong to read this passage entirely straight, as one of Chaucer's best critics has done.[1] The dreamer-narrator may be advocating the reliance on the authority of books – since they are all we have to rely on – but we know by now that he has a particular stake in such a recommendation. As Nietzsche remarked: beware of philosophers who recommend the philosophic life as the answer to all life's problems. In fact, the weight of the passage is evenly balanced on the incisive irony of the phrase: 'Bernard the monk ne say nat al, parde!' Taken at its face value this means: 'Surely men ought to believe more than simply what they see; after all, even Bernard[2] did not see everything he described and surely you don't doubt him?' But of course the passage can be taken in a diametrically opposite sense: 'Since no one has ever been to heaven and hell and returned to tell us about it, everyone is in the same position with regard to what these places are really like, so why should we believe what anyone tells us about it, whether it's Bernard or anyone else?' The effect is similar to the one we find in the Nun's Priest's Tale, where the narrator explains:

> This storie is also trewe, I undertake,
> As is the book of Launcelot de Lake,
> That wommen holde in ful greet reverence.
> 			(*CT* VII 3211–13)

My story is as true as that of Lancelot – but perhaps the story of Lancelot is no truer than my story. Instead of moving from (apparent) confusion to (real) clarity, as with Dante and Langland, these early poems of Chaucer's set up a rigid opposition of experience and authority from the start and never progress towards their reconciliation. They remain for the most part unfinished or badly flawed, as though the poet had been defeated by the contradiction between the two.

But it is not only these early poems that circle compulsively round the problem. Few, if any, of the *Canterbury Tales* do not address themselves to the conflicts it raises, and since there Chaucer is in greater control of his material it may be as well to pause a little and see just what he does with it.

Many of the characters in *The Canterbury Tales*, either the pilgrims themselves or the characters within the pilgrims' tales, raise the question of the relation of experience to authority. They do this either by insisting on their simple down-to-earth reliance on experience and thus making us suspect any reference to authority, or by piling up references to authorities and impressing us with the way their own views tally with those of the great men of the past. Occasionally, as with the Wife of Bath, they miraculously manage to combine the two. A good example of the first approach is the Franklin, who begs the pilgrims to

> Have me excused of my rude speeche.
> I lerned nevere rethorik, certeyn;

37

> Thyng that I speke, it moot be bare and pleyn.
> I sleep nevere on the Mount of Pernaso,*   *Mount Parnassus, home of the Muses
> Ne lerned Marcus Tullius Scithero.*   *Cicero
> Colours ne knowe I none, withouten drede,
> But swiche colours as growen in the mede,
> Or elles swiche as men dye or peynte.
> Colours of rethoryk been to me queynte;
> My spirit feeleth noght of swich mateere.
>   (*CT* V 718–27)

But this we of course know to be itself a figure of rhetoric, cunningly deployed. The implication that because he isn't going to dress up his tale in high-flown rhetoric it will be honest and truthful is one that we will see dramatically challenged in the Pardoner's Tale, but the Franklin's words are sufficient to warn us that he is not as simple as he seems.

More interesting than this *ingénu* approach is the converse, the citing of authority to back up one's private prejudices, or the reliance on authority which reveals to the reader an unwillingness to learn from experience. There is, for example, the carpenter John, in the Miller's Tale, who

> knew nat Catoun,* for his wit was rude,   *Cato, author of school texts
> That bad man sholde wedde his simylitude.
>   (*CT* 1 3227–8)

and all of whose troubles come from an unnatural doting on his young wife. This leads him to accept the false astrology of the clerk Nicholas, with his assurances that the stars foretell a second flood. Although Nicholas tempts him with the notion that after the flood,

> thanne shul we be lordes al oure lyf
> Of al the world, as Noe and his wyf....
>   (*CT* I 3581–2)

he is not, like most of the other characters in Chaucer, really interested in power, lordship. Nonetheless, his willingness to accept unquestioningly the false authority of Nicholas is the direct result of his failure to listen to the proper authority of Cato, and he reaps the consequences of this neglect. With January in the Merchant's Tale the technique grows clearer. He too has not heard of Cato's advice and so marries a young wife, but this time there is a friend at hand to remind him of the wise man's words:

> Avyseth yow – ye been a man of age –
> How that ye entren into mariage,

And namely with a young wyf and a fair.
By him that made water, erthe and air,
The youngeste man that is in al this route,
Is bisy ynough to bryngen it aboute
To han his wyf allone. Trusteth me,
Ye shul nat plesen hire fully yeres thre,
This is to seyn, to doon hire ful plesaunce.
                    (*CT* IV 1555–63)

But this of course is just what January does *not* want to hear:

'Wel,' quod this Januarie, 'and hastow sayd?
Straw for thy Senek,* and for thy proverbes!   *Seneca
I counte nat a panyer* ful of herbes   *bread-basket
Of scole-termes.* Wyser men than thow,   *philosophical terms
As thou hast herd, assenteden right now
To my purpos....
                    (*CT* IV 1566–71)

And January is not altogether wrong. For the puzzling thing seems to be that the authorities contradict one another; however many are produced on one side of an argument, an equal number seem capable of being produced on the other side. And nothing, as we saw in the case of Scripture in the previous chapter, can tell us how we are to arbitrate between the rival authorities. They fill the pages of Chaucer's tales, these classical and patristic writers, they tumble over each other in a riot of profusion; but, unlike the Virgil and St Bernard of Dante and the Holy Church of Langland, they only add to the confusion. It is no longer a matter of a fleshly as opposed to a spiritual reading: all reading seems to be equally fleshly and equally spiritual, depending on the point of view.

What, for instance, are we to make of the debate between Chauntecleer and Pertelote in the Nun's Priest's Tale? The arguments between them are already familiar to us from Chaucer's early dream poems: what is the significance of dreams? Are they warnings sent from God or are they purely physiological in provenance, the mere result of overeating? Pertelote is in no doubt:

'Have ye no mannes herte, and han a berd?
Allas! and konne ye been agast of swevenys?*   *dreams
Nothyng, God woot, but vanitee in sweven is.
Swevenes engendren of replecciouns,*   *overeating
And ofte of fumes* and of complecciouns,*   *stomach vapours *bodily humours

> Whan humours been to habundant in a wight.
> Certes this dreem, which ye han met* tonyght,   *dreamed
> Cometh of the greete superfluytee
> Of youre rede colera,* pardee....   *red choleric humour
>   Lo Catoun, which that was so wys a man,
> Seyde he nat thus, "Ne do no fors of dremes?"*   *Take no account of dreams
>   Now sire,' quod she, 'whan we flee fro the bemes,
> For Goddes love, as taak som laxatyf....'
>   (*CT* VII 2920–43)

But Chauntecleer will not have his dream dealt with in this reductive way:

> 'Madame,' quod he, 'graunt mercy of youre loore.
> But nathelees, as touchyng daun Catoun,
> That hath of wysdom swich a greet renoun,
> Though that he bad no dremes for to drede,
> By God, men may in olde bookes rede
> Of many a man moore of auctorite
> Than evere Caton was, so moot I thee,*   *so may I thrive
> That al the revers seyn of this sentence,
> And han wel founden by experience
> That dremes been significaciouns
> As wel of joye as of tribulaciouns
> That folk enduren in this lif present....
>
>   Dame Pertelote, I sey yow trewely,   *Macrobius, who wrote on dream theory in
> Macrobeus,* that writ the avisioun   his commentary on Cicero's *Dream of Scipio*.
> In Affrike of the worthy Cipioun,*   *Scipio
> Affermeth dremes, and seith that they been
> Warnynge of thynges that men after seen.
> And forthermoore, I pray yow looketh wel
> In the olde testament, of Daniel....
>   (*CT* VII 2970–3128)

and he goes on to cite Joseph, Croesus, Andromache, and many more biblical and classical figures whose dreams *were* prophetic. Our confidence in him is, however, slightly lessened, when he reveals the private and instinctive bias of his learning by translating 'mulier est hominis confusio' as 'woman is man's joy and all his bliss'. Here, surely, we are back with a figure not at all unlike the aged January, whose use of authorities is conditioned by his need to back up his own private desires. In the event, however, Chauntecleer turns out to have been right after all. His dream is prophetic, and his fears turn out to have been justified, since a little later a fox does in fact get hold of him. But it would, I think, be wrong to read the story in this way as a *justification* of prophetic dreams. The effect of the tale on the reader, as I shall try to show later, is to make him laugh at the discrepancy between the importance of the subject (are dreams prophetic? does God really speak directly to us in this way?) and the barnyard incident that illustrates this. Is it *this* story that will allow us to adjudicate between all the learned authorities? It may be as true as the story of Lancelot, but, as we have seen, perhaps Lancelot's story is no more than this, the trivial tale of a farmyard cock. As the Nun's Priest says, in discussing the tremendous issues of free-will and predestination:

> I wol nat han to do of swich mateere;
> My tale is of a cok, as ye may heere.
> (*CT* VII 3251–2)

But this too, as I shall try to show later in this chapter, is only a partial view of the situation.

With the Wife of Bath we are on less slippery ground. Her prologue furnishes us with the *locus classicus* of Chaucer's exploration of the way in which private whim can transform 'authority' into a mere excuse for following one's own interests. She begins by insisting on her *experience* as the source of any wisdom she might now possess:

> Experience, though noon auctoritee* **written authority
> Were in this world, is right ynogh for me
> To speke of wo that is in mariage;
> For, lordynges, sith I twelve yeer was of age,
> Thonked be God that is eterne on lyve,
> Housbondes at chirche dore I have had fyve....
> (*CT* III 1–6)

And yet, as if to demonstrate the psychological fact that we always need to align our experience in some way with that of the rest of mankind if we are to make sense of it, she launches after this opening straight into a lengthy defence of her own character, citing the Old Testament, the Gospels and St Jerome, among others, in defence of her practice. D. W. Robertson Jr has shown in great (and not always convincing) detail how this citing of authority, while intended to provide evidence of the rightness of her actions, would, in fact, have damned her in the eyes of her audience.[3] Here, for example, is the way she treats the authority of Solomon:

> Lo, heere the wise kyng, daun Salomon;
> I trowe he hadde wyves mo than oon.
> As wolde God it were leveful* unto me   *lawful
> To be refresshed half so ofte as he!
> Which yifte* of God hadde he for alle his wyvys!   *what a gift
> No man hath swich that in this world alyve is....
>   (*CT* III 35–40)

Robertson comments:

> The 'yifte of God' (cf. 1 Cor. 7.7) Solomon had is readily discernible in 3 Kings 11: 'And king Solomon loved many strange women.... And he had seven hundred wives as queens, and three hundred concubines; and the women turned away his heart. And when he was now old, his heart was turned away by women to follow strange gods: and his heart was not perfect with the Lord his God....' In fact, the foolishness of Solomon in his old age was proverbial. As Proserpyna observes in the Merchant's Tale,
>> He was a lecchour and an ydolastre,*   *idolatrer
>> And in his elde he verray God forsook.
>
> Five husbands of which she has 'pyked out the beste / Bothe of here nether purs and of her cheste' have been sufficient to bring the wife to a similar position.[4]

The climax of the Wife's prologue beautifully mimes the misreading of authorities involved here. Her fifth husband, it will be recalled, used to read to her continuously out of old authors who dwelt on the evils of women, starting with Eve and moving steadily (and at considerable length) down to the present, so that

> whan I saugh he wolde nevere fyne*   *cease
> To reden on this cursed book al nyght,
> Al sodeynly thre leves have I plyght*   *plucked
> Out of his book, right as he radde,* and eke   *read
> I with my fest so took hym on the cheke
> That in oure fyr he fil bakward adoun.
> And he up stirte as dooth a wood* leoun,   *mad
> And with his fest he smoot me on the heed....
>   (*CT* III 788–95)

After all the citing of learned authorities, after the endless flood of *words* poured out by the Wife of Bath, experience bursts with extraordinary violence into the situation.[5] It is as though the literal and 'non-spiritual' nature of the Wife's interpretation of Scripture had found its true outlet as she leaps forward and tears the leaves out of the old book. And suddenly, with this action, the book is there before us as an *object*, its power dependent entirely on its remaining intact. In a flash we are made aware of the fact that language is only literal when we think of it in purely physical terms – marks on paper – and that otherwise all language is spiritual in that it is in need of *interpretation*. And we see too that not only do the authorities bafflingly range themselves on both sides of any question, but that these 'authorities' speak to us only as marks on paper, never as people. But if *this* is authority, this book coming apart in my hands, how on earth can I trust it to guide me through my life? Yet without authorities to guide us, what sense are we going to make of the world and of ourselves? The climax of the Wife of Bath's prologue shows us that it is useless aligning experience against authority or authority against experience: neither speaks to us directly, both need interpreting, but where are we going to find a criterion for interpreting either?

Notes

1 R. O. Payne, *The Key of Remembrance* (Yale, 1963) 94–6.
2 There is some doubt as to who is meant here.... [Probably Bernard of Clairvaux]
3 *A Preface to Chaucer* (Princeton, 1963) 317ff.
4 Ibid. 323–4.
5 The tale which the pilgrim Chaucer tells of Melibee forms an interesting contrast to the Wife's prologue. In this tale a cruel incident – the deliberate maiming of a man's wife and daughter – is drained of all emotional flavour (it is described in five lines) and made the excuse for an elaborate exercise in rhetorical argumentation (nine hundred lines). The result is that when the evildoers are pardoned at the end we are only confirmed in our feeling that the outrage never really took place at all. Its function in the tale is rather like that of those baths that are perpetually in the process of being filled by hot and cold taps in elementary algebra problems: the fact that the water might well overflow does not make us worry about the contents of the house.

The Audience

Paul Strohm

Brewer and Josipovici focus on the relation of Chaucer's writing to his sources and to medieval literary conventions, although Brewer's biographical detail usefully reminds us of socio-historical as well as literary influences on Chaucer. Paul Strohm's study, Social Chaucer, *considers the ways Chaucer is shaped by the social forces of his time and how his* oeuvre *engages with them. Strohm's approach combines traditional historicism with 'new historicism' and thus emphasizes the ideological forces underlying Chaucer's work, and especially class relations. Strohm* also draws on a range of theorists, in particular Mikhail Bakhtin and his school, for whom the notion of social production of literary texts is essential.[1] In this extract Strohm considers Chaucer's audience, as much in terms of its role in the creation of a text as of its identity. The discussion builds on Chaucer's use of the romance convention of the minstrel addressing his audience (remarked by Brewer), to consider the ways a text is shaped by the expectations and identity of its intended audience, and thus becomes a 'speech act' or 'ideological bridge', both speaking to and, in a sense, spoken by, its listeners or readers. Strohm challenges earlier formalist readings which focus on the textuality of Chaucer – the text as written word – but also Foucauldian readings that place a work as a 'discourse' or strand of communication, in that they are one-sided, ignoring the shaping role of the audience.[2] Reader response theory, too, fails to take account of this two-way process (emphasized by Bakhtin and his circle), for the audience's influence begins prior to the writing of a text, a notion that in many ways reflects medieval rhetorical theory.[3] Strohm turns as well to speech-act theory, which emphasizes the performative and mimetic qualities of literary texts.[4]

Strohm is sensitive to the difficulty of taking this approach beyond the abstract: he considers the variable nature of Chaucer's immediate circles of audience (inner court, royal household, London intellectuals) and the effects of shifting politics on these, as well as the wider readership that manuscripts reached. He also notes the differences between speech and writing: the forces influencing forms of writing are not only social but also literary, as the writer constantly selects from and reworks literary genres and conventions. In the second part of this extract, Strohm analyses the relation between audience and text suggested by the early work, The Book of the Duchess, *a poem that treats the subject of communication in its presentation of a dialogue between the narrator and the Man in Black, who grieves for his lost beloved. Strohm's argument makes clear the influential role played by French courtly writing, a genre that would have been familiar to the audience circles of the inner court and royal household. The poem is unique, however, in its explicit engagement with an historical event, the death in 1368 of Blanche, Duchess of Lancaster and wife of John of Gaunt. The ready identification of the Man in Black with John of Gaunt allows Strohm to tease out the delicate class nuances of the relation between the grieving knight and the narrator. Strohm shows how this centres on a notion of limited equality or civility that takes account of the patronage of one by the other. He cleverly brings to bear historical research on the hierarchy of the royal household and the power of John of Gaunt to argue that social relations, rather than questions of the narrator's comprehension of the knight's bereavement, are central. He also draws on the work of more textual critics to explore the nuances of the forms of politesse exchanged by the Dreamer and the Knight in Black.*

As we shall see, it is equally valid to consider the poem in terms of its psychological and literary insights. Strohm's argument, however, is valuable in its reminder that Chaucer's writings, first read aloud to a familiar audience (though *also intended for a wider readership), are profoundly informed by medieval social relationships. As such, they are especially responsive to social readings.*

Notes

1. The theory of Mikhail Bakhtin emphasizes the dialogic relation between a literary text and the society that produces it: texts represent sites where multiple voices interact, and meaning is constructed through the complex relation between text, social forces producing it and audience.
2. The term 'discourse', now widely used, was adopted by Michel Foucault to describe different types of verbal structure, literary and non-literary; Foucault argued that any discourse was shaped by the power structures of the period in which it occured.
3. Reader response theory, such as that of Roman Ingarden, Wolfgang Iser and Hans Robert Jauss, emphasizes the process of a reader's reception of a text to produce meaning; this process is necessarily shaped by the reader's experiences and ideological assumptions. Jauss stresses the effect of historical change on reading.
4. Speech-act theory was developed by John Austin and taken up by a range of theorists such as John R. Searle and Stanley Fish.

Paul Strohm, from 'The Audience' in *Social Chaucer*. Harvard University Press, Cambridge, MA, 1989

The idea of art without audience would probably have seemed either contradictory or absurd to Chaucer, if in fact he could have entertained it at all. The word 'audience,' as he uses it, remains close to its etymological sense of 'those within hearing,' and his own poems almost always contain references to those who 'hear' or 'harken' or to whom he is 'telling' his 'tale.'[1] Even in his later works, when listeners begin to yield to page turners who 'see' his meaning written out rather than hear it read, these absent readers are as much the objects of admonition and address as if they were literally present. For, whether Chaucer seeks literal audience from listeners or figurative audience from an emerging reading public, the consequences of losing audience would be devastating; in a view that he repeats several times, the narrator who fails to hold the attention of those he is addressing might as well not speak or write at all. In the *Tale of Melibee*, for example, one of the 'olde wise' gains audience or hearing but then loses the attention of the group he wishes to sway: 'alle atones bigonne they to rise for to breken his tale, and beden hym ful ofte his wordes for to abregge.' Chaucer as pilgrim-narrator observes that, "whan this wise man saugh that hym wanted audience, al shamefast he sette hym doun agayn. / For Salomon seith: 'Ther as thou ne mayst have noon audience, enforce thee nat to speke'" (VII. 1037, 1042, 1045–6). A similar moment is about to occur on the pilgrimage itself. The Monk's 'hevy' recital of tragedies is interrupted by the Knight, who is in turn seconded by Harry Bailly: 'Whereas a man may have noon audience, / Noght helpeth it to tellen his sentence' (VII. 2801–2). The sentiment is of course a commonplace. The spurned counselor of *Melibee* and the narrator's accompanying observation are taken directly from the *Livre de Melibe* of Renaud de Louens [fourteenth-century moral treatise],[2] and Harry Bailly's remark has its source in Ecclesiasticus 32.6. Such insistence on the indispensability of attentive hearing to meaningful discourse is commonplace because it was one of the cornerstones of a rhetorical system, elaborated in various places including medieval treatises on preaching, in which Chaucer's work remains securely lodged.[3]

The notion that discourse assumes its full significance – perhaps its only significance – in interaction with an audience has certain corollaries, one of which is that artists should not simply hope for good audition but should shape their discourse with the needs and capacities of an intended audience in view. As Petrarch observes to Boccaccio, in a somewhat condescending explanation of his decision to countenance the free humor of the *Decameron*, the style and language of that work may well be suitable for those who are likely to read such tales. 'It is important,' he continues in a more general vein, 'to know for whom we are writing, and a difference in the character of one's listeners justifies a difference in style.'[4] Chaucer's own allegiance to this precept is not only suggested by his poetic practice but is embodied in words presumbaly close to his own voice when he states his tactical decision to avoid complex argumentation and to reiterate hard points in explaining the astrolabe to little Lewis: 'curious endityng and hard sentence is ful hevy at onys for such a child to lerne ... me semith better to writen unto a child twyes a god sentence, than he forgete it onys' (45–9). A similar tactical decision is made, but announced less discreetly, by the Eagle when he lectures Geffrey about the nature of sound: 'so I can / Lewedly to a lewed man / Speke' (*HF*, 865–7). Such examples might be continued almost indefinitely. Their common denominator is simple: a successful artist adapts both content and style to the requirements and capacity of the intended audience.

Critics have not given much weight to the communicative dimension of Chaucer's work. The formalist or explicatory critics who have produced the largest volume of commentary on his work over the last three or four decades regard his *oeuvre* as autonomous, as a system of signs with no important referents outside itself. More recent criticism, written under the influence of Foucault and other French theorists, has been even more emphatically focused on the textual surface of the poetry and insistent on its status as discourse in a world of discourse, rather than as a form of utterance in a communicative situation.[5]

Other critics have followed the different lead of reception theory, abandoning the assumption that Chaucer's writing is self-contained and concerning themselves with its impact on auditors or readers, whether historical or current. Still, even while acknowledging a communicative dimension to Chaucer's work, these critics tend to view his communication with his audience as proceeding in one direction only: from author to audience. However active the audience's participation in the ultimate determination of meaning, it is presumed to be on the far side of a communicative divide that precludes its influence on the form of the work. Jauss's initial formulation of the matter seems to promise an expanded acknowledgement of the audience's impact at all stages of the creative process, as when he argues that 'in the triangle of author, work, and public the last is no passive part, no chain of mere reactions, but rather an energy formative of history.'[6] But he goes on to restrict the audience's influence to works yet to be created. In his scheme the work enters history only after its production, when the audience's experience of the work issues in new norms and new transgressions; underestimated is the contribution of the artist's understanding of an audience to the very form of the work.[7]

The medieval sense that the requirements of an audience might influence literary creation deserves consideration within the framework of a theory that grants its possible legitimacy. Such a theory would assign to the audience, and to the author's sense of audience, a role not simply founded on passive consumption but on active participation, in determining textual meaning and in influencing the form of texts. One such body of theory exists in the writings of Bakhtin and his collaborator/surrogates Voloshinov and Medvedev. The importance of Voloshinov's sociolinguistics and Medvedev's recasting of formalism in a social context is that these works give full weight to the importance of communicative context for the *formation* of utterances. The utterance, according to Voloshinov, is a 'two-sided act...the product of a reciprocal relationship between speaker and listener, addresser and addressee.'[8] As such, it is to be regarded as the sole property neither of the speaker who frames it nor of the listener who receives it, but as their common property. This is because the utterance is formed and received within the larger social milieu that embraces both speaker and listener and the more particular social relationship that exists between them; the organizing center of the utterance thus lies in the social circumstances and purposes of the discourse.

Literary works cannot, of course, be treated simply as utterances or speech acts.[9] Medvedev and others have long recognized that the literary text is hardly a fresh or pure creation of a speaker and an addressee, but that it represents an artist's selection of an appropriate genre from within a previously existing system of literary possibilities, a system through which any communicative intent is 'refracted' in extremely subtle ways.[10] While the literary work remains a highly specialized form of communication, a communication mediated through the spectrum of existing generic possibilities (for the writer) and generic expectations (for the audience), it remains a form of communication nonetheless. Medvedev's contribution to Voloshinov's theory of the utterance is to argue that the artistic work, like every other form of utterance, 'is a communication, a message, and is completely inseparable from intercourse.'[11] The text is not transmitted from the author to the reader, but is constructed between them as a kind of ideological bridge.[12]

Persuasive as this formulation of the audience's contribution may be in theory, however, its implications for the understanding of particular works of literature are less easily explored – particularly in a case like Chaucer's, where the composition of his actual audience remains a matter of uncertainty. The most plausible supposition about Chaucer's audience is that it consisted mainly of those gentlepersons in service who, together with a few London intellectuals, I have identified as Chaucer's social and literary circle. Owing to the perplexing nature of the available evidence and the peculiarities of the circumstances, however, this conclusion cannot be reached in a straight argumentative line. We must pause at every point to evaluate the character of the evidence itself and its relation to Chaucer's own circumstances.

Starting with the assumption that Chaucer addressed much of his poetry to a circle of social equals and near-equals, I wish to give fair weight to a number of countervailing considerations. We have, for one thing, already seen that the membership of this group was in constant flux and that it played a variable role in his life. To address such a group would have meant one thing in the 1360s and early 1370s, when he was very much a member of a court circle; a somewhat different thing in the period 1374–85/86, when associations with members of the royal household were supplemented by involvements with London intellectuals; quite another thing after 1386, when political friction and Chaucer's removal from Westminster-London would have complicated communications among such a circle; and yet another thing after his return to a reconstituted circle in the fall of 1389.

Not only did this group shift in composition throughout Chaucer's career, but it vied with other groups for his attention. At times he addresses other groups altogether; a poem of clear-cut advice to princes, 'Lack of Steadfastness,' is a case in point. This poem, together with works like *Boece* and *Melibee*, stands as an apt reminder that, although he rarely if ever wrote for patronage, Chaucer conformed in some ways to the career of 'court poet.' Although current consensus regards Chaucer as writing mainly for social equals,[13] we would, as Elizabeth Salter reminds us, be wrong to deny him any audience in the inner circles of the court.[14] At times, too, Chaucer undoubtedly worked concurrently on poems for more than one kind of audience within a single period of his career. The years after 1387, for example, probably involved some simultaneous work on a poem for the most broadly conceived of his audiences (the *Canterbury Tales*) and for one of his least socially diverse (the *Legend of Good Women*). Another competing audience, increasing in importance throughout Chaucer's career, is his audience in posterity. The *Canterbury Tales* numbers people like Bukton and Scogan [two of Chaucer's aristocratic contemporaries, to whom he addressed poems] among its hearers or readers, but they must share his attention along with a larger audience of imagined page turners, encountering Chaucer's work beyond his control.

I do not, in other words, mean to argue that Chaucer addressed one audience alone. In a sense, the thesis of this chapter might be served simply by attributing a communicative aspect to his poetry and tracing it through varied situations of address and varied groups of addressees. But the shifting body of social equals and near-equals I have identified as his core audience continues to stand in *some* relation – however tacit or indirect – to most of his major work. Without exaggerating this audience's role, I will nevertheless trace its continuing importance throughout Chaucer's career by concentrating on several instances from different stages of his career: the *Book of the Duchess*, a poem addressed to a social superior in which this core audience is evoked as a kind of 'secondary' addressee; *Troilus and Criseyde*, in which this audience vies for narrative attention with a host of other implied and intended auditors; the *Canterbury Tales*, in which traces of this audience are pratically lost between the vividly inscribed pilgrim audience on the one hand and an imagined future audience on the other; and a cluster of short poems (and works written under Chaucer's influence) in which the importance of an audience of friends and equals most vividly shows through.

The *Book of the Duchess* as Social Communication

The *Book of the Duchess* is securely grounded in communicative situations, both within the poem (as the grieving Knight in Black pours out his sorrows and recollections to a narrator marked either for his obtuseness or his extreme tactfulness) and beyond the poem as well (in the presumed connection of the Black Knight with John of Gaunt and that of the narrator/dreamer with Chaucer himself).[15] I do not say 'presumed connection' because Chaucer's referential motives are in any serious doubt. Nothing could be more reasonable than the supposition that the young courtier Chaucer between 1368 (the death of Blanche) and 1371 (Gaunt's marriage to Constance of Castile and his assumption of the title 'King of Castile')[16] should write a poem directed to a social superior who was in a position to do favors for him and his wife.[17] Still, certain considerations argue against an exact correspondence between the Black Knight and Gaunt, the dreamer and Chaucer. Commentators wishing to firm up the connection have been forced to some ingenuity by the fact that the Black Knight's age is not right,[18] and the dreamer seems less closely identified with Chaucer's own person than is a narrator such as Geffrey of the *House of Fame*, who makes 'rekenynges' by day (653) and has a weight problem. The relation of the narrator and the Black Knight within this poem is, then, less a replication of that between Chaucer and his eventual patron than a restatement of it, a counterpart refracted through the available literary tradition of the Old French love vision. With this modest distinction, I would argue for a very broad application of the poem to Chaucer's relations with John of Gaunt: that the dream is not only a consolation to John of Gaunt for his loss of Duchess Blanche, but an exploration of Chaucer's own existing and potential relations with Gaunt, in a form at once tactful and quietly self-promotional.

The debates about the dreamer's therapeutic strategy – whether he is obtuse or is giving the Knight a chance to vent his sorrows and replace them with fond memories – are essentially beside the point. The dreamer tells the Knight outright that 'to make yow hool, / I wol do al my power' (553–4), and whatever its motivation and source, his persistent interrogation of the Knight certainly promotes a series of healing recollections. More interesting here is Chaucer's subtle delineation of the Knight's and the dreamer's respective social positions. At every point in their interaction, we are reminded of a certain amicable equity, on the one hand, and of a considerable social gulf on the other; of a polite egalitarianism in that both are gentlepersons and a decided limitation of egalitarianism in that one is an aristocrat and the other is not.

The dreamer is the most gentle of any of Chaucer's narrators. He tells us that, unable to sleep, he 'bad oon reche me a book' (47), a book not only bespoken from a servant in the voice of one accustomed to obedience, but also a book elected from among other gentle leisure-time activities such as 'ches or tables' (51). Once within the dream, he conducts himself as one accustomed to participating in the hunt, addressing a huntsman with a confident, '"Say, felowe, who shal hunte here?"' (366). The Black Knight recognizes his station, warmly addressing him as 'goode frend' (560). But the social divide between them is acknowledged in a number of ways. Having first greeted the Black Knight as best he can, the narrator waits patiently before him, head uncovered, presumably out of respect not only for his grief but for his superior social station ('y stood / Before hym and did of myn hood' – 515–16). As Alfred David points out, the Black Knight addresses the dreamer with the informal 'thee,' while the dreamer retains the more formal 'ye' or 'yow' appropriate for a social superior.[19] The Black Knight's civility is ultimately marked by social condescension; the dreamer's evident pleasure in the fact that the Black Knight addresses him without difficult verbal formulas or verbal artifice ('He made hyt nouther towgh ne queynte,' he gushes – 531) measures both their proximity and their considerable social distance.

The actual relations of Chaucer and John of Gaunt would presumably have been marked by a similar mixture of equity and inequality. On the side of equity, we may note that Chaucer, as a newly appointed esquire of the king, was a gentleperson and hence a member along with Gaunt of the broadly conceived fellowship of gentlepersons and clerks that R. T. Lenaghan has described as embracing all the members of the household and court, from the civil servant most recently elevated to gentle status to the king himself.[20] Moreover, Chaucer was recently married to Philippa, either newly appointed or soon to be appointed as lady in the household of Gaunt's second wife Constance.[21] Eventually, by virtue of Gaunt's third marriage to Philippa's sister, Chaucer would even become a kind of brother-in-law to Gaunt. Yet, on the side of inequality, we must remember that, during the period in which Chaucer's poem was probably composed, John of Gaunt was arguably the most powerful man in England. With his marriage to Blanche in 1359 and her inheritance of 1362, he gained title to the most extensive duchy in the country. With his marriage to Constance in 1371, he gained additional claim to the throne of Castile. With the illness of the Black Prince after 1367, he became the most authoritative of young Richard's uncles and in some ways overshadowed the aged and infirm ruler. Lenaghan reminds us that relations within the court were not only lateral but decidedly hierarchical, and, within the society of gentlepersons constituting the court, Gaunt was situated near the very top and Chaucer near the very bottom.

We cannot know what Chaucer might or might not have felt himself able to say to John of Gaunt in real life, but the poem as a whole and particularly the dream provide a forum within which it can be shown that Chaucer is a fit interlocutor – at once a gentleperson worthy of intimacy and friendly exchange, and a person of discretion who can be trusted not to forget aspects of social difference (including the ultimate separation of the Knight and the dreamer into their respective worlds, as 'this kyng' (1314) returns to his castle and the dreamer to his bed). Chaucer found his format in the love visions of Machaut and Froissart, and he learned much from them. To our relief, he also manages to avoid the pitfalls of bathetic excess, as in Machaut's 'Dit de la Fonteinne Amoureuse,' in which the patron falls asleep with his head in the narrator's lap and the two experience temporary obliteration of social difference by dreaming the same dream.[22] As in Machaut's *Dit*, however, the poem itself – and especially the dream within the poem – provide an imagined arena where some ordinary restraints on the interaction between socially unequal parties may be set aside.

While modeling Chaucer's relation with John of Gaunt in its dream, the *Book of the Duchess* is nevertheless simultaneously addressed to a larger group that the narrator describes collectively as 'ye' or 'yow.' Not only are these people presumed to be auditors of an oral narration rather than readers of a text ('Ryght thus as I have told hyt yow' – 271), but certain shared understandings are taken for granted ('And wel ye woot' – 16) and certain allusions presuming special knowledge of Chaucer's personal state are addressed to them ('there is phisicien but oon / That may me hele' – 39–40). Our sense of this enlarged but familiar audience is sharpest in the frame of the poem, as opposed to the dream with its focus on the narrowed situation of address, and this broadened situation of address permits poetry of correspondingly greater range and tonal variation. Present in the framing narrative of Seys and Alcyone, for example, are shifts in perspective and tone missing in the conscientious and respectful dialogue of the dream, including alternation between serious attention to Alcyone's loss and the buffoonery of the messenger's approach to Morpheus, between the implied consolation for those who know the ending of the Ovidian tale and the narrator's own sly refusal to tell it, between the narrator's presumed reason for choosing a tale of bereavement and his trumped-up suggestion that he has recounted Alcyone's plight because it gave him the idea of praying to Morpheus for sleep.

Chaucer's address to this larger audience also suggests that its membership is encouraging to a new dimensionality in subject matter and tone. Although the composition of this audience cannot securely be known, the confidence with which Chaucer approaches it would argue for relatively greater social equality than that existing between Chaucer and John of Gaunt. In the late 1360s and early 1370s, such an audience could most likely be found among fellow knights and esquires of the household and ladies of equivalent station – persons like Richard Stury, for example, listed with Chaucer in 1368 along with other members of the household of Edward III,[23] someone well situated to appreciate his transformations of poems by Machaut and Froissart.[24] Other evidence of the composition of this enlarged public, with its seemingly expanded capacity for tonal variation, will be pursued in the discussion of Chaucer's subsequent poems. We can certainly say for now that the increased expansiveness in content and tone that marks Chaucer's address to this larger audience suggests his early recognition that alternative situations of address can open alternative narrative and stylistic possibilities.

Notes

1   Middle English *tale* itself conveys a strong and etymologically based sense of oral narration. The bibliography on the oral delivery of literature before the invention of printing is too long for recitation here, but basic texts include: Ruth Crosby, 'Oral Delivery in the Middle Ages,' *Speculum*, 11 (1936), 88–110, and 'Chaucer

and the Custom of Oral Delivery,' *Speculum*, 13 (1938), 413-32; Bertrand H. Bronson, 'Chaucer's Art in Relation to His Audience,' *Five Studies in Literature* (Berkeley: University of California Press, 1940), pp. 1-53; H. J. Chaytor, *From Script to Print* (1945; rpt. London: Sidgwick and Jackson, 1966), esp. pp. 1-21; Albert C. Baugh, 'The Middle English Romance: Some Questions of Creation, Presentation, and Preservation,' *Speculum*, 42 (1967), 1-31. To the extent that a private reading public was fostered by manuscript circulation in the course of the fourteenth and fifteenth centuries, these conclusions must of course be qualified. See Karl Brunner, 'Middle English Metrical Romances and Their Audience,' *Studies in Medieval Literature in Honor of Professor Albert Croll Baugh*, ed. MacEdward Leach (Philadelphia, 1961), pp. 219-27; M. T. Clanchy, *From Memory to Written Record* (Cambridge, MA: Harvard University Press, 1979). Too recent for proper consideration here is Leonard Michael Koff's highly pertinent *Chaucer and the Art of Storytelling* (Berkeley: University of California Press, 1988).

2 See Renaud's 'Livre de Mellibee et Prudence,' in *Sources and Analogues*, pp. 572-3.
3 The rhetorical sense of audience I am describing here is less evident in rhetorical treatises like those of Geoffrey of Vinsauf and Matthew of Vendôme, with their focus on the internal amplification of literary works, than in medieval theories of preaching. On this general subject, see Charles Sears Baldwin, *Medieval Rhetoric and Poetic* (New York: Macmillan, 1928), pp. 1-51; G. R. Owst, *Preaching in Medieval England* (Cambridge: Cambridge University Press, 1926), pp. 331-54; Harry Caplan, 'Classical Rhetoric and the Medieval Theory of Preaching,' *Historical Studies of Rhetoric and Rhetoricians*, ed. Raymond F. Howes (Ithaca, NY: Cornell University Press, 1961), pp. 86-7; and James J. Murphy, *Rhetoric in the Middle Ages* (Berkeley: University of California Press, 1974), pp. 269-355, esp. pp. 294-5. Of particular importance are the later medieval *artes praedicandi*, such as the fourteenth-century *De modo componendi sermones cum documentis* of Thomas Waleys, with its keen attention to matters of effective delivery and its advice that the preacher shape subject matter to the audience ('Necessarium tamen est ut discretionem habeat in loquendo, secundum diversitatem auditorium'). See *Artes Praedicandi*, ed. T.-M. Charland, *Publications de l'Institut d'études médiévales d'Ottawa*, 7 (1936), 339.
4 *Letters of Riper Years* (17, 3); quoted from *The Decameron*, ed. Mark Musa and Peter Bondanella (New York: Norton Critical Editions, 1977), p. 185.
5 Exemplified by H. Marshall Leicester Jr's discussion of the 'self-constructing' voice embodied in the text of Chaucer's *General Prologue*, in 'A General Prologue to the *Canterbury Tales*,' *PMLA*, 95 (1980), 213-34.
6 H. R. Jauss, 'Literary History as a Challenge to Literary Theory,' *Toward an Aesthetic of Reception*, trans. Timothy Bahti (Minneapolis: University of Minnesota Press, 1982), p. 19.
7 The same point can made of those sociologists of art – including Arnold Hauser and others following in the nondogmatic Marxist tradition of Plekhanov – who have written illuminatingly on the importance of a socially defined group of readers in perpetuating an artistic style. In his *Philosophy of Art History* (New York:

Meridian Books, 1963), Hauser argues that a style is confirmed when it finds 'a point of attachment in the support of a socially defined group' (p. 230). This is a valuable theory in its capacity to explain the mixture of styles within the art of a given age or even within a given *oeuvre* (a result of different social and cultural currents within any society) and the phenomenon of stylistic change (a result of the rise of new classes or groups of interested persons). These formulations nevertheless omit the influence of an audience (or an author's sense of an audience) on the process of composition. Hauser's audience can be 'attracted' by what it finds in a work and can 'encourage' a stylistic tendency by means as indirect as approbation or as direct as patronage, but it remains in a consuming role, wholly reactive to what the artist has placed before it.

8   V. N. Voloshinov, *Marxism and the Philosophy of Language*, trans. Ladislav Matejka and I. R. Titunik (New York: Seminar Press, 1973), p. 86.
9   Jonathan Culler, *Structuralist Poetics* (Ithaca, NY: Cornell University Press, 1975), pp. 131–2.
10 M. M. Bakhtin/P. M. Medvedev, *The Formal Method in Literary Scholarship*, ed. Albert J. Wehrle (Cambridge, MA: Harvard University Press, MA 1985), p. 18.
11 Ibid., pp. 151–2.
12 Compare Stanley Fish's compatible argument that the writing of a text is governed by the same community-derived rules that govern interpretation: 'Interpretive communities are made up of those who share interpretive strategies not for reading but for writing texts, for constituting their properties. In other words these strategies exist prior to the act of reading and therefore determine the shape of what is read rather than, as is usually assumed, the other way around.' See *Is There a Text in This Class? The Authority of Interpretive Communities* (Cambridge, MA: Harvard University Press, 1980), p. 14.
13 That such a group, consisting of gentle civil servants and a few Londoners, represents the heart of Chaucer's literary and social circle has previously been argued by Derek Pearsall, 'The *Troilus* Frontispiece and Chaucer's Audience,' *YES*, 7 (1977), 68–74; Paul Strohm, 'Chaucer's Audience,' *Literature and History*, 5 (1977), 26–41; and V. J. Scattergood, 'Literary Culture at the Court of Richard II,' *English Court Culture in the Later Middle Ages*, pp. 29–43. See also P. R. Coss, 'Aspects of Cultural Diffusion in Medieval England: The Early Romances, Local Society and Robin Hood,' *Past and Present*, 108 (1985), 35–79. Evidence pertinent to the existence of such a circle is also presented in Michael J. Bennett, *Community, Class and Careerism* (Cambridge: Cambridge University Press, 1983), pp. 30–3, 67–89.
14 For Salter's warning not to overreact against 'older accounts of Chaucer as court-poet, with patrons among the innermost circles of the English royal family,' see 'Chaucer and Internationalism,' *SAC*, 2 (1980), 79. An argumentative context for the reassertion of Chaucer's connections with royalty is provided by Richard F. Green, *Poets and Princepleasers* (Toronto: University of Toronto Press, 1980). The argument for the continuing importance of Richard and his circle as the primary audience of Chaucer's poetry has been cogently restated by Donald R. Howard, *Chaucer: His Life, His Works, His World* (New York: Dutton, 1987). Howard's

analysis reflects the influence of two arguments for the royal and occasional background of important works: Larry D. Benson, 'The "Love-Tydinges" in Chaucer's *House of Fame*,' *Chaucer in the Eighties*, ed. Julian Wasserman and Robert Blanch (Syracuse, NY: Syracuse University Press, 1986), pp. 3–22, and 'The Occasion of *The Parliament of Fowls*,' *The Wisdom of Poetry*, ed. Benson and Siegfried Wenzel (Kalamazoo, MI: Medieval Inst. Pubs., 1982), pp. 151–76. My argument is by no means intended as a refutation of these studies, which reassert an important element of Chaucer's situation of address to which I have given only brief attention. Chaucer's own activities in royal service provided him with ample incentive to address Richard and other magnates on selected occasions, and works like 'Lack of Steadfastness' (almost certainly addressed to Richard, probably in support of the king's attempt to broaden his popular base by opposing livery and maintenance in 1388–9) leave no doubt that he sometimes took advantage of these occasions. If his inscribed audiences are to be taken at all seriously as indicators of his intended audiences, one of his most ambitious poems – the *Legend of Good Women* – may be addressed almost exclusively to a socially elevated readership....

Several considerations, however, argue that Chaucer's address to his monarchs was occasional and situational rather than constant. One is the fact that he seems rarely to have written for purposes of patronage; James Hulbert argued convincingly as long ago as 1912 that Chaucer's literary efforts can be connected with no marks of royal favor that decisively set him apart from his fellow, nonliterary esquires (*Official Life*, p. 79). Another is the suggestion of booklists and other evidence that Richard's court embraced two tiers of linguistic and literary preference, with Richard and highly placed associates like Simon Burley preferring literature in French and Chaucer and his associates preferring English. On Richard's reading preferences, see Edith Rickert, 'Richard II's Books,' *The Library*, 4th ser., 13 (1933), 144–7; R. F. Green, 'Richard II's Books Revisited,' *The Library* 31 (1976), 235–9; M. V. Clarke, 'Forfeitures and Treason in 1388,' *Fourteenth Century Studies* (Oxford: Clarendon Press, 1937), pp. 120–1; V. J. Scattergood, 'Two Medieval Book Lists,' *The Library*, 23 (1968), 236–9. Even Henry IV appears to have preferred literature written in languages other than English. Henry did, to be sure, address Parliament in English (*RP*, vol. 3, pp. 422–3), but the most concrete illustrations of his reading preferences are his invitation to Christine de Pisan to be his guest in England (see *Lavision-Christine*, ed. Mary Louis Towner [Washington: Catholic University, 1932], pp. 165–6) and his apparent interest in Latin works of disputation and theology (as described in William Dugdale, *Monasticon Anglicanum*, vol. I [London: Bohn, 1846], p. 41). Actually Henry V was the first English king who definitely owned English books. Notable among these volumes is the Campsall MS of *Troilus and Criseyde*, which bears his arms as Prince of Wales (see Robert Kilburn Root, *The Manuscripts of Chaucer's Troilus*, Chaucer Society, ser. I, vol. 98[1914], p. 5), and Edward Duke of York's Englishing of Gaston de Foix's *Livre de Chasse*, addressed to Henry as Prince of Wales (*The Master of Game*, ed. W. A. and F. Baillie-Grohman [London: Chatto and Windus, 1909]). On the other hand, we have good evidence that (excepting a few members of exceptionally elevated station) most knights and esquires of the royal household preferred literature in English. Consider, in this regard, works by Usk and Clanvowe as well as Chaucer, together with such relevant nonliterary evidence as the English wills of the Lollard chamber knights (McFarlane, *Lancastrian Kings*, pp. 209–10).

15 Supported by such details as the connection between the 'ryche hil' and John of Gaunt's estate 'Richemont,' and between the 'long castel' and 'Lancaster.' See F. N. Robinson, *The Works of Geoffrey Chaucer* (2nd edn), note to lines 1318–19.

16 On the death of Blanche, see J. N. N. Palmer, 'The Historical Context of the *Book of the Duchess*: A Revision,' *The Chaucer Review*, 8 (1973–4), 253–61. On Gaunt's remarriage see McKisack, p. 267. But if, as Howard Schless has argued, 'this kyng' (1314) refers to Lancaster's claim on the throne of Castile, the date of the poem may be pushed to the end of 1371 or even to 1372. See 'A Dating for the *Book of the Duchess*: Line 1314,' *The Chaucer Review*, 19 (1984–5), 273–5.

17 A mandate of 30 August 1372 provides for an annuity to Philippa Chaucer for services to the Duchess Constance (*Life-Records*, pp. 85–6).

18 The Black Knight is described as being 'of the age of foure and twenty yer' (l. 455), when the Duke would actually have been 29 when Blanche died. Robinson (note to ll. 445ff.) offers a possible scribal explanation.

19 David, *The Strumpet Muse*, p. 11.

20 Lenaghan, 'Chaucer's Circle of Gentlemen and Clerks,' *The Chaucer Review*, 18 (1983–4), 155–60.

21 The marriage had occurred by 1366; Philippa was in service with Constance by 1372 (*Life-Records*, pp. 67–8, 85–6).

22 *Chaucer's Dream Poetry: Sources and Analogues*, ed. and trans. B. A. Windeatt (Cambridge: D. S. Brewer, 1982), pp. 39–40.

23 *Life-Records of Chaucer*, part 4, ed. R. E. G. Kirk, Chaucer Society Publications, 2nd ser., no. 32 (London, 1900), pp. 162–5.

24 ... Stury knew Froissart and possessed his own copy of the *Roman de la rose*.

3

Dream Vision Poetry: An Overview

The dream vision form evidently held great appeal for Chaucer: he used it in his three early poems, the *Book of the Duchess*, the *Parliament of Fowls* and the *House of Fame*, and returned to it in the later *Legend of Good Women*.[1] Dreams more generally are recurrent subjects in Chaucer's writing and several of his works include inset dream visions.[2] The three early dream vision poems (written between 1368 and 1382) share a number of motifs and themes, but are in some ways very different. The earliest, the *Book of the Duchess*, looks back to French courtly writing and has direct sources and analogues, whereas the *House of Fame* and *Parliament of Fowls* are influenced by Italian writing, and demonstrate a different kind of intertextuality; all three also draw on classical literature. The dream vision tradition itself has two aspects: the philosophical or religious mode of instruction, which finds its origins in the prophetic dreams of the Bible and in classical didactic poems like Cicero's *Dream of Scipio*, on which the *Parliament of Fowls* plays directly; and the courtly dream vision form made popular in French writing, in particular the *Roman de la Rose* of Guillaume de Lorris, in which the protagonist falls asleep, to dream that he is entering a beautiful springtime garden, where he sees a dance of allegorical figures associated with love, such as Delight and Mirth, is struck by the arrow of the God of Love, and falls in love with the beautiful Rose. The *Roman de la Rose* was completed by Jean de Meun, who returned to the philosophical tradition, adding characters like Nature and Reason, and writing a much more satirical, often anti-feminist, scholastic treatise. His realist mode is in direct contrast to the romance mode of Guillaume, and this hybrid text in many ways is a model for Chaucer, who brings together even in the *Book of the Duchess*, the most courtly of the early poems, the strains of romance and realism. Stephen Knight, who lucidly reads Chaucer's poems 'in terms of their social and historical meaning and function', reminds us of the possibility of social criticism in the dream form:

> The dream itself was a basic mode for medieval analysis of society. Dreams were taken seriously as ways of revealing a truth that the waking individual could not attain.... When he adopted the dream mode Chaucer was not only using a form appropriate to a leisured aristocracy: he was enabling himself to adventure into the highest ranges of medieval art and social analysis.[3]

For all its conventions the dream vision form was full of potential, an experimental mode.

The *Book of the Duchess* appears to respond to an historical event in an overt way, the death of John of Gaunt's wife Blanche, Duchess of Lancaster, in 1368, probably from the plague, and it draws very obviously on French conventions – the dream vision, the *dit d'amour*, the complaint and consolation – and on specific works, in particular those of Guillaume de Machaut and Jean Froissart. In the period before 1372 when he visited Italy, the strongest influence on Chaucer was that of the French courtly poets, whose writing was very much the currency of the 'international court culture' to which he belonged.[4] French poets like Froissart and Jean de la Mote spent time in Edward III's court, and the poet Oton de Graunson was, like Chaucer, a retainer of John of Gaunt. But the occasional and derivative qualities of the poem are deceptive: the *Book of the Duchess* is also a remarkably fluid composition, oddly resistant to interpretation. Its use of sources, so self-conscious and overt, is highly original, so that the poem becomes a creative translation of both a whole range of texts and no text. It may have been inspired by a particular death, but its narrative impact in many ways lies quite elsewhere, in the universals of the poem and its reworking of French courtly tradition. It is not irrelevant that one of the poets Chaucer was most influenced by, Machaut, was also a composer: in many ways the *Book of the Duchess* works like a complex piece of polyphonic early music, borrowing movements and motifs, transitional phrases and developments, but combining these in a highly imaginative fashion. The poem is pervaded by images of death, and it is this theme above all that structures the *Book of the Duchess*; it resonates through the story at both a literal and figurative level, and weaves together three stories, of the narrator's illness, of Ceyx and Alcyone, and of the dream of the Man in Black who sits lamenting in the forest. As the Dreamer, perhaps naively, perhaps knowingly, questions him about his loss, he is led through the processes of grief – to remember his lady and place her as lost, although we gain no easy consolation, but only the statement, 'she is ded'. The poem becomes a comment both on personal grief and the reality of death, and on the possibilities of courtly expression.

The *House of Fame* is a very different kind of poem – a difference marked for us by the contrast with the conventional springtime landscape of dream vision poetry. Here, the Dreamer falls asleep in December, and finds himself in a vast desert rather than a beautiful garden. This overturning of expectation sets the tone for the rest of the poem, which both works by undercutting literary convention and takes as its central theme the unstable nature of literary authority, meaning and interpretation. The Dreamer enters first a temple of glass, where he reads the story of Dido and Aeneas. Like the chamber decorated with stories from the *Roman de la Rose* in the *Book of the Duchess*, this image draws attention to the poem as a fiction that both interprets experience and requires interpretation. Chaucer's version of the Dido story offers a new interpretation that contrasts with Virgil's in its emphasis on the sufferings of Dido and on Aeneas's faithlessness. The narrative also points to one of Chaucer's recurring interests, that of the female predicament: the story of Dido will be told again in the *Legend of Good Women*.

In the vast desert, where the temple of the *House of Fame* is set, Geoffrey's guide proves to be rather different from the instructive figures of dream visions – not Virgil or Lady Philosophy, but a great eagle who catches him up in his claws. Unlike Scipio, who is shown the secrets of the spheres in Cicero's *Somnium Scipionis*, the plump and bookish 'Geoffroi' insists that he prefers to read about them instead: he is swept on to the House of Fame, half-solid, half-built on melting ice, and then to the whirling, unstable House of Rumour: in the House of Fame he learns directly of the arbitrary nature of fame and authority, as companies step forward, to be dismissed or rewarded only according to the whim of the goddess Fame. Here Chaucer draws on classical depictions of Fame, in particular that in the *Aeneid*, but again, as with his French material or the earlier strands from Dante and Cicero, he expands and rewrites them into something entirely new, at once classical, medieval and idiosyncratic. The work overturns our expectations of the courtly love vision: Geoffrey is identified as a poet who writes of Love, yet he has no 'tydynges' (644); he sits 'domb as any stoon' (656) at his books, living 'as an heremyte' (659). It overturns too the expectation of serious philosophical instruction, for the guide is a windy eagle and his subject unwilling. The poem is frenetic, almost nightmarish, certainly surreal, full of glittering, witty references to books and authors, constantly undercutting the notion of fame. It is also unfinished, breaking off just as a 'man of gret auctorite' enters: perhaps given the narrative direction, ending was impossible; indeed, some critics have suggested that the break is intentional.

Wholly different again is the *Parliament of Fowls*, where we return to something much closer to the love vision of the *Book of the Duchess* or the *Roman de la Rose*. Yet despite its light-hearted tone the poem is marked by ambiguous, darker implications. The gates at the entrance of the grand park where the Dreamer finds himself combine promises of paradise and perdition, as an inscription echoing that at the entrance of Dante's *Inferno*, 'Abandon hope all ye who enter here', is placed alongside images of bliss, eternal spring and grace. Hell is rewritten as a garden of love – but the garden of love is given its own infernal aspects, most obviously in the figures of suffering and torment that decorate the walls of the Temple of Venus. The stories depicted there are of tragic lovers: Tristan and Isolde, Troilus, Helen of Troy and Cleopatra. Venus herself is a languorous, sensuous figure, and the temple a steamy place of amorous sports. Venus is opposed in the poem by the goddess Nature, whose home is also within this earthly paradise, and who presides over the central narrative episode, the Parliament of Fowls itself, which draws on a familiar courtly tradition of debate between birds. Chaucer presents this as a ritual of Saint Valentine's Day, and may have written the poem specifically for this occasion: he seems to have set the example for subsequent literary celebrations of this festival.[5] This portrayal of natural order would seem the answer to the anguished loves of the Temple of Venus, and yet the parliament too is ambiguous: although the lower birds simply desire fitting mates, the three noble eagles echo the complexities of human love as they attempt to win the hand of the lovely formel eagle. The refined passions of the higher birds, set out in formal argument, are in marked contrast to the robust comedy of the quacking, cackling, chattering lower-class birds, and we are left uncertain of whether 'natural' love is possible when desire is complicated by thought, freedom and choice. We are uncertain too of the genre of the poem: is it an estates satire or a love poem, a love vision or a philosophical debate? Again we receive no answers: the choice of mate is deferred for a year, and the Dreamer wakes only to record his dream. In this third dream vision Chaucer once again merges a set of conventions to create an open-ended, questioning work.

A central issue of all these early poems is the question of the nature of dreams themselves, and hence the relation between dream theory and reality. The *Book of the Duchess* provokes the question of whether the dream arises from the sickness (presumably love) of the narrator, or from the tale of loss he has been reading, or is sent from outside, in response to his prayer to Morpheus. The *House of Fame* offers a serious discussion of the causes and classification of dream in its proem, which draws closely on the theory of Macrobius. And the *Parliament of Fowls* again relates the dream to the book the narrator has been reading – the *Dream of Scipio*. Each plays on courtly convention in using non-realist landscape and tropes. Yet, as well, the poems are wonderfully realistic in their dream-like qualities – their sudden shifts from scene to scene, their lack of logic, and their surreal, intense images. Most of all, the exploration of dreams becomes for Chaucer a means of exploring the creative processes of writing: the poems address the question of inspiration and its origins, the tension between courtly convention and realism, experience and authority, literary reputation and interpretation, and finally, the difficulty of writing, 'which is, like love, a craft so long to lerne' (*PF*,).

Dream Vision Poetry: An Overview

The dream vision form was one that Chaucer was to return to later in his poetic career with the *Legend of Good Women*. This is a rather different work in that it comprises a long dream vision prologue, which establishes the framework of the legends, followed by the nine legends themselves. Like the *House of Fame* and *Parliament of Fowls*, the Prologue raises questions of literary authority, which hint at the fact that in the legends, the focus will be as much on the process of writing as on the nature and truth of women. Like Geoffrey in the *House of Fame*, the narrator presents himself as an avid reader steeped in book knowledge, an absolute believer in literary truth: even when resting from his books to worship the daisy, his most beloved flower, he composes courtly verse. The prologue self-consciously uses all the conventions of courtly writing, to create semi-parodic parallels to the *Roman de la Rose*: the portrayal of the landscape, the adoration of the flower, and the figures of the God of Love and his court. The narrator is not struck by the arrow of love like the dreamer in the *Roman de la Rose*, however, but asked to atone for the offences against women that he has committed in translating the *Roman de la Rose*, the second part of which is so cynical about Love, and in telling the story of Criseyde's faithlessness in *Troilus and Criseyde*. His penance, dictated by the God of Love's queen Alceste, is to occupy the rest of his life 'In makyng of a glorious legende / Of goode wymmen, maydenes and wyves, / That weren trewe in lovyng al hire lyves; / And telle of false men that hem bytraien...' (F Prologue, 483–6).

The legends themselves follow an established literary genre, that of the catalogue of holy or virtuous women, but their subject is as much literary interpretation as the defence of women. We are made constantly aware of Chaucer interpreting and rewriting his sources, sometimes seriously, sometimes subversively, so that we are never quite sure of the status of the legends. Do they defend or condemn the passive, virtuous women they claim to celebrate? Are they comic in their concealment of negative details, and their frequent ellipses? Or is their pathos genuine, their adaptations suggestive of the possibilities of writing the female voice? The work moves between high seriousness and comedy, cliché and intense emotion, convention and originality. Its uncertain status has perhaps inspired more critical debate than any other work – but also less critical writing, for until recent feminist interest, the *Legend* was often considered dull and impossible to place.

While in his own time Chaucer had been viewed as the great poet of love and admired for his courtly writing, subsequent scholarship paid scant attention to the dream vision poetry until critics such as Lewis, Muscatine, Wimsatt and Bennett returned Chaucer to his place as courtly poet. The focus of their studies was most of all Chaucer's experimental use of literary conventions, in order to create what Muscatine termed a 'mixed style'. Below, he discusses the two styles, conventional and naturalistic, both of which Chaucer learned from French poetry:

> Rhetoricians, from classical times, have divided styles into the 'high', the 'middle', and the 'low', according to varying principles. And while these rigid principles of literary decorum seem to have passed out of favour, there is a basis of truth in them. We speak of the 'grand' style and of colloquial style, of formal or artificial style, and of naturalistic style. We speak of levels of usage in language generally. What is particularly significant in the use of this kind of terminology is that it often immediately implies a logical or social or even philosophical relationship among styles. And a perception of this kind of relationship – whether the styles are managed according to prescriptive rules of decorum or not – is often an additional indication of the meaning-function of the style or styles involved. 'High', 'middle', and 'low' about the twelfth century, for instance, indicated not only a difference in traits but also a relative level of social dignity in the subject matter. What we shall apply to Chaucer is perhaps a more sophisticated scale: that which corresponds roughly to the scale by which we classify the levels of human apprehension of experience. Thus we can say that a style which we instinctively call 'elevated' is better adapted than a naturalistic style to support an idealistic attitude toward experience. The non-representational traits of the former – often called the 'conventional' traits – are among the best resources open to the poet who wishes to deal with that level of experience not immediately apprehensible to the senses. Conversely, the adoption in a naturalistic style of certain traits from the idiom of common life, representationalism generally, is a sign of the particular potency of this style in the expression of a phenomenalistic attitude toward experience.[6]

Muscatine's work still stands as seminal in its depiction of the inventive intertextuality of Chaucer's dream poetry.

Extracts from the critical studies of J. A. W. Bennett and Wolfgang Clemen (see pp. 96 and 76) demonstrate a similar interest in placing Chaucer within a sophisticated tradition of literary authorities stretching back through the medieval writers of France and Italy, through theologians and philosophers various, to the great classical writers.[7] Subsequent criticism, such as that of Piero Boitani, has developed the subject of Chaucer's literary inheritance: Boitani's work on the *House of Fame* (represented below) and on the Italian influence more generally, employs T. S. Eliot's notions of literary debt to go beyond the study of sources or 'imitation'. Boitani thus considers Chaucer's imaginative response to writers such as Dante, 'the poet of heaven and hell', to explore 'the three lessons that as a poet "one learns, and goes on learning"' [Eliot], 'the lessons of craft, of speech and of exploration of sensibility (or "width of emotional range")'.[8] Boitani's work rewrites source study as an exploration of the making of the literary imagination.

Dream Vision Poetry: An Overview

As we have seen, the ironies and ambiguities of the dream vision poems rendered them of particular interest to those writing in the New Critical school. Their work, alongside a new historical emphasis, less extreme than Robertson's exegetical criticism, opened the way for further studies that focused on Chaucer's poetics. Sheila Delany offered an influential response to Robertson in her study, *Chaucer's 'House of Fame': The Poetics of Skeptical Fideism* (1972), which emphasized the process of reading and the ways history and ideology might inform it. This also presented the attractive notion of Chaucer as literary sceptic, ready to question cultural assumptions.

Since the 1980s, with the growing influence of postmodern critical theory, critical studies have focused particularly on the play of convention and originality, and on intertextuality. The question of genre recurs, as for instance in James I. Wimsatt's consideration of whether the *Book of the Duchess* is 'secular elegy or religious vision'.[9] W. A. Davenport offers an excellent consideration of Chaucer's use of the complaint genre.[10] Colleen Donnelly develops Muscatine's ideas regarding intertextuality in her consideration of how Chaucer challenges convention in the *Book of the Duchess* to achieve a 'plural, indeterminate vision' that is contained within a tight structural framework; Ruth Morse echoes this in her notion of Chaucer's 'controlled ambiguities'.[11] Jacqueline Miller addresses the specific intertextuality of the *House of Fame* to consider the issues of interpretation, authority and authorship, and relates literary invention to the process of dream. Rosemarie P. McGerr takes a similar perspective in considering the ways Chaucer engages with 'medieval traditions of closure and openness', in particular to resist closure.[12]

Much emphasis has been placed on the ambiguity of the poems and their self-consciousness about the process of writing. Lisa Kiser treats the issues of truth and textuality across Chaucer's *oeuvre* through the lens of 'the thematics of poststructuralism' to consider 'the problems inherent in poetic representation of all kinds'; Kiser, like Strohm, is also interested in 'socio-poetics', the relation of author, text and audience.[13] Robert Jordan considers Chaucer in terms of language theory, emphasizing the potential for 'a rhetorical poetics' represented by the dream vision form: 'In the dream visions Chaucer explored a range of generic forms and tonal registers that his vernacular had never before attempted'; his chapter on the *House of Fame*, 'Writing about Writing,' draws attention to the self-consciousness of this exploration, and the questioning of 'the validity of language and the nature of poetic composition'.[14] Stephen F. Kruger similarly considers the topic of 'self-reflexivity' in highly theoretical terms and relates the tension between earthly and celestial in the poem to its 'self-conscious consideration of its own imaginative processes'.[15] Critics such as Kruger draw both on postmodern linguistic theory and psychoanalysis, as do Judith Ferster and A. C. Spearing in the extracts below.

63

Stephen Knight brings into play the useful notion of the Gothic, arguing that the *Book of the Duchess* is 'written in a fully Gothic mode': rather than following a climactic movement, it states a theme – grief – and plays on this through poetic variation, amplifying it in different ways so that it becomes 'authorized'.[16] This notion of the Gothic works especially well for all Chaucer's dream vision poems. It can readily be applied not only to the *Book of the Duchess*, the *Parliament of Fowls* and the *House of Fame*, but also to the *Legend of Good Women*, which, though originally thought to be of less interest, has gradually come to receive a good deal of critical attention for its extended treatment of women in just this Gothic mode of amplification, variation and intertextuality. The discussion and extracts below point to the divided critical views on the *Legend of Good Women*. The dedication to the queen in the F Prologue has attracted numerous historical readings: early critics argued that the work was written 'in reluctant response to a royal command – an unwilling poet writing on an assigned topic', hence its unfinished state and problematic quality.[17] Such dependence on the truth of the Prologue's fiction is limiting and unpersuasive: it ignores the unlikelihood of close prescription, but also the typically open quality of Chaucer's writing and the complex literary games of interpretation that occur in the poem. Historical readings can, however, be fruitful: Florence Percival's full-length study, for instance, considers the Prologue, with its presentation of the Dreamer's adoration of his beloved daisy and vision of Queen Alceste, in terms of the cult of the marguerite or daisy, and its association with Queen Anne. New interest in Chaucer's writing about writing has also provoked much consideration of the poem in terms of its play on sources and engagement with the nature of 'olde bokes': Robert Worth Frank offered an engaging and sympathetic account of Chaucer's use of paradox, creative translation and combination of comedy and pathos, although Frank saw the work primarily as transitional, as a step towards the *Canterbury Tales* and 'to a poetry more of the world and less of the garden, to a realm of experience beyond the patterned and polite, the limited and predictable emotions and movements of courtly love'.[18] Subsequent criticism has taken the poem more on its own terms. Janet M. Cowen draws attention to the need to consider its genre, that of the 'legend' or collection of saints' lives; Lisa Kiser, whose work is discussed below, examines Chaucer's rewriting of his classical sources.[19] The feminist debate over the poem has been considerable and provocative. Various critics have challenged the work's claim to defend women by demonstrating the reductive effect of its repeated portrayals of passive, victimized women: Elaine Tuttle Hansen, for instance, refutes the notion of Chaucer as 'all womanis frend' in her rebarbative readings, which aim to expose the collusion of the narrator/author with anti-feminist thinkers.[20] Jill Mann's humanist approach, by contrast, offers a perceptive and sympathetic treatment of Chaucer's use of pathos, the complaint tradition,

Dream Vision Poetry: An Overview

and the hagiographic mode to evoke the woman's voice and celebrate feminine virtue. Richard Firth Green writes persuasively of Chaucer's criticism of 'erotic duplicity' in fashionable French courtly writing and the serious moral instruction on the virtue of *trouthe* offered in the *Legend*.[21]

Numerous critical readings focus on the self-consciously literary quality of the work: Alcuin Blamires places the work as 'a poetic manifesto'; Peter L. Allen considers the relationship between narrator and audience, and the ways the reader is drawn to criticize, reject and reform narratorial authority in an 'affirmative' sense; Steven Kruger addresses the ways the poem 'defies ... constraints' and demonstrates 'the inadequacy of schematic literary structures' to convey 'human passions'; Florence Percival considers the work in its literary contexts, as debate poem and palinode, as literary joke and dialogue between genders, as discussion of 'poetic craft' and demonstration of poetic ability in its engagement with the 'matter of Woman'.[22] She persuasively emphasizes Chaucer's adoption of 'a stance, a mask, a strategy' in his use of gender oppositions:

> The 'natural' falseness of men towards women is not unlike a certain inevitable poetic faithlessness towards one's source, one's matter, incurred whenever the poet employs his craft and subtlety, his art and feigning, to translate and make his source new and relevant.

She places special emphasis on 'the role that humourous anti-feminist/feminist debate plays in the self-definition of the learned poet, in the contexts both of courtly recreation and of scholarly *jeu d'esprit*'.[23] Percival's argument is persuasive in bringing together and explaining the anti-feminist/feminist impulses of the poem, which lend it so remarkable and uneasy a tension. Perhaps no other work so clearly demonstrates the subjectivity of reading – an issue with which Chaucer himself was so self-consciously engaged. The poem returns to the concerns of the earlier dream visions and to the subject of women, but in a more deeply ironic, questioning and often disturbing mode.

Notes

1 Helen Phillips and Nick Havely offer an excellent annotated edition, *Chaucer's Dream Poetry* (Longman, London, 1997). A. J. Minnis, *The Shorter Poems* (Clarendon Press, Oxford, 1995), in the *Oxford Guides to Chaucer* series, provides a very good, comprehensive introduction; also invaluable are B. A. Windeatt's collection of sources and analogues, *Chaucer's Dream Poetry* (D. S. Brewer, Cambridge, 1982), and A. C. Spearing's *Medieval Dream Poetry* (Cambridge University Press, Cambridge, 1976), discussed below.

Dream Vision Poetry: An Overview

2. See, for example, the several dreams in *Troilus and Criseyde*, and Chaunticleer's dream in the *Nun's Priest's Tale*.
3. Stephen Knight, *Geoffrey Chaucer* (Blackwell Publishers, Oxford, 1986), 7.
4. Minnis, *Shorter Poems*, 14.
5. For a consideration of the associations of Saint Valentine, see Henry Ansgar Kelly, *Chaucer and the Cult of Saint Valentine* (University of California Press, Davis, 1986).
6. Charles Muscatine, *Chaucer and the French Tradition: A Study in Style and Meaning* (University of California Press, Berkeley, 1957), 3.
7. See also Bennett's study of the *House of Fame*, *Chaucer's 'Book of Fame': An Exposition of the 'House of Fame'* (Clarendon Press, Oxford, 1984).
8. 'What Dante Meant to Chaucer ' in Piero Boitani, ed., *Chaucer and the Italian Trecento* (Cambridge University Press, Cambridge, 1983), 116–17.
9. '*The Book of the Duchess*: Secular Elegy or Religious Vision?' in John P. Hermann and John H. Burke, Jr, eds, *Signs and Symbols in Chaucer's Poetry* (University of Alabama Press, Tuscaloosa, 1981), 1; see also Wimsatt, *Chaucer and his French Contemporaries*: *Natural Music in the Fourteenth Century* (University of Toronto Press, Toronto, 1991).
10. *Chaucer: Complaint and Narrative* (D. S. Brewer, Cambridge, 1988); see also Lee Patterson, 'Writing Amorous Wrongs: Chaucer and the Order of Complaint' in James M. Dean and Christian K. Zacher, eds, *The Idea of Medieval Literature: New Essays on Chaucer and Medieval Culture in Honor of Donald R. Howard* (Associated University Presses, London, 1992).
11. Donnelly, 'Challenging the Conventions of Dream Vision in *The Book of the Duchess*', *Philological Quarterly* 66 (1987), 432; Morse, 'Understanding the Man in Black', *Chaucer Review* 15 (1980-1), 208.
12. McGerr, *Chaucer's Open Books: Resistance to Closure in Medieval Discourse* (University of Florida, Gainesville, 1998), ix.
13. Kiser, *Truth and Textuality in Chaucer's Poetry* (University Press of New England, Hanover, 1991), 10, 13.
14. Jordan, *Chaucer's Poetics and the Modern Reader* (University of California Press, Berkeley, 1987), 22–4.
15. Kruger, 'Imagination and the Complex Movement of Chaucer's *House of Fame*', *Chaucer Review* 28 (1993–4), 128.
16. Knight, *Geoffrey Chaucer*, 9.
17. Benson, *The Riverside Chaucer*, 587.
18. Robert Worth Frank, Jr, *Chaucer and the 'Legend of Good Women'* (Harvard University Press, Cambridge, MA, 1972), 36.
19. Janet M. Cowen, 'Chaucer's *Legend of Good Women*: Structure and Tone', *Studies in Philology* 82 (1985); Lisa Kiser, *Telling Classical Tales: Chaucer and the 'Legend of Good Women'* (Cornell University Press, Ithaca, NY, 1983).
20. Elaine Tuttle Hansen, *Chaucer and the Fictions of Gender* (University of California Press, Berkeley, 1992); see also Sheila Delany, *The Naked Text: Chaucer's 'Legend of Good Women'* (University of California Press, Berkeley, 1994).

21 Jill Mann, *Geoffrey Chaucer: Feminist Readings* (Harvester Wheatsheaf, New York, 1991); Green, 'Chaucer's Victimized Women', *Studies in the Age of Chaucer* 9 (1988), 8.
22 Alcuin Blamires, 'A Chaucer Manifesto', *Chaucer Review* 24 (1989-90), 29; Peter L. Allen, 'Reading Chaucer's Good Women', *Chaucer Review* 21 (1986-7), 420; Steven Kruger, 'Passion and Order in Chaucer's *Legend of Good Women*', *Chaucer Review* 23 (1988-9), 220; Florence Percival, *Chaucer's Legendary Good Women* (Cambridge University Press, Cambridge 1998), 11, 14.
23 Ibid., 18, 19.

4

Dream Vision Poetry:
Critical Extracts

The Lady White and the White Tablet: *The Book of the Duchess*

Judith Ferster

In the last extract of chapter 2, Paul Strohm addressed the Book of the Duchess *in the terms of speech-act theory, to consider the relations between Chaucer and his audience, as well as between Chaucer's writing and his literary sources. While Strohm's approach is firmly socio-political, the poem also lends itself to much more literary approaches, for it is as much about writing as it is about speech. Judith Ferster's book* Chaucer on Interpretation *examines the ways that a literary discourse 'produces new meaning' through a writer's reading, interpretation and rewriting of his sources. The term 'discourse' hints at the subjectivity of reading: interpretation depends upon the reader's preconceptions and biases, rather than representing transparent truths, and writing intersects with other strands of discourse to create new ones. Interpretation thus bridges the gap between 'self and other' (an idea that recalls Strohm's reference to the 'ideological bridge' between text and audience). Such notions reformulate, for example, Josipovici's discussion of experience and authority. Ferster links medieval notions of interpretation with those of modern phenomenological hermeneutics which address the dialectical and ongoing relation between mind and world in the creation of meaning, figured in the concept of the hermeneutic circle.[1] Ferster's approach is influenced too by deconstructive criticism, which tends to present the literary text as ultimately self-reflexive, about writing itself; she also employs psychoanalytical criticism. What is striking is how readily Chaucer's work lends itself to such apparently 'postmodern' analysis, for although the terms are different, the concerns regarding reading, writing and interpretation are similar.*

Ferster, like Strohm, views the topic of conversation as central to the Book of the Duchess. *Unlike Strohm, however, she does not consider the oral aspects of Chaucer, but focuses on conversation as a model for the relation between 'author and reading audience'. Such a relation, she argues, is echoed in the interlocutory relations within the text. For Ferster, the identification of the Black Knight with John of Gaunt is almost irrelevant, whereas for Strohm it is essential and almost self-evident; Ferster finds a considerable distance between the 'embarrassingly self-indulgent mourner' and the powerful noble who was to become king of Castile as well as a ruling force behind the young Richard II. For her, the focus is much more the isolation of the self, and she highlights the ways in which, just as the story of Alcyone reflects on the Dreamer's grief, so too the Man in Black may be seen as a projection of the Dreamer. The voices in the poem replicate each other, presenting a series of shadowy figures of grief. We, like the mourning Dreamer at the start of the tale, are uncertain of the distinctions between external and internal. In the same way, we are unsure of the status of the dream vision: does it arise from the Dreamer's internal state or is it the product of external forces, as the image of Morpheus suggests? And is the effect of the dream, like the sad tale of Alcyone, to enhance or alleviate grief and isolation? Is sleep healing or deathly? Does conversation cure, or recall distance and alienation? Ferster's chapter continues with a consideration of the notion of 'discourse as solution' in its engagement with others: 'we are often trying both to know each other and making each other into white tablets... on which we write our own characters'. She evokes sensitively the play of the poem on the emotions and shows how, like the narrator, Chaucer as reader interprets his sources, Ovid and Machaut, according to the particular emphases of this poem on self-engrossed grief. We are made acutely aware of the* Book of the Duchess *as poignant evocation of existential isolation.*

Notes

See also Judith Ferster's earlier article, 'Intention and Interpretation in the *Book of the Duchess*', *Criticism* 22 (1980), 1–24.

1 The term 'hermeneutics' was originally employed to describe biblical interpretation or 'exegesis'; it is now applied to interpretation generally. The image of the hermeneutic circle describes the circularity of interpretation: the understanding of the whole is dependent on understanding the parts, and vice versa. Phenomenological hermeneutics employs the philosophical perspectives of, in particular, Edmund Husserl and Martin Heidegger, to analyse literary works as fictional worlds created from the author's experience and consciousness. The work of Hans-Georg Gadamer, instanced by Ferster, exemplifies this approach.

Judith Ferster, 'The Lady White and the White Tablet: *The Book of the Duchess*' in *Chaucer on Interpretation*. Cambridge University Press, Cambridge, 1985.

The primary mode of discourse in the *Book of the Duchess* is conversation; the poem takes conversation as its model for the relationship between author and reading audience. The poem comments on both terms in this hermeneutically rich analogy,[1] showing that not only are relationships between authors and distant audiences problematic, but those between interlocutors who are face to face are problematic, too. In the *Book of the Duchess*, interlocutors are often alienated from one another. Every example of conversation emphasizes the difficulties of communication by casting doubts on the ability of the one who is addressed to respond correctly, or even to respond at all. The poem contains speech addressed to a woman who, in dying of a broken heart, seems to have willfully misinterpreted a truthful message, to a god who may not exist, to a knight who may be a projection of the speaker's imagination, and to Death, who does not answer. The woman, Alcyone, is a character in a tale in a book, a fixed form not responsive to its audience, and the mourned White, the topic of conversation between the narrator and the Black Knight, is one of the many medieval examples of women who are important because they are absent. In each case, communication seems to be stymied.

The poem can be seen as a description of the insoluble problem of the isolation of the self, or of successful communication between the narrator and the Black Knight, or of the formation of a new relationship in which two selves mutually influence each other, forming a unit or system larger than either of them alone. Through the ambiguity of the poem, the ease with which it seems to shift back and forth among these readings, Chaucer explores ideas of communication based on the very condition that makes communication problematic: its dependence on interpretation. In the remainder of this chapter, I shall discuss the poem's ambiguity and then the way in which that ambiguity is the key to Chaucer's reading of reading.

The Problems of Discourse

Conversation imperiled by self-enclosure is a metaphor for the danger besetting the relationship between a poem and a distant audience. What's more, the poem raises the possibility that the audience is always removed from the poem and that, indeed, speech is always removed, not only from the listener, but from the speaker. Knowledge of self and knowledge of other are both threatened.

The dream vision is well suited to the portrayal of monadic [isolated] selves. As we have seen [in chapter 3] the two basic kinds of dream in medieval dream theory are carefully distinguished by their sources. Truthful dreams are visitations by an external agent such as a god or an important relative capable of predicting the future; untruthful ones are caused by internal imbalance – for instance, from eating too much or worrying about one's job – and have no predictive value.² The trouble with this system of identification is that it allows for classification of a dream only after what it predicts has or has not happened. Since there are no criteria that permit us to categorize a dream according to form or content, the dream vision is inherently ambiguous: it may reflect external reality or merely an internal condition.

The beginning of the *Book of the Duchess* does nothing to reassure us about the nature of the dream or about the likelihood of the narrator's recounting it successfully. In fact, at the opening of the poem the narrator's inability to sleep has distorted his relationship to the world:

> I have so many an ydel thoght,
> Purely for defaute* of slep, *lack
> That, by my trouthe, I take no kep
> Of nothing, how hyt cometh or gooth,
> Ne me nys nothyng leef* nor looth. *pleasing
> Al is ylyche* good to me – *equally
> Joye or sorowe, wherso hyt be –
> For I have felynge in nothyng,
> But, as yt were, a mased* thyng, *bewildered
> Alway in poynt to falle a-doun...
> (ll. 4–13)

Since he tells us that he takes heed of nothing, we can assume that the 'ydel' thoughts to which he refers in line 4 are not just idle or random, but empty thoughts, with no meaning at all. The phrase, almost an oxymoron, suggests that his disease disturbs his perception and locks him inside his own mind.

The danger of self-enclosure is also reflected in the names for the mental phenomena that 'fill' his empty mind:

> For sorwful ymagynacioun
> Ys alway hooly in my mynde.
> (ll. 14–15)
> Suche fantasies ben in myn hede,
> So I not what is best to doo.
> (ll. 28–9)

Although 'fantasy' was one of the Middle English words commonly used to translate *species*, the image that mediates normal perception, the term had a negative connotation as well.³ The language does not distinguish between an image that mediates knowledge and a device that deceives. There is similar ambiguity in 'imagination'.... The narrator's dream may actually be a product of his diseased mind.

The narrator's account is paradoxical: he presents us with both an insoluble problem and a solution. Language may either cure isolation from the world or intensify it. Language is a cure in that to speak to another, to make a request, to express a need are actions with which he breaks out of the self-enclosed state that threatens his identity. He defines himself as subject with the first word of the poem: 'I.' Writing implies that he is not (or is no longer) in the state he complains of. He is also capable of treating himself as an object, both of self-reflection ('I have gret wonder... / How that I lyve...,' ll. 1–2; 'So when I saw I might not slepe...,' l. 44) and of the attention of others ('But men myght axe me why soo...,' l. 30). Once he has begun to speak the poem, he is not suffering from the disease of apathy. Had he still been apathetic, he would not have been able to request a book, read it, sympathize with the main character, or start his poem. This discrepancy between the content of his complaint and the implication of his ability to complain may signal that he is already at least partially cured of his malady.

The discrepancy, however, may also magnify the problem of loss or absence because it shows that he is absent from himself. The self he refers to when he claims to be apathetic is already past. The poem itself alienates him from his experience. As he reminds us at the very end of the poem (ll. 1330–4), what we experience as we read is not his dream, but his poem, which is now predicated upon the existence of a lost original.[4]

The narrator's relationship to the story of Alcyone is ambiguous in a similar way. If his project, or the project of the poem, is to cure the narrator's malaise, the story of Alcyone both does and does not contribute to the cure. It does because the book is 'other,' but it does not because he absorbs Alcyone into his own mental state. On the one hand, his empathy with the bereaved queen is a response to another. On the other, the empathy merely gives him a new reason to remain unhappy. Empathy with another may be part of the cure, but if the other merely represents the self and if misery merely loves company, empathy is just projecting one's own emotion onto the world.

The story of Alcyone demonstrates the dangers of assimilating others' words or actions into one's own mental set. The mourning queen, who is fasting for grief over her husband's disappearance, is visited by an apparition of her husband (Morpheus disguised in the king's body), which tells her that he is dead and that she should stop grieving. His exact words are 'let be your sorwful lyf!' (l. 202). He then instructs her to bury his body, and leaves. With that, Alcyone falls into a coma and in three days dies.

Her response to the apparition is an example of willful misinterpretation. Her previous promise to Juno – 'Send me certain knowledge of my husband's fate and I will dedicate myself to you' – implies an intention to live after hearing the news. The king's command – 'Bury my body' (l. 207) – implies that 'let be your sorwful lyf' means 'give up your sorrow and get on with your life.' When, instead, she gives up her life, she is simultaneously self-interested and self-destructive – suicide by misinterpretation.

It is instructive to compare this version of the story with its source in Ovid's *Metamorphoses* (Book XI).[5] Whereas Ovid's Alcyone prays for her husband's safe return, Chaucer's is almost hysterical because of her uncertainty about him and prays to Juno for information. Chaucer makes the important issue not safety, but knowledge, one of the important subjects of the poem. Furthermore, when Ovid's Alcyone walks on the beach and sees a drowned body that she does not recognize as that of Ceyx, she weeps in sympathy for both the 'stranger' and his wife. Our sympathy for her is increased by her sympathy for someone she thinks she does not know. The self-enclosed death of Chaucer's Alcyone (she seems never to get out of bed after she learns the truth about her husband) allows no room for feelings for others.

The issue of sympathy, suppressed in Chaucer's version of the story, informs the rest of his poem, starting with the narrator's response to Alcyone. In one way, she is the mirror image of the narrator – she sleeps too much, he too little. In another way they may be just alike in assimilating the messages of others to their own purposes. She misreads Morpheus; he misreads Ovid. One interpretation of the story is that one should not grieve too much. But rather than end his eight-year mourning, the narrator extends it at least one day on Alcyone's account (ll. 99–100). Her story advances him on his self-destructive course rather than recalling him from it. Critics have speculated on whether the narrator 'learns' anything from his dream. We may interpret his announcement of his extra day of sadness as positive if we think it healthy to sympathize with another or negative if we think it unhealthy to use another's pain as an excuse for prolonging one's own.

Our interpretation of the fact that the book leads the narrator to sleep will depend on our assumptions about sleep and the dream. For Alcyone, sleep, which is metaphorical death ('the dede slep,' l. 127; 'dedly slepynge soun*,' [sound] l. 162; 'This cave was also as derk / As helle-pit,' ll. 170–1), leads to literal death. Is the narrator's sleep healing or a form of death? Is the dream an encounter with another person that reintegrates him into society or merely his reproduction of his own situation?

Insofar as the poem is an elegy for Blanche, Duchess of Lancaster, the Black Knight is clearly someone other than the narrator: John of Gaunt, Chaucer's patron. The interview with him marks the narrator's return to a healthy relationship with the outside world. But if the knight is John of Gaunt, what rules of decorum would allow the artist to portray his patron as an embarrassingly self-indulgent mourner who needed to be coaxed back to rationality?[6]

The knight is also a projection of the narrator.[7] When we meet him, he is in a state very much like the narrator's at the start of the poem: he is apathetic and out of touch with the world. He cannot see the narrator or hear his greeting. He is also concerned with death but goes the narrator one better in not merely fearing it, but openly wishing for it:

> Allas, deth, what ayleth the,
> That thou noldest* have taken me,   *did not wish to
> Whan thou toke my lady swete...
> (ll. 481–3)

Juxtaposing the *Book of the Duchess* with one of its sources, Machaut's *Dit de la Fonteinne amoureuse*, highlights the ambiguity of the Black Knight's identity. In Machaut's poem, the narrator meets the knight while still awake, so there is less question about his objective existence. Then the dream appears to be objectively caused when both men dream the same dream.[8] Machaut disallows the confusion about the status of the knight and the dream that is inherent in Chaucer's poem.

The *Book of the Duchess* oscillates between two opposing views: the existence and isolation of the self and the other, and their mutual intelligibility and influence. The self may be alone because it does not know whether the other exists, or it may partially determine and be determined by the other as they interact. The poem may describe either a replicating series of characters who are shadows of each other – the narrator, Alcyone, the narrator's dreamed self, the Black Knight, Chaucer – or powerful encounters between the narrator and his book and the two figures of his dream. There seems to be no easy way to decide. As in the *Parliament*, the solution lies partly in describing the problem.

Notes

1   The comparison between conversation and interpretation is crucial to Hans-Georg Gadamer in *Truth and Method* (London: Seabury Press, 1975), especially pp. 325–41.

> Dialectic as the art of conducting a conversation is also the art of seeing things in the unity of an aspect (sunoran eis hen eidos) i.e. it is the art of the formation of concepts as the working out of the common meaning. Precisely this is what characterizes a dialogue, in contrast with the rigid form of the statement that demands to be set down in writing: that here language, in the process of question and answer, giving and taking, talking at cross purposes and seeing each other's point, performs that communication of meaning which, with respect to the written tradition, is the task of hermeneutics. (p. 331)

The rest of this chapter is a commentary on the analogy.
2 Macrobius, *Commentary on the Dream of Scipio*, 1.3.4, trans. William H. Stahl (New York: Columbia University Press, 1952), p. 88.
3 See *MED*, 1, 2.(a), 3.(a).
4 As J. Hillis Miller argues in 'Ariadne's Thread: Repetition and the Narrative Line,' it is the supposed 'copy' that is the source of the originality of the 'original' (*Critical Inquiry*, 3 [1976], 55–77; see pp. 66–7). This is particularly true in the case of dreams, in which a later recounting provides the only access to the original. The distance between original and copy is also interesting to hermeneutics. Gadamer comments that translations are always somehow 'more' than the original texts. Reproduction is never 'mere' reproduction (see *Truth and Method*, pp. 346–51), and the narrator's poem includes more than just the dream.

The separation of the individual from himself has received attention from both medieval and modern writers, for example, St Augustine, *Confessions*, 10.32, trans. R. S. Pine-Coffin (Baltimore: Penguin Books, 1961), pp. 237–8; Gadamer, *Truth and Method*, p. 385. In 'Limited Inc abc...,' *Glyph*, 2 (1977), 162–254, Jacques Derrida explores the way in which one is alienated from the self by language (see pp. 185, 193, etc.).
5 I have used the Frank Justus Miller translation of *Ovid: Metamorphoses* (Cambridge, MA: Harvard University Press, 1916), as it is excerpted in *Chaucer: Sources and Backgrounds*, ed. Robert P. Miller (New York: Oxford University Press, 1977), pp. 108–11.
6 D. W. Robertson, Jr argues that the Black Knight is not to be identified with John of Gaunt ('The Historical Setting of Chaucer's *Book of the Duchess*,' in his *Essays in Medieval Culture* [Princeton, NJ: Princeton University Press, 1980], pp. 235–56). Robertson cites other studies on p. 235.
7 This view is supported by Gadamer's comment (*Truth and Method*, p. 382) on understanding as dialogue:

> Because our understanding does not embrace what it knows in one single comprehensive glance, it must always produce out of itself what it thinks, and present it to itself as if in an inner dialogue with itself.

Among the critics for whom the Black Knight is a version of the narrator is Robert W. Hanning, who calls the narrator's meeting with the knight 'a confrontation with his own sorrow... in the externalized and idealized form of a black knight.' See 'The Theme of Art and Life in Chaucer's Poetry,' in *Geoffrey Chaucer: A Collection of Original Articles*, ed. George D. Economou (New York: McGraw-Hill, 1975), pp. 15–36, especially p. 16.
8 For a summary of this passage of the poem, see B. A. Windeatt, *Chaucer's Dream Poetry: Sources and Analogues* (Woodbridge, Suffolk: D. S. Brewer; Totowa, NJ: Rowman and Littlefield, 1982), p. 40.

'The Dido Episode' in *The House of Fame*

Wolfgang Clemen

Wolfgang Clemen follows in the footsteps of the great early medievalists, C. S. Lewis, J. R. R. Tolkien and J. A. W. Bennett, in his knowledge of the literature of the Middle Ages and the classical period, and his technical expertise in analysing medieval writing. Like his predecessors, he sees as fundamental to medieval literary studies the question of sources and the use of conventions. Although his terms are more traditional than Ferster's, he is in fact concerned with the same issue: the hermeneutic circle of Chaucer, his sources and his readers. His method is that of close comparison of Chaucer's writings with his sources, in order to elicit critical readings and, often, to demonstrate just how unconventional Chaucer is. This extract focuses on one section of the House of Fame, *the Dido episode, and demonstrates how fruitful imaginative intertextual study can be. Clemen shows Chaucer's recurrent emphasis on the issues of writing and interpretation, and considers a third thematic strand, also present in the* Book of the Duchess, *that of love and gender. Here the important issue of* trouthe *is raised, in particular the respective* trouthes *of men and women. Whereas in the* Book of the Duchess *the enemy who snatched away the Man in Black's 'fers' (654) was death, here it is* untrouthe, *unfaithfulness and betrayal. It is in elaborating this notion that Chaucer most greatly alters his source.*

Clemen begins his consideration of the House of Fame *with a description of Chaucer's exploratory narrative technique: we experience, along with the Dreamer, the exotic setting of the Temple of Venus. The gradual unfolding of detail culminates in the depiction of the wall-paintings telling the story of Dido. Clemen notes the contrast between allegorical French courtly poetry, the conventions of which Chaucer is using, and the story drawn from the* Aeneid. *For Clemen, the telling works through 'ironical contrast', as a familiar story is told with startling shifts, enhanced by the* naïveté *of the narrator. Like Brewer, Clemen is sharply aware of the ways that Chaucer experiments with convention, and he makes the observation, not unlike Strohm's (though not phrased in socio-political terms), that Chaucer deliberately plays with his audience, here by subtly re-presenting a story familiar from the celebrated tellings by both Virgil and Ovid. Clemen notes how swiftly the scene is sketched, through Chaucer's 'condensing narrative technique', but remarks too the early hints of a subjective and empathetic narrator.*

In the second part of the account the tone shifts from swift, broad summary to the minute depiction of Dido's loss. Here, psychological and circumstantial detail create an intense picture of her plight. For Clemen, this shows that Chaucer's focus is not that of a poet of 'courtly love'. Love is not celebrated as an ecstatic triumph, while the betrayal and suicide scenes are vastly reduced, so that we are uncertain quite what the tenor of the narrative is. Although the narrator's choice of phrases makes clear Aeneas's 'feigning,' Dido's passion is portrayed as 'nyce', foolish. For Clemen, the great text is the classical one, whereas this version, he argues, reduces the passionate and noble to the banal; the story is divested 'of the last shreds of romanticism, greatness and magic'. Clemen views the medieval tradition of portraying Aeneas as seducer as reductive, leading to a trite version of a tragic love story.

Yet as he acknowledges in the last part of his discussion, this critical view is also reductive: like the Legend of Good Women *(though not all critics would agree), the work is not a parody or travesty of the classical story, but rather offers a comic contrast, working through irony to provide the type of exemplum regarding male truth that Chaucer offers again and again in his writing. The question of tone is a delicate one. Dido's lament may be seen as poignant in its specificity, and her innocence not as folly but vulnerability: 'we wreched wymmen konne noon art' (335). Questions are undoubtedly raised about the status of a tale of female innocence and male betrayal, told by a male author and narrator, and such ambiguity is Chaucer's hallmark. Yet, as so often, pathos does not seem to be lost, but rather intertwined with irony: a voice of realism or even cynicism directly counters the excessive and sometimes superficial idealism of French courtly poetry, and the male focus of the Dido episode of the Aeneid. Once again, as the rest of the* House of Fame *so clearly demonstrates, we are left with questions of interpretation: how would Dido tell her own story? Analysis of Chaucer's sources like that of Clemen allows for some assessment of Chaucer's response to this question.*

Wolfgang Clemen, '"The Dido Episode," in *The House of Fame*' in *Chaucer's Early Poetry*, trans. C. A. M. Sym. Methuen, London, 1963.

The Dido Episode

Chaucer's rendering of the *Aeneid* which centres round the Dido episode offers several instances of his art of taking over well-known material and then going on to disappoint expectations and introduce an ironical contrast to what had been familiar. The effect of surprise is linked with irony and veiled amusement; in addition, the naive and astonished pose of the dream-narrator adds a particular spice as Chaucer thus skilfully plays with conventions and traditional material, and deliberately influences his audience.

As he himself tells us (378f.), Chaucer used both Virgil and also Ovid's *Heroides* for his episode. At the beginning, however, it is the *Aeneid* that he recalls by quoting its universally familiar opening lines as the 'inscriptio' on the wall of the temple. This serves to emphasize still further the contrast between his version (which then follows) and the tone and spirit of that great epic.

Chaucer's version of the *Aeneid* falls clearly into two sections. In the first he gives a chronological account up to the beginning of the Dido episode, which he relates in the second. The first section is an example of his condensing narrative technique, a few bold lines giving a rapid flexible outline of the outward events. Chaucer divides the complex happenings into six sections, each introduced by 'I saugh'; and he 'paints the picture' by portraying each happening *as* a picture. At the same time the continuous flow of the narrative brings movement into each scene, while numerous verbs of motion carry the story along.

It might seem that this kind of rapid summary, skimming over the surface of things and putting the emphasis on facts, would prevent Chaucer from developing any personal attitude to his material. Yet a characteristic bias does creep in here; the poet abandons his objective attitude as narrator. He does so by his avowals of sympathy ('allas', 157, 183, 'dispitously', 161, 'That hyt was pitee for to here', 180, 189, etc.), and still more by his familiar address to the two goddesses and his way of describing them ('There saugh I thee, cruel Juno...Renne and crye as thou were wood', 198f.; 'Venus, how ye, my lady dere, Wepynge with ful woful chere', 213f.). This brings the lofty tale of Aeneas and the strife among the gods down from its pedestal into a familiar everyday sphere and presents it with an appeal for the sympathy or disapproval of the public. In this first section there are also indications that Chaucer tends to tone down features at variance with his own attitude; when for instance he relates Creusa's counsel to Aeneas to journey to Italy, he writes:

> And seyde he moste* unto Itayle,   *must go
> As was hys destinee, sauns faille;
>
> (187f.)

In this context, 'sauns faille'[1] serves to stress not Chaucer's own conviction but – as he later (427) expressly states – a faint doubt about this 'excuse'.

As soon as Chaucer begins the Dido story itself (239ff.) it is clear that this was the sole episode of importance to him. He alters his whole method of presentation. The facts and outward circumstances are now given briefly, to allow full scope for the psychological action. No longer content with brief asides, the narrator now steps forward to take his place beside his story, commenting on it, suggesting how it may be applied, plainly taking sides and giving his views. One is struck by this eagerness on Chaucer's part to

Dream Vision Poetry: Critical Extracts

appear as interpreter of his own story, his readiness in furthering his public's understanding of it and in directing their attention to certain aspects of it. There is an ironic contrast here, one attitude cutting across the other; we have the dreamer, naive about what he notes and relates, and also the busy commentator, passing remarks on what he recounts, pointing out certain details and keen to use this episode for the edification of his public.

What, in fact, is Chaucer aiming at in this Dido episode? In what tenor does he relate it, and in what light does he show Dido and Aeneas? A few lines are enough to tell how their love to one another came about and what course it took:

> And, shortly of this thyng to pace,
> She made Eneas so in grace
> Of Dido, quene of that contree,
> That, shortly for to tellen, she
> Becam hys love, and let him doo
> Al that weddynge longeth too.
>   (239ff.)

The '*brevitas*-formula'[2] (often employed here and such a favourite with Chaucer), and the topos of modesty or incapacity (247f.) are only an excuse to pass quickly, almost scornfully, over this whole part of the Dido story dealing with the birth, upsurge and ecstasy of their love. Chaucer, unlike the poets of 'courtly love', is averse to expressing this love in 'lofty phrases'.

> What shulde I speke more queynte,*   *elaborately
> Or peyne me my wordes peynte*   *use circumlocutions
> To speke of love? Hyt wol not be;
> I kan not of that faculte.
>   (245ff.)

He dismisses what Dido felt for Aeneas in a line where alliteration and rhythm emphasize the real intention of the words:

> Made of hym shortly at oo word
> Hyr lyf, hir love, hir lust,* hir lord   *pleasure
>   (257)

In the very next lines Chaucer clearly quite abandons the attitude of an objective reporter, giving his own interpretation and verdict as he says of Dido:

Dream Vision Poetry: Critical Extracts

> Wenynge hyt had al be so
> As he hir swor; and herby *demed*
> That he was good, for he such *semed*.
> (262)

The expressions *demed* and *semed* lead Chaucer on to a long discussion on 'appearance and reality', using Aeneas as an illustration. And two lines further on, he anticipates the later course of the episode with:

> For he to hir a traytour was;
> Wherfore she slow hirself, allas!
> (267)

Chaucer seems, then, in great haste to come to what is for him the real point of the tale. He has to leap forward in the story and tell us the end, and only takes it up in its chronological sequence at line 293. Aeneas as a worthless deceiver, a mean fellow who with scornful heartlessness deserts Dido after getting what he wanted; Dido on the other hand as meriting our pity, a tender though foolish and gullible creature easily deceived by a fine show – this is how Chaucer here presents these two famous lovers to us. He continues to break in with his own views and comments, in order to impress this interpretation on his public. He speaks of Dido's 'nyce lest' (287), (her foolish infatuation), states that she loved 'al to sone a gest' (288), and after he has let her lament at length, ends on a dry note:

> But that is don, is not to done;
> Al hir compleynt ne al hir moone,
> Certeyn, avayleth hir not a stre.*   *straw
> (361ff.)

Despite his aim of bringing this love-tragedy to the level of a human and individual story, Ovid had based Dido's lament on genuine feeling common to all mankind. Chaucer however gives us the plaintive lamentations of a girl of middle-class background who has been 'let down' by a man and now bitterly bewails the fact that 'all men are the same':

> Allas! is every man thus trewe,
> That every yer wolde have a newe,
> Yf hit so longe tyme dure,
> Or elles three, peraventure?
> As thus: of oon he wolde have fame
> In magnyfyinge of hys name;

Another for frendshippe, seyth he;
And yet ther shal the thridde be
That shal be take for delyt,
Loo, or for synguler profit.*   *personal pleasure
(301)

Widely applicable banalities of this sort bear no relation whatever to the disillusionment and passionate grief felt by a proud woman of royal blood as described by Virgil. The same, too, applies to Dido's laments at the loss of her good name and her fear of getting herself talked about. People would begin to murmur 'that she will no doubt do with others as she has done now' (358–60). Fame, which appears in Virgil as an independent figure, a mighty personified abstraction (*Aen.* IV, 174), is here reduced to a timorous reflection uttered by Dido herself. Dido's own references to *fama* (a bare hint of Virgil, *Aen.* IV, 321) are expanded by Chaucer into the commonplace anxiety of a woman careful of her good name. Her remarks, like the other passages, show how Chaucer reduces the stature of his lovers, stripping them of all heroism and grandeur. With a kind of shrewd everyday common sense he examines this famous love story under a magnifying glass, subjects it to a coldly disillusioned scrutiny and divests it of the last shreds of romanticism, greatness and magic which the episode may still have possessed at that period.

Chaucer was very well aware that Virgil had represented the episode in quite another way, above all in his unmistakably different portrayal of Aeneas.[3] But when it comes to the most significant point here, the behests of that fateful power which Aeneas was bound to obey before even his love, Chaucer only mentions these in a casual aside thrown out long after he had finished with the whole episode:

But to excusen Eneas
Fullyche of al his grete trespas,
The book seyth Mercurie, sauns fayle,*   *for certain
Bad hym goo into Itayle,
And leve Auffrikes regioun,
And Dido and hir faire toun.
(427)

This explanation 'to excusen Eneas',[4] thus woven in at a later stage, throws light on Chaucer's attitude; and this is more clearly expressed in his *Legend of Dido* which deals with the same theme. In Virgil's version, Cupid in the guise of Ascanius causes Dido to fall in love (and in Chaucer's eyes this 'excuses' Dido); to this, Chaucer remarks:

> but, as of that scripture,
> Be as be may, I take of it no cure.
>
> (*Legend* 1144f.)

It can of course be argued that in Ovid's *Heroides* Chaucer could see the episode detached from its epic and fateful historical connotation.[5] Ovid had already taken the 'heroism' out of Dido; she had forfeited the tragic greatness of Virgil's *Dido* and had acquired a sweet almost sentimental character. The affecting lament, a feature of all Ovid's *Epistles*, may have stimulated Chaucer to stress these aspects still further in his portrait of Dido, and to express them in her speeches, which form the chief part of the episode.[6] There were also hints here for Chaucer, showing Aeneas in the role of a perfidious seducer; these were enlarged upon in the *Roman de la Rose*, by Chrétien and by Machaut;[7] and they were furthermore represented in Germany by the Aeneas Romance and the *Eneid* of Heinrich von Veldecke. But all this is not enough to explain Chaucer's individual portrayal. What he has taken up here is the best-known love story of the Middle Ages,[8] a courtly theme hitherto treated in a polished and conventional style; and what he makes of it – almost like a ballad-monger singing a murder-ditty – is a very ordinary love-affair, a tale not of some fateful entanglement but of the everyday weakness of men and women.

There is direct contrast to Virgil, then; and there is also noticeable divergence from Ovid. For all that, however, it is neither necessary nor appropriate to regard Chaucer's version as an intentional 'parody of Virgil' or as the 'travesty of a myth'.[9] If this were so, then many parts of the *Legend of Good Women*, as well as other retellings of classical tales, would also have to be seen as a 'parody' or a travesty. In the case of a parody, some well-known author's typical themes, stylistic traits and conventions are so imitated and used that through radical alteration and exaggeration they offer a comic contrast with the original. But this is not what Chaucer does; he aims at retelling the story from the very beginning in a new light, on a new plane and with a different intention. What emerges certainly contrasts with tradition and some comic effects may result from it. But the more the hearers or readers were familiar with the Dido story as originally presented, the better they would have been able to appreciate Chaucer's irony that flashes out both here and in the other Books of the *House of Fame*. Moreover, this humoristic effect is only one of many; and to try to see the story from this angle alone would be to take a very biased view.

Notes

1   Cf. the slightly comic use of '*sauns faille*' in the *Man of Law's Tale* II, 501.
2   W. N. Francis, 'Chaucer shortens a tale', *PMLA* 68 (1953).

3   Cf. *Aeneid* IV, 331ff., 340, 361, 393ff., 447ff.
4   For a different interpretation of these lines cf. Muscatine, p. 110. [In Virgil's *Aeneid*, the god Mercury summons Aeneas to leave Dido and follow his destiny of founding Rome.]
5   E. K. Rand, *Ovid and his Influence*, 1925.
6   Cf. also W. F. Schirmer, 'Chaucer, Shakespeare und die Antike', *Warburg Institute Lectures* 1930–1.
7   Cf. *Roman de la Rose* 13192, Machaut, *Jug. Navarre* 2104, Chrétien, *Erec* 5342. This conception of Aeneas as a deceiver was supported by a tradition going back to Dares Phrygius and Dictys Cretensis, whereby the Greeks owed their capture of Troy to the treachery of Aeneas and Antenor. On the Dido story during the Middle Ages, cf. D. Comparetti, *Vergil im Mittelalter*, 1875; George Gordon, *Virgil in English Poetry*, British Academy Lecture 1931.
8   Saint Augustine confesses that on reading the story of Dido he had once been so moved by her death as to forget for the time being to live *in Christo* (*Conf.* I. 1. 53).
9   Cf. I. Besser, p. 63.

Chaucer's Fame and Her World: The Poem

Piero Boitani

In many ways Piero Boitani follows in the footsteps of scholars of literary history such as Wolfgang Clemen: his book places Chaucer's depiction of Fame in the House of Fame *within the vast sweep of European literature, classical and medieval. He does not simply look at Chaucer's use of sources, however, but rather at the ways that images and themes associated with Fame developed in the shift from ancient to medieval, and how Chaucer's work intersects with these – 'the way in which he uses traditional imagery and ideas, creates myth, exploits the marvellous, explores literature and poetry, discusses language'. As in Strohm's and Ferster's studies, though from the rather different perspective of cultural history or history of ideas, we are made aware of the dialectic relation between internal and external, between Chaucer and the literary traditions that at once shape and are shaped by him. The notion of Fame is particularly relevant to any consideration of the process of writing, and it is clear that in the* House of Fame *Chaucer directly addresses the question of literary immortality. As Boitani suggests, it is perhaps not coincidental that the poem is unfinished: such great questions have no answer.*

   In this opening chapter Boitani focuses on the visit to the House of Fame (Book III) and argues that the poem has a more definite structure than is often suggested: whether or not it is finished, its structure can be seen as coherent, though this coherence is often allusive and implicit, like that of dreams. Boitani, like Clemen, explores the ways that Chaucer moves away from the French courtly dream vision form, used in the Book of the Duchess, *to a form more indebted to Dante, and perhaps to other Italian writers. The eagle-guide is a direct reference to Dante's vision of an eagle in* Purgatorio IX, *as well as a comic allusion to Virgil as guide. Such references, direct and indirect, pervade the poem, as when the nervous 'Geoffroi' thinks on the description of the spheres in the books he possesses – the writings of Boethius, Martianus Capella and Alain de Lille – and later, when he encounters the mythical figures who people the House of Fame, and the great authors atop their pillars there. Boitani shows the work to be a kind of literary tapestry, which comically places Chaucer as an unwilling representative amongst the celebrated writers of 'olde appreved stories', and at the same time reveals the arbitrary nature of such approval.*

For Boitani, it is the sensual that structures the movement of the poem and creates its drama. He explores the visual constructs of the Houses of Fame and Rumour, and comments on the parallels between the earlier temple of glass and the fantastic castle, built on the half-melting rock of ice. In particular, he points to the repeated theme of sound: we move from the silence of the pictures in the Temple of Venus, to the eagle's disquisition on the science of sound, to the riot of sound in the House of Fame and the babble of the House of Rumour, a series of crescendos as sound 'goes mad'. Boitani explores Chaucer's portrayal of Fame in terms of his sources and also of the apocalyptic effect of such crescendo; he places Rumour as one manifestation of Fame, and analyses the difference between medieval and later notions of fame, which focused on writers rather than the matters they related. Here again, we return to the notion of interpretation: perhaps unsurprisingly in an age when so many works were anonymous, the telling is more crucial than the myth of the author. For Boitani, Chaucer stands on the cusp, associating yet questioning poetry and fame, setting up the possibility of writers as 'famous folk', but also suggesting the element of chance in their fame. For Chaucer, Fame finally is ambiguous, although his poems again and again return to this topic and the related issue of authority. They weave a complex web of literary relations, ancient and contemporary.

Piero Boitani, 'Chaucer's Fame and Her World: The Poem' in *Chaucer and the Imaginary World of Fame*, Chaucer Studies 10. D. S. Brewer, Cambridge; Barnes and Noble, Totowa, NJ, 1984.

The *House of Fame*, the second of Chaucer's dream poems, is an extremely complex creation, and not only because it is formally incomplete. Its construction has often given the impression of total disorder. At first sight it is impossible to understand. After reading it the least one can say is that it is puzzling. We cannot rule out the possibility that this was precisely one of the effects Chaucer had in mind in presenting it to the public. He sets up a series of problems which are not treated organically, but rather announced, hinted at, withdrawn, and now and then plucked up again from forgotten depths, to emerge finally in one grand question mark that makes us ponder and re-read. Nor can we exclude the possibility that the formal incompleteness of the poem is the sign, more or less conscious, of a work that is 'open' in intent and effect. The *Book of the Duchess* uses the methods of allusion, implicit statement, and ambiguity, and is ruled by the logic of dreams.[1] In the *House of Fame* all these are extended and refined. As in the earlier poem, irony is not only a device for producing humour but also the principle inspiring Chaucer's thought and the measure of his wisdom. In the *House of Fame*, however, the cultural background has been renewed and has acquired greater density. Alongside the continuing French influence appears that of Dante, and perhaps a first acquaintance with Petrarch and Boccaccio. This contact with the Italian writers did not produce a radical alteration or dramatic change of direction in Chaucer's poetry, but it broadened the poet's horizons, and provided a stimulus within his own cultural sphere. It not only suggested the figure of the guiding eagle, but urged a deeper consideration of the activity and the dignity of poetry. For example, the authority and success of Dante confirmed that poetry could be used to discuss even physics; it stimulated a more profound study of the medieval thought with which Chaucer was already familiar (Boethius, Alain de Lille). It contributed to a greater knowledge of the classics, especially of Virgil's works, with which the whole of Book I is imbued, and from which a good part of the *ecphrasis* [extended descriptive passage] of Fame is derived.[2] Indeed, the central nucleus of Book III is born in the shadow of Virgil and Ovid, with the division of Fame into 'Fame' and 'Rumour', whose house is constructed according to the description in the *Metamorphoses*.[3]

The central design of the *House of Fame* is clear: it is a dream which the protagonist has on the night of December 10th, in the course of which he, here 'Geffrey' Chaucer in person, visits certain places in an imaginary world. Modelled perhaps on Dante, the poem is divided into three Books, each of which opens with an Invocation (the first to the god of sleep and to God; the second to Venus, the Muses and Thought; the third to Apollo, god of 'science' and light). Book I begins with a Proem in which the nature and causes of dreams are discussed, and then passes from the Invocation to the description of the Temple of Venus. There, beside the portrait of the goddess and many 'curiouse portreytures, and queynte maner of figures', the poet can read the opening lines of the *Aeneid*, on a bronze tablet, and then admire the whole story of Virgil's poem, especially the episode of Dido, which is painted on the walls. When he comes out of the temple the protagonist finds himself in a sandy desert, and sees a golden eagle preparing to descend towards him. In Book II, the eagle grasps the poet 'in his fet', and transports him, stunned and frightened, higher and higher into the sky. The eagle has been sent expressly

Dream Vision Poetry: Critical Extracts

by Jove to carry Geoffrey to the House of Fame, so that he can have 'som disport and game' in return for his 'labour and devocion' towards Cupid. The eagle explains that the House of Fame is suspended between heaven, earth and sea, and that in it the poet will find 'mo wonder thynges' and 'of Loves folk moo tydynges' than he can imagine. The poet does not believe this, and so to prove it the eagle embarks on a logical-scientific exposition of the theory of sounds, constructed with perfect coherence of argument: in the natural order everything has its own 'kyndely stede' (its own port, Dante would say),[4] towards which it moves by natural inclination. Now, a word is sound, and sound is nothing but 'eyr ybroken'. Like water into which a stone is thrown, it ripples, forming a circle which then produces others, wider and wider. So every word moves the air, which in turn disturbs other air, carrying each sound towards its 'port', suspended between heaven, earth and sea – in other words, to the House of Fame. When this demonstration is finished, the eagle points out to Geoffrey the distant earth, by now no more than a 'prikke', and the Galaxy above with the 'ayerissh bestes'. Finally they come into view of the House, and hear the 'grete swogh' coming from it. The eagle sets the poet down near the palace and says good-bye, promising to wait for him. Book III is devoted to the two Houses, that of Fame and that of Rumour: the first is a castle of fantastic-Gothic architecture, surrounded by musicians and magicians; the interior, all of gold, is filled with coats of arms. In the 'halle' is Fame in person, surrounded by the Muses, with the escutcheons and the names of Alexander and Hercules on her back. On both sides arise metal pillars, on each of which a famous author holds on his shoulders the 'fame' of some subject or 'matere': Josephus Flavius and seven others, then Statius, Homer, Dares, Dictys, Guido delle Colonne, Geoffrey of Monmouth, the mysterious Lollius, Virgil, Ovid, Lucan and Claudian. As he contemplates this scene, Geoffrey witnesses the arrival of nine groups of men, who, kneeling before Fame, ask her in turn to grant them glory, or to cancel their names from the memory of men, or to give them fame contrary to their merit. The goddess, attended by Aeolus (who blows one of his two trumpets, 'Clere Laude' and 'Sklaundre', to broadcast good and bad names respectively), replies to these requests in an extremely voluble manner. The last to arrive is the man who burned the temple of Isis in Athens. A stranger turns to the protagonist, asking who he is and if he has come to acquire fame. Geoffrey says no, he has come

> Somme newe tydynges for to lere,* *learn
> Somme newe thinges, y not* what, *I do not know
> Tydynges, other this or that,
> Of love, or suche thynges glade.
>
> (1886–9)

Following the man, the poet finds himself below the castle, in a valley, before an extraordinary house made of twigs, sixty miles long, and continually revolving. It is full of murmurs, voices, and sounds. At this point the eagle reappears and lifts the poet through a window into the house. There a large crowd is gathered, in which each person is telling his neighbour 'a new tydynge'; news and stories spread rapidly in a continual crescendo, and then fly out through windows and crevices to arrive at the Castle, where Fame gives them a name and a duration 'after hir disposicioun'. This House of Rumour is full of sailors, pilgrims, pardoners and messengers, with packs full of stories. As he moves about and listens to some of these tales, the poet hears a great noise in one corner of the room, 'ther men of love-tydynges tolde'. He approaches, while all the others rush over, crowding and trampling one another, and he finally sees a man whom he does not know, but who seems to be 'of grete auctoritee'. And here, at line 2158, the poem ends, incomplete.

One way of making a first approach to the *House of Fame* is to enjoy its rich surface and movement, the visual element and the sounds that define its atmosphere. This should not be an impressionistic reading, but a necessary exploration of the imaginative and linguistic co-ordinates that govern the poem. As the Proem reminds us with its easy, yet learned, Macrobian discussion, we must never forget that we are in a dream, and that the author's hand is guided by the same dream logic which is at work in the *Book of the Duchess*. The first scene offered to us is that of the Temple of Venus: here silence reigns. Amid the fantastic architecture of the 'chirche', with its extravagant decoration, the frescoed wall paintings stand still and mute – Venus naked in the great sea, garlanded with roses, with a comb in her hand, accompanied by Cupid and Vulcan; the bronze tablet with the solemn opening lines of the *Aeneid*; the painted story of Virgil's poem displayed on the walls, and relived by the poet in his memory. Thus Dido's words and the laments resound, not in space, but in the mind, in an absolute physical silence. They echo in thought, which can then digress and extend to famous cases of betrayed heroines: Chaucer drops the formula 'saugh I grave' precisely at the beginning of the Dido episode, picking it up again as soon as the latter is finished. In silence the *Aeneid* is recreated and lives on the walls, enriched by the poet's pity, external and intimate at the same time. Not even Geoffrey dares to break this silence, and when he marvels at the nobility and the richness of the images, he does so in thought, just as in thought he turns to Christ for salvation 'fro fantome and illusion' when he finds himself in the sandy desert that surrounds the temple. There the complete silence and solitude signify aridity, sterility, the absence of life:

> Then sawgh I but a large feld,
> As fer as that I myghte see,
> Withouten toun, or hous, or tree,

Dream Vision Poetry: Critical Extracts

> Or bush, or grass, or eryd* lond;   *cultivated
> For al the feld nas* but of sond*   *was not *sand
> As smal as man may se yet lye
> In the desert of Lybye;
> Ne no maner creature
> That ys yformed be Nature
> Ne sawgh I, me to rede or wisse*   *advise or direct.
> (482–91)

On the threshold of a *phantasma*, a dream dictated by evil spirits, the poet prays to Christ, raising his eyes, and suddenly the heavens appear 'd'un altro sole adorno' (adorned with another sun): Dante's eagle has arrived.[5] At the appearance of Jove's messenger, the still and silent scene of the now-ended book bursts into life again; the eagle descends like a lightning bolt without thunder, silent and intent, and seizes the poet; images abound (534–44). Then begins the dialogue, or rather the eagle's monologue, broken now and then by the replies of an air-sick Geoffrey. It is a discourse full of humour and verve; life opens out again in the familiarity and the humanity of the communion between the two. As they fly through space the eagle's words ring out – pure voice – speaking of sound and air, of water and natural laws, while below the Earth is seen, diminishing to a point as they move farther and farther away. There is an underlying correspondence between the images of the eagle's speech, the shattered air, the stone dropping into the water and rippling, and the Earth fading away in the distance: little by little words become detached from immediate reality and are rarefied, transported to the plane of pure thought. At first earthly images are still in focus; thus, if the word is reduced to the thin substance of air, if

> Soun* ys nought but eyr ybroken,   *sound
> And every speche that ys spoken,
> Lowd or pryvee,* foul or fair,   *private
> In his substaunce ys but air;
> (765–8)

the comparison is still based on flame and smoke, and the proof by association makes use of musical instruments (774–80). The image of water-ripples is a silent one (788–803). The monologue is interrupted by a lively exchange, and when it begins again, the view broadens out; on one side, the distant world:

> And y adoun gan loken thoo,
> And beheld feldes and playnes,
> And now hilles, and now mountaynes,
> Now valeyes, now forestes,

Dream Vision Poetry: Critical Extracts

> And now unnethes* grete bestes;   *with difficulty
> Now ryveres, now citees,
> Now tounes, and now grete trees,
> Now shippes seyllynge in the see...
>   (896–903)

On the other, the galaxy and the creatures of the air:

> Tho gan y loken under me
> And beheld the ayerissh bestes,
> Cloudes, mystes, and tempestes,
> Snowes, hayles, reynes, wyndes,
> And th'engendrynge in hir kyndes...
>   (964–8)

Thought might be transcending the elements, as the poet himself, recalling Boethius, seems to imagine. This could be the threshold of a higher vision, as the quotation from Saint Paul would appear to indicate,[6] and as in effect happened to Dante. But Geoffrey is thinking of his beloved books, of Martianus Capella, of the *Anticlaudianus*. And the eagle interrupts him with 'Lat be... thy fantasye!' The spell is broken, and the dialogue is beginning again with renewed spirit, when the noise of the House of Fame is heard. The silence, echoing with the two solitary voices, is broken; the eagle describes the new sound, and Geoffrey, finally perceiving it, indulges in two similes:

> 'Herestow not the grete swogh?'*   *sound of wind
> 'Yis, parde!' quod y, 'wel ynogh.'
> 'And what soun is it lyk?' quod hee.
> 'Peter! lyk betynge of the see',
> Quod y, 'ayen the roches holowe,
> Whan tempest doth the shippes swalowe;
> And lat a man stonde, out of doute,
> A myle thens, and here hyt route;*   *roar
> Or elles lyk the last humblynge*   *rumbling
> After the clappe of a thundringe,
> Whan Joves hath the air ybete...'
>   (1025–41)

Thus closes Book II, announcing the tremendous noise which will pervade the following Book. But the first thing to strike the reader in Book III is once again the visual spectacle: the rock on which the castle stands is made of ice, like bright crystallized alum; a cold shadow preserves the names written on the mountain, while the other side melts in the heat; and finally there is the castle itself, a fantastic structure that recalls and surpasses the Temple of Venus:

Temple		Castle	
But as I slepte, me mette* I was	*dreamed	Al was of ston of beryle,	
Withyn a temple ymad of glas;		Bothe the castel and the tour,	
In which there were moo ymages		And eke the halle and every bour,*	*room
Of gold, stondynge in sondry stages,*	*plinths	Wythouten peces or joynynges.	
And moo ryche tabernacles,*	*niches	But many subtil compassinges*,	*devices
And with perre* moo pynacles,	*precious stones	Babewynnes* and pynacles,	*gargoyles
And moo curiouse portreytures,		Ymageries* and tabernacles,	*carvings
And queynte maner of figures		I say; and ful eke of wyndowes,	
Of olde werk, then I saugh ever.		As flakes falle in grete snowes.	
(119–27)		(1184–92)	

Both edifices are products of the same architectural imagination, but the second is perhaps even richer, more extraordinary than the first; and the final simile of thickly falling snowflakes is like a last burst of fireworks, preparing us for the visual feast that follows.

Noises begin at once: minstrels telling 'tales both of wepinge and of game'; harps, pipes, bag-pipes, and trumpets; then the songs of the Muses, the cries of those who praise Fame, the arrival of the postulants buzzing like bees, their prayers, the trumpets of Aeolus, the words of Fame, Geoffrey's exchange with the stranger. These are all human sounds, in some way ordered, sounds which still have meaning – music, words, conversation. The postulants are arranged in groups, as if for an audience; they kneel in courtly ceremony. There are coats of arms of the 'chevalrie' of the whole world and of all times; there are metal pillars for writers – in short, the place is ordered like a catalogue. And, against a background of walls, floor and ceiling covered with gold six inches thick and studded with all the gems of the Lapidary, sits Fame herself on her imperial ruby throne. She is the 'monstrum horrendum ingens' [huge terrible monster] of Virgil: a female creature less than a cubit in height, who grows longer and wider until she touches the floor with her feet and the sky with her head. She has as many eyes as a bird has feathers, or as the beasts of the Apocalypse; her hair is golden and curly; she has innumerable ears and tongues; her feet are winged. She is a capricious woman, the sister of Fortune, quite different from Boccaccio's *Gloria* and Petrarch's 'bella donna' [beautiful

Dream Vision Poetry: Critical Extracts

lady] – an iconographic nightmare, an apocalyptic beast that Chaucer is the first English writer to recreate.

With the *ecphrasis* of Fame, the world of the vision seems to go mad, to explode according to a clearly premeditated plan. This is what happens in the House of Rumour, where the visual fantasy and the 'sound-track' are magnified, where all order is shattered, the space is filled with swarms of people, and the air is full of voices in continual crescendo, an almost Rossinian effect.[7] It continues almost to bursting point, until the 'tydynges' rush out through the window and the cracks in the wall, until the whole building is revealed as a sort of 'faire felde ful of folke' like Langland's, dominated not by activity but by words. The last thing we see is the running crowd, which ends up in a heap of figures trampling each other; their cries are the last thing we hear. Then, mysteriously, appears the man of authority, who remains suspended in our imagination. The Ovidian impulse that lies behind the description now breaks free. The House, 'Domus Dedaly,' [House of Daedalus: a labyrinth] is labyrinthine, marvellous and strange. It is made of multicoloured twigs, with entrances as numerous as the leaves of trees in summer, and a thousand holes in its roof. Open night and day, sixty miles long, it is built to last as long as may please Chance:

> ... ever mo, as swyft as thought,
> This queynte hous aboute wente,
> That never mo hyt stille stente.* *stood
> ... ...
> And the noyse which that I herde,
> For al the world, ryght so hyt ferde,
> As dooth the rowtynge* of the ston *roar
> That from th'engyn* ys leten gon. *catapult
> (1924–34)

Like a cage, then, turning round and round, full of murmurs, stories, whispers and babblings and chatterings; from within, in a curious relativistic effect, it proves to be immobile. There, sound is associated with individual human beings:

> And every wight* that I saugh there *creature
> Rouned* everych in others ere *spoke
> A newe tydynge prively,
> Or elles tolde al openly
> Ryght thus, and seyde: 'Nost not thou* *do you not know
> That ys betyd, lo, late or now?'
> 'No,' quod he, 'telle me what.'
> And than he tolde hym this and that,

Dream Vision Poetry: Critical Extracts

> And swor therto that hit was soth* –   *true
> 'Thus hath he sayd,' and 'Thus he doth,'
> 'Thus shal hit be,' 'Thus herde y seye,'
> 'That shal be founde,' 'That dar I leye'...
>   (2043–54)

This bit of bravura is not an end in itself; it lays the foundation for the description of the 'tydynges' that spread from one person to another and yet another, constantly increasing like the ripples described by the eagle, until

> ...Thus north and south
> Wente every tydyng fro mouth to mouth,
> And that encresing ever moo,
> *As fyr is wont to quyke and goo*
> *From a sparke spronge amys,*
> *Til al a citee brent up ys.*
>   (2075–80)

The *House of Fame* is, then, an extraordinary *tour de force* of language and creativity, in which selected authors set the theme, and serve to spark off an imagination that is always ready to burst into flame: the simile that ends the passage I have just quoted is, as it were, its emblem. This reading of the poem clarifies at least two things: firstly, the *House of Fame* has a precise plan (what else could explain such a careful arrangement of visual and aural effects and images?); secondly, this plan does not correspond to a fixed and rigid unit of theme and mode. Both these aspects make the *House of Fame* a many-sided work – ambiguous, and, perhaps deliberately, in-finite. What is the connection between Venus and the *Aeneid*, between these and Fame and Rumour, and between all of these and the eagle's flight and his science? What are the 'tydynges' which Jove has promised to Geoffrey? What is the relevance of the Proem? Is there an overall meaning in the *House of Fame*?...

We must, however, first ask ourselves other questions. There would have been no reason for Chaucer to call this a 'Book of Fame' – as he did in the 'Retracciouns' – if he had not considered Fame its central subject. Now, the one thing a reader can say about Chaucer's Fame is that it is ambiguous. In the first place, she is divided between the two dwellings, of which the second, the House of Rumour, is but the House of Fame raised to the nth power. In the second place, we are shown two aspects of Fame herself, one passive and one active. The minstrels and the 'gestiours' who swarm round the Castle

> ...tellen tales
> Both of wepinge and of game,
> Of al that longeth unto Fame.
>   (1198–200)

Dream Vision Poetry: Critical Extracts

Wizards, witches and enchanters 'by such art don men han fame'. Above all, poets bear on their shoulders the fame of the various subjects treated in their works. This is how fame is created. C. S. Lewis has compared the attitude of the medieval public with that of the humanists; the latter, exemplified by Pope, shows the 'literariness' of its whole cultural outlook. In the context of his own time, Chaucer's attitude can more significantly be compared...with the 'triumphs' of Petrarch and Boccaccio, who began the tradition to which Pope belonged. The difference emerges clearly, says Lewis, if one compares Chaucer's *House of Fame* with Pope's *Temple of Fame*:

> In Pope the great poets have the place we should expect: they are present because they are famous. But in Chaucer it is not the poets but their subjects that have the fame. Statius is present to bear up the fame of Thebes, Homer to bear up the fame of Troy, and so forth. Poets are, for Chaucer, not people who receive fame but people who give it. To read Virgil sets you thinking not about Virgil but about Aeneas, Dido, and Mezentius.[8]

Fame becomes, for Boccaccio, 'la *Gloria* del popol mondano' (the glory of worldly folk). But although Chaucer's attitude is close to the one identified by Lewis, there is something in the *House of Fame* that slightly modifies it in the new direction: the coats of arms displayed on the armour in the palace are those

> *Of famous folk* that han ybeen
> In Auffrike, Europe, and Asye,
> Syth first began the chevalrie.
> (1338–40)

Fame herself bears on her shoulders

> Bothe th'armes and the name
> Of thoo that hadde large fame:
> Alexander and Hercules...
> (1411–13)

Finally, it is Calliope [Muse of epic poetry] and the other eight Muses who sing the praises of the 'goddesse of *Renoun* or of *Fame*', while their very presence seals the close connection between poetry and fame. The Muses, here depicted in the attitude of the angelic choirs of the *Praefatio* and the *Sanctus*, are, precisely, the *angheloi*, the angels, harbingers of fame.

Dream Vision Poetry: Critical Extracts

On the other hand, there is no clear disjunction between the creation of Fame and her creative and destructive activity. The effects of Fame's action are already seen on the slopes of the rock on which the Castle stands, in the half-cancelled names ('so unfamus was woxe hir fame') and in those that are preserved, 'as fresh as men had writen hem here / The selve day ryght'; and again, in the beryl of the Palace walls, which magnifies everything:

>...walles of berile,
> That shoone ful lyghter than a glas
> And made wel more than hit was
> To semen every thing, ywis,
> *As kynde thyng of Fames is*...
> (1288–92)

And finally on the portal, decorated with unprecedented richness, which reveals the two laws of fame, because

> ...it was be *aventure**   *chance
> Iwrought as often as be *cure*.*   *choice
> (1297–8)

The potential power of Fame is revealed, however, in her figure – and it is shown in action in the audience she grants to the postulants: a small and enormous monster, animal–woman–bird, who sees all, hears all, and repeats all. She is contradictory and voluble, her motives are inscrutable (1541–2), she knows no justice (1820), and bestows her favours with no regard for good and evil. Fame gives or refuses herself impartially to the first group of postulants, who have all done 'good workes', to the indolent of the sixth and seventh groups, and to those in the eighth and ninth groups who, together with the violator of the temple, have sinned, as Dante would say, through 'malizia' and 'matta bestialitade' [mad bestiality]. She cancels a name forever, or spreads it far and wide, truly or falsely:

> Non è il mondan romore altro ch'un fiato
> di vento, ch'or vien quinci e or vien quindi,
> e muta nome perché muta lato.
>
> (Earthly fame is naught but a breath of wind,
> which now comes hence and now comes thence,
> changing its name because it changes quarter.)
> (*Purgatorio*, XI, 100–2)

This, then, is fame – beyond morality. She is Fortune's true sister (1547), omnipresent and fragile, the magnifying beryl and the nullifying silence, a trumpet of gold and black, the creation of poets and the glory radiated by the Muses, a prize won by chance and by effort. She sows and she reaps: the 'grete swogh', the murmur, the sigh, the moan, the grumble, the great 'breath of wind'; *fame*, precisely, *renown*, and *ill-repute*. And now *Rumour*. This is a composite, atomized Fame, reduced to its essential particles, centrifuged in that sort of gigantic cyclotron which is the revolving House in the valley, totally dominated by Chance, the 'moder of tydynges'. *Rumour* is the world in which stories are gathered, hearsay, news, words, true and false, pronounced by human beings, by common mortals – pilgrims, sailors, pardoners. These, now, are the *angheloi*, the 'messengers', who in the Palace were impersonated by the Muses and the poets. It is a world of swarming crowds, broken up into separate voices, reflected in exaggerated stories – not the world of reality, but a mirror of it, a 'boyste crammed ful of lyes' like those carried by couriers, a pack of words to which Fame will give

> duracioun,
> Somme to wexe and wane sone,
> As doth the faire white mone...
> (2114–16)

In the last few pages, we have encountered many images, several myths, and the names of classical and Italian poets – Virgil, Aeneas, Dido and Venus; Dante and the Eagle; the vision of the Earth as a 'prikke' and Boethius, Martianus Capella, Alain de Lille; clouds, mists, storms; sound, wind and ice; the Castle, chivalry, minstrels, magicians, poets and Muses; Aeolus, the cage of Rumour, Ovid, the 'fair white mone'; Dante's 'mondan romore' and Pope's Fame; Boccaccio's and Petrarch's Glory. The question we must now ask ourselves is how much of this *imaginaire* is purely Chaucerian and what is derived from tradition, and how Chaucer uses these images. Other scholars – notably W. O. Sypherd, B. G. Koonce, J. A. W. Bennett, and Sheila Delany[9] – have already given their answers. What I will try to do... is to reconstruct in greater detail and with different emphases the development of the world of Fame in classical and medieval Europe, constantly referring to Chaucer's use of it in his works. The journey we are embarking on is similar to, though slower than, Geoffrey's voyage in the *House of Fame*, and it is an equally fascinating exploration of European culture. At the end of it, we shall be able to assess Chaucer's cultural position *vis-à-vis* Fame, and to study the meaning of his imagery and his poem in greater depth.

Notes

1 For this, see P. Boitani, *English Medieval Narrative in the Thirteenth and Fourteenth Centuries* (Cambridge, 1982), pp. 138–49.
2 *Aeneid*, IV, 173–88; *House of Fame*, 1360–94.
3 *Metamorphoses*, XII, 39–63; *House of Fame*, 713–24 and 1920–2033.
4 *Paradiso*. I, 109–17. This canto was used by Chaucer in the Invocation for Book III.
5 *Purgatorio*, IX, 19–21 and 28–30; *Paradiso*, I, 61–3.
6 II Corinthians, 12.2; *House of Fame*, 981–2.
7 One is also reminded of Calumny's aria [Basilio's aria about Calumny] in the *Barber of Seville*. Calumny stands to Infamy as Rumour stands to Fame.
8 C. S. Lewis, *English Literature in the Sixteenth Century* (Oxford, 1954), p. 27.
9 W. O. Sypherd, *Studies in Chaucer's House of Fame* (London, 1907); B. G. Koonce, *Chaucer and the Tradition of Fame* (Princeton, 1966); J. A. W. Bennett, *Chaucer's Book of Fame* (Oxford, 1968); S. Delany, *Chaucer's House of Fame and the Poetics of Skeptical Fideism* (Chicago and London, 1972).... A short analysis of the tradition and the imagery is also to be found in A. C. Watts, '"Amor gloriae" in Chaucer's *House of Fame*', *Journal of Medieval and Renaissance Studies*, III (1973), 87–113.

Park of Paradise and Garden of Love

J. A. W. Bennett

Unlike the preceding extracts, the following discussion is not readily approachable – yet J. A. W. Bennett, the first to write a full-length study of the Parliament of Fowls, *was too great a scholar to be ignored here. Bennett follows in the majestic humanist tradition of C. S. Lewis and J. R. R. Tolkien, but his work is more relentlessly scholarly, less directed by sympathetic critical analysis. The extract here offers a good example of his distinctive voice, considering and erudite. The plethora of names and references to literatures in different languages is daunting, but reminds us of how learned medieval poet–scholars such as Chaucer must have been. Yet despite Bennett's erudition, he is capable of weaving together literary sources, traditions and conventions so seamlessly that the style seems extremely natural. This naturalistic mode distinguishes the* Parliament of Fowls *and renders it a much more integrated poem than the* House of Fame; *like the* Book of the Duchess, *it fluidly traces the narrator's experience. The* rime royal *form of the poem reflects Italian verse forms and sustains the Italianate influence already evident in the* House of Fame.[1]

In this extract Bennett looks back beyond Dante to trace one specific aspect of the poem, the ideal landscape, to its classical origins. Such minute analysis is typical of the way that Bennett works: he may not offer cohesive critical readings, but his extraordinary scholarship unweaves and evaluates the finest threads of the literary tapestry of the poem. Bennett draws on the ideas of the great German scholar Ernst Curtius, whose work European Literature and the Latin Middle Ages *(1948) underpins the study of literary history and history of ideas. Curtius developed the notion of* topoi, *topics or ideas, that recurred throughout European literature, and found their origins in classical writing. For Curtius, the growth of literature was bound up in the changing use of these themes such as old age, loss of worldly goods, or the wedding. Bennett takes as his way into the* Parliament of Fowls *one of these* topoi, *the ideal landscape, represented in classical literature either as the abundant forest or the* locus amoenus *(place of loving), originally a delightful place amenable to cultivation, but quickly associated with love and the idea of eternal life. The myth of the earthly paradise, Eden, was especially powerful in medieval writing, and it underpins the conventional use of the* locus amoenus, *the beautiful springtime garden and place of love, in courtly poetry. Bennett describes various instances of the* topos *from the fourth century onwards.*

Both forms of the ideal landscape, forest and garden, are represented at the start of the Parliament of Fowls, *as the Dreamer, like the narrator of the* Book of the Duchess, *finds himself in an emerald-green forest, and sees, 'A gardyn...ful of blosmy bowes' (183). Both are placed inside the fateful gates through which Affrican pushes the narrator, and Bennett thus represents the landscape as a kind of 'park of paradise' with its garden of love within. Bennett shows how the garden of the* Roman de la Rose *relates to Chaucer's poem, but also remarks the complexity of the* topos *in its use of a wide variety of sources, in particular, classical works like that of the Silver Age Latin poet, Statius. Bennett notes especially the emphasis on the abundance of Nature, evident in both French and Italian portrayals of idealized forests, and suggests the appeal of this to Chaucer, who follows Boccaccio in his portrayal of teeming wildlife. Such an emphasis is carried through but undercut in the portrayal of the actual birds, and their chaotic parliament.*

Note

1 *Rime royal* employs stanzas of seven ten-syllable lines rhyming ababbcc.

J. A. W. Bennett, 'Park of Paradise and Garden of Love' in *'The Parlement of Fouls': An Interpretation.* Clarendon Press, Oxford, 1957.

'If we look back at Homer, Theocritus, and Virgil, and ask ourselves... what types of ideal landscape could late Antiquity and the Middle Ages get from these poets? we cannot but answer: the mixed forest and the *locus amoenus* [place of loving] (with flowery meadows *ad libitum* [at will]).'[1] Curtius' question and reply may serve to summarize the poetic history of the first part of this 'mater' – the *topographia* that occupies the ensuing forty lines. Curtius sees the origin of such landscapes in the *locos laetos et amoena virecta* [joyful and green places of loving] of *Aeneid* VI, an Elysian scene in the strictest sense; and it happens that the same book describes the forest of pine, holm-oak, ash, and elm from which Statius and Boccaccio (in the *Teseida*) were to borrow largely. But neither *topos* might have had so long a literary history, or have appeared, in blended form, in the *Parlement*, if *amoenus* had not early been derived from *amor* [love]... The *topos* of a delectable region of the earth immune from the touch of time is not in origin identical with that of the *locus amoenus*, but has so much in common with it that the two easily fuse into one. Lactantius' fourth-century *Carmen de Ave Phoenice* offers one of the earliest variants of this paradisal topography in Christian verse, and had inspired an Anglo-Saxon poet to write those lambent lines that read like a rendering of Tennyson's account of the valley of Avalon into Old English.[2] From the outset this blissful place was identified with the lost Eden; and speculation about the seat of Eden contributed much to the pictures of this paradise found in poems as various as *Pearl* and the romances of Alexander.[3] De Lorris, we saw, could describe the Garden in the *Roman* [*de la Rose*] as *seeming* to be a very 'paradis terrestre' [earthly paradise]; but this, on Mr Lewis's exegesis, is no more than a spurious copy of the true Earthly Paradise, which de Meun describes towards the end of the *Roman*. It is in the latter description that Mr Lewis finds de Meun to be most unlike Chaucer. Yet the temperate breeze that

> made in the leves grene a noise softe
> Accordant to the foules songe on lofte[4]

might well have emanated from de Meun's park of good pasture. And there are certain details in de Meun that Chaucer seems to have remembered; his fishes resemble those that in de Meun are depicted on the outer wall of the park; and his *mise en scène* might have been elaborated from de Meun's

> Erbes, arbres, bestes, oiseaus,
> E ruisselez e fonteneles
> Bruire e fremir par les graveles
> E la fontaine souz le pin.[5]

[Grass and trees, animals and birds, streams and springs babbling and splashing over the gravel, and the spring beneath the pine.]

But it is folly to seek for parallels when Chaucer is evoking Nature at her loveliest. If his verses make us think sometimes of de Lorris's mead, where

> Cleer was the water, and as colde
> As any welle is...
> ... ...
> The medewe softe, swote and grene,
> Beet right on the water syde,
>   (Chaucer's *river* (l. 183), i.e. river bank)

or of his garden where the birds

> songe hir song as fair and wel
> As angels doon espirituel;[6]

sometimes, again, of the green valley in the *Purgatorio* where grass is brighter than 'fresh emerald at the moment it is split'; and sometimes of the perpetual paradise as depicted by de Meun or the Scots poet who described Alexander's discovery of it: 'So temperit and sa sobir was 3e are...Na thing bot frute and flouris and spicis was...,

> Thare was na cloude na strublance* in 3e are,   *disturbance
> Bot softe and swete 3e wedder was, and fare;'[7]

the resultant intermingled effect is no more surprising than the ambiguity we have found in this poem at every turn. At first sight, to be sure, the trees in Chaucer's park seem to have been transplanted straight from de Lorris's garden, where most of them are found growing (along with some 'fro the land Alexandrin').[8] But we know, as Pope knew, that such arboreal catalogues derive from a poet as much revered by Chaucer as by Dante: Statius. It is of Statius that any well-read medieval poet would first think when he came to handle this commonplace, though he might also recall the variants in Claudian and in Joseph of Exeter, on whose version of Dares others besides Chaucer relied for certain classical lore.[9] In the hunt for such sources we must not forget the primary effect that Chaucer was aiming at – that of glades composed of noble trees...flourishing 'eche in his kinde' (l. 174); and they are characterized according to use rather than appearance: just as are the birds 'of every kinde' that we shall find in another part of the forest (311 ff.). We may think of them as illustrating Nature's 'simplicity' – in woods, says Boccaccio, is

Dream Vision Poetry: Critical Extracts

nothing artificial, counterfeit, or obnoxious: 'simplicia quidem omnia sunt Naturae opera' [simple indeed are all the works of Nature][10] – but even more her plenitude.

This abundance of Nature as found in a forest had enthralled Chaucer from the first. In the *Book of the Duchesse*, where there are 'many grene greves', 'thikke of trees, so *ful* of leves',

> *many* an harte and *many* an hynde
> Was both before me and behynde.
> Of faunes, sowres*, bukkes, does   *yourg bucks
> Was *ful* the wode, and *many* roes,
> And *many* squirrelles that sete
> Ful high upon the trees and ete
> And in her maner made festes – [11]

'Shortly, it was ful of bestes'. Squirrels and conies were as indispensable to such scenes as they were to the margins of an East Anglian Psalter; and Chaucer had found them playing in de Lorris's trees. So too had Boccaccio; and as Chaucer set about grafting into his poem the stanzas from Boccaccio's *Teseida* that we are about to consider, he added here and there to the forest picture a touch perhaps suggested by a phrase in the Italian (which makes no mention of trees, beyond saying that myrtle abounded). Thus to Boccaccio's 'molti altri carissimi bestiuoli' [many other dear little creatures] he probably owes his 'bestes smale of gentil kinde'; and some of Boccaccio's birds, like some of Chaucer's, were busy 'con diletto i nidi fare' [building nests with delight] (cf. l. 192). On the other hand, no 'smale fishes lighte', 'with finnes rede, and skales silver brighte', swim in the 'fonti chiare' [clear spring] of the Italian poet:[12] Chaucer's fishes (in their life and movement so unlike those gasping in the dried-up weir of ll. 138–40) are here as part of the scale of creatures, the chain of being in which the richness of divine creation is displayed. If we are familiar with the endless lists of trees, fishes, birds ('all the birds from here to Babylon', in Villon's phrase) that clog such poems as Alain Chartier's *Livre des Quatre Dames*, we shall be grateful for Chaucer's restraint here.

Notes

1   Curtius, loc. cit., p. 193. For an earlier, and fuller, discussion of ideal landscapes *v.* Ruskin's *Modern Painters*, IV. xiii–xvi (esp. xiv, sec. 34ff.).
2   *The Phoenix*, ll. 1–84. Cf. also Prudentius, *Cathemerinon*, 3. 101.
3   The conjectures are found as early as Philostorgius (cf. Gibbon, Everyman ed, ii. 243, n. 4) and are still seriously canvassed in Raleigh's *History of the World*, Book I. III. iv, where Peter Comestor, Barcephas, and others are cited. For some references

of intermediate date, and for an account of the incorporation of the paradise into the romances, v. H. R. Patch, *The Other World* (Harvard, 1950); M. M. Lascelles, 'Alexander and the Earthly Paradise in Medieval English Writings', *Medium Ævum*, v (1936), pp. 31, 79, 173; and N. Zingarelli, *Dante* (in *Storia Letteraria d'Italia*, 3rd edn., 1947), ii, p. 1168, for studies by P. Rajna and E. Coli; and B. Nardi, 'Il mito dell'Eden', in *Saggi di filosofia dantesca* (1930), pp. 347-74.

The description of a different kind in the legend of Sir Owain (printed in Scott's *Minstrelsy of the Scottish Border*, 2nd edn., ii. 409) has been overlooked by writers on the subject.

4 ll. 202-3.
5 *RR*, ll. 20342-5. For the precedent of the *Altercatio Phyllidis et Florae* (an English version of which appears in J. A. Symonds's *Wine, Women and Song*) v. Langlois, *Origines et sources du Roman de la Rose*, pp. 10ff.
6 *Romaunt of the Rose*, ll. 116ff., 671-2; *RR*, ll. 110ff., 663-4.
7 B.M. MS. Add. 40732, f. 226r.
8 *Romaunt*, l. 602, following the reading 'la terre Alexandrin(s)' in some MSS. of *RR*, l. 592; 'Alexandrin' conceivably refers to the Earthly Paradise as discovered by Alexander, though this form could equally well mean 'of Alexandria'.
9 Pratt, loc. cit., quotes a gloss on Claudian....Chaucer knew the catalogue in *Teseida*, xi. 22-4 (and uses some of its trees at C.T.A. 2921ff.)....
10 *Gen. Deor. Gent.* XIV. xi. The rest of the passage – which describes woods as places where the earth is covered with grass and flowers of a thousand colours; where there are argent brooks, gay song-birds, playful little animals, and the boughs are softly stirred by the breeze – has affinities with ll. 183-203 of the *Parlement*. For Boccaccio such pleasure soothes the soul 'if it be weary'; and Chaucer depicts himself as in that state before dreaming of the park.
11 ll. 427-33.
12 Skeat prints 'E fonti vive [for "vide"] e chiare', st. 51, l. 6; and Chaucer may have read 'vive', since the 'fonti' become 'colde welle stremes, nothing dede' (l. 187). For 'dede' =sluggish cf. A. S. Napier and W. H. Stevenson, *The Crawford Charters* (Oxford, 1895), p. 79. Chaucer's Scots admirers seized on the details: cf. *The Kingis Quair*, st. 153; Douglas, *Eneydos*, *Prol.* xii. 55-8.

The Parliament of Fowls

A. C. Spearing

The following extract from A. C. Spearing's study of dream poetry offers a rather different kind of reading from that of Bennett: it is relaxed in tone, sometimes deceptively simple, and presents a cohesive reading that employs contemporary psychoanalytical and anthropological theory as well as medieval sources. Yet it is in fact complementary to Bennett, whose scholarship Spearing draws on. He moves from the question of literary history to consider the thematic import of the poem, and its poetic function, and to place it within the contexts both of Chaucer's development as a writer and of fourteenth-century cultural attitudes and history. He notes the links to the earlier dream vision poems, which also use naive narrator figures: like them, this poem again treats the contrast between experience and authority, in the figure of the disappointed lover whose only experience is from books. Spearing hints at the possibility of reading the poem as about both love and poetry: both may be seen as the subject of its opening line, 'the lyf so short, the craft so long to lerne'. Like love, poetry is desirable yet difficult, and both are creative experiences. For Spearing, the poem offers a kind of resolution to the suffering of love - not through rational response of the kind that the Dreamer finds so unsatisfactory in the philosophical book he reads, the Somnium Scipionis, *but through the kind of dream logic that Ferster and Boitani also consider. To explain its working, Spearing employs Jung's notion of dream as containing grand, archetypal symbols, as myth does. In contrast, he also offers a discussion of the dream according to the medieval dream theory of Macrobius, and like Ferster, raises the question of its status: is it a dream sent by Venus, as the narrator suggests, or are we to see it as the fantastic product of his overwrought mind and his reading? This question can apply too to poetry and the process of poetic inspiration. Spearing pursues the issue of the poet–narrator from a different perspective in his more recent study,* The Medieval Poet as Voyeur *(1993).*

In his discussion of the dream itself, Spearing takes a much longer perspective than Bennett: thus, although he places the landscape as ideal, related to the garden of love in the Roman de la Rose, *and to the 'typical paradise-landscape,' he does not offer a detailed discussion of the* topos. *Notably, however, he distinguishes between paradise and this 'pseudo-paradise of idealized desire', where in fact, as the negative inscription on the gates suggests, not everything in the garden is lovely. In the garden, ideal figures are accompanied by more negative ones, and the temple, where Priapus and Venus are found, is a place of 'obsessive sexuality', full of images of tragic lovers. Spearing compares the description to that of Boccaccio, and returns to a familiar theme, that of the self-consciously literary nature of the poem, which plays, for example, on the natural philosophy of the medieval thinker Alain de Lille.*

Spearing cleverly moves between different theoretical perspectives: psychoanalytical, literary historical, and more straightforward literary critical; in the final section depicting the parliament itself, he shifts to a socio-political perspective more akin to that of Strohm, but combines this with anthropomorphization: humans draw conclusions about their society from the animal world, yet, conversely, use this as a safely distancing metaphor (as in Chaucer's beast fable, the Nun's Priest's Tale*). The birds thus become, rather like the Canterbury Pilgrims, a cross-section of the estates of human society and present a stereotypical set of human attitudes to love* *and marriage*. Like Strohm, Spearing considers class issues, and notes too the courtly context of the poem, perhaps composed for Richard II's marriage to Anne of Bohemia, and certainly as a demande d'amour *to which the audience would provide the answer: this allows neatly for the inconclusiveness of the poem. Within the comedy, serious questions are raised, of the nature of a 'parliament', of common profit and its relation to the ideal model of society, of upper- and lower-class attitudes to love and lust, and of choice in marriage, an issue that Chaucer's portrayal of women returns to again and again.*

For Spearing, the poem is finally about 'nature and culture', an opposition that raises recurring questions regarding the distinction between learned and natural behaviour, between desire and its expression in fin'amors. *This topic relates to the themes of experience and authority: experience may be seen as building on natural instincts and desires, and authority as offering culturally derived models of behaviour. The dream responds to the unrequited lover by unifying the two to some degree, though it offers no final resolution.*

A. C. Spearing, 'The Parliament of Fowls' in *Medieval Dream Poetry*. Cambridge University Press, Cambridge, 1976.

Chaucer's third dream poem was *The Parliament of Fowls*, which probably dates from 1382. In style, it is considerably more settled and composed than the two earlier dream poems. Italian influences, which had affected only the content of the *House*, have now been absorbed stylistically too, and it is written not in the octosyllabic couplets of the two earlier poems, but in rime royal stanzas. The effect is less of rapid movement, whether gay or nervous, than in the earlier poems, and more of 'a grave sweetness and a poised serenity';[1] though colloquial touches are by no means excluded, and indeed stand out more sharply in this more dignified setting. Here more than ever Chaucer shows his awareness of the long and complex tradition of visionary writing, but it is now as much a matter of deft and pervasive allusion as of explicit reference. In structure, however, Chaucer remains very close to *The Book of the Duchess*. Indeed, one might guess that, after *The House of Fame*, where, under the impact of insoluble personal problems, he had pushed the use of dream-methods for literary creation so far as to make the poem unfinishable, he now decided to follow more exactly the causal sequence that had proved so successful in his first dream poem. As in the *Book* there is a long introductory section, in which the narrator is still awake and reads a book about a dream, which then provides motivation for his own dream. As in the *House*, the narrator is a devotee of love but

> For al be that I knowe nat Love in dede,
> Ne wot how that he quiteth folk here hyre,

Yit happeth me ful ofte in bokes rede
Of his myrakles, and his crewel yre.
(8–11)

quiteth pays; *hyre* wages

But, in laying its emphasis on the narrator as would-be lover rather than poet of love, the *Parliament* is nearer to the *Book* than it is to the *House*. However, the distinction is not very clear-cut; there are one or two explicit references to the narrator as poet, and there is also a pervasive suggestion that love and poetry can be seen in the same terms, as creative experiences, which are highly desirable and yet difficult of achievement.[2] It is significant that the narrator invokes Venus not only as the cause of his dream, but also for help 'to ryme and ek t'endyte' (119) when he comes to set it down.

The narrator is introduced as reading one particular book, 'a certeyn thing to lerne' (20). What that thing is, we are never explicitly told, and at the end of the poem he resumes his search in 'othere bokes' (695); but here perhaps the poem is truly dreamlike, in that it solves the Dreamer's problems (at least for us) in the very act of reflecting them. The thing sought is surely found in the dream itself, without the Dreamer being aware of it, though if asked to define it one could only say that it is the meaning of the whole poem, which cannot properly be expressed in other terms. To put it more crudely than the poem does, what the narrator is seeking is presumably the meaning of that love which is the major subject of medieval courtly poetry, but which he sees chiefly as a cause of suffering; what he finds in the dream is a subtle placing of love in the larger context of the social order and of the relationship between the natural and the human, nature and culture. But to put it like that *is* to put it crudely, for the poem itself is deliberately enigmatic; it holds back from direct statements and conceptual formulations, and prefers to explore and order experience in the way dreams actually do, through images. Perhaps it would be better to say, through symbols, using 'symbol' in its Jungian sense as 'the expression of an intuitive perception which can as yet, neither be apprehended better, nor expressed differently'.[3]

The book the narrator of the *Parliament* is reading is the *Somnium Scipionis* [of Cicero] itself, 'Tullyus of the dream of Scipioun' (31), of which he proceeds to give a compact summary. It is seen as a threefold vision of judgement, according to the traditional formula embodied in the *Divine Comedy*, except that earth takes the place of purgatory between heaven and hell:

Chapiteris sevene it hadde, of hevene and helle
And erthe, and soules that therinne dwelle.
(32–3)

In the summary the emphasis is on heaven, that 'blysful place' which is the reward of the good; and the word 'blysse' is repeated three times, and the phrase 'blysful place' twice, in this brief passage. Another repeated phrase is 'commune profit': heavenly bliss is the reward above all of those who have pursued the welfare of the community rather than private profit or even personal salvation. Finally the narrator, as it gets dark, puts the book down, dissatisfied with its teaching,

> For both I hadde thyng which that I nolde,
> And eke I nadde that thyng that I wolde.
> (90–1)

nolde did not wish; *nadde* did not have

That is enigmatic indeed, but similar statements are made elsewhere in Chaucer's poems, for example in *The Complaint unto Pity* and *The Complaint to his Lady*, and they always refer to the situation of the unrequited lover, who has the suffering that he does not wish but lacks his lady's mercy, which he does desire.[4] So in one way these lines probably refer to what we already know, the narrator's role as one who has had no success in love. But a similar phrase is also used by Philosophy in the *De Consolatione* to refer to the general state of man, who seeks mistaken means to arrive at that ultimate good which is his goal, and therefore suffers from a perpetual anxiety, because 'the lakkide somwhat that thow woldest nat han lakkid, or elles thou haddest that thow noldest nat han had' (III, pr. 3. 33–6). Thinking of *The House of Fame*, we might feel inclined to see the dissatisfaction as that of the medieval courtly poet, conscious of lacking the 'love-tidings' he needs if he is to produce the expected kind of poetry, and finding in the *Somnium Scipionis* a philosophical doctrine which seems to be of no use to him, because it contains nothing about love (except, significantly, in the phrase 'that lovede commune profyt' (47)). The dream will reconcile these contradictions, and will provide the poet with 'mater of to wryte' (168); but in its immediate context the statement is mysterious, used to express a state in which the mind is dissatisfied for an undefinable cause, weary as night falls, but still seeking for a truth that will answer its longings.

The narrator falls asleep, and dreams that Scipio Africanus stands at his bedside, just as Scipio the younger saw him in the book he has been reading. As in the two earlier dream poems, there is an ambiguity concerning the status of the dream, which implies an ambiguity in the status of the poem itself, and by extension of imaginative fiction in general. The only theory about the causation of dreams which is stated in this poem occurs in a stanza I have mentioned before, which sees all dreams as reflecting states of body or mind: the hunter dreams of hunting, the sick man of drinking, the lover of success in love, and so on. And the narrator seems to assume the truth of this theory at the very end of the poem, where, after his awakening, he goes on reading more books in the hope that they will so affect his mind that one day he will have a dream that will do him good:

> I hope, ywis, to rede so som day
> That I shall mete som thyng for to fare
> The bet, and thus to rede I nyl nat spare. (697–9)
> (Indeed I hope [or expect] some day to read in such a way that I shall dream some thing that will bring me greater success, and thus I will not refrain from reading.)

But he has already expressed doubt –

> Can I not seyn if that the cause were
> For I hadde red of Affrican byforn,
> That made me to mete that he stod there
> (106–8)

– and, as we have seen, he goes on to say that it was Venus who made him dream as he did. Taken literally [according to Macrobius's dream theory], this would imply that the dream was a *somnium coeleste* [celestial dream], inspired by the goddess of love in her planetary form; taken metaphorically, it would indicate that it was a *somnium animale* [animal dream], inspired by the narrator's waking thoughts of love. Then again, a dream which introduces a venerable figure such as Scipio Africanus the elder would count, according to Macrobius, as an *oraculum* [oracular dream], like the younger Scipio's own dream. If this were true, then the *Parliament* would be the kind of vision that *The House of Fame* stopped short of being; on the other hand, as J. A. W. Bennett has remarked, Chaucer 'reduces to a minimum Africanus' oracular function: the latter becomes a benevolent compère rather than the embodiment of divine wisdom'.[5] Are we to see the dream which follows as offering supernatural guidance, or as a fantasy woven by the Dreamer's mind out of his waking preoccupations and his reading? Chaucer does not commit himself to any answer to this question, nor to the question which by implication follows from it: are we to see a poem like this as a mere deceptive fiction, or does it offer access, through imagination, to truth?

Like the waking section, the dream in the *Parliament* follows closely the pattern of *The Book of the Duchess*. A preliminary section describes the dream-place (forest or garden), and then comes what appears to be the real subject of the poem (meeting with Black Knight or gathering of birds). We shall find in the *Parliament* as much as in the *Book* that what may seem merely a preliminary diversion is in fact related to the main subject through the kind of linkage that belongs to dreams. Africanus leads the Dreamer to the gate of a walled park, reminiscent of the walled garden of the *Roman de la Rose*. Over it are written two inscriptions 'of ful gret difference' (125), one at each side. These derive from the single inscription over the mouth of hell in Dante's *Inferno*, which promises grief and despair to all who enter. But Chaucer's inscriptions are, characteristically, more ambiguous. One promises:

> Thorgh me men gon into that blysful place
> Of hertes hele and dedly woundes cure;
> Thorgh me men gon unto the welle of grace,
> There grene and lusty May shall evere endure.
> This is the wey to al good aventure.
> Be glad, thow redere, and thy sorwe of-caste;
> Al open am I – passe in, and sped thee faste!
> (127–33)

hele health; *lusty* joyful

Then the other:

> 'Thorgh me men gon,' than spak that other side,
> Unto the mortal strokes of the spere
> Of which Disdayn and Daunger is the gyde,
> Ther nevere tre shal fruyt ne leves bere.
> This strem yow ledeth to the sorweful were
> There as the fish in prysoun is al drye;
> Th'eschewing is only the remedye!'
> (134–40)

Daunger resistance; *were* weir

The Dreamer is paralysed by the contradiction between the two inscriptions, but Africanus tells him that they are meant to refer only to one who is 'Loves servant' (159), and therefore not to him. And so he 'shof' (shoved) the Dreamer in through the gate, telling him that he can only be an onlooker, not a participant, but that he will at least gain material for his poetry.

What is behind the gate is evidently a garden of love, like that in the *Roman de la Rose* and its successors, and the inscriptions are saying that love is both heaven and hell. It is the 'blysful place' promised to the good in the *Somnium Scipionis*, with imagery of health, flowing water, and greenness; it is also a place of dryness, sterility and death, which can be avoided only by never entering the garden in the first place. The dream of a heaven and a hell is explicable psychologically through the influence of the vision of judgement read about in the *Somnium Scipionis*; but now the heaven and the hell are the same place – an original variant on the traditional pattern of visions. So far as the dream is to be thought of as providing material for poetry, one might also suggest that two contrary states of the imagination are indicated by the double inscription. The imagery of dryness and sterility recalls the desert outside the temple of Venus in book I of *The House of Fame*, which I suggested was a symbol, among other things, of the failure of inspiration; the imagery of growth and flowing water, on the other hand, suggests a renewal of creativity. Love, as the subject for poetry, can provide either or both of these.

The Dreamer enters the garden, and it proves to be a typical paradise-landscape, with a meadow and a river, a temperate climate, leaves that are always green, day that lasts for ever, birds singing like angels, and harmonious music sweeter than was ever heard by God 'that makere is of al and lord' (199). It contains the whole variety of natural species, instanced by lists of trees and of animals. But it soon becomes clear that this seeming paradise, as in the *Roman de la Rose*, is really a pseudo-paradise of idealized desire. In it 'Cupide, oure lord' (212) sharpens his arrows, 'Some for to sle, and some to wounde and kerve' (217), and his bow lies ready at his feet. The Dreamer sees personifications of pleasing qualities such as Pleasure, Courtesy and Beauty, but also others less pleasing, such as Foolhardiness, Flattery and Bribery, and, most forcefully described, with a real shudder in the rhythm of the last line, Cunning:

> ...the Craft that can and hath the myght
> To don by force a wyght to don folye –
> Disfigurat was she, I nyl nat lye.
> (220–2)

can knows how; *don by force* compel

Now he presses further into the garden, and comes upon a temple of brass, the atmosphere of which is at once exotic and sinister. It may have Patience and Peace sitting at the door, but inside the air is hot with lovers' sighs, which make the altar flames burn more fiercely, and which he sees are incited by 'the bittere goddesse Jelosye' (252). The description of this temple is based on that of the temple of Venus in Boccaccio's *Teseida*; but in the *Parliament*, unlike book I of *The House of Fame*, we are not told to whom the temple is dedicated. Chaucer tells us that the 'sovereyn place' in it is held by Priapus, and leaves us to guess that it is his temple rather than Venus's. Priapus is the god of the phallus as well as of gardens, and a recent scholar has suggested that 'Chaucer's direct reference to the story in Ovid's *Fasti* of Priapus' thwarted attempt to make love to the nymph Lotis clearly marks the temple as a place of sexual frustration'.[6] Moreover, the Dreamer tells us that

> Ful besyly men gonne assaye and fonde
> Upon his hed to sette, of sondry hewe,
> Garlondes ful of freshe floures newe.
> (257–9)
>
> (People were eagerly attempting and endeavouring to set on his head garlands full of fresh new flowers, of various colours.)

The emphasis on *attempting* to do this is not in Boccaccio, who says merely that there were garlands of flowers about the temple; and, though the modern reader may think of a notorious incident in chapter 15 of *Lady Chatterley's Lover*, the suggestion Chaucer intends is probably that the cult of sexuality cannot be so easily prettified, however 'besyly men gonne assaye and fonde'. In a dim corner, the Dreamer finds Venus performing a kind of striptease act, which draws an approving snigger from him. The temple is hung with broken bows, symbolizing the lost virginities of those who 'here tymes waste / In hyre [Diana's] servyse' (283–4), and it is decorated with paintings of famous figures from myth and legend who died for love.

From this hothouse atmosphere, the Dreamer re-emerges into the garden 'that was so sote [sweet] and grene' (296), and walks about to recover from his insight into obsessive sexuality. There he sees another goddess, contrasting with Venus. This is Nature,

> ...a queene,
> That, as of lyght the somer sonne shene
> Passeth the sterre, right so over mesure
> She fayrer was than any creature.
> (298–301)

shene bright; *over* beyond

Chaucer does not describe her in detail, but, with another of the poem's allusions to the visionary tradition, simply says that she looked just as Alanus described her in the *De Planctu Naturae*. Now, however, the birds of different species, which in Alanus were pictured on her garments, have come alive, and they are all crowded round her, awaiting her judgement. The day, we learn, is that of St Valentine, when the birds choose their mates; and it is likely that the *Parliament* was composed to form part of the St Valentine's day celebrations in Richard II's court. 1382 was the year of Richard's marriage, at the age of fifteen, to Anne of Bohemia. Nature is later described as God's deputy, 'vicaire of the almyghty Lord' (379), but there is little emphasis on her subordination to some higher realm of values. By contrast with the *Roman de la Rose*, this poem lays its stress not on the limitation of Nature's realm but on its extensiveness, though it is also concerned with the intricate relationships between the natural and the human. Nature is so surrounded with birds, the Dreamer says, that 'unethe was there space / For me to stonde, so ful was al the place' (314–15); and indeed, from this point on, the Dreamer drops almost completely out of sight, as if the birds had squeezed him out of the poem; and so does Africanus, his guide. This is one way in which the *Parliament* is very different from both of Chaucer's earlier dream poems: the subject-matter of the dream itself becomes so solid and energetic that it elbows the Dreamer aside, and instead of a contrast of points of view between Dreamer and guide there is a contrast *within* what the Dreamer sees. There may be a connection between this disappearance of the Dreamer's point of view and the poem's lack of emphasis on the Dreamer as poet; here it is what is seen that is important, not the role of the person who sees it.

The first things seen are all the species of birds, described in five stanzas, each bird with its own epithet or attribute, which serves to humanize it or to align it with some aspect of human life – the noble falcon, the meek-eyed dove, the thieving crow, the gluttonous cormorant, the wise raven, and so on. These are traditional epithets, evidence of the longstanding human tendency to think of birds as constituting a society parallel to human society. We may compare this list with the earlier list of trees in the garden. Both are concerned not simply with description of the natural world, but with the interaction of the natural and the human. The epithets in the list of trees call attention to the usefulness of the different species to men: the oak for building, the box for making pipes, the fir for ships' masts, the yew for bows, and so on. The list of birds, on the other hand, presents them as independent of human beings but parallel to them. The anthropologist Claude Lévi-Strauss has suggested some reasons for this attitude towards birds, which

> can be permitted to resemble men for the very reason that they are so different. They are feathered, winged, oviparous and they are also physically separated from human society by the element in which it is their privilege to move. As a result of this fact, they form a community which is independent of our own but, precisely because of this independence, appears to us like another society, homologous to that in which we live: birds love freedom; they build themselves homes in which they live a family life and nurture their young; they often engage in social relations with other members of their species; and they communicate with them by acoustic means recalling articulated language. Consequently everything objective conspires to make us think of the bird world as a metaphorical human society: is it not after all literally parallel to it on another level? There are countless examples in mythology and folklore to indicate the frequency of this mode of representation.[7]

There are also countless examples in medieval literature, among them Clanvowe's [fourteenth-century poem] *Cuckoo and the Nightingale*, which we shall consider later, and the earlier English poem *The Owl and the Nightingale*, in which the two birds are used to articulate a whole range of binary contrasts among human attitudes.

In *The Parliament of Fowls*, under Nature's arbitration, the birds are choosing their mates. Like men in medieval society, they are divided into several broad classes: the birds of prey, those that live on worms, those that live on seeds, and water-fowl. Fittingly, in terms of the human hierarchy of the Middle Ages, Nature begins with the noblest, the birds of prey, and among these with the highest, the royal eagle. But here there is a difficulty, for there are three candidates for the hand – or wing – of the beautiful female eagle, the formel, whom Nature herself is holding on her hand. They are, naturally, three male eagles, or tercels. Each speaks in turn to stake his claim to her: the first rests his claim essentially on the total humility of his devotion, the second on the length of his service as her admirer, the third on his exclusive loyalty. The statement of these claims, in a style of appropriately courtly amplitude, occupies some time, but meanwhile the other classes of birds are anxious to express their own views. Their attitudes are often less courtly than those of the aristocratic birds, and the poem echoes with cries of 'kokkow' and 'quek quek'; indeed, our last reminder of the Dreamer's presence as an observer occurs just here, when he complains that 'though myne eres the noyse wente tho' (500). Nature determines that each class of birds shall select its own spokesman to offer a solution to the dilemma. The falcon, for the birds of prey, says that there is no further possibility of discussion, and the three tercels must fight to the death, unless the formel can choose among them herself. The goose, for water-fowl, offers the simple solution that any of the tercels who is not loved by the formel should choose another female as his mate – an uncourtly view, which is treated with ridicule by the sparrowhawk and the other 'gentil foules alle' (575). The turtledove, on behalf of the seed-fowl, claims that each of the tercels must show his loyalty to the formel by loving no one else until he dies, even if she should die first – a *reductio ad absurdum* of courtly claims for the transcendent value of personal emotion, in which we are perhaps intended to see a touch of bourgeois sentimentality. The duck agrees with the goose: there are other fish in the sea, other stars in the sky:

'Ye quek!' yit seyde the doke, ful wel and fayre,
'There been mo sterres, God wot, than a payre!'
(594–5)

The last verdict is that of the cuckoo, for the lowly worm-fowl, the *vylayns* of bird-society: since the eagles cannot agree, let them remain solitary all their lives. Another *gentil* bird, the small falcon called a merlin, protests against this in most *ungentil* language, calling the cuckoo 'wormes corupcioun' (614); but at this point Nature intervenes again.

In the paralleling of different types of bird with the attitudes supposed to be appropriate to different social classes, there is a close resemblance to the way in which primitive men use the categories built into nature as means of thinking about their own lives as part of human culture. In many areas of life such habits of thought have been retained by civilized societies too, so that, as Lévi-Strauss puts it, 'The differences between animals, which man can extract from nature and transfer to culture,... are adopted as emblems by groups of men in order to do away with their own resemblances'.[8] In the *Parliament* the poet of a highly civilized society to some extent reverses the original process: the already existing human groupings, and the attitudes which accompany them, are transferred to the realm of the birds, a realm which remains under the dominion of Nature. There are objectively and permanently different species of birds; but they are only birds, after all. One consequence of this is that we can think about their differences of attitude, even towards so central a subject as love, with amused tolerance. The irreducible birdlikeness of the eagle in *The House of Fame* had a similar function, in preventing us from being able to take him too seriously as a figure of authority. This part of the poem, the actual parliament of the birds, is very funny, not least as a parody of the unruly parliament of Chaucer's own time. Its amusing aspects, indeed, have perhaps tended to overshadow the rest of the poem. A second consequence of the way in which the birds remain birds is that Nature, the mother of them all, can call them to order, if necessary somewhat sharply: 'Holde youre tonges there!' (521) or '"Now pes!" quod Nature, "I commaunde here!"' (617). Their different degrees of *worthinesse* are not conceived as a merely historical phenomenon, but are ratified as part of Nature's 'ryhtful ordenaunce' (390). And she is in a position to insist that their mating must be by mutual agreement, by *eleccioun* (621) rather than by the force that the earlier temple of brass seemed to imply.

Finally, towards the end of the dream, a provisional solution to the dilemma of who shall mate with the formel is achieved by moving out of the realm of birds and back into that of men and women. Nature allows the formel to make her own choice – which was what the falcon had originally urged. Nature herself, it appears, is on the side of the *gentil*, even though she 'alwey hadde an ere / To murmur of the lewednesse [coarseness] behynde' (519–20). She advises the formel, saying that were she not Nature but Reason she would counsel her to choose the first of the tercels; but the actual choice she leaves to the bird herself. The formel, however, declines to choose; she does not yet wish to serve Venus or Cupid, and she needs more time to make up her mind. This too Nature grants. She allows her until the next St Valentine's day to make her choice, and meantime the three tercels have a year to prove their devotion to her. With this problem removed for the time being, all the other birds can now choose their mates. They choose immediately, and before their departure they sing a roundel in honour of Nature, the exquisite lyric 'Now welcome, somer, with thy sonne softe' (680). The noise of the birds' 'shoutyng' when the song is finished awakens the Dreamer from his sleep, and the poem ends with him reading still more books, in the hope of one day having a dream that will do him good.

There is a striking contrast between the evident dissatisfaction of the Dreamer with his dream, which he thinks has not given him what he was seeking in his books, and the satisfying completeness which most readers find in the poem that contains the dream. The difference is that between the conscious mind, always seeking for rational solutions to life's problems on the 'bookish' level of philosophy, and the unconscious mind, which achieves mastery over problems by enacting them in the form of concrete images rather than through rational analysis. One scholar writes of all Chaucer's dream poems that 'The great originality of these poems is in their attempt to exploit the possibilities of *dispositio* – over-all structural arrangement – in ways more complex and meaningful than anything the [rhetorical] manuals suggest in their perfunctory treatments of it.'[9] This is particularly true of *The Parliament of Fowls*: the meaning of the poem is conveyed through certain contrasts embodied rather than stated in the dream-experience, and it was surely his sensitive understanding of dreams that enabled Chaucer to go beyond the inadequate treatment of *dispositio* in the *artes poeticae*. There is, for example, the contrast between the temple of Priapus and Venus and the garden of Nature, between love conceived as enslaving obsession and love conceived as natural impulse, operating within the orderly hierarchy of Nature; then there is the further contrast, within the natural order, now seen as mirroring the human order, between different attitudes towards love. We *feel* the contrast between the enclosure of Venus and Priapus and the freedom of Nature (and we may note that the temple is set within Nature's garden: Nature is more inclusive than sexuality). This freedom, always combined with order, is enacted in the parliament, where every attitude is allowed freedom of expression. This is how the 'commune profit' of the *Somnium Scipionis* is achieved in Nature's realm, which in one way encloses and in another way is homologous with the realm of human society. The cuckoo even uses the phrase 'comune spede' (507), which means the same as 'commune profit'. And the freedom of speech and choice includes a freedom not to choose, or at least to defer choosing. The poem ends unexpectedly, so far as the suitors are concerned: this mating season for them brings not the achievement of love but its deferment. This has the advantage of finally transferring the freedom of discussion to the poem's audience. As some scholars have suggested, *The Parliament of Fowls* leads up to a *demande d'amour*, a love-question to be settled by the courtly listeners as *they* think fit. Whom should the formel choose next St Valentine's day? It is for us to decide. Moreover, the deferment of the choice implies a richer civilization than merely seasonal activities might lead us to expect. Human love, the poem implies, involves not merely the gods of sex and their temple of illicit passions, but the possibility of resisting Nature, or at least of gaining a certain margin of freedom within which to choose the time and manner of one's submission. No doubt, as Jean de Meun's La Vieille puts it, quoting Horace,

> qui voudroit une forche prandre
> por soi de Nature deffandre
> et la bouteroit hors de sai,
> revandroit ele, bien le sai
>
> (13991–4)
>
> (if anyone wanted to take up a pitchfork to protect himself against Nature and shove her out of himself, she would come back, I know well).

But human beings, though they may not be able to overcome Nature completely, at least are not like birds in being so absolutely dominated by natural impulse that they cannot resist the mating season. The subject of the poem, as I have argued, is that central subject of anthropological study, the relation between nature and culture. The dream, then, though it does not satisfy the Dreamer, does weave the thoughts that had been preoccupying him, both from books and from life, into a new and more richly significant pattern. Love, heaven, hell, the 'commune profit': all these appear, transmuted, in the dream, which offers, like myth, an imaginative mastery over the problems of human life.

The mastery is only imaginative, of course, and that is one meaning of the poem's dream-framework. Once the dream is over, the Dreamer may still be troubled by problems so fundamental to human nature that they cannot be abolished. Moreover, the poem in its texture, its 'feel', is genuinely like a dream. It may make use of conceptual thought, but it does so in the most tentative way, with conceptual oppositions largely replaced by concrete contrasts, and one contrast merging dreamlike into another. Such a delicate structure could not have been created by a poet who was truly in the dreamlike state in which he represents himself. A superb intelligence is at work in *The Parliament of Fowls*, and some words written about a great poet of the twentieth century would apply equally well to this poem of Chaucer's:

> The poet's magnificent intelligence is devoted to keeping as close as possible to the concrete of sensation, emotion and perception. Though this poetry is plainly metaphysical in preoccupation, it belongs as purely to the realm of sensibility,

and has in it as little of the abstract and general of discursive prose, as any poetry that was ever written.[10]

Notes

1. J. L. Lowes, *Geoffrey Chaucer* (Oxford, 1934), p. 117.
2. In this Chaucer is continuing a tradition that goes far back in medieval courtly poetry, though it rarely achieved conscious realization. Cf. E. I. Condren, 'The Troubadour and his Labor of Love', *Mediaeval Studies*, vol. XXXIV (1972), pp. 174–95: 'Many troubadour lyrics seem indeed to speak about a new and rarefied concept of love – about *fin' amors*. But several of them also use the language of love to describe the poet's search for poetry. Similarly, the poet's anguish and frustration in love are frequently co-subjects with his inability to create songs' (p. 175).
3. *Contributions to Analytical Psychology*, p. 232.
4. Noted by D. S. Brewer, ed., *The Parlement of Foulys* (London, 1960), p. 103.
5. *The Parlement of Foules: An Interpretation* (Oxford, 1957), p. 54.
6. G. D. Economou, *The Goddess Natura in Medieval Literature* (Cambridge, MA, 1972), p. 136.
7. *The Savage Mind* (London, 1966), p. 204.
8. Ibid. p. 107.
9. R. O. Payne, *The Key of Remembrance* (New Haven, 1963), p. 145.
10. F. R. Leavis, 'T. S. Eliot's Later Poetry', in *Education and the University*, 2nd edn (London, 1948), p. 88.

The Narrator as Translator

Donald W. Rowe

That Chaucer's Legend of Good Women *is in many ways the most difficult of the dream visions to apprehend critically is reflected in the very various critical approaches to it. These tend to centre on the question – not so unusual for Chaucerians but particularly relevant here – of whether the work is to be read as serious or ironic. It is inevitable that the most persuasive readings choose some middle ground and present Chaucer as engaging in both 'game and earnest'. Precisely what is game and what is earnest, however, is harder to decide: what seems profound pathos to one reader may appear comic parody to another. The difficulty of assessing the tone is compounded by the apparent gap between prologue and legends: in no other dream vision is the prologue so developed. The prologue contains the conventional elements of dream visions: the ideal landscape, the narrator's love for the flower, and the encounter with allegorical or mythical figures, here the God of Love and his queen Alceste. Its focus, however, is not on love but on Chaucer's heresy against the God of Love in translating the* Roman de la Rose *and writing of faithless women. The result is the uneasy group of legends of faithful women, presented by Chaucer as penance.*

In the following extract, Donald Rowe addresses the issue of how we can make sense of the legends by approaching them through the prologue – not just superficially, as (perhaps unwilling) penance, but rather through the questions of writing and perspective that are raised in this first part of the work. Rowe notes how unsatisfying it is either to read the legends, as some early critics did, as straightforward moral exempla, or to see them exclusively as 'unmerciful satire'; if either was the aim, Chaucer has not succeeded. Rather, Rowe sees the poem as deeply engaged with the notion of 'storyal soth' (702), the question of the truth of authority and interpretation, and as well with the opposition between different poetic ideologies, philosophical and courtly. The God of Love may be seen as demanding a superficial form of writing, which subscribes to the courtly tradition, but is unsatisfactory in that it does not possess the critical depth of the condemned Troilus and Criseyde. *Women are reduced to patterns, although the narrator, perhaps naively, becomes persuaded by the truth of the legends. To read the stories straight is unsatisfying, and yet they do involve genuine feeling: despite the 'ironic intertextuality' of the work, the legends gain their own 'storyal soth'. Rowe argues that the poem is in fact 'about failure' – about failing to fulfil the demands of the God of Love because these are impossible. Yet it is a failure that contains its own truth about writing: the legends move between an acute sense of emotion and human experience, which the narrator has gained from his beloved books, and a deep sense of dissatisfaction at the constraints of the authoritative pattern of the* exemplum *genre.*

As Rowe points out, we return, of course, to the 'perennial problem': what is the relation between Chaucer and the narrator? As in the earlier dream visions, the narrator is a caricature, an 'affable bumbler' who feels love for his daisy, for Alceste and for his 'olde bokes' (Prologue, 25), and who confuses his legends and retells them in ways that directly oppose or conceal their content (for instance, making Medea a saintly victim). Our attention is drawn, sometimes comically, sometimes uneasily, to the possibilities of interpretation, to the question of the truth of 'olde bokes' that the House of Fame *engages with so notably. Rowe presents this from a slightly different perspective: how can the ideas of the past be reconciled with those of fourteenth-century London? He returns to the issue of Chaucer's audience: how can he please his listeners and readers, who desire courtly poetry of love, and yet write the philosophical poetry he himself would choose? This opposition might also be seen as one between idealism and realism, convention and originality. Chaucer's poem seems once again to address the need to find a style that invests 'olde bokes' with new experience, an issue central to all his dream visions, but treated here in a more anguished manner that dramatizes the difficulty of failure.*

Dream Vision Poetry: Critical Extracts

Donald W. Rowe, 'The Narrator as Translator' in *Through Nature to Eternity: Chaucer's 'Legend of Good Women'*. University of Nebraska Press, Lincoln, NB, and London, 1988.

The fundamental problem confronting the reader of the legends is to determine the point of view from which they ought to be read or – to phrase the question another way – to determine their relationship to the Prologue, for one's view of this relationship is bound to govern one's perception of how Chaucer's narratives relate to their sources. Having been commanded in the Prologue to 'speke wel of love' by writing of good and faithful wives and of false men, Chaucer's narrator produces a sequence of legends whose heroines and villains seem highly unsatisfactory. Some critics have chosen to minimize the apparent discrepancies between the demanded and the delivered: Lowes, for example, argues that the heroines are all 'stock *exempla* of fidelity in love,' and Robinson declares them *'good in the only sense that counted for the purpose at hand.'*[1] Others have emphasized the discrepancies to read the legends ironically: Goddard, for example, declares them *'a most unmerciful satire upon women'*; Garrett, *'a masterly set of humorous sketches.'*[2] While Chaucer must have known that these 'stock exempla' were far from ideal representatives of truth in loving, the critical question is whether or not he intended the discrepancies in his versions to be recognized as such, a question that directs us first to the Prologue to see what guidelines it provides.[3] *If Chaucer's intent was 'unmerciful satire,' the critical history of the legends suggests that he was as unsuccessful as he was if he wished us to respond to his heroines with heartfelt sympathy and unqualified respect.*

When Alceste and the god of Love lay down the law, they impose it on the narrator: that is, not on the poet but on the fictive representation of himself that Chaucer creates in the poem. What they impose is the manner and matter of the courtly tradition. The narrator proves an intrusive teller of tales, and though he begins reluctantly, apparently still convinced that men as well as women can be true in love, and admits near the end that he is 'agroted' [surfeited] from telling of false men, his intrusions overwhelmingly reinforce the prescribed attitude. He pities his heroines as innocent victims and denounces their lovers as faithless. Time and again he addresses his audience directly, urging the women in it not to trust men and implicitly indicting the men in it as false. Indeed, the narrator's reactions are so frequent and so frequently extreme that they prove self-dramatizing, even comically so. This fact reinforces our sense from the Prologue that we must distinguish not only technically between the poet and the narrator – the one being inside the poem, the other outside it – but also ideologically. They speak with different voices and represent different points of view. Thus, to address again the old question of the point of view appropriate to the legends is to confront another of the perennial problems of Chaucer criticism: the relationship of Chaucer to his narrator.[4]

R. W. Frank has argued that the question of the goodness of the legends' heroines is in effect a red herring. He contends that Chaucer's purpose in the *Legend* was to introduce his audience to a new and essentially uncourtly subject matter and that the Prologue was his strategy for achieving this end. By making the legends penance for his past sins against the god of Love, even written at the command of the god and his queen, Chaucer 'lends an illusion of orthodoxy to the new kind of story he is introducing' and thus frees himself to 'do almost anything he wishes':[5] namely, to tell stories simply for their own sake.[6] While Frank's approach ignores the crucial fact that these stories have been altered to increase their agreement with the letter of Alceste's demands (often to the detriment of the story) so that they seem anything but free performances, it does implicitly recognize that the problem of the relationship of the legends to the Prologue is not simply a question of whether or not they satisfy Alceste's and the god's requirements. Before we can read the *Legend* as a poetic whole, we must distinguish between what Alceste and the god require the legends to be and the purposes the Prologue as a whole assigns to them. We must distinguish between Alceste's idea for the legends and the poet's.

The first thing the Prologue as a whole indicates is that the legends will not satisfy the demands of the god and his queen. The shallowness of the god's criticisms, the absurdity of much of Alceste's defense, and the contradictory nature of their prescriptions all indicate that the legends must inevitably fail to meet their desires. The god's complaint reveals that what he wants from Chaucer's art is flattery for himself and his servants. If Chaucer intended the legends to be taken at face value, presumably he would not have implied that the desire for such legends was a self-serving denial both of the complexity of reality and the profundity of old books. While each of Alceste's defenses makes good enough sense in itself – that Chaucer may have been falsely accused, there being many liars and flatterers in the god's court; that he may have been translating heedlessly; that he may have been ordered to make the offending translations; that he may have repented; that he was only translating others' words – collectively, they do not augur well for any future efforts. If Chaucer is as simple-minded, as 'nyce,' as she implies, this fact can only be a recipe for further trouble. The difficulties it predicts are guaranteed when the god orders the narrator to begin with Cleopatra, for Cleopatra is impossible in the role of a woman true in loving all her life. Even without this stipulation the narrator's task is impossible, for the requirement that he speak well of love is in conflict with the demand that he depict all men as false lovers. How is one to speak well of a love that has no beneficent effects upon its servants? In defense of love, the narrator has been ordered to deny, at least by implication, that which was thought to prove its worth: its ennobling power, a proof of the value of love repeatedly appealed to in the *Troilus*, we recall.

The fact that Chaucer dramatizes the irrationality of the program he nonetheless has the narrator execute not only predicts inevitable failure but also indicates that this failure is part of his true subject. In effect, the narrator is the author of the legends as courtly poems; he writes the poem Lowes reads. Chaucer wrote the rather more elusive poem that those who read the legends as an ironic intertextuality have been trying to define. What has not been sufficiently realized by those whose footsteps this chapter follows is that the poet's poem is not merely the ironic inversion of the narrator's poem but contains it, is about those translations. By reading the legends as illustrations of Alceste's and the god's inadequate idea, Fyler and Kiser take the first step toward appreciating the significance of this fact. The next step is to realize the importance of the visibility of the narrator, for it implies that the second poem dramatizes his writing of the first poem. Thus the Prologue not only narrates the events that account for the narrator's translations but also presents itself as the narrator's response to those events. The apostrophe to the daisy, invoking its help; the inclusion of the *balade*; the speculations about the value of old books, with the subsequent comment that he will tell us why he spoke of old books when he has time – all these belong to the time of the writing and dramatize that writing. The same must be said of the narrator's apostrophes to his characters and his direct address to his audience in the legends. They dramatize the writing. One implication of this fact is that the conventional problem of the reader, how to reconcile the Ovidian sources with Alceste's and the god's prescriptions, is inside the poem; it is the narrator's problem. Chaucer's legends are about his efforts to deal with this difficulty.

Much of Chaucer's characterization of his narrator in the *Legend* is familiar. While we may hear 'Chaucer the man' protesting in the narrator's insistence in the Prologue that it was always his intention to further truth in loving in his poetry, we also recognize that familiar persona of the affable bumbler by which Chaucer time and again represents himself in his poetry. His denigrating dramatization of himself in the Prologue is evident in the apparent literal-mindedness of the narrator's veneration of the daisy, in the naive credulity of his declaration that he himself gives his old books 'ful credence,' in the obtuse forgetfulness with which he fails to recognize his own Alceste in the dream, in the ineffectuality of his protestations of innocence. When Alceste defends the narrator on the grounds that he is 'nyce' and, hence, may have translated the offending works not from malice but from carelessness simply because 'he useth thynges for to make' (F 364), as though he translated mindlessly and compulsively, she describes precisely what we find in the legends from the point of view of her demands, stories rather carelessly chosen and dubiously interpreted. The narrator is a man who gets little right, and that little is misunderstood. This accord between Alceste's characterization of the narrator and the legends he produces indicates that the lack of accord between the demanded and the delivered is no accident but an integral part of Chaucer's idea. While the Prologue does not require so many tales of Sir Thopas, this accord indicates that the unsatisfactory character of the legends reflects the narrator's comic limitations as well as the artistically counterproductive character of the demands imposed upon him.[7]

All is not comedy, however. The Prologue anticipates a drama of considerable import and poignancy. First, the narrator has two loves: he loves the daisy from the natural world; he loves Alceste, a heroine from old books, and more generally, old books themselves. While his vision reveals that his diverse loves manifest the same truth, the initial presentation of them in opposition implies at least some conflict between authority and experience, between the 'doctrine of these olde wyse' and the way things seem to be in the here and now of fourteenth-century London. Further difficulty is implied by the disparity between the narrator's ideal loves, the daisy and the historical Alceste, and the humanized counterparts that people his dream. The latter are the source of the Prologue's contradictory prescriptions. By depicting their imposition of the courtly ideology as an irrational comedy, one that places the lady of the narrator's dream at odds with her ideal prototypes, Chaucer further intimates the irrationality of that ideology – its commitment to illusion rather than to reality – and implies that the imposed perspective will contradict both experience and the 'doctrine' of old books. The narrator would indeed seem to be trapped among these irreconcilable loyalties and obligations.

It is equally clear that the narrator's drama enacts Chaucer's own dilemmas as poet. Behind him as courtly maker stands an enabling tradition, which – if the god and Alceste can be taken to speak accurately for it – threatens to frustrate his apparent ambition to be a philosophical poet. Before him stands an audience determined that his poetry should pamper its illusions and delusions. If he finds a way of surmounting these impediments, a way of transforming courtly making into philosophical poetry, all the hazards inherent in that high calling await him. 'Storyal soth' is elusive and, discovered, but a dark mirror of transcendent 'trouthe.' As we shall see, the narrator and his courtly poem are both Chaucer's dramatized confession of his own inadequacy for this task and simultaneously his means of realizing it.

Notes

1   Lowes, 'Is Chaucer's *Legend* a Travesty?' 546; Robinson, *Works*, 482....
2   Goddard, 'Chaucer's *Legend*' (1908), 101; Garrett, 'Cleopatra the Martyr,' 67....

3 Kelly implies that Chaucer left the *Legend* incomplete in part because he discovered in the course of writing it the inappropriateness of the heroines listed in the Prologue's *balade* and presumably intended for inclusion (*Love and Marriage*, 113–20), but Chaucer's prior familiarity with the unsuitability of many of these women is clear from earlier references to them (see, for example, the *Book of the Duchess*, 725–34).
4 The classic work on the narrator in the dream visions remains Dorothy Bethurum, 'Chaucer's Point of View as Narrator in the Love Poems,' *PMLA* 74 (1959): 511–20. On the similarity of the persona to the poet, see Donald R. Howard, 'Chaucer the Man,' *PMLA* 80 (1965): 337–43.
5 Frank, *Chaucer and the Legend*, 35.
6 Ibid., 14–15. Frank also denies the poem any 'moral or theological purpose' (p. 15). He does recognize incidental comedy and irony.
7 The present study lends support to Fyler's view that one of the purposes of the legends is to show the deleterius effect on art and morality of an *a priori* point of view (*Chaucer and Ovid*, 98–115).

Chaucer's Classical Legendary

Lisa J. Kiser

Writing, of course, is not the only subject of the Legend of Good Women; *as its title declares, and like so many of Chaucer's works, it is a poem about women. Part of its difficulty for contemporary critics results from the radical shift that has occurred in the understanding of gender between the medieval and modern periods. It is not easy for the contemporary reader to find inspiring the saintly model of womanhood, dependent as it is upon passive suffering and martyrdom, and rejection of sexual desire and worldly ambition. Indeed, one aspect of the ready appeal of Chaucer's writing is his sympathetic presentation of the model of the active woman: he considers the questions of female desire and rationality, rendering his saint Cecilia in the* Second Nun's Tale, *for example, as more skilled in rational argument than her male antagonist. The* Legend of Good Women, *however, does not pursue individual action, but rather reduces its subjects to the saintly, passive pattern of the virtuous woman: to a great extent, these women all represent the same pattern of perfection, and follow the same fates of suffering, betrayal and death, martyrs to the cause of love and victims of men.*

This is the topic addressed in the following extract by Lisa Kiser, one of the critics to whom Rowe refers as emphasizing 'ironic intertextuality'; for Kiser, the purpose of the legends is 'broadly comic', although they also raise serious questions about writing, translation and morality, in particular how Christian writers are to use classical authorities. She combines source study, literary history and genre study

Dream Vision Poetry: Critical Extracts

with a more radical theoretical approach. Her views are in many ways more extreme and provocative than Rowe's, perhaps because of the problematic presentation of women in the poem, and while her exploration of Chaucer's classical legendary is lucid and scholarly, her conclusions are more debatable. The extract below explores Chaucer's use of the model of the exemplum *in ways that often lead to uneasy alignments of classical heroines and Christian saints. For Kiser, these are generally negative, though this is by no means the only way of viewing the text.*

Kiser distinguishes at the start of her discussion the characteristics of exemplum *and establishes hagiography, the writing of saints' lives, as one form of such moral writing: it is into this genre that Chaucer fits his lives of classical women. Kiser emphasizes the apparent 'historical veracity' or 'storyal soth' as well as the moral truth of the legends. The distortion of historical truth is reflected in the distortion of the legends more generally (for Kiser, unsuccessfully), in order to give them the shape of hagiographic exempla. Kiser emphasizes the difference between women dying for God and for love, and draws careful comparisons between Chaucer and Boccaccio, who did not include saints in his lives of famous women. She makes the valid point that from the Christian perspective, secular love is 'unredeeming passion' – and yet, because such love is the subject of perhaps the greatest medieval literature (for instance, the stories of Launcelot and Guinevere, Tristan and Isolde, Troilus and Criseyde), it is difficult to be troubled by its sanctification. Indeed, as C. S. Lewis pointed out early on, this is very much a feature of* fin'amors.

Kiser places Lucrece as the least unsatisfactory of Chaucer's martyrs: the victim of rape, her death is less for love than for honour, and even in classical tellings she appears very much a martyr figure. Yet, as Kiser notes, her suicide was seen as sinful by some Christian writers, Augustine in particular. Chaucer rewrites the rape of Lucrece against tradition by causing her to swoon, with the effect of absolving her from any question of guilt. To Kiser, the telling of the story is still unsatisfactory in hagiographic terms: Lucrece dies from shame; Tarquin is a courtly lover; conventions are violated. Yet her argument ignores the pathos of the legend, which so acutely evokes the predicament of the vulnerable woman:

> No word she spak, she hath no myght therto.
> What shal she seyn? Hire wit is al ago.
> Ryght as a wolf that fynt a lomb alone,
> To whom shal she compleyne or make mone?
> What, shal she fyghte with an hardy knyght?
> Wel wot men that a woman hath no myght.
> What, shal she crye, or how shal she asterte*   *escape
> That hath hire by the throte with swerd at herte?
> (1796–803)

As in this instance, moments of pathos and emotion repeatedly counter the disjunctions of the Legend of Good Women, *reminding us of the power wielded by the interpreter of 'olde bokes'.*

Lisa J. Kiser, from 'Chaucer's Classical Legendary' in *Telling Classical Tales: Chaucer and the 'Legend of Good Women'*. Cornell University Press, Ithaca, NY, and London, 1983.

I have limited my discussion thus far in this chapter to the three general characteristics of the exemplum form that Chaucer parodies in his legendary – its explicit morality, its applicability to life, and its brevity. Chaucer's legendary, however, is constructed to conform to a particular kind of exemplum, that is, the saint's life. As a subtype of the exemplum, hagiography usually shares with other exemplary narratives the three characteristics just mentioned.[1] Its moral purpose is, of course, beyond dispute; saints' lives were plainly designed to represent the struggle between good and evil. Despite the great variety of the individual Christian narratives within it, the genre always has – at bottom – this purpose.[2] Its applicability to life is also commonly stressed; from the narrative usually considered to be the prototype of European saints' legends, Athanasius's *Life of Anthony* [fourth century], to the late medieval *specula* [literally, mirrors] containing large numbers of lives, authors and compilers routinely expressed the usefulness of their narratives as models of behavior.[3] Brevity, too, was a common feature of the saints' lives, especially when more than one was collected into a legendary or when a legend appeared with exempla of other kinds to form a compendium.[4]

Another characteristic typical of hagiographical narratives is a claim of historical veracity, a feature that Chaucer mimics in his legendary.[5] In the clearest example, Chaucer writes of Cleopatra's story that 'this is storyal soth, it is no fable' (702). However, he also suggests the historicity of other legends by mentioning emperors and kings whose reigns were contemporaneous with the ladies' lives and by having the God of Love in the Prologue talk about classical literary women as if they really existed. The women 'in that tyde,' the deity remarks, were far truer than men 'in this world' (G 302–4). These appeals to history are often comic because of the distortion in some of the narratives of the historical truth. *Cleopatra*, in fact, which includes the strongest assertion of historical validity, is one of the least faithful retellings of a classical source in the entire collection.

The most important feature of Chaucer's legendary, however, is its careless disregard for the differences in subject matter between hagiography and classical literature. The stories in the *Legend* combine pagan erotic love and Christian *caritas* in a facile union that corresponds to the God of Love's own artificial synthesis. As we might expect, the results are appalling, and little justice is done to either of the worlds being represented. Chaucer's classical sources are cheapened by his forcing them into an alien hagiographic pattern,[6] and the spirit of hagiography is profoundly violated by Chaucer's implicit suggestion in these stories that pagan women who die for love are somehow morally comparable to saints dying for the love of God. In fact, in many of the most well-known saints' lives, saints become martyrs by dying at the hands of pagans, that is, *because* of the antipathy between the Christian and pagan cultures. Clearly, in Chaucer's mind, the solution to the problem of how Christian artists should use classical material does not include the wholesale adoption of a hagiographical point of view. The idea of 'Cupid's martyrs,' the central conception of Chaucer's legendary, is an extreme and finally unworkable one for a serious artist.

To confirm the perversity of this sort of union, even in the opinion of medieval writers who were actively seeking new syntheses of pagan and Christian topics, we need only to turn to Boccaccio, whose *De claris mulieribus* [*Of Famous Women*] is quite probably one of Chaucer's medieval sources. Boccaccio did not include any Christian saints in his collection because he did not think they were appropriate in the company of pagans. In his preface he writes, 'It seemed that they could not very well be placed side by side and that they did not strive for the same goal.'[7] To Boccaccio, the natural virtue of pagans is somehow different from Christian virtue, and the two must not be confused, or even combined in the same exemplary collection. Furthermore, he reminds us that the virtues of Christian saints had already been described in books reserved for them alone:

> ...not only do Christian women, resplendent in the true, eternal light, live on, illustrious in their deserved immortality, but we know that their virginity, purity, saintliness, and invincible firmness in overcoming carnal desire and the punishments of tyrants have been described in special books, as their merits required.[8]

Though the lives of the saints may have been the generic inspiration for Boccaccio's collection of exempla, he is nevertheless careful to draw a distinction between his own work and the 'special books' devoted to saints. To him, saints and classical women were simply not alike.[9]

Although Chaucer's comic project in the *Legend* is different from Boccaccio's serious one in *De claris mulieribus*, the two authors were faced with the same problem – how to retell the lives of classical women in such a way as to make them useful to Christian readers as 'examples' of behavior. Boccaccio's solution to this problem was to tell, quite plainly, the stories of natural virtue to be found in classical texts. He did not attempt to introduce the conceptions of hagiography into his collection, beyond the simple idea of making his stories roughly conform – in imitative purpose – to the numerous collections

Dream Vision Poetry: Critical Extracts

of the lives of female saints. But Chaucer's project is much more difficult, because he has to ignore the incompatibility of the two narrative types in making saints out of classical women, including classical women who were enthralled in what is, from a Christian point of view, an unredeeming passion.

Only Chaucer's *Legend of Lucrece* is, in some ways, an exceptional case. The poet did not have to alter its plot much, because Lucretia was, quite literally, a martyr for chastity, exhibiting (though only superficially, as we shall see) the same virtue that we find in so many female saints. Lucretia may have been, in fact, the most 'canonical' of Chaucer's ladies, having survived, good reputation intact, the scrutiny of Jerome and other Christian authorities.[10] But for Augustine, whom Chaucer's narrator unwisely names in his opening lines, Lucretia's 'virtue' was actually a crime, for in killing herself, she was killing an innocent victim. As for the motive behind her suicide, Augustine remarks that it was obviously not the 'love of purity,' but the 'overwhelming burden of her shame.' Thus, he concludes, there is a significant difference between the 'true sanctity' of Christian martyrs and the illusory virtue of Lucretia.[11] This problem raised by Augustine does not interfere with Chaucer's enterprise, however. The narrator simply ignores the substance of Augustine's lengthy commentary on Lucretia's case and attributes to him a feeling of 'gret compassioun' (1690) for her. He then introduces a theme common to hagiography – commemoration – by remarking that his story is being told 'to preyse and drawe to memorye' (1685) the event in her life which resulted in her 'martyrdom.'[12]

Chaucer's handling of Lucrece's rape and subsequent death is reminiscent of hagiography in other ways as well. One of his only additions to this story's plot is Lucrece's swoon, which occurs during her rape, and which Chaucer describes as deep and deathlike:

> She loste bothe at ones wit and breth,
> And in a swogh* she lay, and wex so ded,   *swoon
> Men myghte smyten of hire arm or hed;
> She feleth no thyng, neyther foul ne fayr.
> (1815–18)

Lucrece's swoon serves several purposes. First, it renders her oblivious to Tarquin's violence, sparing her the conscious experience of (and, of course, complicity in) such an outrage. It is intended, perhaps, to resemble the otherworldly states in which God allows His beloved saints miraculously to endure physical suffering (in fires that do not burn them, in hot baths that do not scorch, etc.).[13] Second, it worsens Tarquin's character since it suggests to us that his desire for Lucrece has, as its object, what is most 'lifeless' about her

– her mere physical form. And third, it is a primitive example of the typological structure sometimes used in hagiographic narratives in that it 'prefigures' Lucrece's real death.[14]

Finally, Lucrece's story is fairly easy to force into the hagiographical mold since her own compatriots venerated her for her virtue; as Chaucer writes, she was 'holden there / A seynt, and ever hir day yhalwed [blessed] dere' (1870–1). With these lines, the narrator slyly introduces the terminology he needs to make the Christian parallel clear. Moreover, her corpse, carried through the streets to give witness to the spreading story of her 'martyrdom,' is surely meant to recall the relics of a Christian saint, circulated with a legend, so that men 'may see and here' (1867) of miraculous forbearance and power in the face of great suffering.

These hagiographic devices in Lucrece's tale, coupled with the digression (1759–74) that makes Tarquin fully equal in lustful power to the sexually obsessed pursuers of female saints,[15] by no means confer upon her any easy canonization, however. As hard as our narrator may work to make Lucrece fit the mold of a chaste Christian, she is still saintly only by the standards of her own pagan culture, dying, as Augustine says, not for Christian truth but through shame over the result of someone's violent and lustful desire. Tarquin's character, too, is odd in the extreme, for Chaucer has permitted him to display the tender longings of a stricken courtly lover, even though these details do not fit the purpose of hagiographic legend. The lustful pursuers of female saints should never be allowed to show poignant emotion; such a display conflicts with the moral clarity that such tales are designed to convey. Thus Chaucer's attempt to equate Lucrece's life with that of a saint results in an obviously contrived piece of literary deception that violates the generic specifications of both hagiography and courtly narrative. The story also violates its own professed interest in the strict correlation of 'word' and 'dede' (1706–7), 'contenaunce' and 'herte' (1738–9). Chaucer's praise of Lucrece for having beauty 'by no craft...feyned' (1749) does not seem to deter him from feigning the beauty of sainthood for her. And finally, if we can trust Chaucer's words in the Prologue to his own life of St Cecilia, the writing of saints' lives is in part a valid method of preventing idleness, a sin with which the tale of Lucrece is concerned. Both Lucrece and Chaucer work to deter that sin; she spins, while he writes. But one must finally question the validity of Chaucer's labor here, for it can hardly be described as 'leveful bisynesse,' as the Second Nun describes it. He certainly meant for us to notice Lucrece's simple but productive task and to contrast it with his own more complex, more directly 'Christian' one which is, however, ultimately idleness.

Notes

1 Not every saint's life exhibits all three characteristics of the exemplum form; there are, for example, some very long legends. Moreover, not every legend is intended as a model for behavior; Chaucer's legend of Cecilia is a good example. But in spite of the exceptions, most saints' legends were considered to be exempla and were gathered into collections together with other narratives to form exemplary *specula*. For corroboration of this point, see Mosher, p. 74n.: 'These legendary lives of holy men and women and the Virgin furnished more exempla than any other class of material. In a sense, a saint's life or a collection of saints' lives constituted a sort of example-book.' Welter, in *L'Exemplum*, also categorizes saints' lives as exempla, as does Owst, pp. 123–35.

2 On the struggle between good and evil in saints' legends, see Theodor Wolpers, *Die Englische Heiligenlegende des Mittelalters* (Tübingen: Max Niemeyer, 1964), pp. 28–30. See also Alexandra Hennessey Olsen, '"*De Historiis Sanctorum*": A Generic Study of Hagiography,' *Genre*, 13 (1980), 415–25; Charles W. Jones, *Saints' Lives and Chronicles in Early England* (Ithaca, NY: Cornell University Press, 1947), p. 73; and Rosemary Woolf, 'Saints' Lives,' in *Continuations and Beginnings: Studies in Old English Literature*, ed. E. G. Stanley (London: Thomas Nelson, 1966), p. 41.

3 See Owst, pp. 123–4, 134–5. Indeed, Owst sees imitation as the 'chief object' of the saint's life. In Athanasius's *Life of Anthony*, the author twice mentions Anthony's value as a model, once in the Prologue and once in the Conclusion. See also the *Golden Legend*, p. 645: '[The Martyrs] are given to us as models for combat,' and Jaroslav Pelikan, *The Growth of Medieval Theology (600–1300)* (Chicago: University of Chicago Press, 1978), p. 125.

4 See Wolpers, pp. 13, 33: Olsen, p. 411; the *Golden Legend*, p. 687; and Ernst Robert Curtius, *European Literature and the Latin Middle Ages*, trans. Willard R. Trask (1953: rpt. New York: Harper and Row, 1963), p. 160.

5 On the 'historicity' of saints' lives, see Owst, pp. 125–6, where he quotes from a fourteenth-century manuscript as showing this typical claim: 'This is no fabull that I sey you.' See also Olsen, p. 417; William Nelson, *Fact or Fiction: The Dilemma of the Renaissance Storyteller* (Cambridge, Harvard University Press, 1973), pp. 23–4; and Hippolyte Delehaye, *The Legends of the Saints: An Introduction to Hagiography*, trans. V. M. Crawford (1907: rpt. South Bend, IN: University of Notre Dame Press, 1961), p. 9. pp. 65–9.

6 On the single 'pattern' of Christ's life as it is demonstrated in saints' lives, see Olsen, p. 411, who reminds us of Gregory of Tours's comment: 'And it is asked by many whether we should say the Life of the saints, or the Lives.' See also Pelikan, p. 174.

7 *Concerning Famous Women*, trans. Guido A. Guarino (New Brunswick, NJ: Rutgers University Press, 1963), p. xxxviii.

8 *Concerning Famous Women*, p. xxxix.

9 Boccaccio's translator Guido A. Guarino, writes: 'He did not write of saints and martyrs simply because he was not drawn to them, while classical antiquity held

Dream Vision Poetry: Critical Extracts

      him enthralled with its charms' (*Concerning Famous Women*, p. xxv). The issue is probably more complicated than Guarino suggests.

10   For Jerome's approval of her, see *Adversus Jovinianum* 1.46 (*PL* 23, col. 287). Also see Odo of Cluny's *Collationum libri tres*, *PL* 133. col. 557. For examples of the medieval view of Lucretia's story, see *Gesta Romanorum*, trans. Charles Swan and revised by Wynnard Hooper (London: Bohn's Antiquarian Library, 1891). p. 239; *Le Ménagier de Paris*, trans. Eileen Power (London: Routledge and Sons, 1928), pp. 101–5; and the *Romance of the Rose*, ll. 8608ff. Some of Chaucer's alterations of the original story are discussed by Frank, pp. 93–110, and by Edgar Finley Shannon, *Chaucer and the Roman Poets* (Cambridge, MA: Harvard University Press, 1929), pp. 220–8.

11   *The City of God*, 1.19. See also John S. P. Tatlock, 'Chaucer and the *Legenda Aurea*,' *MLN*, 45 (1930), 296–8.

12   See Owst, pp. 123, 125–56, who quotes two typical examples of hagiography being called a means of 'blessid commemoraciouns' and a form of 'remembrance.'

13   See, for example, the *Golden Legend*, pp. 593, 632, 695: and *The South English Legendary* 1, ed. Charlotte D' Evelyn and Anna Mill, EETS e.s. (London: Oxford University Press, 1956), pp. 63–4, ll. 41–5, 56–60.

14   Compare, for example, the 'foreshadowings' of death in the life of St Martha, *Golden Legend*, p. 393.

15   See, for example, the *Golden Legend*, pp. 52, 540, 552, 571; and *The South English Legendary* 1, p. 19, ll. 8–16: p. 293, ll. 43–50; and 2, p. 586, ll. 5–8.

5

Troilus and Criseyde: An Overview

Troilus and Criseyde is arguably Chaucer's greatest single work. It perfects the art of the dramatic narrative and the *rime royal* form of the *Parliament of Fowls*, extending this to a five-book tragedy in verse that moves gracefully from high drama and philosophy to realistic dialogue and comedy. As an epic romance of Troy it occupies a space entirely different from either the literary dream world of the early poetry or the explicitly medieval pilgrimage and social satire of the *Canterbury Tales*, though it also sustains and develops crucial themes – the nature of *fin'amors*, the predicament of women, predestination and free will, chance and fortune, society and the individual, writing and interpretation. In translating Boccaccio's *Il Filostrato* and retelling the story of a celebrated betrayal in love, Chaucer once again engages explicitly with the issue of 'olde bokes', returning to the Trojan epic that he has already used in the *House of Fame* for the story of Dido, and will use again in the *Legend of Good Women*.[1]

In Book V of *Troilus and Criseyde* Criseyde laments: 'Allas, for now is clene ago / My name of trouthe in love, for everemo!/ ... Allas, of me, unto the worldes ende, / Shal neyther ben ywriten nor ysonge / No good word, for thise bokes wol me shende. / O, rolled shal I ben on many a tonge' (V, 1054–61). The words function powerfully to convey Criseyde's regret for her own falseness, but they also draw attention to the self-consciously literary status of the text by recalling the place of Chaucer's telling in a long-standing literary tradition, within which Criseyde's name has already been 'rolled... on many a tonge' as one that epitomizes female unfaithfulness and betrayal – and will continue to be, by writers as diverse as Henryson and Shakespeare. Though Chaucer's Criseyde states that women will hate her name most of all, we become aware of how, ultimately, her reputation is shaped and reshaped by a whole procession of male writers, just as within the text she is passed from one man to another – from father, to uncle, to lover, to father; from Trojan to

Troilus and Criseyde: An Overview

Plate 2 Chaucer reading to a courtly audience. Reproduced by permission of the Master and Fellows, Corpus Christi College, Cambridge, MS 61, fol. 1b.

Greek. Within a strongly anti-feminist tradition no writer, before or after Chaucer, has allowed Criseyde so much space, and no narrator has been so unwilling to admit Criseyde's betrayal: 'she so sory was for hire untrouthe, / Iwis, I wolde excuse hire yet for routhe' (V, 1098–9).

In many ways Chaucer reworks *Il Filostrato* very closely: long sections of *Troilus* are close translations of Boccaccio, and the stanzas frequently follow the same division and line emphasis. But at the same time Chaucer makes notable omissions and additions; as well, his careful, often minute rephrasing and rewriting effect an overall shift in emphasis, focused most of all in his portrayal of Criseyde. While Boccaccio's telling all too clearly moves towards her betrayal of Troilus, Chaucer leaves us uncertain as to her motivation; he both allows us more insight into Criseyde's psyche and is highly selective in the details he offers, ensuring that she remains an enigma.

If this enigma lies at the heart of the work, Criseyde is by no means the only focus. The figures of Troilus and Pandarus are not only essential to the movement of the plot, but also allow Chaucer to explore complex philosophical questions of love and free will. Through Troilus, the work explores the sublimity of love, its capacity to elevate the individual to new realms of being, to open onto the ineffable, and to inspire creativity – Troilus's response to love is to compose songs, which include the first translation of a Petrarch sonnet into English. The counterpart of this extreme passion is an inability to act: the story gains much of its comic momentum through Pandarus's promotion of the love affair, to the extent of physically placing Troilus in bed with Criseyde. This passivity promotes tragedy as well, however, for Troilus views Criseyde's departure as predestined, an inevitable blow of fate, and thus opposes it less than he might.

It is possible to see the three main characters as representative of three philosophical stances, and Chaucer interweaves with his Italian source parts of Boethius's *Consolation of Philosophy*, which he was translating at the same time: Pandarus represents the opportunist, and interwoven into his speeches are optimistic passages on fortune from Boethius; Troilus, by contrast, voices the laments of the imprisoned Boethius, the victim of fortune, never discovering how to reconcile the ideas of free will and predestination; Criseyde is a rationalist, optimistic regarding her power, but dominated by social pressures and fear of public shame. It is essential that the plot unfolds within a pagan universe, for this allows Chaucer to weave a fabric of references to astrological influences, Fortune, Fate and the classical gods, particularly in the grandiose, allusive proems to each book, and thus to create a sinister aura of predestination. This contrasts markedly with the apparent free will of the actors within the story, who seem to make their own choices in the game of love, and whose emotions and decisions provide much of the suspense. Chaucer does not make his figures incompatible with a Christian perspective: Troilus in particular refers frequently to one God and depicts the chain of love that binds the universe, though he also believes in Fate and Fortune. The morals of the poem are certainly those of a fourteenth-century Christian society, and indeed, Boethius was viewed as a great Christian philosopher. Yet the pagan world of *Troilus* lends great force to the notions of looming tragedy and fall, the turning of Fortune's wheel, and the cruelty of the gods, which underpin the existential crisis of Troilus, not resolved until he reaches the eighth sphere of the heavens and recognizes the worthlessness of temporal things. For the reader, this ending is highly problematic, in that the story's power comes precisely from its evocation of the passion and tragedy of the temporal world. The poem thus raises profound existential questions regarding the nature and purpose of romantic love, and of humankind's situation within a callous world, the untrustworthiness of which is finally symbolized by Criseyde's betrayal of Troilus.

The work comments too on the nature of *fin'amors* with its demands of secrecy: are passionate love affairs antithetical to marriage, as Pandarus seems to suppose, or are the social situations of Troilus and Criseyde so different that marriage would be impossible? We are made keenly aware of the power of the notions of honour and reputation, and of the potential shame that elopement represents. Chaucer, by making Criseyde a widow (for Boccaccio, a mark of sexual experience), engages with the issue of female independence, but also with the vulnerability of a woman without a protector in a chivalric world. The poem at once depicts the fictional world of ancient Troy, the material world of fourteenth-century England, and the never-never world of medieval chivalric romance. Troy plays an ambiguous role in the poem: although it provides the impetus for the loss of Criseyde, and the occasion for Troilus's death, it is oddly absent from the narrative, which engages so intensely with the private space of the lovers. Yet the structuring opposition of the poem is that of public and private, and hence the themes of love and war are inextricable. War impinges in other ways: it provides the circumstance for Troilus's triumphant appearance in the streets of Troy and attests to his military worth.

As with the great Arthurian knights Launcelot and Tristan, the combination of extraordinary prowess and the ability to experience the extremes of love to the point of madness and malady proves chivalric excellence. Troilus embodies the experience of *fin'amors* and the behaviour of the courtly lover: love comes upon him unexpectedly, as he is struck by the God of Love's arrow, wounded through the eyes that lead to the heart, to manifest the symptoms of the malady of love – weeping, sighing, swooning, and falling into a physical melancholy and decline. Chaucer leaves us uncertain as to the good of this extreme, inevitable love – raising questions similar to those evoked by the lament of the Man in Black in the *Book of the Duchess*, the pictures of tragic lovers painted on the wall of the Temple of Venus in the *Parliament of Fowls*, or the martyrs of love in the *Legend of Good Women*. Such love inspires both bliss and anguish: as the inscription on the gates in the *Parliament of Fowls* suggests, it is both infernal and paradisal. We are left, as in the *Knight's Tale*, written at about the same time, to ask whether high romantic love, by contrast to the robust mating of the birds or Diomede's assertive seduction of Criseyde, must necessarily be anguished and tragic.

Like the dream visions, *Troilus and Criseyde* engages explicitly with the issue of story matters and story-telling, through its use of a dominant narrator figure who claims that he is too fearful to love and can only serve lovers, in whose cause he retells the story of 'the double sorwe of Troilus' (I, 1). That he names as his source the fictional Lollius draws attention to the literary status of the poem, and throughout the poem the narrator refers to his sources, 'As writ myn auctour called Lollius' (I, 394), 'as telleth Lollius' (V, 1653), 'Men seyn – I not' (V, 1050), 'as bokes us declare' (V, 799); by ignoring his real sources, Chaucer plays a complex literary game, presenting a fictional version of the author who translates and selects from his sources even while he does this himself. We are made acutely aware of the difficulty of interpretation, of the subjective quality of the literary text, filtered as it is through the biases of the writer – and the narrator's bias for Criseyde is shown to be a powerful one. Like the central characters, caught between their own free wills and the events predestined by the fates – the certainty of the fall of Troy, prophesied by Calchas – the narrator is caught between his own affection for Criseyde and desire to portray her favourably, and his knowledge of the fixed end of the story, the 'double sorwe of Troilus'. The story thus creates a complex set of relationships: Pandarus orchestrates the love affair and manipulates the lovers; the gods decide human destiny and manipulate fortune; the writer, like a stage director, manipulates and fleshes out his characters and their choices. Yet at the same time, like Pandarus, his free will is not absolute; he is caught by the fixed points of the tragedy he tells, so that he too is subject to a kind of predestination. On all levels, then, the work engages with the opposition between free will and predestination – both within the fictional sphere of action, and outside it, as the writer who undertakes to tell the stories already written in 'olde bokes' is forced to ask how far subjective interpretation can go.

It is unsurprising that this great poem has generated an extraordinarily wide range of criticism. In *Chaucer's 'Troilus and Criseyde' and the Critics* (1980), Alice R. Kaminsky distinguishes four types of approach: historical, philosophical, formalistic (New Critical) and psychoanalytical. Early criticism of *Troilus and Criseyde* focused in particular on 'courtly love', most famously C. S. Lewis's *Allegory of Love* but also, for instance, William George Dodd's *Courtly Love in Gower and Chaucer* (1913). For Lewis, *Troilus and Criseyde* demonstrated Chaucer in the guise of 'poet of courtly love'.[2] E. T. Donaldson argued that Chaucer surpassed himself on the theme of 'romantic love' in *Troilus*, necessarily turning in the *Canterbury Tales* to other subjects. Donaldson captures well the polyvalency of *Troilus*, its 'multiplicity of interpretations': 'It possesses to the highest degree that quality, which characterizes most great poetry, of being always open to reinterpretation, of yielding different meanings to different generations and kinds of readers'.[3] Donaldson is perhaps most famous for his studies, exemplified below, of character and destiny in *Troilus*, which he often presents in terms of ambiguity. From the 1950s, much critical emphasis was placed on the moral and philosophical aspects of *Troilus and Criseyde* and related issues of character, a topic already well-established early on through studies such as Howard R. Patch's 'Troilus on Determinism' (1929), which considers in particular Troilus's fatalism and the tension between free will and predestination.[4] Related criticism includes that of D. W. Robertson, Jr, who, as we have seen, reads the entire poem allegorically, as an exemplification of the fall of humankind, 'the tragedy of every mortal sinner'.[5] Walter Clyde Curry, in *Chaucer and the Mediaeval Sciences* (1960), looks back to early scholars such as Root and Kittredge to trace Chaucer's 'conception of fate or destiny', examining medieval philosophy and astrology and the influence of Boethius on *Troilus*.[6] Donald R. Rowe considered the poem in terms of Platonic philosophy, to suggest that, through its oppositions (heaven and hell, tragedy and comedy), Chaucer creates 'a sacramental revelation of God, through his dramatization of his narrator's limitations'.[7] There are numerous other studies that engage with similar issues in an effort to resolve the complex existential and moral questions raised by this work.[8] The issue of genre has also played a crucial role in *Troilus* studies, from early explanations of the poem as tragedy, to Monica McAlpine's more recent and searching study of Chaucer's interweaving of different theories of tragedy, and the ways that 'the narrator's generic labelling of his book may be both expected and unexpected, both welcome and unwelcome to the reader'.[9] H. A. Kelly's scholarly *Chaucerian Tragedy* emphasizes the originality of Chaucer's exploration of both the rise and fall of Troilus.[10] Lee Patterson has written interestingly on the embedded use of the related genre of complaint in the poem.[11] All these studies of genre highlight the Boethian influence.

Chaucer's artistry, and especially the ambiguities of both language and theme, has also been the subject of much critical discussion. Morton Bloomfield, for example, writes perceptively of the ways that Chaucer as narrator creates a sense of distance, by emphasizing the historical status of the narrative, and thus engages with the issue of predestination.[12] Dorothy Bethurum treats this issue from another angle, placing *Troilus's* narrator in the context of other Chaucerian works and medieval writing more generally, and compares Chaucer to Dante in his presentation of both real and ideal:

> The effect of Chaucer's insistence on his lack of freedom is that he maneuvers himself into exactly the position of the reader, and his intense involvement is that of the fascinated reader or hearer, knowing how the story must end and dreading to see Troilus sigh his soul out to the Grecian tents where Criseyde lay that night.... like Dante, he can now have it both ways. Dante's poem in its magnificent architecture, the journey, sets out the justice of God; but Dante as a figure moving through the system can express man's pity.[13]

The ambiguities of the text are examined at length by Ida L. Gordon in *The Double Sorrow of Troilus* (1979).

Troilus and Criseyde: An Overview

Since the 1960s, scholars have become especially interested in the cultural context of Chaucer's writing: John Stevens, for instance, wrote of *Troilus and Criseyde* as a romance figuring in the courtly 'game of love', part of the process of 'dalliance'.[14] Later studies have not only pursued the issues of audience and socio-political contexts, but have also reformulated the question of Chaucer's sources into sophisticated considerations of literary history.[15] A series of wide-ranging cultural studies, such as that of C. David Benson, represented below, have considered *Troilus* in light of the literary influences shaping the work, in particular Boccaccio and Boethius, but also Dante, the classical tradition, the romance tradition, and the matter of Troy.[16] There have also been interesting technical studies, such as Stephen A. Barney's *Studies in 'Troilus': Chaucer's Text, Meter and Diction* (1993) and Barry Windeatt's great scholarly edition of the poem, which includes copious annotation and presents the Italian text of Boccaccio's *Il Filostrato* alongside Chaucer's work.

Perhaps unsurprisingly, given the extraordinary psychological realism and intensity of the poem, the characters and emotions at the heart of *Troilus and Criseyde* have received most critical attention. C. David Benson argues that 'the central interest of the poem lies in its exploration of the attempt by two human souls to establish the deepest and most searching of relationships'.[17] Critical views on Troilus have been divided: is he the great hero, whose chivalry combines excellence in love and war, or the comically passive, ridiculed lover? E. G. Stanley places the poem in the context of its sources and story matter to emphasize Troilus's chivalric, warrior status.[18] A complementary approach is that of Stephen Barney, who very persuasively presents Troilus in terms of 'the theme of bondage', to trace his 'snaring and imprisonment' by Fortune, but also by his devotion to 'trouthe'. Barney sees Troilus as 'in some way Romantic and Promethean', 'a model of heroic steadfastness': 'he is bound to the truth and bound by the truth'.[19]

It is, however, Criseyde who has been the perennial subject of critical interest. Most famous of all perhaps is E. T. Donaldson's essay on the narrator's love for Criseyde, which Donaldson relates to the ambiguities and distance of the latter part of the work and to the poem's dramatic irony.[20] From the 1960s, new psychoanalytical approaches also began to be taken. A. C. Spearing, for instance, considers Criseyde's dream both in terms of medieval dream theory, as a *somnium animale*, a dream reflecting the dreamer's psychological state, and in light of modern psychoanalytic theory, arguing for the relevance also of modern approaches: 'In so far as Chaucer has successfully explored human nature in his poem, we should expect it to be open to interpretation in terms of the psychology of any age'.[21] It is through psychoanalytical criticism that Chaucer criticism has most changed, and there has been a special interest in *Troilus and Criseyde* coincident with the growth of feminist studies. As Donaldson's essays demonstrate, however, the character of Criseyde was already in the critical foreground, and her story proved especially fruitful for new historicist and psychoanalytical perspectives. More explicitly feminist criticism ranges from the subtle, historically informed writing on Criseyde of David Aers (exemplified below p. 161), Jill Mann or Priscilla Martin, to the radically, often unpersuasively politicized views of Jane Chance or Elaine Tuttle Hansen.

Maureen Fries persuasively presents Criseyde as 'feminist and victim', emphasizing both her independence and her need for reassurance, her 'subtle conditioning by society'. Fries situates Chaucer's fiction in the context of medieval precepts regarding the protection and behaviour of women.[22] That radical gender studies can be historically grounded is proven by Carolyn Dinshaw's provocative, scholarly and highly sophisticated examination of the feminized Troilus in *Chaucer's Sexual Poetics* (1989). More problematic are some recent considerations of Pandarus's indubitably voyeuristic role in the love affair, and his affection for his niece that can seem rather more than avuncular: the delicacy of Chaucer's suggestive ambiguity is ignored in readings that take for granted an incestuous relationship or even Pandarus's rape of Criseyde.[23] Valuable critical attention has been paid to the social ethics of the poem's fictional world and the relation of these to individual psychology. Thus Barry Windeatt considers Chaucer's treatment of the issue of secrecy by contrast to Boccaccio's, in terms of Chaucer's heightened conception of 'the private life of the individual' and 'how the freedom of his lovers is limited both by the society in which they live and by their willingness to conform their lives to what literature tells of how lovers should behave'.[24] It is a testament to Chaucer's skill that an individual work should inspire such a plethora of criticism of all kinds, and that new readings and research on *Troilus and Criseyde* remain possible.

Notes

1 Invaluable in the study of *Troilus and Criseyde* are Barry Windeatt's comprehensive introduction *Troilus and Criseyde* in the *Oxford Guides to Chaucer* series (Clarendon Press, Oxford, 1992), and his scholarly, parallel-text edition of the poem (1990). For sources, see R. K. Gordon, trans., *The Story of Troilus* (J. M. Dent, London, 1934) and Nick Havely, *Chaucer's Boccaccio* (D. S. Brewer, Cambridge, 1980). Useful collections of essays are Mary Salu, ed., *Essays on 'Troilus and Criseyde'* (D. S. Brewer, Cambridge, 1979), S. A. Barney, ed., *Chaucer's 'Troilus'* (Scolar Press, London, 1980), and C. David Benson, ed., *Critical Essays on Chaucer's 'Troilus and Criseyde' and His Major Early Poems* (Open University Press, Milton Keynes, 1991). A. C. Spearing, *Chaucer: 'Troilus and Criseyde'* (Edward Arnold, London, 1976), Ian Bishop, *Chaucer's 'Troilus and Criseyde': A Critical Study*

(University of Bristol Press, Bristol, 1981), and Allen J. Frantzen, *'Troilus and Criseyde': The Poem and the Frame* (Twayne, New York, 1993) provide helpful introductory studies.

2   See C. S. Lewis, 'What Chaucer Really Did to *Il Filostrato*' (1932) in Benson, *Critical Essays*, 18.
3   E. T. Donaldson, 'Troilus and Criseyde' in *Chaucer's Poetry: An Anthology for the Modern Reader* (1958), quoted in J. A. Burrow, ed., *Geoffrey Chaucer: A Critical Anthology* (Penguin Books, Harmondsworth, 1969), 190.
4   Howard R. Patch, 'Troilus on Determinism' (1929) in Richard Schoeck and Jerome Taylor, eds, *Chaucer Criticism*, 2 vols (University of Notre Dame Press, Notre Dame, IN, 1960–1), vol. 2.
5   D. W. Robertson, Jr, 'Chaucerian Tragedy' in Schoeck and Taylor, *Chaucer Criticism*, vol. 2, 118.
6   Walter Clyde Curry, *Chaucer and the Mediaeval Sciences* (1960 [1926]), quoted in Schoeck and Taylor, *Chaucer Criticism*, vol. 2, 35.
7   Donald R. Rowe, *O Love O Charite! Contraries Harmonized in Chaucer's 'Troilus'* (Southern Illinois University Press, Carbondale, 1976), 172.
8   See, for example, James Lyndon Shanley, 'The *Troilus* and Christian Love' (1939), Alex J. Denomy, C. S. B., 'The Two Moralities of *Troilus and Criseyde*' (1950), and Theodore A. Stroud, 'Boethius' Influence on Chaucer's *Troilus*' (1951–2), all in Schoeck and Taylor, *Chaucer Criticism*, vol. 2.
9   Monica McAlpine, *The Genre of 'Troilus and Criseyde'* (Cornell University Press, Ithaca, NY, 1978), 15.
10 H. A. Kelly, *Chaucerian Tragedy* (D. S. Brewer, Cambridge, 1997), Ch. 3, 92–148.
11 Lee Patterson, 'Writing Amorous Wrongs: Chaucer and the Order of Complaint' in James M. Dean and Christian K. Zacher, *The Idea of Medieval Literature* (University of Delaware Press, Newark, 1992).
12 Morton Bloomfield, 'Distance and Predestination in *Troilus and Criseyde*' (1957) in Schoeck and Taylor, *Chaucer Criticism*, vol. 2.
13 Dorothy Bethurum, 'Chaucer's Point of View as Narrator in the Love Poems' (1959) in Schoeck and Taylor, *Chaucer Criticism*, vol. 2, 225. See also John M. Ganim, 'Consciousness and Time in *Troilus and Criseyde*' in *Style and Consciousness in Middle English Narrative* (Princeton University Press, Princeton, NJ, 1983).
14 John Stevens, *Music and Poetry in the Early Tudor Court* (1961), 'The Game of Love,' quoted in Burrow, *Geoffrey Chaucer*, 239–41.
15 More traditional studies also continue to be written: see, for instance, Chauncey Wood, *The Elements of Chaucer's 'Troilus'* (Duke University Press, Durham, NC, 1984).
16 On Italian influences, see, in particular, the work of Piero Boitani and also Howard H. Schless, David Wallace, Carla Taylor, Michael G. Hanly, Richard Neuse; on classical influences, see John V. Fleming, *Classical Imitation and Interpretation in Chaucer's 'Troilus'* (University of Nebraska Press, Lincoln, NB, 1990); on Troy, see C. David Benson, *The History of Troy in Middle English Literature* (D. S. Brewer, Woodbridge, 1980).

17 C. David Benson, *Chaucer's 'Troilus and Criseyde'* (Unwin Hyman, London, 1990), 18.
18 E. G. Stanley, 'About Troilus', *Essays and Studies* n.s. 29 (1976), 84–106.
19 Stephen Barney, 'Troilus Bound', *Speculum* 47 (1972), 447, 458.
20 E. T. Donaldson, 'Criseide and Her Narrator' in *Speaking of Chaucer* (Athlone Press, London, 1990); see also Donaldson's study of Criseyde's literary past and future, 'Briseis, Briseida, Criseyde, Cresseid, Cressid: Progress of a Heroine' in Edward Vasta and Zacharias P. Thundy, eds, *Chaucerian Problems and Perspectives* (University of Notre Dame Press, Notre Dame, IN, 1979).
21 A. C. Spearing, 'Criseyde's Dream' (1964) in Burrow, *Geoffrey Chaucer*, 272.
22 Maureen Fries, '"Slydynge of Corage": Chaucer's Criseyde as Feminist and Victim' in Arlyn Diamond and Lee R. Edwards, eds, *The Authority of Experience: Essays in Feminist Criticism* (University of Massachusetts Press, Amherst, 1977), 55.
23 See, for example, Richard W. Fehrenbacher (who sees incest as a dominant theme), '"Al that which chargeth nought to seye"', *Exemplaria* 9 (1997), 341–69, and Jane Chance, *The Mythographic Chaucer: The Fabulation of Sexual Politics* (University of Minnesota Press, Minneapolis, 1995), ch. 4, 107–67.
24 Barry Windeatt, '"Love That Oughte Ben Secree" in Chaucer's *Troilus*', *Chaucer Review* 14 (1979–80), 116.

6

Troilus and Criseyde: Critical Extracts

The Ending of *Troilus*

E. Talbot Donaldson

It may seem odd to begin this section with an extract treating the ending of Troilus and Criseyde. *Donaldson's minute discussion of the poem's ending, however, raises a range of central issues, and in particular one immediately relevant to any reading of the poem, that of the narrator and his relation to the story he tells. It is also appropriate to begin with Donaldson in that he has become so much the classic voice on Chaucer. To a certain extent, his open, serious tone may seem dated, yet its warmth, engagement and sensitive scholarship have very much stood the test of time. The poem's enduring power lies precisely in the immediacy and appeal of its characters and emotions recognized by Donaldson (most memorably, perhaps, in Donaldson's celebrated essay on the narrator's love for Criseyde, discussed above): although contemporary criticism tends to analyse these qualities differently, as complex literary constructions, we should not forget that engagement with the poem must begin in subjective, individual terms. What is striking is how this emotional appeal cuts across time and space.*

Here, Donaldson addresses the notoriously problematic ending of Troilus and Criseyde. *In the preceding pages he has considered the familiar Chaucerian ploy of presenting a naive and modest narrator who offers an apparently simple moral: for Donaldson, his 'ineptitudes' are intentionally dissatisfying, raising questions of meaning and complicating the text. This 'questioning of relative values' is also found in the* Legend of Good Women, *towards which the ending of* Troilus *points. The fundamental issue is the opposition between predestination and free will. Foreknowledge of 'the double sorwe of Troilus' runs alongside emotional engagement with the story matter, to force the narrator to take a double perspective. He is, as Donaldson phrases it, both the 'scholar' interested in 'storyal soth' and the 'sentimentalist' concerned with romance and optimism. Much of the drama of the telling is situated in the narrator's emotion and unwillingness to reveal the negative aspects – an effect evidently related to the uneasy narration of the* Legend of Good Women. *Critics will return again and again to issues of narratorial and authorial intention, and to the related topic of precisely how Criseyde is portrayed, both in the fiction of the poem and in its sources. Criseyde's betrayal of Troilus, and his death and disembodied laughter at the fickle nature of the world, necessitate questions regarding the status of the very love that the poem has been celebrating.*

Donaldson's essay works through a ploy like that with which he credits Chaucer: he presents a simplistic moral reading of the poem, 'that human love, and by a sorry corollary everything human, is unstable and illusory'. He then offers a careful, close reading of the poem, very much in New Critical style, to suggest the ways that this moral is both upheld and complicated. Here, it is the sensitivity of Donaldson's attention to language and tone, and his care to render his discussion compatible with the medieval context of the poem, that makes the analysis so persuasive. He outlines the narrator's experiments with a series of stances: epic, moral, anti-feminist, pathetic, devout, ascetic. We are made especially aware of Chaucer's skill in moving from one style to another, and of the way that the poem turns an anti-feminist history into romance. Donaldson identifies a return to the notion of trouthe, *a virtue associated with Troilus throughout the poem, as well as the subject of love and its beauty even while this is rejected and given up. We are reminded of the audience's interest in courtly matter, but also the force of medieval Christianity and the deep sense of transience that pervades much writing of the period, in particular Boethius's* Consolation of Philosophy, *which Chaucer drew on so extensively in* Troilus. *Donaldson's consideration of the final prayer and its human terms is particularly effective, and the piece as a whole demonstrates the power of close reading at its best. He is concerned with the universal, with the meaning of the poem for him and for 'us', and yet his humane approach is so delicate and informed as never to allow this modern meaning to seem at odds with what Chaucer's might have been.*

E. Talbot Donaldson, from 'The Ending of "Troilus"' in *Speaking of Chaucer*. Athlone Press, London, 1970.

It is at the end of *Troilus* that Chaucer, employing the kind of devices I have been discussing, achieves his most complex poetic effect. His narrator has worked hard, from the very beginning, to persuade us of his simplicity, though from the very beginning his simplicity has been compromised by the fact that, apparently unknown to himself, he wavers between two quite different – though equally simple – attitudes towards his story. It is the saddest story in the world, and it is the gladdest story in the world. This double attitude appears strongly in the opening stanzas, when he tells us that his motive for writing is, paradoxically, to bring honour to Love and gladden lovers with a love story so sad that his verses shed tears while he writes them and that Tisiphone is his only appropriate Muse. Yet though he starts out firmly resolved to relate the double sorrow of Troilus

> ... in loving of Criseide,
> And how that she forsook him er she deide,
> (*TC* I.55-6)

as the story progresses he seems to forget all about the second sorrow. The historical perspective, which sees before and after and knows the sad ending, gives way to the limited, immediate view of one who loves the actors in the story, and in his love pines for what is not so desperately that he almost brings it into being. The scholar's motive for telling a sad story simply because it is true finds itself at war with the sentimentalist's motive of telling a love story simply because it is happy and beautiful. The optimism that one acquires when one lives with people so attractive makes a gay future for all seem inevitable. Once launched upon the love story, the narrator refuses to look forward to a future that the scholar in him knows to be already sadly past; at moments when the memory of that sad future breaks in on him, he is likely to deny his own sources, and to suggest that, despite the historical evidence to the contrary, Criseide was, perhaps, not unfaithful at all – men have been lying about her.[1]

For the greater part of the poem the intimately concerned, optimistic narrator is in full control of the story – or rather, the story is in full control of him, and persuades him that a world that has such people in it is not only the best of all possible worlds, but the most possible. When in the fifth book the facts of history force him back towards the historical perspective, which has always known that his happiness and that of the lovers were transitory, illusory, he does his best to resist the implications arising from his ruined story – tries to circumvent them, denies them, slides off them. Thus an extraordinary feeling of tension, even of dislocation, develops from the strife in the narrator's mind between what should be and what was – and hence what is. This tension is the emotional storm-centre which causes the narrator's various shifts and turns in his handling of the ending, and which also determines the great complexity of the poem's ultimate meaning.

So skilfully has Chaucer mirrored his narrator's internal warfare – a kind of nervous breakdown in poetry – that many a critic has concluded that Chaucer himself was bewildered by his poem. One, indeed, roundly condemns the whole fifth book, saying that it reads like 'an earlier draft ... which its author lacked sufficient interest to revise'. According to this critic, Chaucer 'cannot bring himself to any real enthusiasm for a plot from which the bright lady of his own creation has vanished'. And, elsewhere, 'What had happened to the unhappy Criseyde and to her equally unhappy creator was that the story in which they were involved had betrayed them both'.[2] Now this is, in a rather sad way, the ultimate triumph of Chaucer's method. The critic responds with perfect sympathy to the narrator's bewilderment, even to the extent of seeming to suggest that the poet had written four-fifths of his story before he discovered how it came out. But in fact Chaucer's warmly sympathetic narrator has blinded the critic's eyes as effectively as he had blinded his own. It is not true that the bright lady of Chaucer's creation has vanished — Criseide is still very much present in book five. What has vanished is the bright dream of the enduring power of human love, and in a burst of creative power that it is not easy to match elsewhere.

For the *moralitee* of *Troilus and Criseide* (and by morality I do not mean 'ultimate meaning') is simply this: that human love, and by a sorry corollary everything human, is unstable and illusory. I give the moral so flatly now because in the remainder of this paper I shall be following the narrator in his endeavour to avoid it, and indeed shall be eagerly abetting him in trying to avoid it, and even pushing him away when he finally accepts it. I hope in this way to suggest how Chaucer, by manipulating his narrator, achieves an objective image of the poem's significance that at once greatly qualifies and enhances this moral, and one that is, of course, far more profound and less absolute than my flat-footed statement. The meaning of the poem is not the moral, but a complex qualification of the moral.

Let us turn now to that part of the poem, containing the last eighteen stanzas, which is often referred to by modern scholars, though not by the manuscripts, as the Epilogue. I object to the term because it implies that this passage was tacked on to the poem after the poet had really finished his work, so that it is critically if not physically detachable from what has gone before.[3] And while I must admit that the nature of this passage, its curious twists and turns, its occasional air of fecklessness, set it off from what has gone before, it also seems to me to be the head of the whole body of the poem.[4]

The last intimately observed scene of the action is the final, anticlimactic interview between Troilus and Pandarus, wherein the latter is driven by the sad logic of his loyalty and of his pragmatism to express hatred of his niece, and to wish her dead. Pandarus's last words are, 'I can namore saye', and it is now up to the narrator, who is as heart-broken as Troilus and Pandarus, to express the significance of his story. His first reaction is to take the epic high road; by means of the exalted style to reinvest Troilus with the human dignity that his unhappy love has taken from him. The narrator starts off boldly enough:

> Greet was the sorwe and plainte of Troilus;
> But forth hire cours Fortune ay gan to holde.

Criseide loveth the sone of Tydeüs,*   *Diomede
And Troilus moot weepe in cares colde.
(*TC* v.1744–7)

But though the manner is epic, the subject is not: an Aeneas in Dido's pathetic plight is no fit subject for Virgilian style. And the narrator, overcome by the pathos of his story, takes refuge in moralization:

Swich is this world, whoso it can biholde:
In eech estaat is litel hertes reste –
God leve us for to take it for the beste!

How true! And how supremely, brilliantly, inadequate! It has been said that all experience does no more than prove some platitude or other, but one hopes that poetic experience will do more, or in any case that poetry will not go from pathos to bathos. This moral, the trite moral of the Monk's Tale – Isn't life awful? – which the Monk arrives at – again and again – *a priori* would be accepted by many a medieval man as a worthy moral for the *Troilus*, and the narrator is a medieval man. But the poet behind the narrator is aware that an experience that has been intimately shared – not merely viewed historically, as are the Monk's tragedies – requires not a moral, but a meaning arrived at *a posteriori*, something earned, and in a sense new. Moreover, the narrator seems still to be asking the question, Can nothing be salvaged from the wreck of the story? For he goes on once more to have recourse to epic enhancement of his hero, more successfully this time, since it is the martial heroism of Troilus, rather than his unhappy love, that is the subject: there follow two militant stanzas recounting his prowess and his encounters with Diomede. But again the epic impulse fails, for the narrator's real subject is not war but unhappy love, for which epic values will still do nothing – will neither salvage the dignity of Troilus nor endow his experience with meaning. In a wistful stanza, the narrator faces his failure to do by epic style what he desires to have done:

And if I hadde ytaken for to write
The armes of this ilke worthy man,
[But, unfortunately, *arma virumque non cano*]*   *[I do not sing of arms
Than wolde ich of his batailes endite;   and of the man' – unlike Virgil]
But for that I to writen first bigan
Of his love, I have seyd as I kan –
His worthy deedes, whoso list hem heere,
Rede Dares – he can telle hem alle yfere.
(v. 1765–71)

Troilus and Criseyde: Critical Extracts

This sudden turn from objective description to introspection mirrors the narrator's quandary. Unable to get out of his hopeless predicament, he does what we all tend to do when we are similarly placed: he begins to wonder why he ever got himself into it. The sequel of this unprofitable speculation is likely to be panic, and the narrator very nearly panics when he sees staring him in the face another possible moral for the love poem he has somehow been unwise enough to recite. The moral that is staring him in the face is written in the faces of the ladies of his audience, the anti-feminist moral which is at once obvious and, from a court poet, unacceptable:

> Biseeching every lady bright of hewe,
> And every gentil womman what she be,
> That al be that Criseide was untrewe,
> That for that gilt she nat be wroth with me.
> Ye may hir giltes in othere bookes see;
> And gladlier I wol write, if you leste,
> Penelopeës* trouthe and good Alceste.*   *models of faithfulness in love

While anticipating the ladies' objections, the narrator has, with that relief only a true coward can appreciate, glimpsed a possible way out: denial of responsibility for what the poem says. He didn't write it in the first place, it has nothing to do with him, and anyhow he would much rather have written about faithful women. These excuses are, of course, very much in the comic mood of the Prologue to the *Legend of Good Women* where Alceste, about whom he would prefer to have written, defends him from Love's wrath on the grounds that, being no more than a translator, he wrote about Criseide 'from innocence, and knew not what he said'. And if he can acquit himself of responsibility for Criseide by pleading permanent inanity, there is no reason why he cannot get rid of all his present tensions by funnelling them into a joke against himself. This he tries to do by turning upside down the anti-feminist moral of the story:

> N'I saye nat this al only for thise men,
> But most for wommen that bitraised* be...   *betrayed

And I haven't recited this exclusively for men, but also, or rather but mostly, for women who are betrayed:

> Thrugh false folk – God yive hem sorwe, amen! –
> That with hir grete wit and subtiltee
> Bitraise you; and this commeveth* me   *moves

> To speke, and in effect you alle I praye,
> Beeth war of men, and herkneth what I saye.

The last excursion into farce – in a poem that contains a good deal of farce – is this outrageous inversion of morals, which even so has a grotesque relevance if all human love, both male and female, is in the end to be adjudged unstable. With the narrator's recourse to comedy the poem threatens to end. At any rate, he asks it to go away:

> Go, litel book, go, litel myn tragedye,
> Ther* God thy makere yit, er that he die,   *May
> So sende might to make* in som comedye....   *compose

(Presumably a comedy will not blow up in his face as this story has, and will let him end on a note like the one he has just sounded.) There follows the celebrated injunction of the poet to his book not to vie with other poetry, but humbly to kiss the steps of Virgil, Ovid, Homer, Lucan, and Statius. This is the modesty convention again, but transmuted, I believe, into something close to arrogance. Perhaps the poem is not to be classed with the works of these great poets, but I do not feel that the narrator succeeds in belittling his work by mentioning it in connection with them; there is such a thing as inviting comparison by eschewing comparison. It seems that the narrator has abandoned his joke, and is taking his 'little book' – of more than 8,000 lines – seriously. Increasing gravity characterizes the next stanza, which begins with the hope that the text will not be miswritten nor mismetred by scribes and lesser breeds without the law of final *-e*. Then come two lines of emphatic prayer:

> And red wherso* thou be, or elles songe,   *wherever
> That thou be understonde, God I biseeche.

It is perhaps inconsiderate of the narrator to implore us to take his sense when he has been so irresolute about defining his sense. But the movement of the verse now becomes sure and strong, instead of uncertain and aimless, as the narrator moves confidently towards a meaning.

For in the next stanza, Troilus meets his death. This begins – once again – in the epic style, with perhaps a glance at the *Iliad*:

> The wratthe, as I bigan you for to saye,
> Of Troilus the Greekes boughten dere.

Such dignity as the high style can give is thus, for the last time, proffered Troilus. But for him there is to be no last great battle in the West, and both the stanza, and Troilus's life, end in pathos:

> But wailaway, save only* Goddes wille: *except that it was
> Despitously him slow the fierse Achille.

Troilus's spirit at once ascends into the upper spheres whence he looks down upon this little earth and holds all vanity as compared with the full felicity of heaven. The three stanzas describing Troilus's afterlife afford him that reward which medieval Christianity allowed to the righteous heathen. And in so doing, they salvage from the human wreck of the story the human qualities of Troilus that are of enduring value – most notably, his *trouthe*, the integrity for which he is distinguished. Moreover, this recognition by the plot that some human values transcend human life seems to enable the narrator to come to a definition of the poem's meaning which he has hitherto been unwilling to make. Still close to his characters, he witnesses Troilus's rejection of earthly values, and then, apparently satisfied, now that the mortal good in Troilus has been given immortal reward, he is willing to make that rejection of *all* mortal goods towards which the poem has, despite his resistance, been driving him. His rejection occurs – most unexpectedly – in the third of these stanzas. Troilus, gazing down at the earth and laughing within himself at those who mourn his death,

> ... dampned* al oure werk that folweth so   *cursed
> The blinde lust, the which that may nat laste,
> And sholden al oure herte on hevene caste.

Up until the last line Troilus has been the subject of every main verb in the entire passage; but after he has damned all *our* work, by one of those syntactical ellipses that make Middle English so fluid a language, Troilus's thought is extended to include both narrator and reader: in the last line, *And sholden al oure herte on hevene caste*, the plural verb *sholden* requires the subject *we*; but this subject is omitted, because to the narrator the sequence of the sense is, at last, overpoweringly clear. When, after all his attempts not to have to reject the values inherent in his love story, he finally does reject them, he does so with breath-taking ease.

He does so, indeed, with dangerous ease. Having taken up arms against the world and the flesh, he lays on with a will:

> Swich fin hath, lo, this Troilus for love;
> Swich fin hath al his grete worthinesse;

> Swich fin hath his estaat real* above;   *royal
> Swich fin his lust, swich fin hath his noblesse;
> Swich fin hath false worldes brotelnesse:*   *undependability
> And thus bigan his loving of Criseide,
> As I have told, and in this wise he deide.

But impressive as this stanza is, its movement is curious. The first five lines express, with increasing force, disgust for a world in which everything – not only what merely *seems* good, but also what really *is* good – comes to nothing in the end. Yet the last two lines,

> And thus bigan his loving of Criseide,
> As I have told, and in this wise he deide,

have, I think, a sweetness of tone that contrasts strangely with the emphatic disgust that precedes them. They seem to express a deep sadness for a doomed potential – as if the narrator, while forced by the evidence to condemn everything his poem has stood for, cannot really quite believe that it has come to nothing. The whole lovely aspiration of the previous action is momentarily recreated in the spare summary of this couplet.

The sweetness of tone carries over into the next two stanzas, the much-quoted ones beginning.

> O yonge, freshe folkes, he or she,
> In which that love up groweth with your age,
> Repaireth hoom* fro worldly vanitee,   *Return home
> And of youre herte up casteth the visage
> To thilke God that after his image
> You made; and thinketh al nis but a faire*   *i.e. temporary pleasure
> This world that passeth soone as flowres faire.

The sweetness here adheres not only to what is being rejected, but also to what is being sought in its stead, and this marks a development in the narrator. For he does not now seem so much to be fleeing away, in despair and disgust, from an ugly world – the world of the Monk's Tale – as he seems to be moving voluntarily through this world *towards* something infinitely better. And while this world is a wretched one – ultimately – in which all love is *feined*, 'pretended' and 'shirked', it is also a world full of the young potential of human love – 'In which that love up groweth with *oure* age'; a world which, while it passes soon, passes soon as flowers fair. All the illusory loveliness of a world which is man's only reality is expressed in the very lines that reject that loveliness.

In these stanzas the narrator has been brought to the most mature and complex expression of what is involved in the Christian rejection of the world that seems to be, and indeed is, man's home, even though he knows there is a better one. But the narrator himself remains dedicated to simplicity, and makes one last effort to resolve the tension in his mind between loving a world he ought to hate and hating a world he cannot help loving; he endeavours to root out the love:

> Lo, here of payens* cursed olde rites; *pagans'
> Lo, here what alle hir goddes may availe;
> Lo, here thise wrecched worldes appetites;
> Lo, here the fin and guerdon* for travaile *reward
> Of Jove, Appollo, of Mars, of swich rascaile;* *rabble
> Lo, here the forme of olde clerkes speeche
> In poetrye, if ye hir bookes seeche.

For the second time within a few stanzas a couplet has undone the work of the five lines preceding it. In them is harsh, excessively harsh, condemnation of the world of the poem, including gods and rites that have played no great part in it. In brilliant contrast to the tone of these lines is the exhausted calm of the last two:

> Lo, here the forme of olde clerkes speeche
> In poetrye, if ye hir bookes seeche.

There is a large imprecision about the point of reference of this couplet. I do not know whether its *Lo here* refers to the five preceding lines or to the poem as a whole, but I suppose it refers to the poem as a whole, as the other four *Lo here*'s do. If this is so, then the form of *olde clerkes speeche* is being damned as well as the *payens cursed olde rites* – by parataxis, at least. Yet it is not, for the couplet lacks the heavy, fussy indignation of the earlier lines: instead of indignation there is, indeed, dignity. I suggest that the couplet once more reasserts, in its simplicity, all the implicit and explicit human values that the poem has dealt with, even though these are, to a medieval Christian, ultimately insignificant. The form of old clerks' speech in poetry is the sad story that human history tells. It is sad, it is true, it is lovely, and it is significant, for it is poetry.

This is the last but one of the narrator's searches for a resolution for his poem. I have tried to show how at the end of *Troilus* Chaucer has manipulated a narrator capable of only a simple view of reality in such a way as to achieve the poetic expression of an extraordinarily complex one. The narrator, moved by his simple devotion to Troilus, to Pandarus, above all to Criseide, has been vastly reluctant to find that their story, so full of the illusion of happiness, comes to nothing – that the potential of humanity comes to nothing. To avoid this – seemingly simple – conclusion he has done everything he could. He has tried the epic high road; he has tried the broad highway of trite moralization; he has tried to eschew responsibility; he has tried to turn it all into a joke; and all these devices have failed. Finally, with every other means of egress closed, he has subscribed to Troilus's rejection of his own story, though only when, like Gregory when he wept for Trajan, he has seen his desire for his hero's salvation confirmed. Once having made the rejection, he has thrown himself into world-hating with enthusiasm. But now the counterbalance asserts its power. For the same strong love of the world of his story that prevented him from reaching the Christian rejection permeates and qualifies his expression of the rejection. Having painfully climbed close to the top of the ridge he did not want to climb, he cannot help looking back with longing at the darkening but still fair valley in which he lived; and every resolute thrust forward ends with a glance backward. In having his narrator behave thus, Chaucer has achieved a meaning only great poetry can achieve. The world he knows and the heaven he believes in grow ever farther and farther apart as the woeful contrast between them is developed, and ever closer and closer together as the narrator blindly unites them in the common bond of his love. Every false start he has made has amounted, not to a negative, but to a positive; has been a necessary part of the experience without which the moral of the poem would be as meaningless and unprofitable as in the form I gave it a little while ago. The poem states, what much of Chaucer's poetry states, the necessity under which men lie of living in, making the best of, enjoying, and loving a world from which they must remain detached and which they must ultimately hate: a little spot of earth that with the sea embracéd is, as in Book Three Criseide was embraced by Troilus.

For this paradox there is no logical resolution. In the last two stanzas of the poem Chaucer, after asking Gower and Strode for correction, invokes the power that, being supra-logical itself, can alone resolve paradox. He echoes Dante's mighty prayer to the Trinity, 'that al maist circumscrive', and concludes with the lines:

So make us, Jesus, for thy mercy digne,*   *worthy
For love of Maide and Moder thyn benigne.

The poem has concerned a mortal woman whose power to love failed, and it ends with the one mortal woman whose power to love is everlasting. I think it is significant that the prayer of the poem's ending leads up, not to Christ, son of God, but to his mother, daughter of Eve – towards heaven, indeed, but towards heaven through human experience.

Notes

1 *TC* iv. 20–1.
2 Marchette Chute, *Geoffrey Chaucer of England* (London, 1946), pp. 179, 180 and 178.
3 The extreme exponent of detachability is W. C. Curry in his well-known essay, 'Destiny in *Troilus and Criseyde*', *PMLA*, xlv (1930), 129ff., reprinted in his *Chaucer and the Mediaeval Sciences* (second revised and enlarged edn, 1960): see especially pp. 294–8.
4 I believe that this is the opinion of many Chaucerians. See, for example, Dorothy Everett, *Essays on Middle English Literature* (1955), pp. 134–8, and Dorothy Bethurum, 'Chaucer's Point of View as Narrator', *PMLA*, lxxiv (1959), 516–18.

The Heart and the Chain

John Leyerle

In this essay, John Leyerle employs the notion of a 'poetic nucleus' in order to provide a new perspective on Chaucer's writings: his approach combines the New Critical emphasis on structure, theme and ambiguity with the study of literary and intellectual contexts. The term 'nucleus', with its double meaning of seed of thematic growth and structural centre of the work, provides a powerful organizing idea. Chaucer's nuclei often find their origins in philosophical notions and are ambiguous, rooted in contradiction. Leyerle considers several of Chaucer's works in terms of such poetic nuclei: in the Knight's Tale, *for example, images of binding recur and the text is structured around the idea of the 'faire cheyne of love'; the* Miller's Tale, *by contrast, centres upon images of holes or apertures, and the* Parliament of Fowls *employs a sequence of places. This extract demonstrates how* Troilus and Criseyde *similarly employs a nucleus, the image of the heart. Leyerle uses a method of close textual reading to demonstrate in detail how this nucleus functions in Book I. He illustrates how Troilus and Criseyde are both defined in terms of the heart – but whereas Troilus's is stable, Criseyde's is 'slydynge'. Leyerle explores, too, the several medieval metaphors for falling in love: the wounding of the heart through the eyes, the imprint on the heart, the exchange of hearts, the seizure of the heart. The notions of the eyes as the way to the heart, and of love as a physical malady or wound, were particularly prevalent in this period: eyes were envisaged as sending out rays that entered the other's eyes and descended to the heart. Thus the many* descriptions of love occurring through the eyes have a literal as well as symbolic import.

In the pages not reproduced here, Leyerle continues his exploration of the heart in the subsequent four books of the poem, to show how the image recurs as a focus in Chaucer's depiction of Criseyde falling in love, the consummation of the affair, Troilus's sickness and Criseyde's betrayal of Troilus. Each episode is realized in terms of its effect on the heart, each character in light of his or her heart, so that the physicality of love, and its situation in the heart rather than the mind, becomes crucial. Unlike reason, love is a physical force that strikes from outside and cannot be controlled.

After establishing the tissue of references to the heart in the text, Leyerle turns to other medieval writing to contextualize Chaucer's work: he shows the exchange of hearts to be a convention of religious writing, and reminds us of the parallels between divine and profane love. Particularly powerful is his discussion of Catherine of Siena, who like Criseyde imagined her heart removed from her body – but by Christ himself. These analogies make especially clear the complex relation of human and divine love, in which the earthly may become either a dark mirror of the celestial, as at the end of Troilus, or a window onto the sublime, as in Troilus's hymns to love. Once again, the complex relation between convention and originality in the Middle Ages is clear: Chaucer brings his creative mind to familiar material – and rewrites it in new and provocative ways. Leyerle argues finally that Chaucer's use of the poetic nucleus of the heart corresponds to the medieval literary theory that the poet sends his heart out in the act of creating – an observation that returns this analysis to the topic of many previous studies, that of the art of writing itself. In Troilus, as in the early poetry, Chaucer is as much engaged with the process of literary creation as he is with the history of the lovers. Leyerle's discussion demonstrates especially well the way that Troilus and Criseyde is rooted in familiar philosophical and literary traditions, and constructed with minute art so that the structural nucleus of the heart binds the poem together like the chain of love it depicts.

John Leyerle, from 'The Heart and the Chain' in *The Learned and the Lewed*, Harvard English Studies 5 (1974), 113–45.

This tendency in Chaucer's poetry to leave conflicting viewpoints unresolved must be kept in mind in discussing any of the texts that are organized about a nucleus so as to avoid reductive interpretations. Indeed, the nucleus itself is usually ambiguous in significance. Each nucleus has a contradiction within itself: the hunting of the *hert* is accomplished when its loss is finally recognized; the *prisoun* of order imposes a restrictive captivity; and the holes of license produce a love that famishes the craving. A nucleus does not, of course, explain everything in a poem where it is found, but it does reinforce from the core the ambiguities present in the whole. Each nucleus has a literal sense, but as the poem develops, each also tends to become invested with metaphoric sense representing the main abstract ideas present.

Here one sees Chaucer as the poet of ideas; he was not a philosopher, and his ideas in abstract statement are commonplace, because so many of them are taken from *The Consolation of Philosophy*, a work of wide influence throughout the Middle Ages. In his imagination, however, these ideas produced a creative reflex in which abstract conceptions took specific form in the nucleus. Perhaps this formation was a carefully worked-out process; more likely, it was the way his imaginative perception instinctively worked. Either way, a nucleus, once identified, provides a very powerful tool for discovering the center and seed of a narrative poem and the way the poet perceived ideas. The nucleus is, of course, very different from the passages of versified ideas inserted into a poem, such as the soliloquy of Troilus on free will and foreknowledge, set down like a lump in Book IV of *Troilus and Criseyde*.

Troilus has an extremely simple and pervasive nucleus, the heart. It is the cause of love and its variable fortune in the poem, thus subsuming both of the main themes. There is a significant difference between the two lovers' hearts, however. Troilus has a stable heart, and this steadfastness in love accounts, I think, for his ascent from the mutable love of the world to the stable love of the heavens. Criseyde, on the other hand, is 'Tendre-herted, slydynge of corage' (V. 825) and moves to the arms of another man, the 'sodeyn Diomede' (V. 1024). References to the heart abound in the poem and are prominent at every crucial development of the love affair. Owing to the length and complexity of this work, arguably the finest narrative poem in the language, there is need to trace the nucleus in some detail, for it is less obvious than the others discussed above.

In the temple of the Palladion Troilus scoffs at the men in his company whom he suspects of showing signs of love, conduct that betrays his ignorance of the strength of love and its application as a universal bond. He supposes that

>   nothing hadde had swich myght
>   Ayeyns his wille that shuld his herte stere,*   *steer
>   Yet with a look his herte wax a-fere.*   *on fire
>   (l. 227–9)

In falling in love he becomes one more example of the power that love has as the binding force of the world (I. 253–9). At the end of Book III Troilus acknowledges this bond in his song in praise of love and its binding force, a passage translated from meter 8 of Book II of *The Consolation of Philosophy* and already noted in connection with *The Knight's Tale*. Love in terms of a bond or knot is also present in *Troilus*, and the discussion of the nucleus of *The Knight's Tale* should be kept in mind here.[1] As Troilus looks about him, his glance penetrates the crowd and falls on Criseyde. 'Therwith his herte gan to sprede and rise' (I. 278); a deep and fixed impression of her sticks 'in his hertes botme' (I. 297). In Book II he uses the same expression of himself, saying

> so soore hath she me wounded,
> That stood in blak, with lokyng of hire eyen,
> That to myn hertes botme it is ysounded.*   *plummeted
> (II. 533–5)

The process follows the traditional pattern of 'loveris maladye': the 'subtile stremes' (I. 305) from Criseyde's eye enter the eye of Troilus, sink to the root of his heart, and cause love, which is regarded as a disease.[2]

> hym thoughte he felte dyen,
> Right with hire look, the spirit in his herte.
> (I. 306–7)

This is the first part of the 'double sorwe' that Chaucer announces as his subject in the opening line of the poem. The connection between eye and heart is taken further when the narrator states that Troilus' 'herte, which that is his brestes ye, / Was ay on hire' (I. 453–4).[3] ...

There are repeated, specific textual references that show how the heart is the nucleus of *Troilus and Criseyde* and controls the main narrative development of the poem. The word is so ordinary that readers miss its pervasive force and frequency in the text; first reaction to the data, once they are presented and analyzed, tends to be surprise. The analysis here is incomplete, because less than half the more than 350 occurrences of the word are discussed. The significance of this nucleus is clear, nevertheless. The heart is source and seat of love and makes man subject to love's universal bond. Since earthly love is imperfect, love's bond may, for a time, be mocked, as Troilus mocks, or it may allow for some sliding, as Criseyde slides. The self-absorbed Troilus mocks what he does not understand, and for a time he suffers unrequited love for Criseyde; this is his first sorrow. She loves him for a time, but her sliding heart lets slip the bond. Again he suffers unrequited love for Criseyde; this is his second sorrow. He dies, and his soul ascends to the stable love of the heavens. In the process sorrow is revealed as a means to higher love, as the narrator observed, 'sondry peynes bryngen folk to hevene'

(III. 1204), both worldly and divine. The poem shows the continuity as well as the progression from worldly to divine love, a progression not unlike the one presented in *The Divine Comedy*, if less explicit and systematic in the English poem than in the Italian.

Chaucer's use of the heart and chain as nucleus metaphors for love and order belongs to long-existing literary traditions. Lovejoy's classic study... is a systematic history of the idea of the chain as a metaphor for order and degree. There is no equivalent single work on the heart as the seat of love, but enough studies have been written to make clear the long history of the idea.[4] One aspect of this tradition does need some attention here, the tradition of the movable heart exchanged in love.

The exchange of hearts is implicit in the *hert-huntyng* of *The Book of the Duchess* and explicit in *Troilus and Criseyde*. Not surprisingly, the idea of a movable heart occurs in religious writing long before the rise of aristocratic love poetry. An example is a passage in a homily by Gregory the Great on the Ascension.

> Unde, fratres charissimi, oportet ut illuc sequamur corde, ubi eum corpore ascendisse credimus.[5] [Therefore, dearest brothers, it is fitting that we follow there with the heart, where we believe him to have ascended in body.]

The actual exchange of hearts with Christ can be found in saints' lives, notably in that of Catherine of Siena, whose experience of 1370 is recounted in considerable detail by her contemporary biographer, Raymond of Capua. Christ appeared to her while she prayed, and he removed her heart; she reported the event to her confessor, who merely laughed. She maintained her story, however, and several days later as she finished praying and was emerging from an abstracted meditation, Christ reappeared to her, holding a radiant heart in his hands; he opened her left side again and inserted the heart, telling her that he had given her his own heart which she had prayed to have. Christ then healed her side, but an elongated scar remained as a visible token, afterward seen by many, of the exchange.[6] Exchanges of hearts recounted in medieval literature either have such miraculous aspects of divine intervention or else they are metaphors; there seems to be no indication in medical literature of the period that the heart, like the womb, could move.[7]

As so often happened in the Middle Ages, the religious tradition of the exchange of hearts in divine love has parallels in profane love. Sometimes the religious aspects are explicit, such as those evident in *Troilus and Criseyde*. In the first book Troilus prays to the god of love and remarks that he does not know whether Criseyde is a goddess or a woman, a confusion also apparent in Palamon's reactions to Emelye in *The Knight's Tale*; the religious vows that

Troilus makes in the consummation scene (III. 1254 ff.) and his apostrophe to Criseyde's empty palace as a 'shryne, of which the seynt is oute' (V. 553) are other examples, and the list could be extended. Sometimes the religious aspects are only implied, and the exchange itself indicates a religious devotion in love and the deep bond existing between the man and the woman, especially when they are forced by circumstances to conceal their love or must spend much of the time apart. A familiar example occurs in Chrétien's *Lancelot* when the knight must leave Guenievere after spending the night with her in Meleagant's castle.

> Au lever fu il droiz martirs,
> tant li fu griés li departirs,
> car il i suefre grant martire.
> Ses cuers adés cele part tire
> ou la reïne se remaint.
> N'a pooir que il l'an remaint,
> que la reïne tant li plest
> qu'il n'a talant que il la lest:
> li cors s'an vet, li cuers sejorne.[8]

> It cost him such pain to leave her that he suffered a real martyr's agony. His heart now stays where the queen remains; he has not the power to lead it away, for it finds such pleasure in the queen that it has no desire to leave her: so his body goes and his heart remains.

An extended treatment of the motif of the exchange of hearts occurs in a work of the fifteenth century, *Le Livre du cueur d'amour espris*, written about 1457 by King René d'Anjou, an allegorical prose account of love interspersed with verse and written in the tradition of the first part of *Le Roman de la Rose*.[9] The exchange of hearts also occurs in more than one fabliau, an indication that the motif was well enough known to make its cynical employment an amusing parody.[10]

Chaucer's use of the heart as the nucleus of a poem about human love, its mutability, and its capacity to lead to divine love thus has historical probability. Both the narrative and the nucleus of *Troilus and Criseyde* are drawn from well-established literary traditions of great antiquity; Chaucer does not so much invent his material as reimagine it. With characteristic economy of means Chaucer put a traditional metaphor at the core of his poem and thereby transformed complex, abstract ideas about love and its relative stability into a nucleus that is so apt and simple that it has remained all but invisible to readers despite its appearance, often in repeated statement, at every crucial turn in the narrative.

In Chaucer's immediate source, *Il Filostrato*, the heart is mainly mentioned in casual references to inner thought or in connection with the affliction of love sickness. There are, however, three times where Troilo refers to Criseida as *cor del corpo mio*, 'heart of my body,' and two times where Criseida refers to him the same way.[11] This expression implies the exchange of hearts, a motif explicit only in Troilo's dream of Criseida and the boar.

> E poi appresso gli parve vedere
> Sotto a'suoi piè Criseida, alla quale
> Col grifo il cor traeva, ed al parere
> Di lui, Criseida di così gran male
> Non si curava, ma quasi piacere
> Prendea di ciò che faces l'animale.
> (VII. 24)

> And then afterward it seemed to him that he saw
> beneath its feet Cressida, whose heart it tore
> forth with its snout. And as it seemed, little
> cared Cressida for so great a hurt, but almost
> did she take pleasure in what the beast was
> doing.

In Chaucer's poem Troilus dreams that Criseyde lies with a boar, but no mention is made of losing her heart. Chaucer uses the motif in Criseyde's dream of the eagle, an episode which is not in *Il Filostrato*. This shift seems to indicate that the episode in *Il Filostrato* provided Chaucer with a hint for his treatment of the heart. Certainly, the shift from animal to bird is indicative of the delicacy of Chaucer's poem in contrast to the vivid sensuality of his source, evident here.

If the hint came from *Il Filostrato*, sustained use of the heart as the nucleus of *Troilus and Criseyde* may be explained by Geoffrey of Vinsauf's advice near the beginning of his *Poetria Nova* [thirteenth-century treatise] on how to start a poem, a passage Chaucer repeated at the end of Book I of *Troilus*.

> For everi wight that hath an hous to founde*   *build
> Ne renneth naught the werk for to bygynne
> With rakel* hond, but he wol bide a stounde,*   *hasty* while
> And sende his hertes line* out fro withinne   *cord
> Aldirfirst* his purpos for to wynne.   *First of all
> (I. 1065–9)[12]

The Latin phrase translated in line 1068 is *intrinseca linea cordis* [the line of the heart within], which applies the heart and the bond to the initial act of writing poetry. The suggestion made earlier that *The Canterbury Tales* form a 'faire cheyne of love' may have a basis in poetic theory known to Chaucer. If so, the links of *The Canterbury Tales* appear more aptly named than might be thought. The extent of this specific debt to the *Poetria Nova* must not be pressed, however. *The Consolation of Philosophy* has so many passages on order described in terms of bonds and *The Romance of the Rose* sufficient passages on love described in terms of the heart that one need look no further for Chaucer's source of the heart and the chain as organizing metaphors for love and order than in those two works which he translated, works that influenced him profoundly throughout his entire poetic career from first to last.

Chaucer's use of a poetic nucleus illustrates a medieval literary theory that is of more significance than the few lines from the *Poetria Nova*. The heart as nucleus of a poem about love and its variance and the chain as nucleus of a poem about order and its confinement are significant instances of a medieval attitude toward poetic language in which key metaphors such as these were apprehended as we would apprehend abstract statement; the metaphor of the chain would thus be thought to have the same literal truth about the organization of the cosmos that we would find in abstract statements about order and degree. This attitude toward poetic language is the subject of an important paper by Judson B. Allen. Using evidence from medieval *accessus* [handbooks] especially those on hymn collections dating from Hilarius in the twelfth century to Johannes Baptista Cantalycius in the fifteenth, Allen presents evidence that in late medieval poetic theory, the transfer of meaning inherent in metaphor was thought of as the literal truth, because the cosmos 'was already, in modern terms, so poetic that there was no need to claim for the poet greater powers than those of an honest reporter.'[13] The chain of order and the heart of love were as real to the medieval mind as, for example, were the crystalline spheres of the Ptolemaic universe [according to Ptolemaic theory the universe was constructed of concentric spheres], which are only metaphoric to us. The analysis here presents independent support and illustration for Allen's analysis by showing that what he suggests about poetic theory can be documented with extensive citation from several works of one of the major philosophical poets of the late medieval period. Chaucer has long been recognized as a philosophical poet, but the centrality of philosophical thought in his poetry has not been grasped, because the essence of his thought has been expressed in the highly creative form of a poetic nucleus. The modern separation of poetic language into concrete and abstract vocabulary is misleading in Chaucer's poetry because of the way that the poetic nucleus is given abstract significance even as it continues to be concrete.

Use of a nucleus in a long text may be a fairly rare occurence and is difficult to detect in a poem of any considerable complexity.[14] Once found, however, a nucleus can provide a lucid perception 'of a work's centre, the source of its life

Troilus and Criseyde: Critical Extracts

in all its parts, and response to its total movement' which is Helen Gardner's lucid definition of the purpose of critical activity.[15] The molecular cohesion and focus of the work are, so to speak, apprehended from within, and the reader's basic experience of the text alters as a result. An apprehension of the functions of the heart and the chain in Chaucer's poetry provides a new perspective on familiar material as when the city dweller, long used to a night sky hazy with reflected artificial light, goes into the country and sees, as if with new eyes, the stars come out in the evening sky until the dark is full of light.

Notes

1 In *The Parliament of Fowls* love is twice described in terms of a knot, ll. 435–8 and 624–8.
2 The standard study remains John Livingston Lowes, 'The Loveres Maladye of Hereos,' *Modern Philology*, 11 (1913–14), 491–546. Lowes is mainly concerned with the medical doctrine behind the lines of *The Knight's Tale*, which, like so much else in the poem, is directly relevant to *Troilus*. A late, but clear, statement of the process occurs in Book III of Castiglione's *Il Libro del Cortegiano*. See *The Book of the Courtier*, trans. Sir Thomas Hoby, intro. W.H.D. Rouse (London: Dent, 1928), pp. 246–7.
3 The idea that the heart was the eye of the breast, or that the heart itself had eyes, is interesting because of the explicit connection of vision with the seat of love. The heart is often reported in Middle English texts to have eyes; see the relevant citations in the *MED* under *eie*. The usage is traditional and is common in the fathers. It occurs, for example, in Jerome's commentary on Isaiah: 'Istos cordis oculos et sponsa habebat in Cantico canticorum, cui sponsus dixit: *Vulnerasti cor meum, soror mea sponsa, uno ex oculis tuis*,' *S. Hieronymi Presbyteri Opera*, Pars 2, *Commentariorum in Esaiam Libri I–XI*, Corpus Christianorum, Series Latina, vol. 73 (Turnholt: Brepols, 1963), Book I. I, ll.42–5, p. 6. The verse from the Song of Songs, 4: 9, may be the most important single source for the idea of love as a wound in the heart inflicted by the eyes of the beloved. References to *oculi cordis* are common in Augustine; see, for example, *Sermo* 159 (Caput 3.3) *Patrologia Latina*, ed. J. P. Migne, 38, col. 869, *Sermo* 286 (Caput 8.6) *PL* 38, col. 1300, *Epistola* 147 (Caput 17.41), the famous *De Vivendo Deo*, *PL*, 33, col. 615, and other references given in the index to Augustine in *PL* 46, cols. 469–70.
4 Of particular help are two long papers by Xenja von Ertzdorff, 'Das Herz in der lateinisch-theologischen und frühen volkssprachigen religiösen Literatur,' *Beiträge zur Geschichte der deutsche Sprache und Literatur*, 84 (1962), 249–301, and 'Die Dame im Herzen und das Herz bei der Dame. Zur Verwendung des Begriffs, Herz in der höfischen Liebeslyrik des 11. und 12. Jahrhunderts,' *Zeitschrift für deutsche Philologie*, 84 (1965), 6–46. Von Ertzdorff traces the literary use of the heart from

the Bible through the fathers up to the high Middle Ages. The apparatus provides useful bibliographical information. I am indebted to Prof. James Rochester Shaw of the University of Rochester for these references and helpful advice on medieval medical views on the heart.

5   Sermon 29, In Ascensione Domini, *PL* 76, col. 1219. This passage is the source for Cynewulf's *Christ II*, lines 751–5:

	Is us þearf micel
Þæt we mid heortan	hælo secen,
Þær we mid gaeste	georne gelyfað
Þæt Þæt hælobearn	heonan up stige
mid usse lichoman,	lifgende god.

The Exeter Book, ed. George Philip Krapp and Elliott van Kirk Dobbie (New York: Columbia University Press, 1936), p. 24. For a discussion of this connection, see Colin Chase, 'God's Presence through grace as the theme of Cynewulf's *Christ II* and the relationship of this theme to *Christ I* and *Christ, III*,' *Anglo-Saxon England*, 3 (1974), 87–101.

6   The material is discussed by Pierre Debongnie, 'Commencement et recommencements de la devotion du coeur de Jesus,' in *Le Coeur*, Les Etudes carmélitaines, 29 (1950), 147–92. For the text of the story, see *Acta Sanctorum Aprilis*, ed. J. Carnandet (Paris: Victor Palmé, 1866), III, 907. The feast day of St Catherine is April 30; the account of her exchange of hearts with Christ is in Part II of her *Vita*, ch. 6, secs. 178–80. See also Jean Leclercq, OSB, 'Le Sacré-Coeur dans la tradition bénédictine au moyen âge,' in *Cor Jesu*, ed. Augustinus Bea, SJ, Hugo Rahner, SJ, Henri Rondet, SJ, and Friedrich Schwendemann, SJ (Rome: Casa Editrice Herder, [1959]), ll. 3–28. Other papers in this collection are also of interest to the subject here.

7   Alfredus Anglicus, for example, in his tract *De Motu Cordis*, written about 1210, reflects medical opinions then current and ultimately derived from Galen; he has nothing whatever about a shift or transfer of the heart; *Des Alfred von Sareshel (Alfredus Anglicus) Schrift De Motu Cordis*, ed. Clemens Baeumker, Beiträge zur Geschichte der Philosophie des Mittelalters, 23 (Münster: Verlag der aschendorffschen Verlagsbuchhandlung, 1923). See also James Otte, 'The Life and Writings of Alfredus Anglicus,' *Viator*, 3 (1972). Nor does 'the cursed monk, daun Constantyn' (*CT*, IV. 1810) allude to any exchange of hearts; see Paul Delany, 'Constantinus Africanus' *De Coitu*: A Translation,' *The Chaucer Review*, 4 (1969), 55–65. For medieval medical opinion on the movable womb see Vern L. Bullough, 'Medieval Medical and Scientific Views of Women,' in *Marriage in the Middle Ages*, ed. John Leyerle, *Viator*, 4 (1973) pp. 485–501.

8   *Les Romans de Chrétien de Troyes*, vol. III: *Le Chevalier de la Charrete*, ed. Mario Roques, Les Classiques Français du Moyen Age, 86 (Paris: Honoré Champion, 1958), ll. 4689–97. The translation is from Chrétien de Troyes *Arthurian Romances*, trans. W. W. Comfort (London: J. M. Dent, 1914), 329. The motif also occurs in Chrétien's *Yvain* (ll. 2635ff.) and, from there, in Hartmann von

Aue's *Iwein*. For other examples of the exchange of hearts, see *La Mort le Roi Artu*, ed. Jean Frappier, 10th edn (Geneva: Droz, 1956). p. 35, and Juan Ruiz, *Libro de Buen Amor*, ed. and trans. Raymond S. Willis (Princeton: Princeton University Press, [1972]), stanzas 209ff.

9 For a miniature illustrating this text showing Amour entrusting the heart of the sleeping king to Vif-desire, see Germain Bazin 'En quête du sentiment courtois,' in *Le Coeur*, Les Etudes carmélitaines, 29 (1950), 129–46, pl. 1 facing p. 138. Bazin also gives three other plates of late medieval/early renaissance illustrations of the exchange of hearts, or the offer to make such an exchange. In Jeanine Moulin, *Christine de Pisan* (Paris: Seghers, [1962]), the plate facing p. 113 shows Venus, in a circle of stars, collecting hearts in her skirt held up to form a lap; her votaries, both men and women, offer to her their hearts which they hold in the hand.

10 For example, see *Fabliaux: Ribald Tales from the Old French*, trans. Robert Hellman and Richard O'Gorman (New York: Thomas Y. Crowell, [1965]), pp. 137 and 148–9. One of these fabliaux is by Rutebeuf and the other by Gautier le Leu.

11 *The Filostrato of Giovanni Boccaccio: A Translation with Parallel Text*, Nathaniel Edward Griffin and Arthur Beck with Myrick (Philadelphia: University of Pennsylvania Press, 1929); the expression occurs in the following stanzas: III. 50, IV. 90 and 145, V. 25 and 59. The *cor/corpus* trope in love poetry is found widely in romance languages and may be no more than an ornament arising from the verbal closeness of the words.

12 For the Latin text see Edmond Faral, *Les Arts poétiques du XIIe et du XIIIe siècle* (Paris: E. Champion, 1924), 198: 'Si quis habet fundare domum, non currit ad actum / Impetuosa manus: intrinseca linea cordis / Praemetitur opus....' A useful English version is *Poetria Nova of Geoffrey of Vinsauf*, trans. Margaret F. Nims (Toronto: Pontifical Institute of Mediaeval Studies, 1967).

13 'Commentary as Criticism: Formal Cause, Discursive Form, and the Late Medieval Accessus,' in *Acta Conventus Neo-Latini Lovaniensis: Proceedings of the First International Congress of Neo-Latin Studies Louvain 23–28 August 1971*, ed. J. Ijsewijn and E. Kessler (Munich: Wilhelm Fink Verlag, 1973), p. 39. The present paper was in substantially finished form when Allen's work first came to my attention as a conference lecture.

14 *The Shipman's Tale* has *dette* as a nucleus, but the poem's relative lack of the usual Chaucerian complexity makes its existence very clear. In this tale *dette* operates at both a commercial and sexual level; the reckoning of the *dette* is another pun with *tailles* referring to tallies, tails, and, perhaps, tales. The point has been discussed before; see Albert H. Silverman, 'Sex and Money in Chaucer's Shipman's Tale,' *Philological Quarterly*, 32 (1953), 329–36. Janette Richardson, *Blameth Nat Me: A Study of Imagery in Chaucer's Fabliaux* (The Hague: Mouton, 1970), pp. 100–22, discusses image clusters in the tale including those pertaining to *dette*.

15 *The Business of Criticism* (Oxford: Clarendon Press, 1959), p. 23.

Criseyde: Woman in Medieval Society

David Aers

In this extract David Aers takes a rather different approach from Leyerle, yet sustains the emphasis on the importance of careful textual reading. Whereas Leyerle's interest is in structural unity, that of Aers is in social and ideological contexts, and is perhaps most reminiscent of Strohm's, discussed above. Aers challenges the 'historical scholarship' of D. W. Robertson and his followers, which emphasizes the allegorical significance of medieval texts, according to which Criseyde may be read, for instance, as 'the lovely vanity of human wishes'. Aers identifies such scholarship, which can be erudite and interesting, as a response to the reductive humanist readings of the early twentieth century, with their emphasis on naturalism rather than the complex web of literary conventions and social realities of medieval writing. There can be no doubt that while Troilus and Criseyde *is not a novel, its situations and emotions are conveyed in immediate and realistic terms: to read the central figures as allegorical is to strip them of their humanity and hence their appeal, even while it is crucial to recognize Chaucer's use of literary conventions such as the chivalric code and* fin'amors *in his construction of character.*

Aers explores how Chaucer engages profoundly with the social and ideological discourse of his time in the creation of a complex figure such as Criseyde. He proposes a new approach, bringing together the minutiae of the text with the general social and cultural context of the period. A close reading of Troilus *demonstrates a complex web of social relations and expectations that shape Criseyde's behaviour and thus defend her from any superficial charge of falseness: her betrayal of Troilus may be seen as deeply rooted in her own vulnerability and objectification by a male and patriarchal society. In creating such a narrative, Chaucer employs an apparently remote classical romance to comment on contemporary social mores and gender roles, specifically, the constraints experienced by aristocratic women. In one sense, romance is an escapist mode, presenting idealized situations where women are adored and served by knights; in another it is mimetic, engaging with social structures and ideologies, according to which noble women must make arranged marriages and authority belongs to men – an issue present in a different way in the* Legend of Good Women. *Like this engagement with the predicament of women, the tension between romance and reality recurs in Chaucer's writing, as for instance in the* Parliament of Fowls.

In this section of his essay, Aers analyses Criseyde's position at the start of the poem in terms of her isolation and vulnerability: he emphasizes the realistic nature of her fears and the way that authority passes from Calchas, to Hector, to Pandarus, to Troilus, and eventually to the parliament that decides Criseyde's fate, then to Calchas once again, and to Diomede. Aers conveys well the patriarchal ethos of a work centred upon war. Criseyde's power is limited to the sexual sphere, and it is in this context that the work engages with the literary conventions of fin'amors. *In the remainder of his essay, Aers goes on to consider the manipulation of Criseyde by Pandarus, her social position as widow, the status of Troilus, and Criseyde's commodification. His discussion of Criseyde's reasons for refusing to flee with Troilus is especially persuasive in its elaboration of how she subscribes to the power of society, embodied both by parliament and by notions of honour and status. For Aers, she is a product of her conservative culture, unable, unsurprisingly, to see beyond the structures and strictures that contain her. Aers's perspective is deeply sympathetic: he views Criseyde's fears as comprehensible, valid and pitiable, and her betrayal of Troilus as an inevitable result of the social constraints placed on her: 'It is not mere idiosyncratic timidity that guides Criseyde, but official (male) ideology about women and values'. For Aers, unlike some more recent feminist critics, Chaucer is 'womanis frend', his text a subtle one of 'insight and art' that both depicts and exposes the social forces of a patriarchal society and the vulnerability of a woman caught within these.*

David Aers, from 'Criseyde: Woman in Medieval Society', *Chaucer Review* 13 (1978–9), 177–200.

Anyone attempting to contribute to the understanding of Chaucer's achievement and meaning in creating the figure of Criseyde will be well aware that, in a necessary reaction to much previous criticism, influential commentators in recent decades have eschewed all interpretation which might seem to treat medieval writing as though it was a nascent form of the kind of 'naturalism' associated with some nineteenth-century novels. Thus, in his important study of Chaucer, Robert O. Payne praised Charles Muscatine and Arthur Mizener for evolving approaches to 'the patterns of characterization which remove it from the realistic and motivational-psychological categories in which earlier criticism had sought to define it.' He himself wished to demonstrate that there is no ground in the poem for any 'naturalistic reconstruction of "personalities",' nothing approaching 'individual psychologies.'[1] In common with other leading critics, such as D. W. Robertson, Jr., Payne assumed that all late medieval poetry was governed by unambiguous 'ultimate moral principles,' that the past was viewed as an unambiguous 'series of illustrations of intellectual abstractions,' and that 'the controlling ideas in the presentation of character' for many medieval poets, including Chaucer, were 'fixity and fitness – character established and unchanging, given typical significance.' So in *Troilus and Criseyde* the characters are discussed in terms of 'their conventional fixity' which allegedly allowed them 'to work out the logic of their positions without the chance inconsistencies and non sequiturs of actual existence': Criseyde, for example, 'is a way of saying something about the lovely vanity of human wishes.'[2] In such approaches, now widespread, all medieval art, including Chaucer's, tends to be seen as one aimed at transforming the multifarious forms of existence into a set of abstractions, at constructing a world of univocal signs and ideas where individuals have been eliminated. It seems to me, however, this more recent critical model has blinded us to central currents in Chaucer's art, and I shall argue that in constructing Criseyde Chaucer was developing a social psychology which comprised a profound contribution to the understanding of interrelations between individual and society, between individual responsibility and given social circumstances and ideologies. Before developing this case it may be worth making some general observations about the enterprise.

All students of medieval literature will readily acknowledge how much has been learnt about medieval conventions and basic frameworks from scholars pursuing the kind of approach pointed to in the previous paragraph. Nevertheless, it is now becoming clear that in at least two vital areas a very different emphasis is needed for the further progress of medieval scholarship. The first concerns the much-debated issue of appropriate 'historical criticism' in the study of medieval texts. Thanks to a growing and increasingly detailed body of work on the diverse developments and conflicts in the social and intellectual history of the fourteenth century, critics can readily free themselves from the mythologized version of a non-dimensional, coherent, static and harmoniously pious late Middle Ages handed on by Robertson and his followers as 'historical' scholarship.[3] The expansion of this work by social and intellectual historians should help literary critics become more open to complexly diverse currents, contradictions, and new energies within their own field of medieval studies. Moving into closer contact with the actual practices, confusions, and aspirations of late medieval women and men, we will be less prone to impose *a priori* schemes on texts which were actually engaged with, and part of, a highly complex, dynamic, and shifting historical reality. The second area I have in mind is related and focuses on the 'close reading' of medieval poetry. Theoretically, most critics are always in favour of this, but practice has not always taken the slogan seriously. Doing so demands scrupulous attention to the specific movements of language and feeling in texts, with the resolute refusal to substitute traditional ethical formulae, ideologies, or pieties for the particular literary product being examined.[4] In this area the critic needs to be open to the possibility that a text may involve important and unresolved divisions, that it may partly affirm but partly negate dominant ideas in the author's period and social group; he will bear in mind the possibility that such divisions or contradictions may be at the heart of the work's power and have their roots in the social and intellectual world with which the writer's imagination is engaged.[5] Ideally, the two general areas mentioned here should be drawn together, criticism moving from the closest attention to the particulars of the text, to the writer's social group, to the widest relevant cultural and social situation and back to the text with enriched and sharpened awareness of its historical and universal meaning.[6] Of course this is an *ideal* for transcending distortion and partiality, and one probably best achieved by collaborative work between scholars trained in different disciplines. Still, however short the present essay may fall of this ideal, it is worth clarifying and pursuing, and this I shall now do in relation to Chaucer's Criseyde.

With regard to *Troilus and Criseyde* the second area just referred to has recently received admirable attention. This is well illustrated by Alfred David's exceptionally sensitive book, *The Strumpet Muse*. As in Elizabeth Salter's fine seminal essay on the poem, David pays careful attention to the specific movements of feeling in the text, and argues that 'Chaucer was of Criseyde's party without knowing it.' He sees *Troilus* manifesting a basic division between Chaucer's intellectual commitment to a Boethian–Christian moral and his emotional commitment to the human reality created by his own art, an art which attaches us more strongly than ever to the world that the intellectual scheme would detach us from. When he treats the breakdown of the central relationship, David sees Chaucer thinking in terms of Nature's cycles, claiming that Criseyde survives because she is 'more like Nature herself – she is the stick that bends.... The weakness, the flexibility of her character paradoxically gives her the strength to survive.'[7] While I believe that a reading such as David's is illuminating, I wish to show that it too still distorts and underestimates the nature of Chaucer's achievement in making Criseyde. For this actually involves a profound exploration of the ways in which individual action, consciousness, and sexuality, the most intimate areas of being, in fact, are fundamentally related to the specific social and ideological structures within which an individual becomes an identifiable human being. And far from thinking that Chaucer was either straightforwardly transporting his readers 'away from contemporary reality to a distant and romantic Troy,' or exemplifying preexistent and well-known ethical universals,[8] I believe he was *exploring* the position of woman in aristocratic society, ideology, and literary convention. Choosing Boccaccio's story placed in Troy certainly made it easier for him to write about love and sexuality without constant attention to the ready-made judgements of traditional institutionalized Christianity.[9] This helped, at least partially, to free his imagination from the dominant religious codes of the period by encouraging detailed and loving explorations in spheres where the inquisitor's handbook held out no such encouragement. But it did not entail a flight from the world of his own audience. Quite the contrary, his handling of Criseyde shows concern with *women in* the social group for which he wrote – the expectations they cherished, the manipulative pressures they had to accept and use, the contradictory self-images, ideologies, and realities with which they were presented, their own complex mixture of opposition and complicity in a situation where women, at all social levels, were a subordinate group.

In the chief traditions of romance and court literature it seems true to say that love is quite removed from 'contemporary reality,' its confusions, compromises, and inescapable miseries. Conventional romances offered a welcome escape from its audience's world, not a painful and earnest examination of it.[10] The formula of an outstanding knight committing his existence to the devoted service of a woman fulfilled a psychological need to create a more satisfying alternative to the real organization of Eros and marriage in medieval society. For upper-class woman was totally subordinate to man and to land, aristocratic marriages being primarily land transactions, and child marriages commonplace. Social practices and ideology (secular as well as ecclesiastical) demanded total obedience and submission of woman to man and land in marriage. It is in this context we should see the contradictory images and conventions of courtly literature in which the normal relations between women and men are inverted, the knight serving the woman, paying her homage and devotion.[11] The role of female patronesses in shaping this courtly literature is no coincidence, and the compensatory role of such conventions and fictions is not obscure. Certainly, as Eileen Power pointed out, such courtly conventions did little to elevate the actual position of woman, and the cost of their fictional development was to banish most human life and activity from the genre. In fact, Eileen Power's suggestion that such courtly conventions and genres served a psychological function for the upper-class women not dissimilar to that served by modern romantic stories and magazines for working-class women seems plausible, for the image of woman as goddess to be worshipped by aristocratic knight sorted very ill with the actual treatment and position of women in the period, dictated by a male aristocracy and a male church.[12] Now it seems to me that Chaucer was fascinated by these contradictions and was not prepared to leave them flaccidly coexisting. In *Troilus* he used the romance genre and the conventions of courtly literature to explore the anomalies between upper-class literary conventions and realities, to explore the anomalies between the place women occupied in society and the various self-images presented to them, and to imagine his way into the psychic cost for men and women in the relevant situation. He returns romance to society and locates Criseyde firmly within it.

At the very opening of the poem Chaucer shows that he wants his audience to take Criseyde's social situation seriously in any assessment of her.[13] He

Troilus and Criseyde: Critical Extracts

emphasizes her isolation in Troy, her danger as daughter of a traitor in a long war, and the aspects of her widowed state that meant she lacked a male protector. Having reported the general view that not only her father but all his kin 'Ben worthi for to brennen' (I, 90–1), Chaucer writes of Criseyde that

> ... of hire lif she was ful sore in drede,
> As she that nyste* what was best to rede;*   *did not know   *do
> For bothe a widewe was she and allone
> Of any frend to whom she dorste hir mone.
> (I, 95–8)

Before critics venture any remarks about her 'weakness' or her being 'slyding of corage' they need to immerse their imaginations in this situation – as Chaucer did. Her fear is fully justified, her weakness is a genuine aspect of a social reality not of her own making, and her isolation is an essential part of her vulnerability. In these circumstances her only asset, her only leverage on the powerful, is her sexuality. She understands this well enough and, 'Wel neigh out of hir wit for sorwe and fere,' approaches Hector, one of the most powerful men in the city:

> On knees she fil biforn Ector adown
> With pitous vois, and tendrely wepynge,
> His mercy bad, hirselven excusynge.
> (I, 110–12)

It is interesting to contrast this scene with conventional courtly images of the male prostrate before the female, images we later see enacted by Troilus and by the arch-manipulator Pandarus (III, 183–4, 953, 1079–80). Indeed, Chaucer already invites such contrasts by preceding her homage with a conventional description of her 'aungelik' beauty and her appearance as 'an hevenyssh perfit creature' (I, 102, 105). We immediately see the heavenly woman desperately on her knees in a totally subordinate role before the all-powerful male. (It is tempting to observe that if she is angelic, then Hector is deific – a fair social projection.) To survive in this society the isolated woman needs to make use of her sexuality and whatever courtly sexual conventions or fictions as may serve her.[14] She does so, and we should not miss the way Chaucer has begun his poem by placing the whole matrix of courtly forms of sexual relations and language in a setting which stresses the 'aungelik' female's totally subordinate position and her urgent need for protection in order to survive.[15] It is Hector, responding to her sorrow and beauty, who guarantees 'hir estat' (I, 113–31). The esteem in which she is held by Hector and the royal family is of great importance to her, and it is not surprising that during her first discussion with Pandarus in Book Two she asks directly after Hector, the potentate whose goodwill and existence appear necessary for her well-being. Similarly when later it seems that there is a threat to her property we see the importance of the royal family as patrons to deliver Criseyde from trouble (II, 1414–91, 1611–36). And being reliant on this group, Criseyde is influenced by their opinions, whether about Troilus in Book Two, when her mixed feelings are soothed by hearing these powerful people sing his praises (1583–94), or in Book Four, when she considers Troilus's proposal that they elope.

The first interview between Pandarus and Criseyde confirms Chaucer's interest in the detailed process of interaction between individual consciousness and various social pressures, manipulations, and values, often bewilderingly conflicting (II, 87–597). Chaucer relocates her fears and natural impulses in the particular situation he had drawn for us in his first book. It is May, and Pandarus invites her to cast aside her self-possession and dance (II, 110–12). At once Criseyde turns to one possible social role (in Chaucer's own society) to protect herself from risks that could be involved in her uncle's suggestion:

> 'I? God forbede!' quod she, 'be ye mad?
> Is that a widewes life, so God yow save?
> By God, ye maken me ryght soore adrad!
> Ye ben so wylde, it semeth as ye rave.
> It sate me wel bet* ay in a cave   *it would benefit me much better
> To bidde* and rede on holy seyntes lyves;   *pray
> Lat maydens gon to daunce, and yonge wyves.'
> (II, 113–19)

We saw before how well founded were her fears (both of her own people and, as she now says, the Greeks [II, 124]), and met one strategy for confronting them. But a widow's situation also allowed another – the posture of contemplative withdrawal from the life of the world and the overcoming of natural instincts.[16] Of course, Criseyde does not claim this is what she positively wants, only that it would be decorous and would fulfil certain, very different, social values. Later, we shall see, she can assess the situation of widowhood and its acknowledged values in yet another way.

As the conversation proceeds the war is the central topic until Chaucer tells us that Pandarus discussed 'hire estat, and...hire governaunce' (II, 211–20). Here he focuses on his relationship to her [183] as uncle, elder male relative, and guide to subordinate female (II, 232–52, 295–8: the *authority* relations here should not be missed, for as the narrator notes, at III, 581, nieces should obey uncles). Having shifted the relationship into these roles, he uses his position to push Troilus's interest at her. Chaucer's handling of Criseyde's situation here is, as so often in this work, extraordinarily delicate. Its vulnerability has been stressed, and Pandarus's circumlocutions play on her fears (II, 278–315). When this has been done he introduces the core of his matter:

> Now, nece myn, the kynges deere sone,...
> The noble Troilus, so loveth the,
> That, but ye helpe, it wol his bane* be. *death
> (II, 316, 319–20)

Pandarus emphasizes the social status of the lover (the personal name follows three lines *after* the social identification), the king's son, using this as a bait but also as a threat. For what would become of Criseyde if she should be held responsible for his death (II, 320–50)? In a similar manner, Pandarus adds to the pressure by stating that if she does not acknowledge Troilus, then he, her uncle, will cut his own throat (II, 323–9). This added threat has a double force, for Criseyde is not only subordinate to him but also genuinely fond of his company. She plays for time and seeks clarification, using the social roles Pandarus has chosen – '"Now em [uncle]," quod she, "what wolde ye devise? / What is youre reed [advice]...?"' (388–9). Pandarus's reply is unequivocal and recommends total fulfilment of Troilus's sexual desires (390–406). Criseyde tries to forestall this demand by appealing to his identity as her quasi-father (408–28). This tactic fails badly, for Pandarus renews his previous threats, now getting up and setting off to carry them out (429–47). Criseyde's response is fully comprehensible and carefully traced in the next three stanzas (II, 449–69). Her great fear has again been given a thoroughly sufficient social basis, and there is no reason to treat it as a peculiar flaw. Thinking of her uncle's suicide, she thinks of its social repercussions, trying to balance her own social survival with her uncle's personal survival – 'my estat lith now in jupartie, / And ek myn emes lif is in balance...' (II, 465–6). Her comment (to herself) that 'It nedeth me ful sleighly for to pleie' (462), suggests how aware she is that her uncle is manipulating her, but it is not women who are final arbitrators of the games' rules, and she simply cannot dissolve the realities and constraints of her position and her past. What she can do is concede gracefully and so shift to the more favourable ground of 'Love.' Here, as mentioned earlier, convention allowed woman a seemingly dominant role, and also legitimized expression, however discreet, of those natural sexual impulses so despised in official church teaching. This enables her to assert that she cannot love anyone against her own will, taking a certain initiative in the role of powerful beauty knowledgeable in the mysteries of love and able to bring even a king's son to woe (II, 477–9, 499–504). But by the time this

Troilus and Criseyde: Critical Extracts

occurs, Chaucer has taken us far into one of the major problems he was exploring – the contradiction between the aristocratic love conventions in which woman was an exalted and powerful figure, and the social reality in which she was a totally subordinate being to be used, manipulated, and taught obedience. Furthermore, and this cannot be given too much weight, he explores the problem concretely as it affected Criseyde's own consciousness and actions, showing subtle concern with the interactions between individual, conflicting ideologies and social situation. This concern is at the heart of Chaucer's imaginative, intellectual, and moral achievement in *Troilus and Criseyde* ...

Notes

This study would never have been written without the contribution, both written and spoken, of Yvonne McGregor, many of whose ideas have been incorporated in my own thoughts.

1 Robert O. Payne, *The Key of Remembrance* (New Haven, CT: Yale University Press, 1963), pp. 182–3, 222, 226. See Arthur Mizener, 'Character and Action in the Case of Criseyde,' *PMLA*, 54 (1939), 65–79, and, very similarly, Robert M. Jordan, *Chaucer and the Shape of Creation* (Cambridge, MA: Harvard University Press, 1967), pp. 99–100.
2 *Key of Remembrance*, pp. 221, 81, 181–2, 223, 226.
3 A fruitful start on these lines has been made by Sheila Delany, *Chaucer's House of Fame: The Poetics of Skeptical Fideism* (Chicago: University of Chicago Press, 1972) and Charles Muscatine, *Poetry and Crisis in the Age of Chaucer* (Notre Dame, IN: University of Notre Dame Press, 1972). I am currently completing a book on Langland, Chaucer, and creative imagination in just such contexts, to be published by Routledge and Kegan Paul. An earlier version of the first chapter appeared as 'Imagination and Ideology in *Piers Plowman*' in *Literature and History*, 7 (1978), 2–19. The kind of work I have in mind as of great help to literary scholars may be exemplified by the following: R. Hilton, *Bond Men Made Free* (London: Temple Smith, 1973): R. W. Southern, *Western Society and the Church in the Middle Ages* (Harmondsworth: Penguin, 1970); G. Duby, *Rural Economy and Country Life in the Medieval West* (London: Edward Arnold, 1968); H. A. Miskimin, *The Economy of Early Renaissance Europe* (Englewood Cliffs, NJ: Prentice-Hall, 1969); Ruth Bird, *The Turbulent London of Richard II* (London: Longmans, Green, 1949); Silvia L. Thrupp, *The Merchant Class of Medieval London* (Chicago: University of Chicago Press, 1948); H. J. Hewitt, *The Organisation of War under Edward III* (Manchester: Manchester University Press, 1966). As examples of useful studies in intellectual and religious history I would cite C. Trinkaus and H. A. Oberman, eds, *The Pursuit of Holiness in Late Medieval and Renaissance Religion* (Leiden: E. J. Brill, 1974); R. E. Lerner, *The Heresy of the Free Spirit in the Later Middle Ages* (Berkeley and Los Angeles: University of California Press, 1972); Gordon

Leff, *William of Ockham* (Manchester: University of Manchester Press, 1975) and *Heresy in the Later Middle Ages*, 2 vols (Manchester: Manchester University Press, 1967).

4   See, for example, E. T. Donaldson, 'Patristic Exegesis in the Criticism of Medieval Literature: The Opposition,' reprinted in *Speaking of Chaucer* (London: Athlone Press, 1970); A. C. Spearing, *Criticism and Medieval Poetry* (London: Edward Arnold, 1964), Chapters one and two; D. Aers, *Piers Plowman and Christian Allegory* (London: Edward Arnold, 1975).

5   For some illuminating general comments on this dialectic of affirmation and negation, see H. Marcuse, 'Art and Revolution,' in *Counter-Revolution and Revolt* (Harmondsworth: Penguin, 1972).

6   See L. Goldmann's description and application of this method in *The Hidden God* (London: Routledge, 1964), esp. parts one to three.

7   Alfred David, *The Strumpet Muse* (Bloomington: Indiana University Press, 1976), chapter two, esp. pp. 29–36; Elizabeth Salter, '*Troilus and Criseyde*: A Reconsideration,' in *Patterns of Love and Courtesy*, ed. John Lawlor (London: Edward Arnold, 1966), pp. 86–106.

8   Karl Young, 'Chaucer's *Troilus and Criseyde* as Romance,' *PMLA*, 53 (1938), 38–63; see also Morton W. Bloomfield, 'Distance and Predestination in *Troilus and Criseyde*,' *PMLA*, 72 (1957), 14–26.

9   In the current essay I have not the space to carry out the useful comparison with Boccaccio's text in relation to the present argument, but it is worth noting how Chaucer deliberately turns Boccaccio's setting into a courtly, aristocratic one. Similarly it is significant that it is Chaucer who gives such careful attention to Criseyde's social situation and its ideological pressures, a central part of his transformation of Boccaccio's one-dimensional heroine. I intend to develop these comments in a future study.

10 See Eileen Power, *Medieval Women* (Cambridge: Cambridge University Press, 1975), pp. 16–28, 35–6; J. Stevens, *Medieval Romance* (London: Hutchinson, 1973), pp. 16–28, 35–6; Alfred David, *The Strumpet Muse*, pp. 17, 55–6.

11 See Eileen Power, *Medieval Women*, chapters one and two. In these areas, H. A. Kelly's *Love and Marriage in the Age of Chaucer* (Ithaca, NY: Cornell University Press, 1975) is no help.

12 Eileen Power, pp. 23–8, 36. A useful anthology is *Not in God's Image*, ed. J. O'Faolain and L. Martines (London: Temple Smith, 1973), parts 5 to 8.

13 All quotations from Chaucer are from *The Works of Geoffrey Chaucer*, ed. F. N. Robinson, 2nd edn. (Boston: Houghton Mifflin, 1957); here, I, 85–135.

14 As Yvonne McGregor points out, the fact that Criseyde chooses not to channel her request through her uncle (transformed by Chaucer into an older man and apparently the only male relative left to her in Troy), could argue a measure of strong-willed independence; but the fact is that she will get a better deal by prostrating her own sex and beauty before the top man.

15 This emphasis, here and throughout, is peculiarly Chaucer's and in my view comprises an ongoing critique of Boccaccio's superficial presentation of female being. Compare here *Il Filostrato*, Canto Two.

16   One recalls the commonplace exegesis of Matthew 13: 8 as applying to marriage (thirtyfold fruit), widowhood (sixtyfold), and virginity (hundredfold).

Coda: The Narrator

C. David Benson

In this short extract Benson considers twentieth-century approaches to the narrator, in particular the idea that the narrator may be seen as a character in his own right in the poem. This concept seems to originate with Donaldson, who argued that the narrator was himself in love with Criseyde, so that the story was related from a highly sympathetic perspective until the last books, when the narrator's suffering was reflected in a kind of poetic disintegration. This approach illuminates the interventionist mode of the narrator who is so partisan to the lovers and who urges on the affair in a manner reminiscent of Pandarus. The poem gains its immediate quality in part from direct narratorial addresses to the reader, particularly in the first books. As the narrator becomes disillusioned, however, his comments are fewer and often relate to disbelief or uncertainty: 'Men seyn – I not – that she yaf hym hire herte' (V, 1050). Chaucer interweaves close involvement and historical distance: while the narrator's perspective moves from one to the other, a sense of history is also maintained through the Trojan background and references to the war. It is, however, the narrator's evocation of the emotional relations between characters and his empathy for them that engages the reader most: the narrator may thus be seen as playing a crucial role in the drama.

Yet as Benson points out, the narrator cannot be considered to function as Troilus, Criseyde or Pandarus do, although like Pandarus he directs the narrative and manipulates the events told in his sources. We know little about him other than that he is not a successful lover, and even this situation is not explored in the way that it is in Boccaccio's Il Filostrato. *Nor is Chaucer's narrator an authorial figure of the kind used by Dante in his* Divine Comedy. *Nevertheless he plays an important role in interpreting events and reminding us of what we do and don't know. He moves from comic commentator to rhetorician, and from pathos to tragedy. As Benson emphasizes at the end of this extract, the self-consciousness of the poem is largely rooted in the narrator's repeated reminders of the status of the narrative as poetic text, of its fictional status. In a phrase like 'men seyn, I not' we become aware of the many interpretations of the story and the impossibility of deciding, finally, on its significance. We, like Chaucer, are readers of old books who make choices each time we interpret a work. The narrator draws attention to the issue of authority and experience, even while we receive his own reading of authority, coloured by his shadowy experience. The question is how does this voice relate to that of Chaucer the poet? Benson's analysis is salutary in reminding us that although the distinction between poet and narrator is a useful and necessary one, in* Troilus *the line is more blurred than in either the earlier poetry or the* Canterbury Tales. *We are given few details to allow us to envisage the narrator, and if we are made aware of the subjectivity of his telling, and sometimes of his unwillingness to reveal 'historical fact', it is impossible to state categorically that he is 'not Chaucer'; he is rather a performative projection of Chaucer, a voice through which Chaucer tells his tale, sometimes set up against and sometimes creating the interpretation that is the final outcome of the engagement of text and reader.*

C. David Benson, 'Coda: The Narrator' from 'Character' in *Chaucer's Troilus and Criseyde.* Unwin Hyman, London, 1990.

The narrator, a figure who has often been considered a fourth major character in *Troilus and Criseyde*, must also be discussed, however briefly, in this chapter, if only to show that he does not really belong. Although his many comments on the action provide some justification for linking him with Troilus, Criseyde and Pandarus, he never becomes a fully developed, independent human character. He plays no part in the action itself, despite his emotional involvement, and it is often impossible to distinguish his statements from those of the poet. The narrator in *Troilus* is better seen as a flexible literary voice than as a human personality – a rhetorical element of the text that Chaucer uses to create a number of different effects. The most important function of this voice may be to reveal the silences and uncertainties of the poem and thus encourage the interpretive role of each reader.

Despite the autobiographical claims of Boccaccio's *Filostrato*, its narrative unfolds with remarkable objectivity... Not so *Troilus and Criseyde*, to which Chaucer has added an intricate layer of narrative commentary. Substantial invocations precede each book except the last, and the reader is frequently addressed in casual asides: after a familiar proverb, for instance ('This, trowe [believe] I, knoweth al this compaignye', I.450), or to mark a change of scene ('Now lat hire slepe, and we oure tales holde/Of Troilus...', II.932–3). We are also frequently told about the process of composition: the narrator discusses his source (a certain Lollius), announces his approach (the love-story rather than the war), admits gaps in his information (even when, as in respect to Criseyde's children, *Filostrato* is perfectly clear [it states that she has none]) and justifies his abridgements. Even more striking are direct expressions of enthusiasm about the progress of the narrative and of the love-affair. The narrator urges on Pandarus's first visit to Criseyde ('Now Janus, god of entree, thow hym gyde!', II.77) and wishes he had experienced such a night of amatory joy ('Why nad I swich oon with my soule ybought', III.1319). Criseyde is an object of special concern; to choose two famous examples among many, the narrator defends her against possible accusations of falling in love too quickly (II.666–79) and is sympathetic even after her betrayal (V.1093–9).

For a long time, when they thought about it at all, critics assumed that such first-person comment, some of which is obviously comic, was in the poet's own voice. Donaldson seems to have been the first to treat the Chaucerian narrator as a separate character. In an influential study of the *Canterbury Tales* ('Chaucer the Pilgrim'), he argued that the portraits in the General Prologue were drawn not by the poet himself but by an independent *persona*, who was enthusiastic, naive, and not wholly to be trusted. In subsequent articles and in his edition of Chaucer, Donaldson posited an equally independent and unreliable narrator for *Troilus and Criseyde*, whose sentimental opinions, especially in defence of Criseyde, we are meant to question. In order to make this point, Donaldson was forced to posit a fully fictionalized character, who is described in psychological metaphors that endow him with will and emotions. In one article the narrator, whose masculinity Donaldson insists upon, is portrayed as acting 'irritably', 'knowing' something, and wanting the audience to 'share his enthusiasm' ('Masculine', 54–5); in another as experiencing 'one of his tenderest moods' ('Criseida', 71); and in a third as suffering 'internal warfare' that results in 'a kind of nervous breakdown in poetry' ('Ending', 91).

At about the same time Robert Jordan also argued that the narrator in *Troilus* plays a 'role...central to the life of the poem' ('Narrator', 237). Jordan's narrator is as fully personalized as Donaldson's and similarly unreliable. A good storyteller, performer, reporter of facts and dispenser of commonplaces, he is finally 'a man of no wisdom': 'Although warm hearted and ingratiating, he is remarkably obtuse, completely imperceptive of the esthetic and moral grandeur of his own creation' (254). In response to the objections of Bertrand Bronson, Jordan later denied that he meant the narrator to be taken as a genuine character of the same order as Troilus, Criseyde and Pandarus (*Shape*, 67), but many subsequent critics have conceived of him in just this way.[1] Often linked with Pandarus, the narrator is treated by some as a disturbed personality suffering from voyeurism or prurience.[2] More positive interpretations also see him as an independent and coherent being. While discussing several different views, Ida Gordon, a critic in the Robertsonian tradition, approvingly cites Muscatine, a decided non-Robertsonian, to support an interpretation of the *Troilus*-narrator 'as a *persona* distinct from the poet' who, like Boethius, is 'brought gradually to a clearer vision as the story proceeds to its inevitable end' (*Double*, 61). Wetherbee also sees *Troilus* as the autobiography of the narrator, and a recent article by Carolyn Dinshaw using the insights of feminism and contemporary theory continues to accept the narrator of *Troilus* as a discrete and consistent consciousness.[3]

Despite the emotions and opinions he expresses, the narrator of *Troilus and Criseyde* is a character or independent *persona* only in a very limited sense. Unlike the narrators of the *Divine Comedy*, *Pearl*, *Piers Plowman* or Chaucer's earlier dream visions, whose experiences truly are central to their respective works, the voice we hear in *Troilus* is never given physical shape and does not participate directly in the events of the poem. He remains, like us, only a reader, isolated in time and space from the genuine characters in the poem, whom he cannot affect and who remain oblivious to him.

A more radical problem with the narrator is the difficulty of defining the extent of his presence in *Troilus*. Is he there only when directly addressing us in the first person or is he responsible for the entire exposition of the poem?[4] William Provost attempts to distinguish five narrative modes in *Troilus* (direct narrative, summary narrative, description, narrator's comment, and invocation), but he is forced to admit that these 'five modes, alas, are not always as distinct as we might wish' (56–8). That is surely the point. How can we hope to distinguish between neutral description and subjective comment in *Troilus*? It is not difficult to identify an unreliable narrator in the various defences of Criseyde, but is the summary of the Trojan War (I.57–98) equally suspect (it contains strong opinions about Calchas) and what about the following portrait of Criseyde that describes her as angelic and heavenly (I.99–105)? It is hard to know where to draw the line. The ending of *Troilus* has been a particular problem in defining narrative presence. Whereas many have seen a retreat into conventional moralizing in the conclusion, and Donaldson imagines the narrator undergoing a nervous breakdown ('Ending'), others hear the voice of the poet himself at last. And there is further disagreement among those who hold this last position: Gordon finds the 'mature, humane poet himself' taking over from the naive narrator as early as V.1093 (*Double*, 87), whereas Jordan argues that it is not until the last twelve stanzas that Chaucer speaks in his own voice ('Narrator', 253).

Mehl suggests that little is gained, and much lost, by anachronistic attempts to separate clearly poet from naive narrator ('Audience', 180), a rigid division called 'more convenient than true' by Salter ('Poet', 282), who warns that the identification of an unreliable narrator as the source of the poem's quandaries may fail to recognize 'what may be the poet, making his own statements, tentative as they may sometimes be, about the problematic background to his artistic decisions and procedures' (286). The narrator is certainly not very consistent. He never becomes a familiar companion, like Conrad's Marlow; but, rather, in Payne's phrase, offers a 'multiplicity of perspectives' (*Chaucer*, 85). As Bloomfield first demonstrated ('Distance'), the narrative voice moves between close involvement and historical distance, nowhere more abruptly than in the three formal portraits in book V (799–840); and the voice is much more prominent in the first three books of *Troilus* than in the last two. If the narrator sometimes sounds sentimental and naive, he can also be authoritative, especially in the poems and in such summary judgements as 'And thus Fortune a tyme ledde in joie / Criseyde and ek this kynges sone [of Troye]' (III.1714–15). Other first-person passages, such as his comment during the consummation that 'Resoun wol nought that I speke of slep, / For it acordeth nought to my matere' (III.1408–9), are comically self-conscious and highly sophisticated.

David Lawton has recently proposed that we regard the narrator of *Troilus* not as a consistent *persona* but as a variable rhetorical device used to emphasize different moments in the text. Even the shift in mood and value at the very end of the poem is not a shift in voice: 'It does what the first-person narratorial voice has done throughout: it responds appropriately to the particular stage of the work's unfolding' (*Narrators*, 82). Lawton rejects the idea that this device is a fourth major character; instead he sees it as the neutral 'voice of performance': 'almost the voice of the poem itself speaking from the time and continuum of its own performance' (89). Lawton's formulation, which somewhat resembles Wayne Booth's conception of the 'implied author', may minimize the extent to which the narrative commentary complicates as well as supports other aspects of the poem, but he seems quite right to regard the voice as textual rather than personal.

If the narrator never becomes a distinct and coherent character in *Troilus and Criseyde*, the effects of his various comments are important and multiple, especially for the reader. The first-person passages that celebrate the love-affair and empathize with both the joys and sorrows of the lovers increase the emotionalism of Boccaccio's story. These invitations to empathy are a genuine element in the poem, which cannot be dismissed as merely ironic, though ironies of various kinds may also be present. The sympathy extended to Criseyde after she decides not to try to return to Troilus is especially poignant. The regretful pity expressed for one both reviled and miserable is neither naive nor sentimental, but mixes pathos with tragedy:

> Ne me ne list* this sely womman chyde *I do not wish
> Forther than the storye wol devyse.
> Hire name, allas, is publysshed so wide
> That for hire gilt it oughte ynough suffise.
> And if I myghte excuse hire any wise,
> For she so sory was for hire untrouthe,
> Iwis, I wolde excuse hire yet for routhe.* *pity
> (V.1093–9)

In addition to stirring our emotions, the narrative voice also tests our judgement. Its comments force us to question not only the ultimate meaning of the story but also its very telling. Did Criseyde have any children and how closely does the poem follow Lollius? Admissions of ignorance about particular facts and the inability to describe the full joy of the lovers remind us that we are reading a fiction that we must interpret. Recognition of the narrator's unreliability does not make our job any easier. We are right to be suspicious of narrative claims that defend the pace of Criseyde's wooing or that certify the characters' good intentions, but these suspicions do not automatically point to a specific 'right' answer, although this is what critics in the tradition of both Donaldson and Robertson often suggest.[5] The narrative voice in *Troilus* creates openness rather than certainty. No deconstructionist is needed to point out the gaps, subjectivity and contradictions in the text as long as the narrator insists on them himself. Through this voice Chaucer renounces any claims to authorial omniscience and empowers the reader. The central experience of the poem is not the narrator's but ours.

Notes

1. Almost a decade after Jordan's retraction, Michael Frost claims to be following him in believing that the narrator 'is a full-fledged *dramatis persona*' (35); other proponents of the personalized narrator, not necessarily following Jordan, include Shepherd, who says that it could be claimed that he 'is the only fully-developed character in the poem' ('*Troilus*', 71), and Osberg, who calls him 'a consistent character with a major thematic function' (258).
2. Spearing, *Troilus*, 46–7. An extreme example of giving the narrator a complex, even pathological inner life can be found in the interesting article by Carton; for instance: 'The narrator's disclaimers of control and responsibility, like Pandarus' equivalent self-extrications, are the increasingly desperate evasions of a character who recognizes his deep complicity in a series of events that features seductions and culminates in betrayal' (49).
3. Like others, Dinshaw uses psychological terms to describe the narrator's erotic response to the narrative. Although Dinshaw stresses the act of reading, her dramatic conception of the narrator, which derives directly from Donaldson, makes his reading (not ours) central.
4. Chatman notes how easy it is to confuse the narrator with the implied author, the figure parallel to the implied reader who can be imagined to have invented everything in the narrative, including the narrator (148).
5. For instance, Gordon says that one function of the narrator is 'a vehicle for the wit by which the poet *expresses his own commentary* in the ironic ambiguities' (*Double*, 62; my emphasis). Similarly, Donaldson imagines that Chaucer stands behind the narrator and occasionally 'jogs his elbow' so that the reader will be encouraged 'to see Criseida in a light quite different from [and therefore truer than] the one that the narrator is so earnestly trying to place her in' ('Criseida', 69).

History versus Romance

Lee Patterson

Patterson's study of Chaucer may be classified as 'new historicist': like Strohm, he is interested in placing Chaucer within the social networks of his time and place. His particular emphasis, however, is on the ways that Chaucer employs 'historical' material, the 'olde bokes' that offer authority, and the relation of these to Chaucer's historical present. This extract focuses on Chaucer's use of history in Troilus and Criseyde *to explore how Chaucer retells classical history to conceal, subvert or rewrite the historical, even while, finally, the poem is dependent on its Trojan matter. Patterson echoes several of the points made by Benson regarding the play between immediacy and distance in* Troilus and Criseyde, *although Patterson employs a different binary opposition, that of history and romance. Patterson (following Strohm and various others) defines romance as being about the individual, whereas epic and history tend to be about nations. The matter of Troy was one of the great epic subjects: it formed the background to Virgil's* Aeneid *and was recounted by the classical historians Dares and Dictys. Troy was of particular interest for English writers of legendary history, for the Trojan Brutus was the legendary founder of Britain: there had even been a move to rename London 'Troynovant'. Chaucer's Troy is thus both historically distant and resonates with medieval London and with the legendary history of the British.*

A critical commonplace regarding Troilus and Criseyde, *however, is that Trojan history is strangely absent from the poem, which is so much dominated by the love story and the three (or four, including the narrator) individuals involved: the erotic emphasis and the interest in individual character, Patterson argues, render the poem a romance despite its historical matter. Chaucer in fact labels the poem a 'tragedy', a term that in the medieval period refers to moral* exempla *of the fall of great men through the turning of the wheel of fortune. Moral readings arguing that Troilus falls through foolish trust in mutable fortune, and that Criseyde is the emblem of mutability and fleeting worldly happiness, such as those of Robertson and others, seem as inappropriate and reductive as a reading that emphasizes the events of the Trojan war. As Patterson emphasizes, the poem resists an historical reading: the narrator states directly that this is not his project. Instead, the subject is love and 'the inner world of erotic action'. It is the intrusion of the public that finally destroys the private world of the lovers. Patterson effectively analyses Chaucer's use of space to show that the lovers are placed within a series of 'walls', from those around Troy to the bed itself.*

Troilus and Criseyde: Critical Extracts

Yet although in a sense the poem is always attempting to 'suppress the historical consciousness', history is crucial to the narrative. Troilus, for instance, performs martial deeds throughout: he is not passive and cowardly, as some critics have suggested, but rather his love forms a corollary to his military glory. Patterson teases out the historical subtext to show that, despite its apparent marginality, the war does play a crucial role in the construction of the love narrative. Not only does it account for Criseyde's departure, but also it underlies a whole series of episodes: Calkas's treachery, the feast of Palladion, Troilus's triumphant return to Troy, Pandarus's pretext of a lawsuit against Criseyde, the meeting at Deiphebus's house. Patterson writes suggestively of the sequence of negative historical images and characters: the Palladion, which will be stolen by the Greeks; Calkas, Criseyde's traitor father; Antenor, who plotted against the Trojans; Poliphete his friend; Helen, the cause of the war; Deiphebus, whose later liaison with Helen ends in his betrayal; and Polyxena who later betrayed her lover. Chaucer hints at a 'darker truth' of betrayal by referring to characters who ultimately participate in the fall of Troy. Patterson emphasizes, however, the unsatisfactory nature of a moral reading: the lovers are victims of their own fraught world, rather than active destroyers. Neither Troilus nor the Trojans seem foolish, even if according to the eye of God all human action is folly, and their present actions do not seem to necessitate their falls. Yet, at the same time, like the narrator retelling what he knows is the 'double sorwe of Troilus', we are not allowed to forget the tragic outcome. For Patterson the coincidence of the falls of both Troy and Troilus seems at first to suggest the meaninglessness of history, in that they are not contingent events; he will pursue this question with regard to medieval historiography. Patterson's argument exemplifies well Chaucer's clever interweaving of genres, and suggests once again the subjectivity of history and the choices that must be made by its teller, here choices that are illuminated by Chaucer's use of a self-conscious narrator.

Lee Patterson, 'History versus Romance' from 'Troilus and Criseyde and the Subject of History' in *Chaucer and the Subject of History.* Routledge, London, 1991.

There is, it must be acknowledged at the outset, something inherently paradoxical about either a historiographical or a historical reading of *Troilus and Criseyde*. For the action of the poem seems conspicuously, even aggressively, to resist the attention to either its Trojan or its contemporary context that would encourage us to regard history as its ultimate reference. The poet defines his project at the outset in entirely amorous terms: he addresses his bidding prayer to 'ye loveres, that bathen in gladnesse' (1, 22), defines his subject as 'swich peyne and wo as Loves folk endure' (1, 34), and calls himself 'the sorwful instrument, / That helpeth loveres, *as I kan*, to pleyne' (1, 10–11). And he shortly issues a polemical statement explicitly disclaiming any historical interest:

> But how this town com to destruccion
> Ne falleth naught to purpos me to telle;
> For it were a long digression
> Fro my matere, and yow to long to dwelle.
> But the Troian gestes,* as they felle,   *deeds
> In Omer, or in Dares, or in Dite,*   *Dictys
> *Whoso that kan* may rede hem as they write.
>   (1, 141–7)[1]

This disclaimer is then matched at the end of the poem by an analogous stanza that justifies the poet's lack of interest in the martial deeds that comprise the public record:

> And if I hadde ytaken* for to write   *undertaken
> The armes of this ilke worthi man,
> Than wolde ich of his batailles endite;*   *compose
> But for that I to writen first bigan
> Of his love, I have seyd *as I kan*, –
> His worthi dedes, whoso list hem heere,
> Rede Dares, he kan telle hem alle ifeere.*   *together
>   (5, 1765–71)

Having initially defined his project in wholly amorous terms, the narrator feels justified in referring us elsewhere for historical details that are, for him, simply distractions from the matter at hand.

But before assuming that the narrator's dehistoricizing of the Troy story represents a straightforward Chaucerian initiative, we should take note of two other textual facts. One is that in subordinating the historical world of events to the inner world of erotic action the narrator's behavior imitates that of his protagonists, thus following a program that we know better than to regard as exemplary. When Troilus first falls in love, 'Alle other dredes weren from him fledde, / Both of th'assege [siege] and his savacioun' (1, 463–4). This does not mean, however, that he abandons his martial duties. As soon as Pandarus leaves Troilus at the end of Book 1, Chaucer adds a passage to the *Filostrato* to tell us that

> Troilus lay tho no lenger down,
> But up anon upon his stede bay,
> And in the feld he pleyde tho leoun;
> Wo was that Grek that with hym mette a-day!
>   (1, 1072–5)

And this martial prowess continues even during the height of the love affair:

> In alle nedes for the townes werre,
> He was, and ay, the first in armes dyght* *ready
> And certeynly, but if that bokes erre,
> Save Ector most ydred of any wight;
> And this encrees of hardynesse and myght
> Com hym of love, his ladies thank to wynne,
> That altered his spirit so withinne.
> (3, 1772–8)

'Bokes' – the 'Troian gestes' of Homer, Dares, and Dictys are doubtless meant – testify to Troilus's bravery, and the narrator here explains its inner meaning. A matching phrase later locates in the *records* of heroism ('As men may in thise olde bokes rede' [5, 1753]) the fact that Troilus continues his martial ferocity after Criseyde's departure, though now motivated by rage and jealousy. Inspired first by love and then by hate, Troilus enacts throughout the narrative a heroism that is admirable (historically worthy of record) because it both testifies to the intensity of his amorous feelings and shows him fulfilling his role as an *alter Hector* – 'and next his brother, holder up of Troye' (2, 644).

In effect, then, the narrator manages to provide for the 'Troian gestes' a rich texture of private motivation and psychological depth without ignoring their significance as history. He thereby protects his story from the simplistic moralization that characterizes so much medieval historiography – and too much modern criticism.[2] The problem with moralizing Trojan history, whether Chaucer's or those of Benoît and Guido, is not that it is wrong, in the sense that it ignores another, more obviously correct understanding, but that categorical moral judgments reduce complex patterns of motivation to simple ideas of choice, or, more seriously, make all stories alike. For, while this narrative foregrounds private amorousness, it also resists the structure of blame. It not only refuses to draw any straightforward causal connections between Troilus's failed love and the fall of Troy, but seems to imply that there is no connection between these two events at all. As I shall argue, in this poem the private stands wholly apart from and seeks to efface the public, just as, at the level of genre, romance, a story focused on the fate of a single individual, seeks to preempt tragedy, a story about (in the definition of Isidore of Seville) *res publicas et regum historias* [public things and histories of kings].[3] And at a still further level of complexity, the reader is so entangled in the inward world of eroticism and delicate feeling that, if he or she has learned anything from modern discussions of reading, the experience should be one not of moral superiority but rather complicity. For the characters, their narrator go-between, and the poem's audience all come to share the desire to suppress the historical consciousness.[4]

At certain points this inwardness is dramatized within the poem itself and thematized in particularly intricate ways. One telling instance is the scene at Deiphoebus's house, where Pandarus's manipulations have succeeded in momentarily creating a space within which the lovers can, in a necessarily constrained and tentative way, begin to express their love. Pandarus's busy weavings create a bustle of activity, both physical and interpretive, that allows for the brief appearance of a local enclave of pure privacy, and one which not even the reader is fully able to penetrate.[5] The same process is at work in an even more elaborately articulated form in the consummation scene, where we are simultaneously made complicit in the eroticism enacted before us and yet denied full access precisely by the ostentatious mediations of both Pandarus and the narrator, a series of multiform goings-between designed to persuade us that at their center is a moment of utterly unmediated confrontation. In part our conviction derives from the sense of progressive inwardness that the very topography of the setting communicates. Situated within a room that is itself surrounded by another room, itself surrounded by the house and its walls, by the city and *its* walls, then by the besieging Greeks, and with the whole encased within a rainstorm, the lovers retreat first to a bed, then to a mental space that only they share, and finally to a wordless union that leads them (and perhaps us) to believe that they have passed beyond the world of history to a transcendent 'Love, that of erthe and se hath governaunce' (3, 1744).

We are likewise made aware throughout the first three books of the poem that the historical is both unavoidably present and nonetheless placed at the service of the erotic action. Although the poem opens with Calkas's defection to the Greeks because of his understanding of the shape that events will assume, this dark premonition is quickly preempted by the theatrical scene of Criseyde pleading before Hector. And Calkas is reduced in these opening lines from 'a lord of gret auctorite' (1, 65) and 'a gret devyn' [diviner (1, 66) to a 'traitour' who has committed a 'false and wikked dede' (1, 87, 93) – a reduction in which the narrator himself participates with his trivializing pun, 'whan this Calkas knew by calkulynge' (1, 71). As I have already suggested, by describing Calkas as a 'lord of gret auctorite,' Chaucer recalls the final line of the *House of Fame* – 'A man of gret auctorite' (2158) – and invokes in this new context the questions of literary authority with which that earlier poem deals. These questions, moreover, become insistent a few lines later when Chaucer states, both gratuitously and disingenuously, that his sources do not tell him whether or not Criseyde had children; in fact, of course, Boccaccio explicitly describes her as childless (*Filostrato* 1, 15). In dispensing with Calkas's authority, therefore, the poet opens the way for other forms of deviation from authority, implying that the story as a whole can be told only if both the Trojan history that is its context (presided over by Calkas) and the literary history that provides its materials (here represented by Boccaccio) can be set aside.

Yet – and this is our second textual fact – if the events of the war seem to enter the narrative only as occasions for erotic action, the historical consequence that is excluded nonetheless reenters by the textual back door. Criseyde's first sight of Troilus is as he returns from battle, and her romantic admiration fastens on, but hardly effaces, the signs of his heroic achievement. Pandarus uses as a pretext to visit Criseyde the arrival of a Greek spy with news (2, 1111–13), and while he never tells her, or us, what the news might be, it remains a disturbing possibility. More tellingly, the gathering at Deiphoebus's palace is called to solve a problem whose triviality seems to efface the larger historical crisis it displaces: Pandarus imagines some kind of legal action against Criseyde managed by 'false Poliphete', an obscure figure whom Criseyde fears only because of 'Antenor and Eneas, / That ben his frendes' (2, 1467, 1474–5) – although even then she regards the threat as insignificant: 'No fors of that; lat hym han al yfeere' (2, 1477). Yet in fact this confected conspiracy is derived from a real conflict. Antenor and Aeneas will shortly join together in a plot against Troy itself, and there is evidence that Chaucer thought of Poliphete as a co-conspirator. For the name derives not from medieval versions of the Troy story but from Virgil's 'Polyphoetes [or Polyboetes] sacred to Ceres' in *Aeneid* 6, one of the fallen Trojans whom Aeneas sees in the underworld.[6] There Polyphoetes is linked with the group Virgil calls 'tres Antenoridas [three sons of Antenor],'Glaucus, Medon and Thersilochus, and Servius's gloss says that 'multi supra dictos accipiunt quod fals[os] esse Homerus docet, qui eos commemorat [Many believe false those named above, which Homer teaches, who remembers them.]'[7] However Chaucer may have understood this gloss, he seems to have believed that 'false Poliphete' was an associate of Antenor, and that the conspiracy Pandarus imagines against Criseyde, and which she here dismisses as trivial, was later to be enacted in a darker, less fictive form. Similarly, just as a crucial moment in Trojan history is here prefigured in a trivialized form so does the 'tretys and ... lettre' with which Troilus distracts Helen and Deiphoebus involve a public matter of grave importance – 'If swych a man was worthi to ben ded, / Woot I nought who' (2, 1699–1700) – that serves as a pretext to occupy two of the leaders of Trojan society who have themselves, we suspect, an amorous agenda that will also figure in the final catastrophe.[8]

This dynamic of simultaneously invoking and suppressing the crucial issues of Trojan history also shapes the exchange between Troilus and Criseyde in the temple that initiates the erotic action in the first place. The event takes place on the feast of the Palladion, here represented as a moment of natural impulses, as

>   the tyme
> Of Aperil, whan clothed is the mede*   *meadow
> With newe grene, of lusty Veer* the pryme,*   *Spring *beginning
> And swote smellen floures white and rede.
>   (1, 155–8)

Because the Greeks 'hem of Troie shetten, / And hir cite biseged al aboute' (1, 148–9), the Trojans are denied access to the extramural world of nature where springtime celebrations traditionally take place; and yet they nonetheless continue to perform their 'observaunces olde' (1, 160). To those familiar with Trojan history, however, the feast of the Palladion signifies more than springtime release. For at its center is the 'relik' (1, 153) whose theft, according to Trojan historians, is one of the conditions of the fall of Troy.[9] The Trojans' turn away from the war into a sanctuary where they can celebrate the reappearance of a springtime from which they are excluded – a turn then reenacted by Troilus in his retreat into first his chamber and then the 'mirour of his mynde' (I, 365) – is thus shadowed by a linear temporality that will finally overcome them. However brave or persistent, their attempts to evade the demands of the historical world are evidently bound to fail.[10]

If Books 1 through 3 show us lovers, and a society, determined to avoid their implication within a tragic history, Books 4 and 5 show instead that the local enclave of love can neither withstand nor transcend the pressures of history. 'It shal be founde at preve' (4, 1659), says Troilus as Criseyde leaves Troy, and the proving of the affair is devastating in its results. For what is revealed is a fatal weakness not just in Criseyde but in the constitution of the affair as whole: whatever it is that makes her unwilling either to stay or to return has been an element of her character that has, from the beginning of the story, been both manipulated and overlooked by a devious Pandarus and an enamoured Troilus. Is the weakness of the private world of love then morally identical with (if not responsible for) the weakness that brings down Troy? Not only the narrative symmetry between the fate of the city and the fate of the lovers solicits such a question. For the exchange of Antenor for Criseyde fulfills another of the dark prophecies about Trojan history, that Troy would not fall as long as Troilus lived: in removing from Troilus his reason for living, the exchange removes as well a necessary condition for the survival of the city.[11] Are we then to think that Troilus, falling in love in such a way and with such a woman, rendered himself vulnerable to a loss that served to undermine the city to which he owed his largest allegiance?

The poem forces us to ask this question, but it declines to provide a clear answer. Chaucer's narrative persistently resists the equation of the erotic and the martial, even at the level of analogy or synecdoche – as Troilus, so Troy.

Rather, the fate of the city is seen to be overdetermined by a multitude of causes, and Troilus's behaviour, if anything, to be *less* culpable, more genuinely heroic, than Trojan society in general. We have already seen how even after the loss of Criseyde Troilus maintains his heroic defense of the city (5, 1751–7); more to the point, the events surrounding the exchange of Criseyde for Antenor are themselves embedded in a set of explanations that preclude Troilus's culpability. In describing the capture of Antenor at the beginning of Book 4, Chaucer returns to the 'authentic' accounts of Benoît [de Saint Maure] and Guido [de Columnis] that show that Antenor was captured not *with* the other listed Trojans but *despite* – 'maugre' – their presence.[12] His purpose is evidently to present this event as a military misadventure caused by an overly aggressive Trojan militarism: the Trojans themselves initiate the battle – 'Ector, with ful many a bold baroun, / Caste on a day with Grekis for to fighte' (4, 33–4) – and yet (in a passage original with Chaucer) 'The folk of Troie hemselven so *mysledden* / That with the worse at nyght homward they fledden' (48–9). Yet another explanation for the fall of the city, and one that also posits a general Trojan culpability, is provided by Calkas immediately prior to the scene of exchange: he explains to the Greeks (in a passage also added by Chaucer) that because Laomedon failed to recompense Apollo and Neptune for building the walls of the city the gods will now bring down vengeance on the 'folk of Troie' (4, 122). And yet a third explanation is then provided by the account of the Trojan parliament (another of Chaucer's additions), in which the expediency of the 'folk' (4, 198, 202) overrides the moral force of Hector's blunt objection: 'We usen here no wommen for to selle' (182). In sum, the event that Chaucer presents as decisive for the fall of Troy – the ironically designated 'deliveraunce' (202) of Antenor – is *also* represented as a function of Trojan folly in a wide variety of forms.

Moreover, while we are certainly entitled to see Troilus's love for Criseyde as self-deluded, the poem is careful to exculpate its protagonist from simple selfishness. For just as Hector seeks by his intervention to protect Criseyde (as he had promised), so does Troilus by his silence. 'With mannes herte he gan his sorwes drye' (154), and his thought is '*First*, how to save hir honour' (159). At the very moment Criseyde is being sold by his fellow citizens, Troilus is seen as preferring 'resoun' to 'love' by choosing silence over speech (162–8), an act that defines his devotion to Criseyde – his 'trouthe' – as very different from the narrow self-interest that motivates the 'peple' (183) of Troy. Far from being complicit in the process that is to bring about their downfall, the lovers are here represented as victims, set apart at the levels of both practice and morality from the world of military, religious, and political action that will serve to drive them apart.

In sum, Chaucer forces upon his historiographically informed reader an interpretive dilemma that allows no easy solution, perhaps even no solution at all. Ostentatiously setting aside the historical context, he then persistently if surreptitiously reinvokes it; and yet having done so, he not only fails to impart any clear sense of its relevance but offers explanations that insist upon its irrelevance. In allowing the collapse of the local enclave of love and the civic world in which it is nested to be occasioned by the same event, Chaucer establishes a connection at the level of event that is then denied at the level of causality. This denial is all the more unsettling because he implies that both events are motivated by a self-destructive blindness: 'O nyce [foolish] world, lo, thy discrecioun' (4, 206) he apostrophizes the Trojan parliament, echoing his earlier apostrophe to the love-struck Troilus – 'O blynde world, O blynde entencioun!' (1, 211). But then by here setting Troilus's 'reasonable' silence (further legitimized by Hector's high-minded defense) against the clamorous 'noyse of peple' (183), the poet insists upon the moral difference between two similar acts of self-destruction.

The effect of this juxtaposition is to bring the reader to an interpretive impasse. We have been encouraged to see the complex erotic relationship that constitutes the subject matter of the poem as providing an interpretive purchase upon the large historical event in which it is embedded; but then at this moment of crisis we are denied the means to do so. Troilus's love fails, Troy fails: these symmetrical events come finally to provide a statement not about the meaning of history but instead about its profound meaninglessness. We can of course find reasons for each individual failure, but it is the lack of connection that is distressing, especially since the narrative seems to assert it so insistently. At best, we are allowed only a metaphoric relation: both Troilus and the Trojans behave foolishly. Not only is this conclusion banal, but it leads to the monkish conclusion that history is by definition simply a record of human folly. Denied a stance within the historical world itself, then, the only critical purchase we can gain upon the action is one that stands outside history altogether – a position that necessarily denies the significance that the poem, by its very definition as a Troy book, seeks to express. How far this impasse can be attributed to a structural weakness in medieval historiography (as distinct from looking beyond Chaucer's poem to its own historical environment) must be our next question; and the first route to its answer is an investigation of previous Trojan history writing, especially that of Benoît de Sainte-Maure in the *Roman de Troie*.

Notes

1 'Whoso that kan:' while this gently qualifying phrase seems in the first instance directed to those without Latin, since Homer was unavailable to virtually *every* medieval reader, Chaucer begins by invoking one of the original accounts of the

Trojan War only to remind us of its absence. The phrase, and the preceding 'as I kan' of 1, 11, also echoes the opening 'if I kan' of the *House of Fame* ('I wol now synge, if I kan, / The armes and also the man' [143–4]), a phrase that simultaneously marks the difference between the medieval minstrel and the classical poet and registers, in John Fyler's words, 'the uncertain ability of art to be true to the facts,' especially when – as in the case of the Dido–Aeneas episode – those facts are notoriously in dispute (Fyler, *Chaucer and Ovid*, 33; see A. C. Spearing, *Medieval to Renaissance in English Poetry* [Cambridge: Cambridge University Press, 1985], 22n. 18). Moreover, the phrases prefigure the nervous 'I have seyd as I kan' with which the poem concludes; see the next citation in the text.

2 In 'The Trojan Scene in Chaucer's *Troilus*,' *ELH* 29 (1962), John P. McCall ascribes the fall of the city to 'the criminal lust of Troy' (263n. 3), claiming that this interpretation is common in 'the medieval encyclopedic tradition' (264n. 4). This may well be so, but it is almost entirely absent from historiographical accounts, including those of Benoît de Sainte-Maure, Joseph of Exeter, Guido delle Colonne, and the various prose histories (e.g. *L'Histoire ancienne jusqu'à César*), the primary means by which classical history was transmitted to the medieval aristocratic world within which Chaucer wrote. Modern readings of the poem in these terms are offered by such diverse critics as D. W. Robertson, Jr., *A Preface to Chaucer* (Princeton, NJ: Princeton University Press, 1962), 472–502, and 'The Probable Date and Purpose of Chaucer's *Troilus*,' *M & H* 13 (1985): 143–71; Chauncey Wood, *The Elements of Chaucer's Troilus* (Durham, NC: Duke University Press, 1984), especially 32–3 and 63–98; Winthrop Wetherbee, *Chaucer and the Poets*, for whom 'an excessive preoccupation with love is the folly at the heart of the *Troilus*, ... and the ultimate downfall of Troy is foreshadowed by the intensity of this preoccupation, the importance assumed by the "siege of Criseyde" in the midst of the larger war' ([Ithaca, NY: Cornell University Press, 1984], 118); and Eugene Vance, 'Mervelous Signals: Poetics, Sign Theory, and Politics in Chaucer's *Troilus*,' *NLH* 10 (1979): 293–337, who argues that 'the heroic young prince is not only reenacting Adam's loss of primal innocence, but Mars's erotic downfall in a coma of heroic inactivity as well' (324). But Chaucer takes pains to show us that Troilus is far from inactive.

3 In medieval literary discussions private and public concerns are generically distinguished in terms of comedy and tragedy, as in the authoritative definition by Isidore cited in the text... Paul Strohm has shown that the term *romaunce* is most often used to designate a narrative about an individual rather than a society: 'the majority of the works designated in this way recount the chivalric (martial and occasionally amatory) deeds of a single notable hero' ('The Origin and Meaning of Middle English *Romaunce*,' *Genre* 10 [1977], 13); see also Strohm's important '*Storie, Spelle, Geste, Romaunce, Tragedie*: Generic Distinctions in the Middle English Troy Narratives,' *Speculum* 46 (1971): 348–59. In terms of medieval genre theory, the *Troilus* wants to be a romantic comedy but is reluctantly constrained to the form of a historical tragedy; and when Chaucer at the conclusion designates his poem 'litel myn tragedye' (5, 1786) he has implicitly acknowledged the triumph of history.

4   A fifteenth-century example is described in Patterson, *Negotiating the Past*, 115–53; for twentieth-century instances, see E. Talbot Donaldson, ed., *Chaucer's Poetry*, 2nd edn (New York: Ronald Press, 1975), 1129–44, and his 'Criseide and Her Narrator,' *Speaking of Chaucer* (London: Athlone Press, 1970), 65–83; Evan Carton, 'Complicity and Responsibility in Pandarus' Bed and Chaucer's Art,' *PMLA* 94 (1979): 47–61; and Richard Waswo, 'The Narrator of *Troilus and Criseyde*,' *ELH* 50 (1983): 1–25.

5   The phrase 'local enclave' is taken from Norbert Wiener, *The Human Use of Human Beings: Cybernetics and Society* (Garden City, NY: Doubleday, 1954): 'While the universe as a whole, if indeed there is a whole universe, tends to run down, there are local enclaves whose direction seems opposed to that of the universe at large and in which there is a limited and temporary tendency for organization to increase. Life finds its home in some of these enclaves' (12).

6   'Cererique sacrum Polyphoeten [Polyboeten]' (6, 484); for an earlier version of this suggestion, see G. L. Hamilton, *The Indebtedness of Chaucer's Troilus and Criseyde to Guido delle Colonne's Historia Trojana* (New York: Columbia University Press, 1903), 97 n. 3. As I discovered after completing this chapter, the reference to Virgil's Polyphoetes is also proposed by John Fyler, '*Auctoritee* and Allusion in *Troilus and Criseyde*,' *Res Publica Litterarum* 7 (1984): 73–92.

7   G. Thilo and H. Hagen, eds (Leipzig: Teubner, 1884), 2: 72–3.

8   These suspicions are discussed by McKay Sundwall, 'Deiphoeus and Helen: A Tantalizing Hint,' *MP* 73 (1975): 151–6, and by John V. Fleming, 'Deiphoebus Betrayed: Virgilian Decorum, Chaucerian Feminism,' *ChR* 21 (1986–7): 182–99. On Helen's thematic function in the poem, see Christopher C. Baswell and Paul Beekman Taylor, 'The *Faire Queene Eleyne* in Chaucer's *Troilus*,' *Speculum* 63 (1988): 293–311.

9   In his commentary to *Aeneid* 2, 13, Servius says that the survival of Troy was dependent upon the preservation of three things: the Palladion, the tomb of Laomedon, and the life of Troilus; see E. K. Rand et al., eds, *Servianorum in Vergilii Carmina Commentariorum* (Lancaster: American Philosophical Society, 1946), 2: 316–17. In the *Filostrato* Boccaccio refers to this relic as 'il Palladio fatale' (1, 18); and in his gloss to *Aeneid* 2, 166, Servius has a long discussion of the theft of the Palladion by Ulysses and, significantly, Diomedes; see Rand et. al., 2: 367–9.

10 Another echo of an excluded but visible Trojan history are the ominous suggestions of a connection among Criseyde, 'Eleyne [and] Polixene' (1, 455), all of whom brought their lovers to disaster. Helen appears at Deiphoebus's house, and in circumstances that disturbingly prefigure her later liaison with (and betrayal of) her host; and Polyxena is then referred to explicitly by Troilus when, in Book 3, he offers to be a go-between for Pandarus with 'my faire suster Polixene' (409). Perhaps it is also Polyxena who is the composer of the song Antigone sings in Book 2. The song is written, we are tantalizingly told, by 'the goodlieste *mayde* / Of gret estat in al the town of Troye, / And let hire lif in moste honour and joye' (2, 881–2) and is addressed to an absent lover ('Now good thrift have he, whereso

that he be!' [2, 847]). These are conditions that would seem to fit particularly aptly a Polyxena who was pining for Achilles.

11 Chaucer could have found this prophecy implicit in the ecphrasis in the temple of Juno in *Aeneid* 1, 474–8, where not only does the *infelix puer* Troilus stand for all the victims of the Trojan War, and of the Italian Wars to come, but his death fits into a larger pattern of prophecy that Aeneas reads but fails to understand. An example of a medieval history that promotes the military role of Troilus in order to link his death to the city's destruction is the *Chronique Martinienne*, a translation of the *Cronica* of Martin of Poland made in 1458 by Sébastien Mamerot (Pierre Champion, ed., *Cronique Martiniane* [Paris: Champion, 1907], xlvi). The connection between the eponymous Troilus and his city is exploited by a number of Trojan texts: for instance, Albert of Stade's *Troilus* establishes in its proem an analogy between the fact that Troilus was named after the city and that the poem is also called *Troilus* because it is named after the Trojan War, which is its subject: 'Troilus est Troilus Troiano principe natus / Et liber est Troilus ob Troia bella vocatus' (Albertus Stadensis, *Troilus*, ed. T. Merzdorf [Leipzig: Teubner, 1875], 9: these lines may be an interpolation into Albert's original). According to the *Compendium historiae Troianae-Romanae*, Troy was named after Troilus: first it was called Neptunia, but 'que post modo, a Troiulo eius nepote, Troia apellata fuit' (ed. Simonsfeld, 242).

12 On the revision of 4, 50–4, see Stephen Barney's notes in the *Riverside Chaucer*, 1044–5.

7

The *Canterbury Tales*: An Overview

> Whan that Aprill with his shoures soote
> The droghte of March hath perced to the roote,
> And bathed every veyne in swich licour
> Of which vertu engendred is the flour;
> Whan Zephirus eek with his sweete breeth
> Inspired hath in every holt and heeth
> The tendre croppes, and the yonge sonne
> Hath in the Ram his half cours yronne,
> And smale foweles maken melodye,
> That slepen al the nyght with open ye
> (So priketh hem nature in hir corages),
> Thanne longen folk to goon on pilgrimages,
> And palmeres for to seken straunge strondes,
> To ferne halwes, kowthe in sondry londes;
> And specially from every shires ende
> Of Engelond to Caunterbury they wende,
> The hooly blisful martir for to seke,
> That hem hath holpen whan that they were seeke.
> (1–18)

The brilliant fictional device of the Canterbury pilgrimage allows Chaucer to create a unique work in the *Canterbury Tales*, the influence of which on later readers and writers can scarcely be over-estimated. In this work Chaucer's interest in experimentation with different literary genres, his self-conscious narratorial play, and his engagement with the opposition between experience and authority, as well as with themes such as love and the predicament of women, all come to fruition. Yet, as well, they take a wholly new form, for here in a much more direct manner than in his early writing, Chaucer engages with his own social reality to portray both the ideals of his society and the

The Canterbury Tales: An Overview

Plate 3 A party of pilgrims leaving Canterbury, from the *Prologue* to *The Canterbury Tales*, 1516. The Art Archive/British Library, London.

distance of these ideals from its reality. The work presents us with a cross-section of medieval society in the Canterbury pilgrims, whose imagined voices we hear in the tales. By including himself among the pilgrims, Chaucer creates a complex, multi-layered narrative, full of the potential for irony: Chaucer the author tells the tale of Chaucer the pilgrim who narrates the tales told by his companions on the road to Canterbury. This develops further the literary device of the narrator already central to the dream visions and *Troilus and Criseyde*.

The *General Prologue* draws on the traditional theory of society as made up of 'three estates', the nobility, the Church and the peasants: those who fight, those who pray and those who work. Chaucer plays with the genre of 'estates satire', which conventionally depicts members of the estates with their typical vices and virtues. The Knight, the Parson, and the Plowman are idealized representatives of the three estates; to the aristocracy belong too the Squire, the Knight's son, and the Franklin, a member of the lesser, country gentry; to the Church, the Clerk, an ascetic Oxford scholar, the Nun's Priest and the undescribed Second Nun; and to the workers, the Yeoman, the Squire's servant, a forester or game-keeper. We are also presented with deeply flawed members of the religious estate: the worldly Monk, Prioress and Friar, and the corrupt parasites of the Church, the red-faced Summoner and the sinister Pardoner. Yet the *General Prologue* also moves beyond the notion of the three estates to depict the growing middle classes. The strong spirit of commercial enterprise in medieval England is evident in the figures of the Shipman, with his own ship the 'Maudeleyn', the Reeve, the manager of a northern estate, and the Miller, affluent from his dishonest sale of corn. The emerging bourgeois class is represented by the Merchant, but also by the Wife of Bath, who has her own cloth-making business, and Harry Bailly himself, the keeper of the Tabard Inn at Southwark. Other, more elevated civic figures, members of the professional classes, are present too: the Physician, the Man of Law and the Manciple, a business agent of an inn of court. The pilgrimage also includes a group of working-class city dwellers: a Haberdasher (hat-dealer), a Carpenter, a 'Webbe' (weaver), a Dyer, a 'Tapycer' (weaver of tapestries), and the Cook. Thus Chaucer interweaves the notion of the city and the spirit of bourgeoisie with the traditional model of the three estates to create a vision of medieval society in all its variety.

The story-telling competition that ensues, like the *General Prologue*, plays on an established literary convention. Chaucer would have been familiar with many kinds of story collections – legends, saints' lives, fables, classical myths, in particular Ovid's *Metamorphoses*, and the Bible itself. None of these, however, uses a frame narrative like the pilgrimage, nor does any use individualized narrators, or the range of genres of the *Canterbury Tales*. Most similar is Boccaccio's *Decameron*, written in the 1340s and presented as a collection of stories told by a group of Italian nobles to while away their stay outside the plague-ridden city of Florence. This contains a number of tales analogous to the *Canterbury Tales*, though Boccaccio does not develop the relations of tellers or the possibilities of literary variation – and it is by no means certain that Chaucer knew his work. The idea of the story-telling competition is original to Chaucer, and it allows for the natural inclusion of a large number of diverse tales which captures the diversity of pilgrims: 'Diverse folk diversely they seyde' (*The Reeve's Prologue*, 3857). At the same time, the fiction of the story competition excuses Chaucer from responsibility in the 'immoral' tales. The reader can always 'Turne over the leef and chese another tale' (*Miller's Prologue*,

3177); 'Blameth nat me if that ye chese amys,' says Chaucer (*Miller's Prologue*, 3181).

The interplay between pilgrim and tale, but also between pilgrims, is a crucial part of the *Canterbury Tales*: we do not know, however, what form the final drama would have taken, since Chaucer, perhaps unsurprisingly, did not finish the projected design of two tales told by each pilgrim, one on the way, another on the way back (24 tales survive, not all completed, none by the same pilgrim), and there is some evidence that the links between tales and narrators were not yet definite. Nor was manuscript culture like book culture: the 55 manuscripts of the *Canterbury Tales* are copied in different ways by scribes, with different spellings, often lacking parts, and in different orders. We know only the order of small groups of tales or 'fragments' that are found consistently together (for example, the Knight's, Miller's and Reeve's tales), and thus the notion of the interaction between pilgrims cannot be taken too far. Despite this, camaraderies and rivalries, already hinted at in the prologue, are evident: the Miller and Reeve, like the Friar and Summoner, tell tales against each other; the Miller responds to the Knight, the Clerk addresses the Wife of Bath in his story of patient Griselda. The tales serve to illuminate their narrators, sometimes in surprising ways: we do not necessarily expect the Prioress to tell a highly anti-Semitic, graphic tale of the violent death of a little boy, or the Wife of Bath to tell an Arthurian romance. Just as we cannot see the work exclusively in terms of the drama of the pilgrims, so it is reductive to see individual tales purely as a function of their narrators, about whom, in some cases, we have little or no knowledge – the Second Nun or the Nun's Priest, for instance. The tales are complex, sophisticated pieces of writing in their own right, which frequently move beyond characterization of their tellers. The *Canterbury Tales* allowed Chaucer to experiment with all extant medieval genres: romance, *fabliau*, beast-fable, saint's life, miracle story, sermon, moral treatise. Frequently, tales are not quite what they seem: they subvert convention, or gain an ironic quality through their relations to their own narrators and to other tellers and tales.

The *General Prologue* not only establishes the notion of pilgrimage and hence the inclusion of different narrators and genres, but also, in its opening lines, introduces two crucial themes – secular and divine love – that recur across the tales. Spring inspires new life, warmth and sexual desire (one meaning of 'corage'); yet it can also kindle desire for another kind of regeneration, that of the spirit, and hence the intention to set forth on pilgrimage. The Canterbury pilgrimage encompasses the two extremes, opposing figures like the ascetic Clerk and Parson, and the virtuous Knight freshly back from the Crusades, with the Wife of Bath, seeking a sixth husband, or the corrupt Pardoner, hoping to fill his purse. The secular and the sacred, and particularly secular and sacred love, function as leitmotifs in the *Tales*, from the *Knight's*

Tale onwards – here, desire opens onto the sublime and raises existential questions, while in the Miller's bawdy parody, *fin' amors* and high idealism are replaced by the most basic of sexual urges, and in the *Reeve's Tale* sexuality becomes an economic transaction. Other tales – the Second Nun's, the Man of Law's, the Prioress's, the Clerk's – deal directly with divine love, and sometimes with the rejection of human love. The question of different kinds of love and related questions of gender, marriage and religious vows of chastity, recur across the *Canterbury Tales*.

The idealism of the Knight is balanced by the corruption of the Pardoner, the asceticism of the Parson by the worldliness of the Prioress, the bookish authority of the Clerk by the experience of the Wife of Bath. The tales, like their narrators, span the different spheres of society, from secular to religious, from the lower-class world of the Miller's tale to the aristocratic one of the Knight's; they span too the sweep of history, from the world of ancient Greece to the fourteenth century. Chaucer plays at realizing his own society on the page, with an objectivity that allows him to shape a most distinctive voice, sometimes ironic, often sympathetic, always credible. Like Shakespeare after him, he is a writer of dazzling diversity, who balances wit and learning with a startling immediacy and ability to range from robust comedy and light-heartedness to profound emotion and existential questions.

It is the *Canterbury Tales* that of all Chaucer's works has most attracted critical attention. Helen Cooper's *Oxford Guide* (1989) is an invaluable tool and there are various other good introductions to the *Canterbury Tales*, in particular those of Derek Pearsall, Helen Phillips, and Alcuin Blamires, who summarizes the critics' debates as well as offering his own readings.[1] The *Oxford Companion to Chaucer Studies* and the *Cambridge Chaucer Companion* offer useful collections of essays; the original and *New Casebook* series offer anthologies of earlier and contemporary criticism on the *Tales*, as do Malcolm Andrew's *Critical Essays on Chaucer's 'Canterbury Tales'* (1991) and Steve Ellis's *Chaucer: 'The Canterbury Tales'* (1998).[2] Gail Ashton's *Chaucer: 'The Canterbury Tales'* (1998) and Peter Brown's *Chaucer at Work* (1994) give discussion, practical examples and helpful exercises in critical study.

As we have seen, early readings such as that of Kittredge emphasized the 'human comedy' and 'roadside drama' of the *Canterbury Tales*.[3] For the New Critics, the *Tales* were an excellent example of sophisticated literary irony, created through the interplay of tales and tellers. The open-ended, ambiguous structures of the work lent themselves especially well to this kind of literary analysis. Robertson and his school, by contrast, offered exegetical readings, while the 1960s brought new interest in theoretical approaches to the tales, especially in terms of rhetoric and poetics; subsequent criticism opened out to consider socio-political and aesthetic contexts, as well as literary ones, while psychoanalysis, feminism, gender and queer theory offered new modes of analysis.[4] More technical studies have also continued: N. F. Blake and Charles A. Owen have both written full-length studies of the manuscript tradition.

The issue of the unity of the *Canterbury Tales* stands out as having received the most critical attention over the course of the last century. Thematic studies fall into two kinds: those that eschew or to some extent circumvent this question to concentrate on individual tales, and those that address either the tales as a whole, or a representative group of tales. Central to the issue of unity has been the question of order: critics have argued both for the order of the Ellesmere manuscript (used in the *Riverside Chaucer*), and for that of the Chaucer Society text.[5] Allen and Moritz in *A Distinction of Stories* (1981) root their argument in medieval notions of unity; Helen Cooper in *The Structure of the Canterbury Tales* (1983), by contrast, presents Chaucer as experimenting with juxtaposition of tales, and the order therefore as inherently unstable. Jerome Mandel, in *Building the Fragments of the 'Canterbury Tales'* (1992), presents a new theory of order based on the traditional groupings of tales. Critical studies have also addressed the issue of unity more generally, as in Donald Howard's *The Idea of the 'Canterbury Tales'* (1976). The notion of the roadside drama sustained, for example, in R. M. Lumiansky's *Of Sondry Folk* (1955), was developed by Ralph Baldwin in *The Unity of the 'Canterbury Tales'* (1955), who presented the notion of pilgrimage and the accompanying moral development as the ordering principle; such interpretations are related to the allegorical interpretations offered by D. W. Robertson and his school.[6] More recently, William E. Rogers in *Upon the Ways* (1986), has offered a useful study of the progression of the thematic emphases of the fragments.

C. David Benson goes beyond the traditional dramatic theory to argue that the 'extraordinary variety [of the tales] ought not to be attributed to the psyches of the pilgrims but to the different styles of the poems'; '*The Canterbury Tales* is not a dramatic clash of different pilgrims but a literary contest among different poets'.[7] Alfred David considers the interrelation of morality and poetics, 'sentence and solaas', to suggest that by using the frame narrative of the pilgrimage, Chaucer provides himself with a range of social types and associated literary conventions, and thus 'is able to escape his moral obligations as a poet'.[8] For David, Chaucer can both 'hold the fundamental beliefs of his age and nevertheless create an image of man that exists beyond all faiths and all times...a vision that has the energy and vitality of life itself'.[9] Paul Ruggiers, in *The Art of the 'Canterbury Tales'* (1965), links the drama and moral aspects of the *Canterbury Tales* to the notion of Gothic structure, and examines the interplay of different kinds of tale – comedy, irony and romance. This notion of the Gothic has been an especially powerful one in criticism of the *Canterbury Tales*, since it allows neatly for the multiplicity and encyclopedic nature of the tales.[10] Robert M. Jordan's *Chaucer and the Shape of Creation* (1967), discussed in chapter 8, employs medieval aesthetic theory to analyse the tales. Related to this approach is V. A. Kolve's study of the first five *Canterbury Tales* (1984) in terms of medieval iconography.

Recent considerations emphasize especially the play between Chaucer's unique vision and the conventions of his time, particularly in terms of genre. The *Canterbury Tales* can very persuasively be viewed as an experiment in literary genre, and genre theory has played an important role in contemporary criticism of the *Tales*, just as it has in criticism of the dream vision poetry. Helen Cooper (quoted in chapter 8) considers the notion of the story collection; Jill Mann discusses the *Tales* as medieval estates satire, 'a neglected medieval genre', placing Chaucer's pilgrims in relation to the social stereotypes of such satire, and the attitudes associated with them – anti-clericalism, anti-feminism, chivalry.[11] Various critics have written on Chaucer's use of particular genres. T. W. Craik, in *Chaucer's Comic Tales* (1964), offers lucid, sympathetic readings that demonstrate the sophistication of Chaucer as poet, and the ways the tales move beyond their imagined tellers; John Hines considers the comic tales in terms of the English *fabliau* tradition.[12] Susan Crane (1994) offers a thought-provoking study of gender and romance in the *Canterbury Tales*. Robert W. Hanning considers how the story collection both gave Chaucer the possibility of 'mimetic accuracy' and represented 'a literary structure offering maximum possibilities to demonstrate artistic virtuosity and control'.[13] As we have seen, there have also been numerous studies of Chaucer's 'auctoritees', the writers that so often underlie his own work, and of the intellectual contexts more generally.

Historical criticism is flourishing, as the numerous critical studies of Chaucer's sources and social, literary and intellectual contexts demonstrate.[14] Early historical studies, which sought either to identify the pilgrims, such as that of Manly's *Some New Light on Chaucer* (1926), or explain the tales through detailed historical reference, as did Curry's *Chaucer and the Medieval Sciences* (1960) and Bowden's *Commentary on the 'General Prologue'* (1967), have largely been superseded by more sophisticated and theoretically informed considerations of the various discourses with which the tales engage – religious, philosophical, legal, as well as literary. S. H. Rigby's *Chaucer in Context* (1996) surveys different approaches to historical contexts, and the very different 'Chaucers' who emerge – allegorical and humanist, misogynist and feminist. Terry Jones adds a new twist to contextual criticism in his study *Chaucer's Knight* (1980), which aims to demonstrate that the Knight would in fact have been a mercenary, whose reputation was a good deal less 'parfit' than it seems and whose tale is thus to be questioned. W. A. Davenport's *Chaucer and His English Contemporaries* (1988) considers Chaucer in light of his English literary contemporaries. David Wallace, in *Chaucerian Polity* (1997), treats mercantile and artistic exchange and relations between country and city, England and the Continent; Seth Lerer in *Chaucer and His Readers* (1993)

The Canterbury Tales: An Overview

examines the relation of Chaucer and his fifteenth-century readers. Particularly interesting is the study by Peter Brown and Andrew Butcher, *The Age of Saturn* (1991), which both argues for the value of traditional scholarship and employs a range of contemporary perspectives to effect 'the reintegration of Chaucer's writings with the social and political life of the later fourteenth century', and thus create a sense of 'the *mentalité* which informs both Chaucer and his audience'.[15]

Jones's study of Chaucer's Knight not only shows the power of historical criticism, but also the desire to read the tales in terms of the individual psychologies of their tellers – to the extent that H. Marshall Leicester feels the need to argue directly: 'there is no Wife of Bath'.[16] Undoubtedly, it is the Wife of Bath who has attracted most criticism of the psychological type, with the Pardoner a close second. Leicester's study *The Disenchanted Self* (1990) aims to deconstruct the notion of the Canterbury pilgrimage, to demonstrate the absence of apparently 'real' characters in the narrative tissue of rhetoric and poetics, and to show that 'the poem is a set of texts that are about the subjectivity of their speakers in the technical sense'.[17]

Perhaps most fruitful in recent considerations of the *Tales* as drama has been the notion of game, which usefully captures the interplay of tales and tellers. Charles A. Owen writes:

> The literal reality of a road, of men and women, of the storytelling and the comment it occasions, of, finally, an organized game, a contest, imitates successfully the complex interrelationships of a society; it generates experienced values that transcend the society and even rational definition.[18]

This idea has been taken up by various critics since, in terms of its socio-historical and poetic relevance. Peggy Knapp views the work as a 'social contest', its discourse related to the social relations and dialects of the speakers: she examines, for instance, how the *Knight's Tale*, which 'enunciates the official medieval representation of its social organization', becomes part of the pilgrims' 'game' and thus 'how texts interact with the social formations within which they function'; Carl Lindahl considers the play of 'folkloric patterns'.[19] John Ganim in *Chaucerian Theatricality* (1990) uses Bakhtinian notions of carnival to offer a dramatic reading. Laura Kendrick in *Chaucerian Play* (1988) employs psychological, psychoanalytical and anthropological models to analyse the 'play' of Chaucer's pathetic and comic fictions and the subversive nature of game-playing.

Closely related to the notions of drama and theatre in Chaucer are ideas of performance and rhetoric, the subjects of Jordan and Patterson (see chapter 8), as well as David Lawton in his study of *Chaucer's Narrators* (1985). Storytelling and performance are examined in, for example, Leonard Michael

Koff's *Chaucer and the Art of Storytelling* (1988). In one sense, to analyse rhetoric deconstructs a text, but in another it allows for critical engagement with precisely the facet of Chaucerian character that has proven fascinating across the ages – its realism. Rhetoric can readily be seen as a kind of game, and Chaucer's fictional games or poetics have been the subject of various studies, from Robert Burlin's *Chaucerian Fiction* (1977) to Earle Birney's *Essays on Chaucerian Irony* (1985), which offers a sophisticated New Critical approach to Chaucer's ambiguities by analysing the use of seven different types of irony. Robert Myles examines the *Canterbury Tales* in metaphysical terms in *Chaucerian Realism* (1994); J. E. Jost's study of *Chaucer's Humor* (1994) contains an interesting collection of essays, such as Judith Tschann's discussion of Chaucerian scatology and its evocation of a sense of temporality, of 'our time-bound life in the flesh'.[20]

Unsurprisingly too, consideration of individual themes has been sustained – most of all, those of love and marriage, though through the lenses of feminist and gender theory they have been rewritten in ways that Kittredge, the first to note the 'marriage group' of tales, might scarcely recognize. Arlyn Diamond was one of the first to question the truth of Gavin Douglas's statement about Chaucer, 'For he was evir (God wait) all womanis frend', and there have since been numerous studies for and against this view.[21] Central to criticism on the *Canterbury Tales* have been the general works on Chaucer's writing of women and gender by Carolyn Dinshaw, Priscilla Martin, Jill Mann and Elaine Tuttle Hansen; Mann and Dinshaw are discussed in chapter 8. Margaret Hallissy considers medieval states of womanhood in *Clean Maids, True Wives, Steadfast Widows* (1993). Anna Laskaya addresses gender more generally: for her, 'Chaucer's text is homosocial – written by a man, primarily about men, and primarily for men', although many critics have found a proto-feminist in Chaucer.[22] Religious themes have also attracted a good deal of interest, most particularly in terms of how they are both undercut through tales like the Pardoner's and upheld in devout tales such as that of the Second Nun. Roger Ellis considers 'the tension between the content and meaning of a narrative' as 'a vital and informing principle of religious art'; John M. Hill attempts to reconcile the moral and experimental Chaucer.[23]

Studies of individual tales, like those treating the work as a whole, range through various approaches: technical (considering, for example, sources, manuscripts, language), historical, exegetical, iconographic, cultural, socio-historical, political, thematic, deconstructionist, psychoanalytical, post-colonial, feminist or queer. The bibliography includes a selection of journal articles using a variety of critical perspectives. Despite the importance of the issue of unity, close reading of individual tales or groups of tales has played an essential role in Chaucer criticism, demonstrating the sophistication of the tales in their own right, and proving how far the *Canterbury Tales* is from simply being a 'roadside drama'. Indeed it is a paradox of the tales that despite their realism and the strength of different narratorial voices, their complexity and literary originality far exceeds that of any but the most skilled, inventive and literate of tellers, Chaucer himself. Thus the *Knight's Tale* is both an appropriately epic romance and undercuts romance convention; the *Miller's Tale* is a brilliant *fabliau* in its own terms and a witty subversion of the *Knight's Tale*, a subversion further enhanced by the *Reeve's Tale*. The *Franklin's Tale*, far from being that of a 'burel man', raises complex existential questions regarding the self, human relations and morality; the *Merchant's Tale* is both bawdy and full of literary play on clerical misogyny. The *Wife of Bath's Tale*, contrary to the Wife's bold and frankly sexual persona, is a subtly questioning romance from a proto-feminist perspective. Religious tales, too, move in and out of their fictional contexts: the unknown *Second Nun's Tale* represents a masterful, empowering legend of Cecilia; the *Prioress's Tale* exploits melodrama and religious conventions in ways that disturbingly oppose her self-presentation; the *Pardoner's Tale* exposes his fraudulence and offers a chilling portrayal of sin and death. The drama of the pilgrims is undeniable, but equally the art of the tales challenges and moves beyond this fictional frame, to leave us, finally, with a sense of Chaucer's literary genius.

Notes

1   See also Winthrop Wetherbee, *Chaucer: 'The Canterbury Tales'* (Cambridge University Press, Cambridge, 1989), J. Norton Smith, *Geoffrey Chaucer* (Routledge, London, 1974), and the older but sound introductions of Trevor Whittock, *A Reading of the 'Canterbury Tales'* (Cambridge University Press, Cambridge, 1968), and Derek Traversi, *'The Canterbury Tales': A Reading* (Bodley Head, London, 1983). There is an excellent Norton Critical Edition of nine tales and the *Prologue*, ed. V. A. Kolve and Glending Olson (W. W. Norton, New York, 1989), which includes source material and extracts from some influential critical works.
2   For the original casebook, see J. J. Anderson, ed., *Chaucer: 'The Canterbury Tales'* (Macmillan, Basingstoke, ed., 1974); for the *New Casebook*, see Valerie Allen and Ares Axiotis, eds, *Chaucer* (Macmillan, Basingstoke, 1997). See also Burrow, ed., *Geoffrey Chaucer: A Critical Anthology* (Harmondsworth, Penguin Books, 1969), Richard Schoeck and Jerome Taylor, eds, *Chaucer Criticism* (University of Notre Dame Press, Notre Dame, 1960–1), and George D. Economou, *Geoffrey Chaucer: Contemporary Studies in Literature* (McGraw-Hill, New York, 1975). Source material may be found in W. F. Bryan and G. Dempster, *Sources and Analogues of Chaucer's 'Canterbury Tales'* (Routledge and Kegan Paul, London, 1958) and Robert P. Miller, ed., *Chaucer: Sources and Backgrounds* (Oxford University Press,

New York, 1977). On the *Canterbury Tales* and Boccaccio's *Decameron* see N. S. Thompson, *Chaucer, Boccaccio and the Debate of Love* (Oxford University Press, Oxford, 1996).

3 See also William Witherle Lawrence, *Chaucer and the 'Canterbury Tales'* (Columbia University Press, New York, 1950); Helen Storm Corsa, *Chaucer: Poet of Mirth and Morality* (University of Notre Dame Press, Notre Dame, IN, 1964).

4 The collection of essays edited by Donald M. Rose, *New Perspectives in Chaucer Criticism* (Pilgrim Books, Norman, OK, 1981), engages with the relation between Chaucer and literary theory.

5 See N. F. Blake, *The Textual Tradition of the 'Canterbury Tales'* (Edward Arnold, London, 1985), Charles A. Owen, Jr, *The Manuscripts of the 'Canterbury Tales'* (D. S. Brewer, Cambridge, 1991), and the work of Benson in the *Riverside Chaucer*.

6 See also Christian Zacher, *Curiosity and Pilgrimage: The Literature of Discovery in Fourteenth Century England* (Johns Hopkins University Press, Baltimore, ML, 1976), and R. E. Kaske, 'Chaucer's Marriage Group,' in Jerome Mitchell and William Provost, eds, *Chaucer the Love Poet* (University of Georgia Press, Athens, 1973): Kaske sustains Kittredge's notion of a marriage group.

7 C. David Benson, *Chaucer's Drama of Style: Poetic Variety and Contrast in the 'Canterbury Tales'* (University of North Carolina Press, Chapel Hill, 1986), 20.

8 Alfred David, *The Strumpet Muse: Art and Morals in Chaucer's Poetry* (Indiana University Press, Bloomington, 1976), 76, 75.

9 Ibid., 5.

10 See also the work of Muscatine and David, as well as Robert O. Payne, *The Key of Remembrance: A Study of Chaucer's Poetics* (Greenwood Press, Westport, CT, 1973 [1963]), Donald Howard, *The Idea of the 'Canterbury Tales'* (University of California Press, Berkeley, 1976), Joerg Fichte, *Chaucer's 'Art Poetical': A Study in Chaucerian Poetics* (Gunter Narr, Tübingen, 1980), Traugott Lawler, *The One and the Many in the 'Canterbury Tales'* (Archon Books, Hamden, CT, 1980) and L. M. Sklute, *Virtue of Necessity: Inconclusiveness and Narrative Form in Chaucer's Poetry* (Ohio State University, Columbus, 1984).

11 Jill Mann. *Chaucer and Medieval Estates Satire* (Cambridge University Press, Cambridge, 1973), 1.

12 See also Janette Richardson's study of imagery in the *fabliaux*, *Blameth Nat Me: A Study of Imagery in Chaucer's Fabliaux* (Mouton, The Hague, 1970).

13 Robert W. Hanning, 'The Theme of Art and Life', in Economou, *Geoffrey Chaucer*, 20

14 See chapter 1, p. 16.

15 Peter Brown and Andrew Butcher, *The Age of Saturn: Literature and History in the 'Canterbury Tales'* (Blackwell Publishers, Oxford, 1991), 1, 18.

16 H. Marshall Leicester, 'Of a Fire in the Dark: Public and Private Feminism in the Wife of Bath's Tale', *Women's Studies* 11 (1984), 157–78.

17 H. Marshall Leicester, *The Disenchanted Self: Representing the Subject in the 'Canterbury Tales'* (University of California Press, Berkeley, 1990), 15.

18 Charles A. Owen, *Pilgrimage and Storytelling in the 'Canterbury Tales': The Dialectic of 'Ernest' and 'Game'* (University of Oklahoma Press, Norman, 1977), 9.

19 Peggy Knapp, *Chaucer and the Social Contest* (Routledge, New York, 1990), 15, 17; Carl Lindahl, *Earnest Games: Folkloric Patterns in the 'Canterbury Tales'* (Indiana University Press, Bloomington, 1987).
20 Judith Tschann, 'The Mind Distended: The Retraction, Miller's Tale and Summoner's Tale', in J. E. Jost, ed., *Chaucer's Humor: Critical Essays* (Garland, New York, 1994), 350.
21 Arlyn Diamond, 'Chaucer's Women and Women's Chaucer', in Arlyn Diamond and Lee R. Edwards, *The Authority of Experience: Essays in Feminist Criticism* (University of Massachusetts Press, 1977).
22 Anna Laskaya, *Chaucer's Approach to Gender in the 'Canterbury Tales'* (D. S. Brewer, Cambridge, 1995), 4.
23 Roger Ellis, *Patterns of Religious Narrative in the 'Canterbury Tales'* (Croom Helm, London, 1986), 37; John M. Hill, *Chaucerian Belief: The Poetics of Reverence and Delight* (Yale University Press, New Haven, CT, 1991).

8

The *Canterbury Tales*: Critical Extracts

The Unity of the *Canterbury Tales*

Robert M. Jordan

In this extract Jordan addresses the seminal issue of unity in the Canterbury Tales. *The first part of his analysis considers the attempts of several decades of critics to 'unify' the poem. Jordan notices the difference between this work and the modern fictional forms with which we are familiar – novels or collections of short stories: the* Canterbury Tales *'invites piecemeal criticism; it also invites the total view'. While it is possible and fruitful, indeed necessary, to analyse individual tales, they must also be seen as part of a whole. Jordan sets the example for much recent criticism by emphasizing the limits of the 'roadside drama' approach, particularly given the uncertain order of the tales, and notes too the problematic nature of allegorical readings: 'the editors' desire to smooth the road to Canterbury eventuated in a journey Chaucer's pilgrims never made'.*

Jordan argues that the Canterbury Tales *should be seen in terms of 'medieval aesthetic theory' and 'Gothic structure'. As we have seen, the notion of Gothic, asymmetrical beauty, often dependent on contrasts and disjunction rather than formal unity, is particularly useful in relation to Chaucer's work, and nowhere more so than the* Canterbury Tales. *Jordan characterizes the parts as not fused together but 'accommodated', complementary rather than forming an organic whole, so that the tales themselves maintain their integrity just as the frame narrative does. This kind of fiction differs radically from the modern novel, which depends upon a unity of perspective (Jordan identifies this principle as post-Jamesian) and a creation of 'consistent, unbroken illusion'. In many ways the* Canterbury Tales *is more like a postmodern novel, drawing attention to its fictional status in a self-conscious manner. This is achieved through the narrator's over-insistence on his truthfulness and the repeated references to readers or audience. As Jordan notes, this is also a feature of* Troilus and Criseyde, *where the narrator's commentary filters the story:*

Jordan endorses unquestioningly Donaldson's distinction between Chaucer the poet and Chaucer the narrator. Yet although in the Canterbury Tales *the narrator is fleshed out as a Canterbury pilgrim, and his approach is conspicuously naive, there still is a sense in which he is a performative voice: his voice surely merges with Chaucer's in the telling of the tales, and in some of the ironic commentary, while we often draw our conclusions from the gap between his interpretation and the material he records. Jordan argues for the* Canterbury Tales *as a writerly text, though he notes that the work aims in part at an audience familiar with Chaucer the poet; his argument suggests the status of the tales both as book and oral text.*

Jordan brings out well the reductive nature of analysing the work as a 'human comedy', especially the attempt to explain the tales by inventing fictional lives for the pilgrims, a process that can lead to extreme flights of fancy – from Kittredge's vivid imaginings to Manly's attempt to identify each of the pilgrims. Rather, Jordan argues, the work moves back and forth between the Chaucerian voice and the fictional voices of the pilgrims: discrepancies are not explained by imagining them as real people with complex pasts, but by recognizing that the illusion is never complete. The interchanges between pilgrims cannot be seen as organic, unified pieces of fiction, but instead move in and out of fictive voices. Similarly, the tales cannot be seen purely as a function of their narrators, about whom, in some cases, we have little or no knowledge – the Second Nun or the Nun's Priest, for instance. The tales are complex, sophisticated pieces of writing in their own right, which frequently move beyond characterization of their tellers. The narrative works like a medieval painting, using a series of different perspectives and combining the symbolic and the naturalistic.

Robert M. Jordan, from 'The Unity of the *Canterbury Tales*' in *Chaucer and the Shape of Creation: The Aesthetic Possibilities of Inorganic Structure.* Harvard University Press, Cambridge, MA, 1967.

Our study of the principles of medieval aesthetic theory and Gothic structure would rather suggest that the basis for a valid unified view of the *Canterbury Tales* is to be found not in the idea of 'fusion' but in that of 'accommodation.' From a Gothic viewpoint the *Tales* can be understood both as a pilgrimage (literal *and* spiritual) and a compound of tales. The mode of relationship between whole and parts can be one which does not at any time rob the parts of integrity and completeness within their own formal outlines. Nor need the part, in its wholeness and complexity, detract from the integrity of the whole. In order thus to have it both ways, Chaucer's art must pay a price, or so it may seem to the modern reader; the price is hard outlines, imperfect resolutions, exposed seams, contradictory viewpoints – in short, conspicuous absence of the primary attributes of post-Jamesian fiction.

I think the most fundamental of [the] distinctions between Chaucerian and Jamesian canons of literary art concerns attitude toward fictional illusion. There is ample evidence to indicate that Chaucer was thoroughly indifferent toward a quality which modern theory has conditioned us to regard as indispensable to good fiction, namely, consistent, unbroken illusion. In fact, we have seen that illusion-breaking is as essential to Chaucer's artistry as illusion-making. It is in this context that I wish to reexamine the 'roadside drama' theory. Since that concept of the *Tales* posits a consistent dramatic illusion, it provides a convenient measure of Chaucer's departures from his assumed practice.

Efforts to show how consistently 'in character' are the actions, expostulations, and narrations of the pilgrims are based upon the assumption that Chaucer is projecting an illusion unified in fictionalized time and space. The fact that some of the pilgrims, notably the Pardoner and the Wife of Bath, talk a good deal about themselves and are therefore 'characterized' by what they say adds support to the 'dramatic' view. The logic of this concept has created an attractive image of the poem as 'an organic whole, and that whole ... essentially dramatic.'[1] To the focal point of the Canterbury road on an April evening all persons and events are supposed to be referable; and, more important, incidents and speeches are supposed to characterize the pilgrims and thereby substantiate meaningful dramatic action. The General Prologue in many ways encourages these assumptions, but a close look at what goes on in some prominent passages, first in the General Prologue and then elsewhere, will indicate that Chaucer's sense of illusion is more flexible – not to say inconsistent – than the dramatic theory would allow.

The realistic illusion of the Canterbury road in April is supported by a passage near the end of the General Prologue in which Chaucer appears to be moving out of fiction altogether and into journalism:

> But first I pray yow, of youre curteisye,
> That ye n'arette* it nat my vileynye,*   *attribute   *rudeness
> Thogh that I pleynly speke in this mateere,
> To telle yow hir wordes and hir cheere,
> Ne thogh I speke hir wordes proprely.
> For this ye knowen al so wel as I,
> Whoso shal telle a tale after a man,
> He moot reherce as ny as evere he kan
> Everich a word, if it be in his charge,
> Al speke he never so rudeliche and large,
> Or ellis he moot telle his tale untrewe,
> Or feyne* thyng, or fynde wordes newe ...   *feign
> (725–36)

It has been evident from the very beginning of the narrative that the role of objective witness is being assumed by the poet, and therefore, strictly speaking, the present passage is totally superfluous according to the requirements of illusion. Here Chaucer deliberately raises the issue of 'truth' by insisting so strongly and so unnecessarily upon the authenticity of his report. The effect is, of course, calculated, and here as in innumerable other instances we recognize the presence of the poet behind the reporter. The humor of the passage arises from the play of these two viewpoints, since the excess of the reporter's earnestness in expounding the obvious is apparent only from the more knowing viewpoint of the poet, the latter, 'superior' viewpoint being the one which governs the passage. The reader's imaginative experience is complicated and active, almost violent, for it consists not only of being absorbed in the immediate surface that is the reporter's perspective, but also an abrupt *disillusionment* and ultimate transference of imaginative focus to the poet's perspective, that of better sense, finer discrimination, and fuller awareness of propriety. At places like this the poem in a sense divides. The effect is similar to what we have observed in *Troilus* and similarly can be explained in two ways, depending upon one's feelings about Chaucer's role as narrator in the poem. Donaldson has differentiated between the undramatized, 'invisible' poet, standing outside the fiction, and the concrete pilgrim-reporter projected into it.[2] Then it becomes possible to describe a characteristic quality of Chaucer's fiction in terms of an observable shifting of focus, as the reader's attention is frequently shifted from illusion to actuality, from Chaucer the wide-eyed pilgrim-reporter to Chaucer the wise and witty poet. Bronson, on the other hand, chooses to effect an imaginative shift of the entire enterprise from a reading experience to a listening one.[3] We then imagine ourselves an audience of Chaucer's contemporaries attending a court recitation by the poet. When Chaucer apologizes – in the name of authenticity – for certain forthcoming 'rude' passages we perceive the twinkle in his eye and we smile because *we know* Geoffrey Chaucer and we know he is not a short-witted reporter but a shrewd and playful poet who has written many a lecherous lay. Though I believe, for reasons indicated earlier, that the more fruitful critical approach is one that deals with the poem as a reading experience rather than as a listening one, I find the differences between Donaldson and Bronson of less than fundamental importance, for both critics perceive, each in his own manner of analysis, the doubleness of focus which plays one sense of the facts against another.

Such a perception is not available, however, from the standpoint of the roadside-drama interpretation, with its exclusive focus on the level of the pilgrim-reporter. The passage in question, when seen in the single focus of the drama theory, is deprived of its range of playfulness. It is explained thus: 'The effect of this mock-apology is ... a whetting of the reader's appetite for what is to follow.'[4] But who is the reader whose appetite is whetted by this means? True enough, we are all irresistibly drawn to the account of the night's happenings, and the mock apology is one means of increasing its appeal. But this is only the direct and obvious appeal to a reader or listener like Harry Bailly, whose wit, like the speaker's, is short, and whose appetite for unusual and lurid truths — especially if they are firmly authenticated — is unlimited. Chaucer's deliberate juggling with illusions makes it clear that he is reaching beyond the naive to readers whose wit is long.

Chaucer would expect his reader — as he expected his own immediate audience — to recognize the deception and appreciate the artistry behind it. Chaucer is not simply disclaiming responsibility for the tales; he is disclaiming art. But even as he insists upon his fidelity to fact he has ensnared us in fiction. The pilgrim designated 'Chaucer' is no more and no less 'real' than those among whom he moves, who are designated Knight, Miller, Harry Bailly, etc. The poet whose art has lived gloriously for six centuries is not the maker of the Tale of Sir Thopas, but the maker of the maker of that tale. Though the distinction between the poet-and pilgrim-selves of Chaucer is rejected by some critics on the ground that it makes a factitious or overly subtle fragmentation of a normal, complex personality, such a distinction at least prevents the error of taking 'Chaucer' as a real person walking among imagined figures. And it prevents the complementary misconception which the 'roadside drama' theory has proliferated, namely, that the fictional characters are real persons consorting with the poet Chaucer. In such a view there is no fictional illusion at all, and the only limits to interpretation are the limits of the critic's understanding not of Chaucer's poetry but of 'people' or life in general.

Rather than accept the pilgrim-Chaucer's protestations of truth at face value, the critic must make the effort to define Chaucer's sense of illusion and the distinctive assumptions it was based upon. It is instructive to see how far the roadside-drama theory has deterred us in this enterprise and carried us into psychological and historical speculation.

A severely compressed synopsis of the development of the drama theory must run somewhat as follows: The *locus classicus* is Kittredge's pronouncement that 'the Canterbury Pilgrimage is...a Human Comedy, and...the stories are merely long speeches expressing, directly or indirectly, the characters of the several persons.'[5] Eleven years after Kittredge, in 1926, Manly published *Some New Light on Chaucer*. Despite the author's frequent efforts to emphasize Chaucer's artistry and poetic skill, the effect of the book was to advance interest in the real persons upon whom Chaucer based his pilgrims. Thus, Bowden's *Commentary on the General Prologue to the Canterbury Tales* of 1948 could cite a large body of historical data which, as in the typical case of the Pardoner, 'inclines us even more decidedly to the belief that the Pardoner must have been known to the poet and at least to some of his audience.'[6] Clearly our subject has become people Chaucer knew, and in this dialectic the means for evaluating art has been usurped by the means for verifying chronicle. Finally, Lumiansky's *Of Sundry Folk* of 1955 establishes 'The Dramatic Principle of the *Canterbury Tales*' and elucidates 'the dramatic techniques by means of which the Pilgrims are kept as the center of focus throughout the *Tales*.' Furthering our absorption in the 'reality' of the roadside drama is this critic's manner of speaking of the tales as 'performances' by actor-pilgrims. And finally we have Baldwin's appropriation of the dramatic principle, as described above.

The drama theory can illuminate only what goes on among the pilgrims, since it limits itself to the perspective of the 'stage' as viewed by one of the participants, the pilgrim-reporter Chaucer. The dramatic critic can point out that the interplay between Host and Pilgrims 'is characterized by interesting dramatic overtones that include a rather subtle play of human relationships...'[7] But he cannot include the subtle play of human relationships between ourselves and the lively-minded poet. Chaucer is indeed one of the actors, but we are expected to see through this often gauche figure to the artful poet, who is delicately shaping illusion and inviting our appreciation of his skill. I do not suggest that this typically Chaucerian posturing is completely accounted for as an appeal to the reader's sophistication – there is more behind it, as I shall try to show presently – but it should be recognized that this dimension of the poem is inaccessible to the reader who is too deeply involved in the 'drama.'

To caution against imaginative surrender to a fictive scene may seem perverse, but not so, I think, when we understand that art can – and Chaucer's does – appeal to responses other than those isolated and identified by Coleridge. Chaucer induces us *un*willingly to suspend disbelief. His is an art of the conscious mind, and though much of the time we can't help responding instinctively, in the manner of Harry Bailly, Chaucer makes certain that we come out of it and recognize where we have been. Nor is this simply a quibble over the obvious. Of course we all know it is all fiction, but the *Canterbury Tales* is not to be read as though it really were drama, that is, as though the exclusive locus of involvement were the road to Canterbury and the ideal reader a Harry Bailly. Nor can the *Tales* be read as though it were a post-romantic novel, which *is* dramatic to the extent that artistic success depends upon unmitigated immersion in the world of the fiction. With Faulkner we really are there, on the road to Jefferson. And with Conrad we really are confronting Marlow who really was there. But with Chaucer we are there, on the road to Canterbury, only some of the time, since Chaucer is there, in the role of reporter, only some of the time. The rest of the time, with his larger sensibility, he is standing back and remarking, virtually out loud, how wonderfully convincing fiction is. Such doubleness of attitude, if judged from a naturalistic point of view, would indicate one of two unfavorable verdicts: either Chaucer is too naive and limited to be able to sustain an illusion, or he is too perverse and unromantic to be willing to accede to the spell of his own fiction. But Chaucer has not been called naive ("rude") or perverse since the prenaturalistic eighteenth century. And although the roadside drama has been read as a sustained illusion, this has been accomplished only at the cost of ignoring the many clear instances in which Chaucer consciously undermines his own achievement of illusion. Only recently has the question of illusion been seriously raised.[8]

Injudicious involvement in the drama has led to some bizarre interpretations of the poem, interpretations based upon a credulousness comparable to that of Harry Bailly lamenting the fate of the Physician's Virginia, or the Reeve taking up arms against an account of a carpenter cuckolded. The significant fact is, of course, that Chaucer has built this level of naïveté into the poem. A proper reading requires that this level of awareness itself be taken into critical account. But the larger perspective must be recognized, that in which we make contact with the poet and acknowledge, with him, the limits of the illusion. However convincing the scene is – and it is wonderfully convincing – Chaucer continually, and in varying ways, calls attention to the boundaries of the fiction. In Gothic fashion, he capitalizes the lineaments of construction, openly displaying his maker's art and achieving thereby a range of aesthetic effect not possible in organicist fiction. In Chaucerian fiction, in which illusion itself is often the subject and is *ipso facto* limited, it is inappropriate to exercise the kind of 'creative' criticism that collaborates with the writer of naturalistic fiction in piecing together hints and symbols which explain the effects of an undepicted and obscure past upon the depicted, vivid present. Rather than approach Chaucer naturalistically, criticism ought to elaborate this very distinct difference: the limitations which Chaucer imposes upon illusion sharply curtail commerce with past time, whereas in later fiction the effect of unlimited illusion is to open the past to the reader's scrutiny. Critical reading of later fiction becomes in many respects an exercise of imaginative ingenuity comparable to the writer's creative effort. Chaucer's pilgrims have been subjected to 'creative criticism' of this kind, and as a result many of them have moved outside their illusionary characters entirely.[9] They have assumed the infinite and unpredictable variety of 'real life,' including psychological life, and life determined or explained by a past assumed to be accessible to the critic.

The assumptions of the drama theory are that inconsistencies of characterization are due to natural causes, not to the limitations of a particular literary mode of representation. A good case in point is provided by explanations of the quarrel between the Miller and the Reeve. Following is one 'dramatic' critic's approving paraphrase of another's findings: 'It seems likely that the

Miller–Reeve acquaintanceship must be of long standing, that the Miller worked years ago as servant boy in the Reeve's household at the time when the Reeve, then a carpenter, was made a cuckold by a cleric...the Reeve probably knows the content of the coming story and is therefore able to tell the Miller that he will be both sinful and foolish to ridicule or insult any man and to circulate such a rumor about a wife.'[10] Clearly we have leapt over the boundaries of fiction as we pursue the 'motivations' of this quarrel down the murky corridors of the past, the real historical past, be it noted, not a past that is part of Chaucer's illusion. And indeed this is no longer illusion at all. We have fallen into Chaucer's enticingly baited trap and taken game for earnest. A moment's further examination of the passage in question will make even clearer that the primary interest lies not in what takes place between Miller and Reeve but in what takes place between the double-visaged Chaucer and his audience.

There is no doubt about the outcome of this exchange: the Miller retains complete mastery; the Reeve makes a fool of himself. The measure of the Reeve's foolishness is his readiness to commit the primary error of perception, to confuse fiction with reality, game with earnest. The Miller has only to announce the subject of his tale – '...a legende and a lyf / Both of a carpenter and of his wyf, / How that a clerk hath set the wrightes cappe' – and the Reeve leaps to protest, not on the possibly legitimate grounds that ribaldry is offensive, but on the irrelevant and indefensible grounds that the unheard tale is not a tale at all. The Reeve's impulsive and violent protest against what he takes to be public charges of cuckoldry and adultery reveals his own churlish inability to distinguish between actual instance and fictional generalization. In this exchange the Miller gains superiority not through his knowledge of the Reeve's past experience of matrimony – as maintained by dramatically oriented criticism – but by the immediate demonstration of a higher quality of mind. It is the shrewd and urbane play of the Miller's logic that proves him the master of his blustering antagonist. Says the Miller, with a very delicate play of nuance:

>   Leve* brother Osewold,   *dar
>   Who hath no wyf, he is no cokewold.
>   But I say nat therfore that thou art oon.
>   (3151–3)

The lines which follow, and conclude the Miller's Prologue, embody the pilgrim-reporter's second 'apology,' in which we are cautioned against attributing the Miller's ensuing 'harlotrie' to the conscientious intermediary. Our reporter concludes, 'Avyseth yow, and put me out of blame; / And eek men shal nat maken ernest of game.' The humor emerges from the clash of two discernible points of view. Chaucer counts on the reader to distance himself sufficiently to perceive Chaucer the reporter trying to deny the identity of Chaucer the poet. Commenting in the single perspective of the drama theory, Lowes has seen here simply 'Chaucer' warning squeamish readers to skip over the harlotry of the churls.[11] But squeamishness is not the *poet's* point – if it were he obviously could not have written the tales. The deluded reader is in a position exactly analogous to that of the Reeve. He, too, takes game for earnest, skips over the 'indecent' tales, and remains the unaware victim of a superior wit. Of course, no actual reader is completely taken in – despite Lowes' fears to the contrary – but the drama theory posits this level of involvement as the ideal. Though this surrender to the 'reality' of the journey is a large and essential part of the reading experience, it is not all of it. We should be equally responsive to the appearances of the illusion-making poet, however deceptive these appearances may be.

The scene we have been considering illustrates another weakness of the drama theory with respect to the very quality of urbanity we find displayed in the Miller. By all accounts the Miller is a man of no intellectual endowment, and in addition he is drunk. The narrator tells us three times how drunk he is; the Host says to him, 'thy wit is overcome'; and the Miller himself says, '...first I make a protestacioun / That I am dronke, I knowe it by my soun [voice].' How, then, do we explain the Miller's cool, masterful toying with the Reeve? The customary explanation is 'dramatic irony,' as illustrated by this comment: 'It may be that the Miller is...more sober than he pretends; under the guise of drunkenness he has enjoyed overriding the Host, and now he is having the fun of discomfiting the Reeve.'[12] The difficulty with this interpretation is that it indiscriminately rejects not just some but all the evidence of the text. There is no reason to suppose the Miller sober if we are told by two observers and by himself that he is drunk. If we say that his treatment of the Reeve proves him to be sober, as many critics do, we are proceeding upon the untenable premise that the pilgrims are 'real' people acting upon motives of their own which are inscrutable, even to Chaucer. The alternative is to acknowledge that the characterization of the Miller is inconsistent. On the one hand we have, in the present instance, explicit assertions, from three points of view, that the Miller is drunk; on the other hand we have his extremely adroit handling of the Reeve.

I think we move a long way toward understanding Chaucer's art when we acknowledge that disparities such as this one do occur, and quite frequently. To 'interpret' Chaucer in such a way that consistency is achieved either by suppression or by negation of data is fruitless and leads to limitless proliferation of 'versions.' We must conclude, in the present instance, that both elements of the contradiction are valid. In one moment we see the Miller as a hopelessly drunken churl, and in the next moment we see the same person as a sober and sophisticated wit. Similar shifts of characterization abound in the *Canterbury Tales*, and they cannot be brushed away in the name of such subtle effects as might be attained in another mode of fiction through dramatic irony. The Miller is not an internally motivated, organically unified character; rather is he an externally shaped composite. That he is a vital, utterly compelling figure attests not only to Chaucer's artistry but also to the possibilities of inorganic form.

The 'compositional' character of the Miller indicates the boundaries of Chaucer's narrative technique. Within this field he composes not only the pilgrim-characters but also the tales they tell and the characters and events within those tales. In the same composite fashion he brings together tales and tellers, on some occasions being more meticulous than on others in adjusting the details for consistency. Though this compositional method may appear limited and simplistic from the standpoint of organicism, it results – especially when practiced by a master like Chaucer – in a sparkling variety of formal structures, verbal styles, and moral perspectives. Sometimes the artifact, whether teller, tale, or character, seems peculiarly out of balance with itself, as in the case of the Miller, where the parts do not form a consistent whole. At other times a firmer consistency prevails, as in the case of the tale the Miller tells, though even here the unity is not of the kind which organicist criticism seeks in its own image. Within the framework of his inorganic technique, Chaucer's varieties of structural unity are many. But they follow the Gothic principle of juxtaposition. Gothic art is like a 'panoramic survey, not a one-sided, unified interpretation dominated by a single point of view.'[13] Characteristically, the total form is determined by the accumulation of individually complete elements. From this standpoint it can be said that in the *Canterbury Tales* the elements of a roadside drama are convincing in themselves; but it must also be said that the focal points they establish are constantly subject to displacement. We can say that the links of the framework at many points strain toward a naturalistic and dramatic ordonnance; however, the aesthetic character of the poem is determined by the dissonance between the dramatic and the static, not exclusively, or even mainly, by 'drama.'

Wölfflin's definition of two kinds of unity in painting clearly fits the situation confronting us in the *Canterbury Tales*. He distinguishes between 'multiple unity' (*vielheitliche Einheit*) as in a head by Dürer, whose features are sharply individuated, and 'unified unity' (*einheitliche Einheit*) as in a head by Rubens, whose features subordinate themselves to the total impression.[14] Following Wölfflin, Wylie Sypher has characterized the organizing principle of Gothic art as a multiple unity which brings together distinct but incongruent perspectives. It is a commonplace observation about paintings of the late Middle Ages that naturalistic figures are juxtaposed against symbolic background; they are not organically fused with it. Thus Sypher, speaking of a fifteenth-century painting, can point out that the Gothic figures are secular but their world is not, and that 'the proportions of the scene are alien to the men who inhabit it.'[15]

What the art historian can remind the 'dramatic' critic of Chaucer is that the background is larger than life, and also that it is part of the picture. In Chaucer's Gothic vision man's environment was not simply the English countryside but nature juxtaposed against supernature. The reality that exists beyond appearances was no less the concern of Chaucer than it was of Dante or Langland or the painters of Gothic miniatures. Chaucer's Canterbury pilgrimage, though exhibiting many of the lineaments of physical reality, was at the same time but the visible, severely limited representation of the spiritual pilgrimage of man.

Notes

1 J. L. Lowes, *Geoffrey Chaucer* (New York: Oxford University Press, 1934), p. 164.
2 E. Talbot Donaldson, 'Chaucer the Pilgrim,' *PMLA*, 69: 928–36 (1954). See also Ben Kimpel, 'The Narrator of the *Canterbury Tales*,' *ELH*, 20: 77–86 (1953); and Ralph Baldwin, *The Unity*, ch. 4, 'The Poet and the Pilgrim.'
3 Bertrand H. Bronson, *In Search of Chaucer*, pp. 25–30, 66, 67. Donald R. Howard, 'Chaucer the Man,' *PMLA*, 80: 337–43 (1965), emphasizes, with Bronson, the presence of the poet. Howard's article is further evidence that disagreement over the relationship of poet and 'narrator' is less divisive than provocative of thoughtful and illuminating analysis. Howard recognizes that Chaucer often 'masquerades' but argues that the man is always present in the stylization of his person and that this presence is dynamic, arising from the relationship between the bourgeois poet and his aristocratic audience. On the other hand, Morton W. Bloomfield, 'Authenticating Realism and the Realism of Chaucer,' *Thought*, 39: 356 (1964), though maintaining that 'the creator of these titles and comments [i.e. interruptions of the narrative] is not the pilgrim who is reporting the Canterbury pilgrimage,' nevertheless recognizes that 'he is related to him very closely,' and that in these externalized passages Chaucer 'is speaking to us from another part of his being.'
4 R. M. Lumiansky, *Of Sundry Folk: The Dramatic Principle in the Canterbury Tales* (Austin: University of Texas Press, 1955), p. 24.
5 G. L. Kittredge, *Chaucer and His Poetry* (Cambridge, MA: Harvard University Press, 1915), pp. 154–5.
6 Muriel Bowden, *Commentary on the General Prologue to the Canterbury Tales* (New York: Macmillan Company, 1948), pp. 283–4. Chaucer's real people have been further pursued by George Williams, *A New View of Chaucer* (Durham, NC, 1965).
7 *Of Sundry Folk*, p. 25.
8 See Bloomfield, 'Authenticating Realism,' which clearly defines the problem by relating Chaucer's method of 'authenticating' his fictions to the practices of other

authors and to fictional technique in general. Bloomfield points out (pp. 355–8) that Chaucer 'continually reminds us...that the poem is his creation and his world and that he is master of both,' and he observes that Chaucer is showing us both the reality *and* the unreality of his *Canterbury Tales*. My ensuing comments on the subject of illusion follow closely my earlier study, 'Chaucer's Sense of Illusion: Roadside Drama Reconsidered,' *ELH*, 29: 19–33 (1962).

9   Paull F. Baum's discussion of commentary on the Pardoner is a trenchant corrective of this kind of excess. *Chaucer: A Critical Appreciation* (Durham, NC, 1958), pp. 44–59. See also Malone, *Chapters*, pp. 172, 163–235.
10 *Of Sundry Folk*, p. 51.
11 Lowes, *Chaucer*, p. 175.
12 *Of Sundry Folk*, p. 52.
13 Arnold Hauser, quoted in Muscatine, *Chaucer and the French Tradition*, p. 167.
14 Heinrich Wölfflin, *Kunstgeschichtliche Grundbegriffe* (Munich: Hugo Bruckmann, 1915), pp. 167–210.
15 Wylie Sypher, *Four Stages of Renaissance Style* (Garden City, NY: Doubleday and Company, 1955), p. 54.

The Esthetics of this Form

Donald R. Howard

In this short extract from his study of aesthetics and unity in the Canterbury Tales, *Howard demonstrates the relation between visual and written forms, extending the frequently repeated comparison between medieval texts and Gothic architecture. Earlier in his consideration Howard explores medieval conceptions of memory as a book or encyclopedia, or a series of chambers, accessed through particular keys – images or words. Such ideas were particularly powerful in a world where oral culture remained so strong and books were rare. Much learning had to be committed to memory and the art of memory could itself be learned. In reading the* Canterbury Tales, *Howard emphasizes, memory is crucial, for the work depends on recollection of the larger frame narrative of the pilgrimage, the interaction between pilgrims, and other tales: the tales work in conjunction with each other, through echoes, contrasts and a process of accretion. In this extract Howard considers the ways in which the idea of memory gives a material form to the* Canterbury Tales: *like a 'hall of mirrors' the work is filtered through the (imagined) memory of the narrator, and in turn through the memories of individual pilgrims as they tell their tales more or less perfectly. Howard emphasizes the 'mentalistic realm' of the tales: despite the naturalistic details of the descriptions of the pilgrims, the road to Canterbury, the day and the hour, the frame is stylized and symbolic; it does not stand up to realistic scrutiny any more than the characters of the pilgrims do.*

The concept of memory allows us to perceive the tales as literary artefacts comprising 'a world of story', and hence to accept their various disjunctions and distortions, and their multiple perspectives. This notion links neatly to the idea of the Gothic, a mode that accepts, indeed demands, disjunction. At the same time, and again rather in the sense of a Gothic architectural construction, the work depends too on shared knowledge – of society, authority, books and conventional wisdom. Howard, like other critics, stresses the incompatibility of the work with a modern desire for 'clean lines', the equivalent of Jordan's notion of organic unity. He points persuasively to the enormously decorative nature of the medieval cathedral and castle, also a resonant image in literature and art. Howard also offers a more specific visual model of the way the Canterbury Tales *functions, that of a medieval illuminated initial, where the larger form of the letter is complemented, even dominated by, the inset images and stories that its shape contains. This notion of an inner and outer form is a particularly useful one for a work such as the* Canterbury Tales, *although it is not the only model. In the latter part of this chapter, Howard considers three other models, based on the images presented in the* General Prologue: *performance, pilgrimage and the image of the flower evoked by the description of springtime. He links the latter to the great rose windows of the period: the rose suggests both mutability, the fading flower of the temporal world (echoed in the comparable image of the wheel of fortune), and the circle of eternity, the celestial rose.*

Howard's discussion is valuable in its demonstration of how the principles and dominant images of medieval art can illuminate literature and add definition to the concept of the Gothic form.

Donald R. Howard, 'The Esthetics of this Form' from 'Memory and Form' in *The Idea of the 'Canterbury Tales'*. University of California Press, Berkeley, 1976.

I know the form I have described must seem like a puzzle whose parts cannot be made to fit, like a hall of mirrors reflecting everything from angles multiplied upon themselves, like a maze. The most attentive and patient reader in the world might well ask at this point, 'the esthetics of *what* form?' I rush forward with a résumé. At base the form is that of a memory: in the General Prologue it is a memory as the Middle Ages conceived of memory, a set of 'places' structured on principles of order and association. This memory is presented as the narrator's own, and the narrator is identified with the author. He remembers a group of pilgrims interrelated in such a way that they make up a society in little, remembers the game they planned, and remembers the tale each told. But the pilgrims did not follow the plan; their tales tumbled upon one another in an apparently random order dictated by group dynamics and interpersonal relations, by the characters and moods of the individuals. Hence a new form takes shape: the narrator's memory serves up the seemingly disordered quality of experience itself. Each tale becomes detachable, can be read for itself: each was in the pilgrim's memory before it was in the narrator's. We experience a memory of others' memories and thus lapse into a mentalistic realm, a world of story, of reality remembered, distorted, tendentious. This 'mentalistic' quality shows in the pilgrimage frame. It is far from 'realistic': the pilgrims progress at a remove from civilization, passing through a wilderness from the outskirts of one city to the outskirts of another within the arc of an artificial day. Such a figural representation of the pilgrimage would make the work seem unfinished, however many tales might have been added.

This 'outer' form contains and hovers over the inner form, the series of tales. These consist chiefly of curiosities and fabrications, discredited by their tellers, their arrangement, or their tone and content. The endings of the tales tend to leave matters open, throwing attention back to the outer form of the pilgrimage, forward to the next tale, or at key points into realms of discourse beyond the literary realm of the work itself. These multiple viewpoints and multiple degrees of closure make the inner form of the tales seem a maze of contradictions in which the reader is left to find his own way, to participate as hearer and judge. But the guidelines for our participation are suggested in the work. The role-playing narrator points our attention to the pilgrims, with whom we share a social and national milieu; to the authorial self behind his role-playing, with whom we share a world of books and ideas; and to proverbial lore, for which we share a taste and a capacity to weigh and select.

Some will no doubt throw up their hands and say that such a form is impossibly abstract. But is it any the less abstract when we talk about dramatic or climactic or episodic form, about rises and falls, turnabouts, ironic twists? Is it less abstract when we choose a simile to describe form, when we say a form is like a circle or a spiral or the building of a house? If we talk about form at all we are talking about something imposed upon or abstracted from the particulars of a work, and the problem is that in modern times *we* like form to be simple, unadorned, pure. We want 'clean lines' in our buildings, single colors, the simple majesty of aluminum and glass. If Chaucer believed with Geoffrey of Vinsauf that the form of a work is like the builder's *archetypus*, that it becomes a reality through a process of construction like that of building a house, must we not ask what kind of houses were admired in Chaucer's time? Must we not remind ourselves that their best and greatest houses were not quaint homes of wattle-and-daub but grand stone castles, walled and pinnacled and wondrously turreted? It has become a cliché to compare a medieval poem with a Gothic cathedral, yet the comparison is just: the Gothic cathedral was a complex structure with outer and inner forms that could be viewed from multiple perspectives, by its very nature unfinished in execution but complete in design. 'Gothic' form was enormously abstract (the mysteries

The Canterbury Tales: Critical Extracts

of number and light played a part in it) and endlessly complicated – worlds apart from the 'clean lines' we admire. Yet the Gothic cathedral was the medieval idea of a house *par excellence*, for it was the house of God.

Some will say still that this is all very theoretical – that I have let my thesis ride me hard. But here I must protest with vehemence: what I am arguing is far *less* theoretical than other approaches. Those who find a simple form like the metaphor of the pilgrimage must fall back on elaborate theories about scriptural exegesis, esthetic response, medieval culture. Those who find simple realism 'breaking with convention and going direct to life' must accept modern theories about 'life' and representation. I do not offer a theory at all. I claim to have done my best to experience a work as it was written and meant to be read, and to have described that experience in a straightforward way. I have done with the poem what I did with the Ellesmere drawing of Chaucer – I have looked at it as sympathetically as I know how, resisting any attempt to explain it away, and have written down what I saw. If what I have written *sounds* theoretical, that is because what I have seen is itself abstract and complicated; but my 'method' is inductive and descriptive, its spirit tentative and pragmatic.

'Yes, yes,' the objector will reply, 'but then wouldn't you be better off to talk about *ideas* instead of *the* idea, about *forms* instead of *a* form?' But – my answer is – if we resort to these plurals, would we not then be talking about *works* rather than *a* work? My thesis has to do with an idea which I take to be unique and inclusive, many faceted, an idea hard to grasp – yet an idea.

The real problem with such a thesis, when it comes to discussing form as part of an idea, is that we are discussing something definite and describable which is hard to *visualize*. That is generally true of form; hence we are always using visual images to clarify our notions – we say the General Prologue is like a portrait gallery or a cross-section, the pilgrimage like a frame, a poem like a house. I am going to call these comparisons 'models.'[1] In trying to grasp a complicated idea or a puzzling set of observations, we can of course use any model we please if it helps us. But we need to be aware that it can limit us too. The world we see around us prompts us to explain that world, but the models we use to explain it shape what we see. In literary study we often use historical models as a means of comparison: we compare *The Canterbury Tales* with a Gothic cathedral or *The Divine Comedy* with a summa. Isn't there some model which would illustrate the principle of an inner form so complex and variegated in its interrelations that it seems to overburgeon, to dominate and obscure the presumably dominant outer form? I will propose such a model, one much closer to the book: a characteristic initial capital from an early fourteenth-century English manuscript, the Tickhill Psalter.[2] If the reader will look at the full-page initial S of Psalm 68 (plate 4) he will see a set of six medallions divided by the cross-stroke of the S into two sets of three, each

The Canterbury Tales: Critical Extracts

framed in circles which interlock chain-fashion. These represent the story of 2 Sam. 6: 2–7: 3. Essentially the form is a capital S; it is clearly framed in a rectangular border whose corners are carefully interlocked so that they themselves are a chain. Yet our attention goes to the story depicted, to the decorations which surround the pictures, to the 'channels' which lead from inside each drawing to the margin (where it was intended that captions and quotations be written). The outer form, the capital S, frames and seems to dominate, but the inner form, the narrative, draws our attention: we ask at once where it begins, what its episodes represent, how it is put together or 'structured.' We need rules or theories to perceive this structure – need to know where to begin, in what direction to proceed, how to relate the drawings in the frame to those at the bottom of the page. Look at the design one way

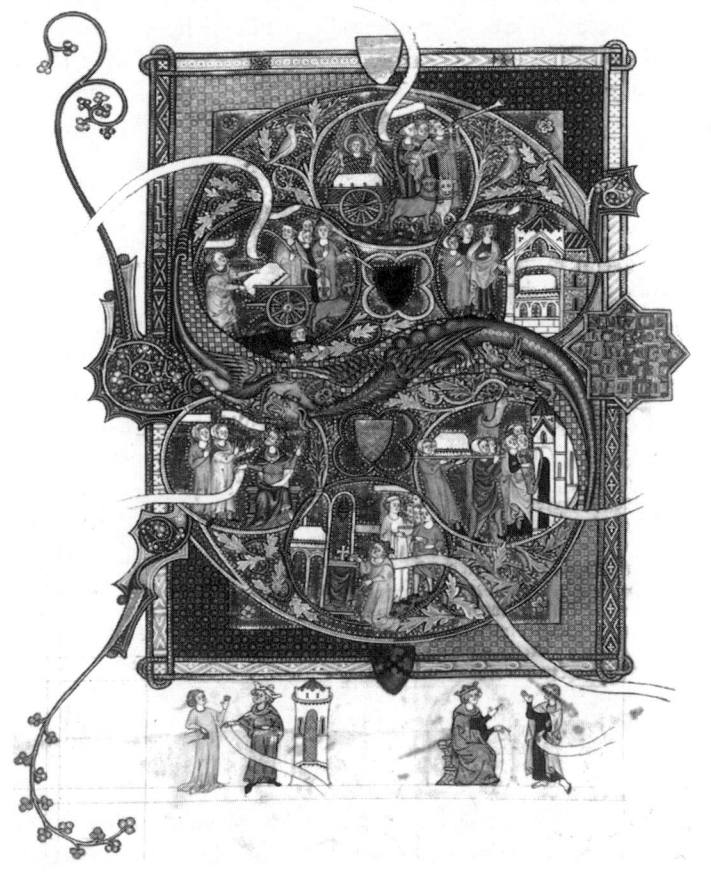

Plate 4 Initial S of Psalm 68 from *The Tickhill Psalter*, MS 26, folio 64v. Spencer Collection, the New York Public Library. Astor, Lenox and Tilden Foundations.

and it is a decorated capital. Look at it another way and it is a world of story framed by a circular design which seems to have no beginning and no end, and yet which seems to have a remarkable unity. Like the Ellesmere portrait of Chaucer it may be seen in either of two ways.

I do not claim any expertise as an art historian, and I offer this 'model' because it is suggestive and illustrative of an esthetic effect which seems abstract and exotic. In what follows I wish to offer three models for which I claim more than the advantage of convenience: they are explicitly stated in *The Canterbury Tales* in its opening passage. I claim they were in the author's mind and were part of his idea. Hence I claim that what follows is descriptive and concrete, not theoretical. About structure, which will be the subject of the remaining chapters, I make no such claim. Form may be abstract but it can be stated in a work and kept palpably present in the reader's mind; structure involves the piecing together of parts, is experiential rather than abstract, and requires extrinsic rules and theories to be perceived. But *stated* models of a form provide an intrinsic key to perception.

That a literary work should state its own models of form is a convention of western literature which modern authors inherited from the Middle Ages. In late medieval literature the example which comes to mind is the dream-vision, which conventionally states its own form by introducing a dreamer who falls asleep. The opening passage of *Piers Plowman* states its own form, that of recurrent or cyclical dreams, in a startling image of swirling waters. Such statements often use visual images from traditional iconography. In *Troilus and Criseyde* Chaucer states the form of the work – 'Fro woe to wele, and after out of joye' – and associates this rise and fall with the image of Fortune's Wheel. These are what I mean by stated models; they can be as straightforward as Dante's 'book of memory' in the *Vita Nuova* or as subtly entwined with the texture and content of the poem as the image of the margarite in *Pearl* or that of 'gomen' in *Sir Gawain*.

If Chaucer agreed with Geoffrey of Vinsauf that a work is an *archetypus* before it is a reality, found by the inner man who casts out his heart's line, this initial 'purpose' (as Chaucer called it) is what I call form. There is every reason to suppose that an author would have been aware of such a purpose. And Chaucer might have found a purpose newly conceived: he is often praised for originality, and the praise is justified, as Egeus would say, 'in some degree.' Yet the three models he stated at the beginning of the work are familiar medieval images. These models are not different from the form I have described; on the contrary, they precisely visualize three aspects of that form. They are like emblematic directions telling us what we should look for as we read. And each had a heritage in medieval ideas about art.

Notes

1 On the term see C. S. Lewis, *The Discarded Image* (Cambridge: Cambridge University Press, 1964), pp. 11–21. The term is borrowed from the sciences; a model is a device used for its convenience in explaining evidence, in 'saving appearances,' and is judged not for its intrinsic or objective truth but for its usefulness – if it helps us it is a good model, and for that reason two or more models may be adopted if they help us better. As the medievals had a 'model of the universe' which explained the appearance of the universe to them, medieval poets conceived models of their own poems – so I am arguing here – which explained the form of the poems.
2 On the Tickhill Psalter, see Donald Drew Egbert, *The Tickhill Psalter and Related Manuscripts: A School of Manuscript Illumination in England during the Early Fourteenth Century* (New York Public Library and the Department of Art and Archeology of Princeton University, 1940), which affords a full description of all details.

An Encyclopedia of Kinds

Helen Cooper

Helen Cooper's book argues for the necessity of treating the Canterbury Tales *as a whole, rather than looking at individual tales in isolation. While the terms in which she examines the tales are different and more specific than those employed by Jordan and Howard, she raises similar issues. Her model is literary rather than visual, but relates closely to the notion of the Gothic put forward by other critics, and to the idea of the book of memory central to Howard's argument. Cooper envisages the tales in terms of a medieval* summa *or encyclopedia – not a work to be used in dictionary fashion, but rather 'a bringing together of all knowledge'. Such* summae *were common, collecting different aspects of moral existence (the sins and virtues, the sacraments, issues such as desire, will and intention, marriage and virginity); there were also encyclopedias of natural philosophy summarizing the workings of nature and addressing topics like medicine and astrology. The image of the encyclopedia parallels that of the medieval castle with its plethora of architectural features, or the Gothic cathedral with its rich variety and contrasts. Plenty and comprehensiveness were viewed as desirable qualities in the Middle Ages: literary works often employ catalogues or lists – of kinds of trees, elements of dream theory, names of knights in a tournament, types of arms; similarly, they are often episodic and full of rhetorical flourishes. In a larger sense the* Canterbury Tales

The Canterbury Tales: Critical Extracts

works as a kind of literary compendium. Whereas writers such as Dante and Langland are encyclopedic in that their span is the universe from heaven to hell, Chaucer's more secular work runs the gamut of medieval genres: romance, fabliau, beast-fable, saint's life, moral treatise, sermon.

Cooper, like Jordan, compares the Canterbury Tales to modern literature, pointing up the poverty of generic possibility in the present day, but also emphasizing how Chaucer, somewhat like a novelist, uses the mode of naturalism. She is emphatic about the impossibility of interpreting the Canterbury Tales metaphorically and the need to consider the substance of individual tales as well as general principles of construction. For Chaucer critics, the challenge is to analyse the parts as sophisticated literary works in their own right, yet also to view them in terms of the whole. Cooper demonstrates the need to employ a multiple perspective of a kind to which the modern reader is not accustomed.

In addition to the issues of genre and kind, Cooper considers the relation between tellers and tales and Chaucer's construction of character. Chaucer does not deal in psychological realism as a novelist would tend to do, but rather deploys a range of character types, models drawn ultimately from medieval estates satire. Cooper explores how Chaucer plays with this tradition in his portraits of both ideal and highly flawed members of the estates, to create a whole range of characters, to whom are added members of the growing middle and professional classes. The pilgrims are immediately and vividly realized, yet this realism occurs in the context of familiar literary types rather than individuals.

While the characters depend on an understanding of the ideal, the tales depend on a knowledge of medieval literary conventions. They range from secular to religious and through various spheres of action, and are both individually complex and contingent. Cooper offers a useful summary of different generic features, such as the ideal beauty of the romance heroine, to show the centrality of the notions of convention and originality to the tales. Chaucer both rewrites and subverts familiar concepts such as chivalry or fin 'amors, and his tales are as much literary experiments as characterizations of their tellers. Cooper treats the same issue as Jordan in exploring the way that tellers, rather than being wholly fleshed out in their descriptions, become the voices of their tales: there is an ongoing, fluid relationship between teller and tale. Each contributes to the understanding of the other, as Cooper demonstrates with regard to the most three-dimensional of tellers, the *Wife of Bath*. She, like the other pilgrims and despite the realism of her portrayal, is constructed from literary conventions: there is no wife of Bath even while Chaucer's literary skill creates her as something that is larger, almost more persuasive, than life itself.

Helen Cooper, 'An Encyclopedia of Kinds' in *The Structure of the 'Canterbury Tales'*. Duckworth, London, 1983.

The Canterbury Tales: Critical Extracts

Plate 5 The Wife of Bath, from *The Ellesmere Chaucer*. The Art Archive/Victoria and Albert Museum, London.

Chaucer's handling of his greatest story-collection gives it strong similarities to another kind of medieval writing: the *summa*. The word implies less a genre than an attitude to life or learning. The *summa* is, in effect, an encyclopedia, a bringing together of all knowledge; but the notion of *togetherness* is important. One uses a modern encyclopedia to look up a single item, and some of the works of the great medieval encyclopedists, Vincent of Beauvais or Thomas Aquinas, could be similarly used; but that was not their point. A *summa* was intended to show the wholeness, the unity, of all creation and all abstract or intellectual thought in all their diversity. The same ideal was pursued by many scholars and, in a different way, by many poets. Alan of Lille in Latin and Jean de Meung in French, both writers whose works were known to Chaucer, were attempting something of the kind. So was Dante, in his great survey of humanity *sub specie aeternitatis*; and there the importance of the unity of the work is especially apparent. One cannot pick out an episode from the *Divine Comedy* and read it in isolation: an understanding of it depends on its placing in the entire scheme. In Chaucer's own time, Gower presented his three major works as a *summa*, and Langland's survey of good life in the world and the revelations of faith is another. The *Canterbury Tales* has the same all-encompassing intention, though the means for achieving it are more overtly literary: for Dante's anagogical range of Hell, Purgatory and Paradise, Chaucer gives a generic range. His work barely touches on such ultimate religious experience as the beatific vision (the Second Nun's Tale comes closest), but as an exploration of life through literature it is unsurpassed. His method is to juxtapose the different perspectives offered by different genres and to allow them to define or tell against each other. The effect is cumulative, and selection or concentration on a single tale goes against the tenor of the work. To read one story alone is a little like reading the Murder of Gonzago without *Hamlet*.

Literature is in a poor way these days so far as form and content are concerned. The range and number of kinds of writing that can be recognized as 'literature' have been getting smaller and smaller ever since the Middle Ages. Chaucer was singularly fortunate in writing at the time when the generic variety was at its richest. A consideration of the genres he uses will indicate our present impoverishment. Many of them have now been assigned a place on the very fringes of 'serious' literature. The romance has become the stuff of women's magazines, or science fiction. The beast-fable has become the staple of children's literature, or if it is more adult (as *Watership Down* is, for instance), it is still regarded with suspicion by the critical establishment, and such suspicion is based primarily on genre, not on the degree of skill with which the genre is handled in a particular work. Few sermons have been accepted as significant literature since the seventeenth century. A modern epic, in poetic form, is all but unthinkable. The *fabliau* has descended to the rugger club or the pub; the saint's life, if it still exists at all, exists as a vehicle for ideological propaganda.

Almost all we are left with now is the novel – and although there are a good many varieties of that, they do not come with the richness of convention and tradition that the various genres of the Middle Ages did. The links between the stories in the *Canterbury Tales* deserve a special mention here. All novels until some of the most recent experimental examples – and perhaps even they – do set out to 'imitate life' in some fairly direct and naturalistic sense, however great the debates about what naturalism is and how one imitates nature in a verbal and structural form. It is this naturalism that distinguishes novels, historically and even at the present, from romances or beast-fables. In the links, Chaucer is providing something of the same extension from art towards life. This does not mean that the *Canterbury Tales* is a novel *manqué* or a forerunner of the novel or anything else of the kind: rather, that Chaucer identified the one area not covered by the traditional generic range, and allowed the trivial amoral non-order of everyday living to play its part alongside the various orderings proposed by the stories. The pilgrimage imposes some kind of overriding structure on the frame narrative, but the deeper meanings of the idea of pilgrimage, to which Chaucer directs attention in the first and last of the tales, impinge singularly little on the pilgrims themselves, or on their stories.[1] They are blissfully unaware of any role they may have in a greater spiritual allegory, and Chaucer is not going to allow a single meaning to emerge from the progression of tales. To do that, as he does in the Monk's Tale, would be to deny too much.

To interpret the pilgrimage in too exclusively spiritual a sense is to overlook the strong claims of the world. The *Canterbury Tales*, most of the time, is much more a secular work than a religious one. The claims of the spirit are not entirely disregarded, however, even outside the overtly secular tales. The famous opening, with its description of the fertile April showers engendering the flowers, the birds wakeful with the pricking of their 'corages', and men and women setting out on pilgrimage, is more than ironic in its association of the sexual and the spiritual, though the irony is there. There is also beyond that an entirely serious level on which it is right and fitting that at the time of the springing of new life pilgrims should set out

> The hooly blisful martir for to seke,
> That hem hath holpen whan that they were seeke.
> (17–18)

The pilgrimage has a potential for spiritual renewal to match the physical regeneration of the sick. The secular is given a generous weighting, but it is balanced by the sacred.

The same kind of all-inclusiveness of perspective is found throughout the General Prologue, and throughout the *Canterbury Tales* as a whole. Some examples of the way Chaucer works in the Prologue may help to demonstrate the kind of richness of approach that he uses later with greater complexity in the stories. Some of the pilgrims are ideal figures; some are villains; most are described in superlatives, with a surface *naïveté* coupled with a precise moral pointing that overtly leaves all judgment to the reader but in practice leaves little room for manoeuvre. Some of the pilgrims are to be judged in two ways at once: the Prioress, for instance, is delightful as a woman, but she is far from being the ideal embodiment of her office. None of the portraits is psychological or character-oriented after the fashion of characterization in the classic novel. All the pilgrims are placed through reference to systems beyond themselves as individuals: to the offices they hold and the standards demanded by those, to their function in society, to their approximation to, or distance from, the ideals set out in those medieval anatomies of the social order, the estates satires. On a larger scale, the stories are handled in the same multiplicity of ways. Some of the tales give an idealized portrayal of the world, emphasizing human nobility or the providential order; others give a kind of debased caricature. If the pilgrims are all the best of their kind, so are the tales, and if moral judgment is harder to reach in this inner fictional world it is not held in suspense. Some of the tales too must be evaluated in two ways at once, not least where aesthetic and didactic values part company; the Pardoner's Tale demands a particularly complex response since it demands two mutually exclusive moral readings, and the *Melibee* presents a complexity that is still to be untangled. None of the tales has the characteristics or concerns of the traditional novel; they are defined by their particular genre and must be read with all the literary sophistication suggested by that, with an alertness to where they are fulfilling conventional expectations and where and why they leave those behind.

It follows that the relationship between teller and tale is a good deal more complicated than the traditional notion of dramatic projection. Chaucer was certainly keenly aware of the relationship between speech and the man who speaks it: so much is not merely a matter of deduction from the *Tales*, but is given a distinctive formulation in the *House of Fame*:

> Whan any speche ycomen ys
> Up to the paleys, anon-ryght
> Hyt wexeth* lyk the same wight   *grows
> Which that the word in erthe spak,
> Be hyt clothed red or blak;
> And hath so verray hys lyknesse
> That spak the word, that thou wilt gesse
> That it the same body be,
> Man or woman, he or she.
>   (1074–82)

The interesting thing about this is that the speech recreates the speaker: the character is a projection of the thing said, not the other way round. In much the same way the stories of the *Canterbury Tales* can be seen as defining or creating their speakers. Mario Praz suggested many years ago that the pilgrims 'sprung up from the stories themselves' through 'an embodiment of the spirit of each work in a concrete person'.[2] This is obviously not the whole story, as the shifting around of tales from teller to teller indicates, and the final fit is still not always very good, dramatically or generically. It may none the less be much less misleading than a reading based on character alone.

The way in which both pilgrim and speech can be grounded in literary sources is demonstrated particularly clearly by the Wife of Bath. Estates satires analysed society into its constituent parts, from the pope or emperor downwards, and defined the shortcomings and abuses of each. In this scheme, women constituted a social order to themselves, and the Wife is nothing if not archetypal woman.[3] As Jill Mann has pointed out, some of the details of her portrayal become additionally delightful when she is set in this conventional context: where the satirists inveigh against the expense of women's clothes, and especially head dresses, the Wife's Sunday 'coverchiefs' for her head did not *cost* ten pounds but *weighed* ten pounds. All medieval anti-feminism was focused in the estates satires; and the Wife is every anti-feminist's dream (or nightmare) come true. She is sexually predatory, extravagantly dressed, ultra-sensitive to her social position, and, worst of all, irresistibly attractive. The 'confession' she gives in the Prologue to her tale is of a piece with this. It is only incidentally autobiographical: all the details of her life, and of her arguments with all her husbands, not least the Oxford clerk Jankin, are drawn from the traditions of anti-feminist literature. The result of all this is something infinitely more rich and delightful than any portrayal of a historical Wife of Bath, such as scholars still occasionally try to find, could ever be. Her Tale itself, of the young knight who marries an old hag, is all the more surprising for this background. Its theme of women's sovereignty is predictable enough; its motif of the old woman regaining her youth is entirely appropriate. What one might not have expected is the romance treatment of the fairy-tale, so that the story becomes an assertion, and a forceful one, of the good to be found in this world. That too is appropriate, but at a deeper level than the rest. After the Wife's exposition of matrimonial woe, the image of secular bliss of the end of the tale demands a reorientation from the reader.

The richness of the *Canterbury Tales* does not spring only from the relationship of tale to teller, whether this is seen in psychological or literary terms. If the Wife, her Prologue and Tale all define and redefine each other, a similar process also goes on between different stories, or different pilgrims. A more detailed look at some of the portraits of the General Prologue may serve to illustrate in miniature these poetic and conceptual relationships.

The stories of the *Canterbury Tales* can be very roughly divided into three spheres of action and interest: the exotic world of chivalry and courtesy in the romances, the everyday world of the *fabliaux*, and the spiritual world of the pious tales. Social analysis divided men according to their three main functions, parallel to these worlds: those who fight, those who work, and those who pray. Both Langland and Chaucer recognize this primary grouping, though it was of course acknowledged that society is a good deal more complex than that – the genre of the estates satire existed to demonstrate the point. Chaucer, however, makes the representatives of those three estates the ideal characters of the pilgrimage: the Knight, the Ploughman and the Parson. A fourth character who comes close to setting a similar pattern for his profession is the Clerk: perhaps Chaucer felt the lack of a place for learning, the labour of the intellect as distinct from the body or soul, in the model of the three estates. Knight, Parson and Ploughman, however, are archetypal figures for the estates.

The Ploughman is described in terms very close to Langland's ideal ploughman:

> A trewe swynkere* and a good was he, *worker
> Lyvynge in pees and parfit charitee.
> God loved he best with al his hoole herte...
> He wolde thresshe, and therto dyke* and delve, *make ditches
> For Cristes sake, for every povre wight.
> (I, 531–7)

Langland's Piers, who in his first and most human manifestation speaks of being Truth's pilgrim at plough for poor men's sake,[4] embodies exactly the same ideal. Some influence is possible, given the popularity of Langland's poem, and indeed the fact that he and Chaucer must have lived within a mile of each other for some years;[5] but it is not necessary to assume it. These are the accepted traditions of the labourer's virtues, though the close connection of duty to the church and duty to the poor is found in no other character in either work.[6] The presence of the Ploughman is a salutary reminder that human perfection should be the norm.

The Parson is the Ploughman's brother: their blood relationship is symptomatic of their equal moral standing in their separate worlds, symbolic of their social functions as labouring to support the body and the soul. Where Chaucer describes what the Ploughman *is*, however, he describes what the Parson is *not*. After the opening lines, the portrait of the Parson is the portrait of a bad priest, annulled throughout by negatives:

> Ful looth were hym to cursen* for his tithes*...   *excommunicate   *rents
> He sette nat his benefice to hyre*   *farm out
> And leet his sheep encombred in the myre
> And ran to Londoun unto Seinte Poules
> To seken hym a chaunterie for soules*...   *appointment as a chantry priest
>   to pray for souls
>
> He was to synful men nat despitous,*   *spiteful
> Ne of his speche daungerous ne digne*...   *haughty
>   (516–17)

By the time Chaucer ends his portrayal of the ideal priest, we have a very good idea of the abuses practised by the beneficed clergy.

The Knight is more complex than either of these other estates ideals. Chaucer puts him first, at the head of the series of portraits, not only for reasons of social precedence but also because the standards by which the Knight is described as living are to be relevant to many of the portraits that follow. Terry Jones, in a fascinating study of the Knight's campaigns, has recently argued that the portrait is a travesty and that the Knight is far from ideal.[7] This is not, I think, what Chaucer is doing. That war is always and inevitably a bloody business in every sense of the word was perfectly well known in the Middle Ages (and is emphasized in the Knight's Tale), but that did not affect the almost universal assumption that the proper function of knights was to fight: even Langland, with all his moral stringency, never questions that.[8] It was generally acknowledged that the killing of Christians was a bad thing (though that rarely stopped anyone from doing it), but only a small group in the late fourteenth century, the Lollard knights at the court of Richard II, some of them closely known to Chaucer, were opposed to the killing of pagans. Whatever his own views may have been, Chaucer in his portrait of his own Knight is recalling the solid tradition of Christian chivalry. The Knight does not fulfil the lower form of his role, of fighting for his feudal lord, but the highest form, of fighting for God. Jones would have him fighting for money – he subtitles his book 'The Portrait of a Medieval Mercenary' – but Chaucer, who can so unerringly identify the ecclesiastics who substitute Mammon for God, never hints at that.[9] There is a curious critical assumption that since Chaucer is often ironic in the *Canterbury Tales*, he must always be ironic. If that were so, there would be little bite left in the irony. It is precisely because the Knight is an ideal that the imperfection of some of the later characters tells so strongly; and most of the characteristics Chaucer gives him have an immediate, and a positive, function in the General Prologue itself.[10]

The Knight, whom one might expect to be portrayed as the well-to-do secular country gentleman, is in fact an ascetic who has devoted his life to the service of Christianity. The Monk, who follows shortly afterwards, and whom one might expect to be portrayed as an ascetic who had devoted his life to the service of Christianity, is in fact portrayed much more as a well-to-do country gentleman. R. E. Kaske has set out the close verbal parallels that Chaucer uses in the two portraits:[11] the Knight who

> fro the tyme that he first bigan
> To riden out, he loved chivalrie,
>
> (I, 44-5)

the Monk 'an outridere, that lovede venerie'; the Knight's 'good' but not 'gay' horses, the Monk's 'ful many a deyntee hors', 'his hors in greet estaat'; the ascetic plainness of the Knight's clothing, the Monk's fur sleeves and gold pin. The contrast extends to internal qualities as well as attributes: the Knight is 'of his port [deportment] as meeke as is a mayde', the Monk 'a manly man, to been an abbot able'. We are made aware of how the world values the Knight: he has been 'evere honoured for his worthynesse', 'everemoor he hadde a sovereyn prys', and the voice is Chaucer's echoing a wider valuation, with no room for irony. In the Monk's portrait, however, it is perpetually his own estimate of himself that we keep hearing in the lines. That he is fit to be an abbot follows too suddenly on the reference to his hunting for it to be acceptable at face value, and his own voice is so distinct later in the description that his qualification for promotion – 'to been an abbot able' – gets infected by it. We never hear the Knight's voice: he is entirely reticent about his exploits, and Chaucer does all the speaking for him. The Knight is summed up in terms of the achievements of his career and his moral qualities; the Monk is described in terms of his attributes, his clothing, his fondness for good hunting, good horses and (above all) good food, and his cheerful contempt of the old-fashioned monastic rule.

Apart from his horse, no animal is mentioned in the portrait of the Knight. The Monk comes surrounded with them: not only the fine horse he rides and the others back home in the stable, but greyhounds 'as swift as fowel in flight' (a simile that suggests hawking to add to his fondness for hunting), the hare he chases; and when he is not hunting he is eating, with the fat swan as his favourite roast, and at the other extreme, as expressions of worthlessness, the plucked hen and the oyster. All this gives the portrait a very different texture from the abstract moral adjectives – 'worthy', 'wys', 'meeke' – used for the Knight, or the Miltonic roll-call of the names of the places where he had fought. Animal imagery is used in a number of other portraits to make an effect different again from the Monk's. In a description such as that of the Miller the animals are not ones he possesses or uses as speech idioms, but are used as similes to associate him with beasts: his beard 'as any sowe or fox was reed', the bristles on his nose are 'reed as the brustles of a sowes eeres'. In a selection of similes full of nastier implications,[12] the Pardoner's eyes are like a hare's, his voice like a goat's, he himself 'a geldyng or a mare'. His holy relics are mere pigs' bones, and he reduces the people he dupes to the sub-human level of 'apes'.

The General Prologue is a very complex piece of writing, and one could analyse these differences of poetic treatment indefinitely; how characters fulfil, or more commonly fail to fulfil, their estates ideals, how far their attributes are conventional (a surprising number of them are) and which are individual, how the different tones and textures of the various portraits are achieved. What emerges from even such a brief survey as I have given here, is how few psychologically individualizing elements there are. The pilgrims are not characters of post-Freudian depth, but individualized types controlled by convention – whether they fulfil expectations or contradict them – and by the poetic manipulation of language and imagery.

As in the General Prologue, so in the tales: the aims and methods are not those of psychological exploration, but of poetry: of imagery, language, genre, manipulation of convention and so on. The 'confessions' of the Wife of Bath and the Pardoner in their respective prologues are clearly tailored to fit the characters, but even they are deeply rooted in convention, in well-known social and ecclesiastical abuses or in the familiar traditions of anti-feminism, and none of the tales shows as tight a connection with its narrator as do these first-person passages. The primary reason for assigning a tale to a particular teller is likely to be rhetorical, not psychological: the ascription derives from the story rather than the pilgrim. Rhetoric demands decorum, 'appropriateness'; and first and foremost it is a fit at that level that Chaucer offers. Even the 'cherles tales' are decorous in this sense:

> The Millere is a cherl, ye knowe wel this;
> So was the Reve eek and othere mo,
> And harlotrie they tolden bothe two.
> (I,3182–4)

At one level this can imply a social ranking: high romance for the Knight, bawdy *fabliaux* for the low-class ruffians. Per Nykrog established some years ago that *fabliau* and romance do not in fact belong to different authors and audiences,[13] and the *Canterbury Tales* is the perfect illustration of that; but Chaucer will pretend that the division is true, and divide his pilgrims into 'cherles' and 'gentils'. Decorum can also provide a contrast, sometimes a subtle one, between the religious and the lay members of the pilgrimage: pious romance for the Man of Law, Miracle of the Virgin for the Prioress. But just as easy divisions of this kind are blurred in the General Prologue, with the

Monk's secularity, the Pardoner's greed and the social climbing of almost everyone except the ideal figures, so the assignment of genre to particular kinds of pilgrims gets confused. The tales are less significant for what they tell us about the characters of the individual pilgrims than for what the assignment to a particular narrator tells us about the kind of story it is. Just as in the General Prologue one has to be alive to expressions of the ideal and departures from it, to levels of imagery, to the play of conventions, to links and reflections and contrasts between portraits, so the tales work in the same way. Just as the portrait of the Monk is qualified by the portraits of the Knight and Parson, so every tale is qualified by the presence of the others.

The process is most clearly visible at the level of genre. Medieval literary genres are very sharply differentiated – in essence, at least: there are always grey areas – and Chaucer is keenly aware of the points of differentiation. Every other writer of a story-collection works to bring his tales towards a common generic centre, to give them a tonal and stylistic consistency and to reduce their differences of narrative outline or thematic import. Chaucer works in exactly the opposite way, to enhance the differences and point them up in every way he can.

The points of difference he exploits are explicit in the genres themselves. The leading genre of secular literature, the romance, idealizes the world and those who live in it. Its heroes are young, strong, handsome and noble, its heroines young, beautiful, noble, and chaste before marriage. There are no romances of adultery in Chaucer,[14] and indeed very few in Middle English. (The main exception is the story of Lancelot and Guinevere, and that was invented by the French. It was in France, not England, that adultery was a common romance motif – though it was still less common in French romances than it is in French novels.) The bulk of any romance is likely to be devoted to the suffering and hardship endured by its characters, but a happy ending is guaranteed, and rewards are dealt out in this world to ensure a happy-ever-after ending. Romances are set far away or long ago, well apart from the triviality of everyday living, and their scope is large both geographically and temporally. They are, above all, stories. Narrative is what counts in romance; but in the more courtly or self-aware romances there is also a deeper level of implied meaning, the *sens* or *sentence* underlying the *matière*. Courtly romance is also concerned with ideals of human behaviour; and the highest value is set on human love.

In the saint's life, the highest value is out of this world: its absolute is a divine imperative. The worldly end of its hero – or more often heroine, since the qualities of being young, beautiful and chaste are again essential, and these have more sensation value in women than in men – the worldly end of its heroine is likely to be a sticky one. The setting is again often exotic: more typical than St Thomas à Becket with his historically and geographically identifiable context would be St Margaret of Antioch, who was swallowed by a dragon which split when she made the sign of the cross (Jacobus a Voragine, [author of *The Golden Legend*, thirteenth century], to give him due credit, doubts whether it actually ate her), but duly martyred by beheading with a sword. What happens to the body is, luckily, unimportant: the soul is what matters. Rewards in the saint's life, by way of spiritual enlightenment in this life and salvation after death, are unmeasurable, or even invisible, to the worldly eye.

The romance stresses the highest earthly ideals, the saint's life the highest spiritual ones; in the *fabliau*, men and women leave all ideals far behind, and act with an eye to instant gratification that allows no postponement of the reward to a distant happy ending or to life after death. The ruling code in the *fabliau* is animal instinct. The physical functions of the body, especially sex (and as a close second in Chaucer, farting), provide the primary plot motifs. In *fabliaux* there is none of the nobility of blood or exoticism of setting associated with romance: the characters are at best middle class, and the plots are worked out in a single house in a local town or village. Further meanings are minimal or non-existent. If medieval fictions are supposed to teach and delight, the authors of the *fabliaux* were not listening to the first half of the injunction. Entertainment value is all.

Beast-fables are also delightfully entertaining; but traditionally they come with their morals firmly attached. If the *fabliau* scarcely distinguishes human action from animal instinct, the beast-fable has its animals imitate rational human action. In contrast with the courtly ideals of the romance or the spiritual absolute of the saint's life, the beast-fable teaches worldly common sense.

And so one might continue through the various genres of medieval literature, and the *Canterbury Tales*. If romance emphasizes the upward movement of Fortune's wheel, *tragedie*, in the medieval non-dramatic definition derived from Boethius, is concerned solely with its downward turning:

> What other thyng bewaylen the cryinges of tragedyes but oonly the dedes of Fortune, that with unwar strook overturneth the realmes of greet nobleye?
> Glose. Tragedye is to seyn a dite of a prosperite for a tyme, that endeth in wrecchidnesse.[15]

If romance concerns itself with marvels and the irruption of the supernatural into the world, miracles of the Virgin, even more than saints' lives, concern themselves with miracles and the irruption of the divine into the world. Between the saint's life and the romance lies an area of secular hagiography, the realm of Custance and Griselda, which examines standards of divine perfection operating within the world; and the Physician's Tale will give another such story a pagan setting. Didacticism can take the form of discursive prose, or, in the Pardoner's Tale, a lengthy sermon *exemplum* can become a gripping murder-story. Traditional wisdom can be embodied in the actions of irrational beasts, or in proverbs and the maxims and *sententiae* of the great teachers of the past.

If the *fabliau* is all entertaining story and no moral instruction, the penitential tract is all moral instruction and no entertaining story. Robert Mannyng [author of fourteenth-century poem on sin] may have enlivened his poem on the good Christian life with an abundance of exemplary tales, but Chaucer's Parson will allow no such compromises with the world:

> Thou getest fable noon ytoold for me;
> For Paul, that writeth unto Thymothee,* *Timothy
> Repreveth hem that weyven soothfastnesse,* *give up truth
> And tellen fables and swich wrecchednesse.
> Why sholde I sowen draf* out of my fest, *chaff
> Whan I may sowen whete, if that me lest?
> For which I seye, if that yow list to here
> Moralitee and vertuous mateere...
> (X, 31–8)

Verse, whether rhymed or alliterative, is excluded along with fiction; Chaucer's exploration of the limits of genre results finally in the rejection of poetry and fiction – in the rejection of creative literature.

Until the very end of the *Tales*, there is the constant alternation of the world of poetry and the imagination, in the stories, and the imitation of real life, with all its apparent disorder and triviality, in the framework. The frame is in fact of course as highly wrought and fully imagined as any of the tales; but where the stories look away from everyday life towards their own worlds, or perhaps look at this world from the perspective imposed by their genre, the frame looks at ordinary life from a point of view within it.

This matter of perspective, of point of view, becomes crucial for any understanding of the *Canterbury Tales*. To ascribe the attitudes expressed in the tales to the narrators is an over-simplification and denies much of the richness of what Chaucer is doing. It is precisely because so many of the differences in perspective are already inherent in the kinds of story told that they can work together for an effect much greater than the sum of its parts. The similarities and contrasts between the different genres that I have set out above are implicit or explicit in every leaf of the *Canterbury Tales*. Chaucer plays off these differences against each other, not just by using so many different genres, but by drawing on an extensive stock of ideas and motifs that recur throughout the work, each time treated from a different angle appropriate first of all to the tale and only secondarily, through the tale, to the teller. The pilgrims may be allowed their say in the links, but in very few of the stories does the voice of any of the ostensible narrators replace Chaucer's. The pilgrims are as much part of his fiction as are their stories.

The recurring themes of the *Canterbury Tales* are enormously various. They include such things as ideas about literary theory, the nature of fiction, and the relation of art and morality; they include metaphysical speculation about divine justice or the balance between Fortune and Providence. Modes of human behaviour, especially the perennially fascinating topic of sex versus chastity, are perpetually discussed. Marriage is one such issue, and the one that every reader of Chaucer knows all about; it is certainly important, but not as all-important as is sometimes implied, nor do the tales of the 'marriage group' stand out in isolation from the rest as the only ones to be thematically linked. There is a vast pattern of similarly related themes woven throughout the whole fabric of the tales. Narrative and rhetorical *topoi* come in for the same kind of treatment: female beauty, or gardens, or sworn brotherhood, or the concept of meeting one's fate by the wayside, and many others, are repeated many times throughout the *Tales*, each time from a different angle suggested by the nature of the story. The interplay of themes and ideas can cover everything from details of style to the discussion of what men – or women – most desire, whether it be love, money, sovereignty or salvation.

The objection may be raised that there is such variety here that all literature is going to cover such themes, and that their presence in the *Canterbury Tales* is both accidental and unavoidable. Chaucer often goes to some trouble to point out the similarities, however; and a comparison of his tales with their sources or closest analogues shows up very precisely how he stresses or develops or adds characteristics of this kind. A collection of the sources of the tales would show very few of these links. Neither Boccaccio's *Teseida* nor his *De Casibus*, for instance, reveals any of the hard metaphysical questioning of the nature of Providence and the relationship of worldly misery to guilt or innocence that Chaucer examines so persistently in the Knight's and Monk's Tales; and it is impossible to imagine any source for the portrait of Alisoun that would provide its detailed counterpointing of the portrait of Emily. Even when tales do have traditional elements that are used by Chaucer in this way – the ruling passions of the Pardoner's and Wife of Bath's tales, for instance, *cupiditas* and women's love of sovereignty – the very selection of such tales can be seen as deliberate. The only proof possible must lie in the text, and this will be the concern of the later chapters of this book; I believe that the precision and detail with which the interrelationships between these various themes are worked out must be seen as conclusive. As Kolve comments on visual imagery, 'It is context that turns a sign into a communication, defining its exact and immediate intent.'[16] The context provided by the *Tales* is very rich indeed, and its communications all the more significant, and precise.

The next question must be, what is the point of writing the *Canterbury Tales* in this way? There are many possible answers to this, some practical and technical, others more profound and far-reaching. The most immediate practical point relates to the question of coherence that the compilers of so many story-collections had come up against: this process of interrelation locks the tales together, and with each additional story the edifice becomes not more diffuse and disordered, like a child's magazine collage, but tighter and firmer, like building an arch. The thematic implications are more significant. The *House of Fame* had suggested that multiplicity of tidings must take the place of the poet's attempt to find an undiscoverable single truth; the Monk's Tale suggests how inadequate a single moral must be. The *Canterbury Tales* is a presentation of the world, and of men's apprehension of the world, in all its richness and relativity. The very diversity of attitudes enforced by the division of literature into different genres means that there cannot be any authoritative 'answers'. There is one answer given by romance, another by *fabliau*, another by saint's life.

Even this way of proceeding is not without precedent, or indeed without generic classification. The anatomy, or Menippean satire, works on just such a basis.[17] Northrop Frye gives the classic account of the form:

> The Menippean satire deals less with people as such than with mental attitudes. Pedants, bigots, cranks, parvenus, virtuosi, enthusiasts, rapacious and incompetent professional men of all kinds, are handled in terms of their occupational approach to life as distinct from their social behavior. The Menippean satire thus resembles the confession in its ability to handle abstract ideas and theories, and differs from the novel in its characterization, which is stylized rather than naturalistic, and presents people as mouthpieces of the ideas they represent.[18]

It 'deals with intellectual themes and attitudes', and in its simplest form will take the shape of a dialogue or colloquy. Boethius's *Consolation of Philosophy* is one such dialogue example well-known to Chaucer: its clash of ideas and its pattern of alternating prose and verse are both typical of the genre. If there are many speakers involved, 'the setting then is usually a *cena* or symposium' – a symposium in its Greek sense of a drinking-party as well as its modern meaning. Frye cites Apuleius, Rabelais, *Gulliver's Travels* and the Alice books as instances of the form; but his account is also a perfect description of the *Canterbury Tales*, which is a symposium in both senses – an intellectual debate between opposing attitudes, and with the promised supper at the Tabard Inn to look forward to. The 'anatomy' basis of the General Prologue has long been recognized; but the anatomy of literary attitudes and of ways of understanding the world extends throughout the work, and adds up to something much larger than the social anatomy of the Prologue.

Such a process might imply that all the tales should be seen on a level, as all equally valuable or 'meaningful'. This is not in practice what happens. The audience's moral judgment is kept perpetually on the alert throughout the *Tales*, just as it is in the General Prologue: that the Knight, Monk, Friar and Parson are there all described in superlatives does not mean that they are all to be taken at face value. There is a clear level of irony at work in the tales as in the Prologue; but very often it is an irony arising primarily from context, from the counterpointing of one tale with another. The *Melibee* was a favourite tract throughout Europe, and taken in isolation Chaucer's translation is entirely faithful; the Prioress's Tale, compared with other miracles of the Virgin, is atypical only by virtue of being so much better. The section on *Sir Thopas* in Bryan and Dempster's *Sources and Analogues* is one of the longest in the work, and demonstrates amply that similar doggerel was being perpetrated in abundance. Put the tales together, however, and rather different things start to happen. The Miller's Tale does not cancel out the Knight's, but the vigour and detail of its parody prevent us from taking the Knight's Tale as the only word to be said on its subject. The difference in stylistic level between the poetics of *Sir Thopas* and the other Canterbury tales damns it instantly.

The notion that the stories are to be told in competition with each other enhances this series of contrasts and relationships. The idea of competition may direct the audience to appreciate the high poetic qualities of the tales; but within the fiction it affects the pilgrims rather differently. The word Chaucer uses – or has his characters use to describe their understanding of the competition is *quite*, 'requite' or 'repay'. The narrators very often set out not to surpass the previous story but to *answer it back*. The stories parody, comically or seriously, each other's generic conventions and attitudes. The high idealism of the Knight's Tale is answered by the cheerful earthiness of the Miller's:

'By armes, and by blood and bones,
I kan a noble tale for the nones,*   *occasion
With which I wol now quite the Knyghtes tale.'
(I, 3125–7)

The Miller's tale of the carpenter is taken by the Reeve as a personal insult, and he insists three times over[19] that his story will 'quite' the Miller's. It does so by more than just reversing the insult, however: there is a more literal overgoing of the Miller's Tale, too. There, one student slept with one woman; in the Reeve's, two students sleep with two women. Oxford is 'quited' by Cambridge, in a fourteenth-century equivalent of the Boat Race, and Cambridge wins by a length. The three tales of the first fragment, to summarize, respond to the 'competition' element, first, in the Knight's Tale, with sheer poetic quality; then by generic parody; then by an elaboration and multiplication of identical plot motifs. The generic contrasting of the tales, here and throughout the work, is backed up by its dramatic projection from the framework, from the pilgrims and their rivalries, but its implications go far beyond individual psychology or dramatic conflict.

Generic contrast can work at many levels, from pervasive themes of cosmic import down to single lines and phrases. It shows in the attitudes to Providence or to authority adopted in different tales; it shows in the various ideals, or lack of them, by which men can live; it highlights different attitudes towards women, marriage and sex. It also gives a sharper point to such a line as

Allone, withouten any compaignye.
(I, 2779, 3204)

Once it is used for Arcite contemplating the grave, at the end of the Knight's Tale; at the beginning of the next story, it describes the amorous Nicholas in his lodgings, preparing to get together with Alisoun. The repetition is too closely juxtaposed, and too brilliantly contrasted, for it not to be intentional.

Not every repetition is significant, however. There is a strong formulaic element in medieval literature: conventional plot motifs, rhetorical *topoi* and proverbial or oral formulae abound, in Chaucer as in every writer of his time. The existence of certain resemblances between different sections or lines of the *Canterbury Tales* therefore in itself proves nothing; some may be significant, others equally clearly are not. There is a genuine difficulty here which every reader will solve in a different way, drawing the line between an incidental relationship and a more profound one in a different place. Chaucer's intentions as to which mean something and which do not must remain speculative when the evidence of the text is inconclusive; and reflections or repetitions that he may not have inserted deliberately still throw a good deal of light on the way the *Tales* work. A few examples will illustrate the various processes and problems.

Some verbal formulae remain at that minimally formulaic level, and their repetition will be incidental and not incremental. That the Knight's Yeoman, the statue of Cupid in the Knight's Tale, and the yeoman-devil in the Friar's Tale, all bear 'arwes brighte and kene',[20] is an example of this kind, where the repeated phrase remains formulaic. Proverbial similes also need carry no significant weight: 'as fayn as fowel is of the brighte sonne' is used by the Knight, and, with only small variations, by the Shipman and the Canon's Yeoman.[21] On other occasions a simile of this kind can help to define the differences between tales even though it seems too much to ask that any audience, or Chaucer himself, should have the earlier usage in mind when the

235

second occurs. 'As drunk as a mouse' is a simile used by both the Knight and the Wife of Bath (mice having had the habit of falling into beer vats). To the Knight, the phrase is a simile for the state of mankind:

> We witen nat what thing we preyen heere:
> We faren as he that dronke is as a mous.
> (I, 1260–1)

The Wife uses it to insult her husbands:

> Thou comest home as dronken as a mous!
> (III, 246)

The use of the same words in the two different contexts epitomizes the differences between the sections: the Knight's Tale with its deep philosophical reach, ready to use the humblest similes in the service of the search for truth; the Wife's Prologue with its vivid colloquialism and concern for the everyday domestic world. When the Wife says 'drunk as a mouse', she means just that; when Arcite says it, it is a simile within a simile – '*as* he that drunk is *as* a mouse' – and ideas of inebriation and small furry animals are alike distanced by his agonized questioning of the nature of human life.

Single lines or aphorisms can present similar problems. Chaucer was not a man to avoid using a good line twice, or even four times.

> Pitee renneth soone in gentil herte

occurs not only in the Knight's, Merchant's and Squire's Tales, and with a slight variation in the Man of Law's, but also in the Prologue to the *Legend of Good Women*.[22] If a poem outside the *Tales* can contain the same line, it would seem to weaken the case for the usages within the *Tales* being significant. This does not necessarily follow, however. The line in the *Legend* confirms that the idea was a lasting concern of Chaucer's – the theme, if not the actual wording, is found again in *Troilus and Criseyde* – and so enforces the likelihood that he was aware of the repetitions in the *Tales*. Given the detailed counterpointing of the Knight's and Merchant's Tales, the uses of the line in those strike particularly hard: it is used once for Theseus tempering anger and ruthless justice with compassion, the second time for May deciding to have an affair with her husband's squire. In the Squire's Tale the line again occurs in the context of a love affair, but here there is no irony: the heroine Canacee's true pity and *gentillesse* are contrasted with the unfaithful tercelet's hollow imitation. The repetition gains extra weight from the likelihood that Chaucer intended the Squire's Tale to follow the Merchant's; but its significance does not depend on the juxtaposition. The Knight's Tale uses the line straight, to mean what it says. The Merchant's turns it inside out, so that *pitee* and *gentil* are both ironically redefined, and even 'soone' has a cynical ring in view of how closely May's plans for adultery follow her marriage. In the Squire's Tale the line has a double meaning: it applies literally to Canacee, but given the context of a lover's unfaithfulness it carries a reminder that its opposite is also true.

Lines and phrases such as these illustrate on a small scale what Chaucer is doing with motifs of every size from a few words to ideas of cosmic import. In order to be perceptible to the listeners, even to ones so alert to literary meaning as late fourteenth-century audiences seem to have been, significant repetitions must be given in a way that will make them noticeable. Adjacent tales can rely on finer cues, or more detailed 'quiting', than more widely spaced stories. For all Chaucer's invitation to turn over the leaf to a different tale, there is a presumption that they will be read in sequence. The locking together of one tale to the next within the fragments by both thematic relationship and narrative connection suggests that a sequential reading of linked tales is preferable, from Chaucer's point of view, and likely, from the reader's. When a motif reappears in tales from different fragments it must be more prominent. The occasional cross-references (such as those to the Wife of Bath) help here, but there are few of them. Chaucer's use of literary conventions helps more: since they would already be familiar to the audience, his variations on them, or his refusal to fulfil the expectations they arouse, would be all the more noticeable. In addition, many of the themes and motifs found pervasively throughout the work are given their first clear statement in the opening tale, the Knight's. The rest can then build on the foundations laid there.

Notes

1 See Ralph Baldwin, *The Unity of the Canterbury Tales* (Anglistica 5, Copenhagen, 1955). Baldwin would deny that the tales are independent of the pilgrimage framework, but the one weakness of his work – and it is a crucial one – is that his account of the *Canterbury Tales* leaves out the stories almost entirely. The Parson's Tale is the only one that can be significantly linked to the pilgrimage.
2 'Chaucer and the great Italian writers of the Italian Trecento', *Monthly Criterion* VI (1927) 50. Similar points are made by Allen and Moritz pp. 186–7, and Gabriel Josipovici, *The World and the Book* (2nd edn., London, 1979) pp. 82, 86.
3 Mann p. 121; the following reference is to pp. 124–5.

The Canterbury Tales: Critical Extracts

4 *The Vision of William concerning Piers the Plowman* ed. Walter W. Skeat (2 vols, 1886/London, 1965) B. VI. 104.
5 Chaucer lived in 'a dwelling above the gate of Aldgate' from 1374 to 1386 (*Chaucer Life-Records* ed. Martin M. Crow and Clair C. Olson (Oxford, 1966) pp. 144–7); Langland speaks of his cottage on Cornhill in a famous passage in the C-text (C. VI. 1–4), written probably in the late 1370s. For a fascinating study of the links between Chaucer and Langland see J. A. W. Bennett, 'Chaucer's contemporary' in *Piers Plowman: Critical Approaches* ed. S. S. Hussey (London, 1969) pp. 310–24.
6 Ibid. pp. 317–18. See also the discussion in Mann pp. 67–74.
7 *Chaucer's Knight: The Portrait of a Medieval Mercenary* (London, 1980).
8 See C. VI. 72–5; he does also, of course, recognize other social functions, such as maintaining justice and hunting vermin (B. VI. 28–46).
9 Jones's arguments are largely based on the fact that there were a great many English mercenaries around in Europe in the fourteenth century, and that the word 'armee' was used for a mercenary army. But Chaucer could easily have dropped a word that the Knight had been in one of the mercenary groups if he had wished to; he does not – the Knight's campaigns are all on the fringes of Christendom. 'Armee' (a disputed reading, as Jones acknowledges) is, on Jones's own evidence, not used in the sense of 'mercenary army' in the derogatory sense he would have it: the examples he gives suggest that 'armee' means a host made up of fighters who are not the lord's own vassals – and since the King of England was not fighting in any Crusades, Chaucer's Knight necessarily has to serve under a different lord.
10 The details of the Knight's clothing and horses appear highly suspicious to Jones; but that they should be interpreted positively becomes unquestionable when they are set against the description of the Monk (see below).
11 'The Knight's interruption of the Monk's Tale', *ELH* XXIV (1957) 249–68, esp. pp. 256–8.
12 See Beryl Rowland, *Blind Beasts: Chaucer's Animal World* (Kent, Ohio, 1971), esp. pp. 100–2.
13 Per Nykrog, *Les Fabliaux* (1957/Publications Romanes et Françaises 123, Geneva, 1973) ch. I.
14 *Troilus and Criseyde* is sometimes described as if it were, but that would be unimaginable if Criseyde had a living husband. The Merchant's Tale is not a romance, partly because the adultery reduces it far below any ideal: see below, pp. 142–3.
15 *Boece* Book II pr.2.67–72.
16 'Chaucer and the visual arts' in *Writers and their Background: Geoffrey Chaucer* ed. Derek Brewer (London, 1974) p. 312.
17 There is a valuable discussion of this aspect of the *Tales* in Derek Brewer's article 'Gothic Chaucer' in his *Writers and their Background*, esp. pp. 27–9. F. Anne Payne's *Chaucer and Menippean Satire* (Madison, WI, 1981) concentrates on *Troilus and Criseyde*, the Knight's Tale and the Nun's Priest's Tale as individual examples of the form and does not develop any ideas about the *Canterbury Tales* as a whole.

18 *Anatomy of Criticism* p. 309; the further quotations are from pp. 311 and 310.
19 I, 3864, 3916, 4324.
20 I, 104, 1966, III, 1381.
21 I, 2437, VII, 38, 51, VIII, 1342.
22 I, 1761, IV, 1986, V, 479, II, 660; *Legend* F 503.

The Knight's Tale and Its Settings

V. A. Kolve

Kolve sustains the emphasis of Howard on the visual analogies to Chaucer's writing in his interesting and scholarly study, Chaucer and the Imagery of Narrative. *He examines with regard to the first fragment of the* Canterbury Tales *how the tales work through 'symbolic images' which 'allow truth to speak through fable'. Such images, for Kolve, are both naturalistic in their relation to the world of experience, and symbolic in their expression of a deeper truth. Thus the pilgrims progress towards a material object, the tomb of St Thomas à Becket in Canterbury, but this is also a sign of spiritual renewal, penance, grace, and the mysterious working of God in the world. Just as this image hovers above the* Canterbury Tales, *so other images stand at the heart of individual tales and link groups of tales – rather as the image of the heart forms a poetic nucleus in* Troilus and Crisyede. *The first group of tales with their several symbolic images has its own cohesion, particularly evident in the close structural links between the Knight's romance and the Miller's and Reeve's parodic* fabliaux, *the echoes in the low-life, bawdy fragment of the* Cook's Tale, *and the rewriting of romance motifs and the theme of love from a female, Christian perspective in the* Man of Law's Tale. *The range of genres, settings, tellers and themes in this group of tales anticipates the rest of the work. Kolve notes the unexpectedness of Chaucer's decision to begin with an epic romance, although it is also the case that a work set in the classical world, with all its grandeur, high rhetoric, and elevated courtly ideals, is entirely suitable to the Knight. As we have seen, the use of 'olde bokes' associated a work with the great literature of antiquity, with an elevated, established tradition of literature rather than with the newer, less respected vernacular writing. Yet this tale, set in the world of classical gods and goddesses, cannot offer Christian resolution or the promise of the eternal. Rather, it becomes a narrative about 'human limitation', setting the scene for a series of stories on this theme.*

In the Knight's Tale *the constraints on the protagonists are closely related to their devotion to high ideals. Kolve discerns two central formative motifs: one, the linked images of the prison and garden (explored below), the other that of the* amphitheatre where the tournament takes place. The two are related, for both prison and amphitheatre represent different kinds of bond – the former forcible and painful, the latter a civilized construction that creates order out of chaos. Yet although the building of the amphitheatre creates a tournament out of an anarchic battle and symmetrical temples out of the disorder of the forest, and thus represents an attempt to rule the unruly passion of love, this order ultimately yields death rather than life: Arcite, riding out in triumph, falls and is mortally wounded. The tale raises existential questions about the human predicament and the possibility of free will: man in the end is at the mercy of the whims of the gods, and all Theseus's power becomes futile. Such questions touch deep veins of human doubt, while the classical setting silently reminds us that faith in a Christian universe offers another, more optimistic perspective on the human pilgrimage of life.

Kolve explores evocatively Chaucer's use of contrasts, and links the prison and garden imagery to conventional portrayals of Fortune as inhabiting a house half rich and decorated, half dilapidated and mean, an emblem of the 'wele' and 'wo' of life that are so much the subject of the Knight's Tale. *In a similar way, a manuscript illumination of Chaucer's source, Boccaccio's* Teseida, *exploits the contrast between dark and light, freedom and bonds. Kolve argues that the wounds of love experienced by Palamon and Arcite go beyond the conventional, representing an instinct towards the freedom they do not possess. Paradoxically, however, love is also a prison – half-painful, half-pleasurable – and the bonds of the literal prison are both painful and pleasurable, for it is here that the lovers are near to Emilye. Kolve demonstrates how Chaucer, as in* Troilus and Criseyde, *draws on the familiar medieval conception of love in terms of oppositions, employed most memorably in the love poetry of Petrarch, which so evocatively uses the images of thirst and drink, heat and cold, life and death. In the* Knight's Tale *these paradoxes move beyond convention: the bonds of Palamon and Arcite are literal, as is Emilye's freedom, and this combination of imprisonment and freedom comes to be an emblem of life itself, where free will is always limited by fate, fortune, the gods, providence or simply chance. For if the world of the* Knight's Tale *is one of unfamiliar gods, its constraints on freedom and the angst of being are not. Such are the questions raised in the philosophical work that most influenced Chaucer, Boethius's* Consolation of Philosophy, *which Chaucer was translating at about the same time as he wrote the* Knight's Tale. *Unlike the prisoner Boethius, however, the protagonists in the* Knight's Tale *are offered no answers.*

V. A. Kolve, from 'The Knight's Tale and Its Settings' in *Chaucer and the Imagery of Narrative: The First Five Canterbury Tales*. Edward Arnold, London, 1984.

Chaucer's pilgrims journey toward the most important Christian shrine in England, the tomb of St Thomas à Becket in Canterbury Cathedral. A great variety of motive has brought them together, and we hear from them as they 'talen' along the way a great diversity of story, ranging from bawdy *fabliaux* to a miracle of the Virgin, from metrical romance to prose sermon, from Ovidian myth to a saint's legend. Because *The Canterbury Tales* exists only in fragments, some more fully articulated than others, our guesses about its internal organization must always remain to some degree tentative. In the great middle of the work – the record of the middle journey – it is very difficult to talk about formal intention, for we are dealing with material that Chaucer, had he lived, might later have revised, replaced, or repositioned. And we know nothing of the plans that never found their way into verse at all.

But the larger 'idea' of *The Canterbury Tales*, in Donald Howard's phrase, can be investigated more confidently, for we have from Chaucer the first tale and the last – those of the Knight and the Parson – and incremental to each a series of tales that together create a substantial frame for the whole. The first of these groups is the subject of this volume, which will argue that the tales of the Knight, Miller, Reeve, Cook, and Man of Law formally begin the journey, constituting a narrative sequence at once coherent in its own right and prophetic – typologically anticipatory – of the shape of the literary pilgrimage as a whole. This sequence of tales looks toward three distinct historical periods – the pagan world of classical Greece, the transitional world of sixth-century Europe, and the contemporary world of late fourteenth-century England. It does so through the lenses of three literary genres – romance, *fabliau*, and artistically elaborated chronicle – each capable of registering a particular area of human experience with maximum precision. But the larger design is also self-reflexive, concerned with the nature of poetry itself. The beginning of the journey offers a carefully structured demonstration of the several ways in which poetry can relate to truth.

The tale the pilgrim company hears first on its journey is dignified, eloquent, and serious in its intent,[1] but it is, for all that, a strange choice of tale to begin a Christian pilgrimage. Within such a story, set in pagan Athens, centuries before the birth of Christ and the continuing witness of his saints, the deepest truths known to the teller and his audience – the very truths they have become pilgrims to honor – cannot be expressed. In this chapter I shall argue that Chaucer chose it as his first tale precisely for its exclusion of Christian material, and for the self-limitation that such a choice entailed for him as poet. A sense of human limitation, apprehended on many levels, is at the heart of the tale, and constitutes its essential contribution to the first day's pilgrimage.

Chaucer's subject is nothing less than the pagan past at its most noble and dignified, imagined from within. As in the *Troilus*, generally thought to have been written at about the same time in his career, his purpose is to discover – through an act of the sympathetic imagination – what it was like to be human then, and what kinds of poetry can be made of that experience. In *The Knight's Tale*, he communicates his vision of the pagan past most powerfully through two great images essential to the narrative, the prison/garden and the tournament amphitheatre, settings that the poetry invites us to visualize in our minds and that rise readily to memory when we think about the tale. Around them it is possible to reconstruct and meditate upon the narrative experience as a whole. Let us look first at the prison/garden, for within that setting the love story has its beginning. As an image it undergoes a grave and beautiful metamorphosis in the poem.

The facts are initially very simple. Palamon and Arcite have been condemned by Duke Theseus 'to dwellen in prisoun/Perpetuelly, – he nolde no raunsoun' (I.1023). They are held captive in a tower, 'in angwissh and in wo,' and it is from that prison some years later that they first see Emelye:

> ...in the gardyn, at the sonne upriste,
> She walketh up and doun, and as hire liste*   *pleases
> She gadereth floures....
>   (I.1051)

The action requires that the garden be within sight of the prison tower, but Chaucer (following his original, the *Teseida* of Boccaccio)[2] goes beyond that, to insist on their architectural contiguity. He joins them in an emblematic way:

> The grete tour, that was so thikke and stroong,
> Which of the castel was the chief dongeoun,
> (Ther as the knyghtes weren in prisoun
> Of which I tolde yow and tellen shal)
> Was evene joynant to the gardyn wal
> Ther as this Emelye hadde hir pleyynge.
>   (I.1056)

In this striking juxtaposition of structures, the prison and garden are 'evene joynant': they share a common wall. The setting is reminiscent of, and may ultimately have been suggested by, the House of Fortune in *The Romance of the Rose*, one part of which is high-towered and gorgeously decorated, with walls of gold and silver set with precious jewels; the rest is low and crumbling, with walls of mud and a thatch roof falling into ruin. (Plate 6, from about 1400, shows Lady Fortune turning her wheel within.)[3] That dual structure is analogous to the prison joined to a garden in *The Knight's Tale*, for both are ways of talking about the 'wele' and 'wo' of human life, about the bewildering range of experience that lies within Fortune's gift.

The Canterbury Tales: Critical Extracts

A remarkable manuscript painter, known after his patron as the Master of René of Anjou, responded vividly to this double setting in a miniature he made around 1455 for a French translation of the *Teseida*. It is part of a remarkable sequence of illustrations (some by a less gifted artist), which we shall examine closely in this chapter. He shows us (plate 7) Emilia in the pleasure garden,* sitting on a turfed bench and weaving a garland of flowers, while the two knights look out upon her through the bars of their prison window.[4] The room behind them is in darkness, whereas the garden, delicate in its colors and open to the heavens, is washed by the light of spring. The double setting immediately establishes the *ethos* of the action, the themes the action will explore. The same may be said of a handsome presentation tray that Mariotto di Nardo, a Florentine painter, decorated some time in the first quarter of the fifteenth century, or of a drawing illustrating the scene in a Florentine manuscript from about 1450.[5] The contrast between the two places, for these artists as well, serves as an entry into the meaning of the

Plate 6 The House of Fortune, from *The Romance of the Rose*, Paris, *c.* 1400. Bodley MS Douce 371, fol. 40v. Bodleian Library, Oxford.

243

The Canterbury Tales: Critical Extracts

Plate 7 Emilia in the pleasure garden; Palemone and Arcita in prison. Illustration to Boccaccio's *Teseida*, French, *c.* 1455. AKG London/Vienna Austrian Nationalbibliothek, Cod 2617, fol. 53.

event, not merely a transcription of narrative detail. And that contrast suggested to Chaucer – as the first in a series of transformations he would work upon this image – a new approach to the young knights' discovery of passionate love, an approach more searching than anything in the *Teseida* or in these pictures based upon it.

In Boccaccio's poem, the two knights at this moment are moved above all by the beauty of Emilia's person and her song. On seeing her, Arcita exclaims, 'She is from paradise!' and Palemone echoes, 'Surely, this is Venus!' (III, vv. 12, 14). They have never seen anyone so beautiful, so pleasing, so gracious – the usual superlatives, given a certain force by the skill of Boccaccio's rhetoric and by the correlative beauty of the *giardino amoroso* in which she is seen. These attributes of Emilia – including the conviction she must be a goddess ('But Venus is it soothly, as I gesse') – are important to Chaucer's version as well. But he works with something distinctive besides, narrating the process by which they fall in love in terms of a formula based on the verb 'to roam,' which owes nothing to Boccaccio and is repeated so often as to shape decisively our understanding of the event. In Chaucer's version (italics added), Palamon, by leave of his jailor,

> Was risen and *romed in a chambre an heigh*,
> In which he al the noble citee seigh,
> And eek the gardyn, ful of braunches grene,
> Ther as this fresshe Emelye the shene
> Was in hire walk, and *romed up and doun*.
> This sorweful prisoner, this Palamoun,
> Goth in the chambre *romynge to and fro*,
> And to hymself compleynynge of his wo.
> (I.1065)

When Arcite notices his friend grow pale, Palamon explains the cause:

> 'The fairnesse of that lady that I see
> Yond in the gardyn *romen to and fro*
> Is cause of al my criyng and my wo.'
> (I.1098)

A moment later Arcite is at the barred window:

> ...with that word Arcite gan espye
> Wher as this lady *romed to and fro*,
> And with that sighte hir beautee hurte hym so,
> (I.1112)

that he speaks of being wounded as deeply as Palamon.

> 'The fresshe beautee sleeth me sodeynly
> Of hire that *rometh in the yonder place.*'
> (I.1118)

There are few places in Chaucer's writings where a single word is used so insistently. The repetition is surely a key to something central in the poem.

The convention of love at first sight that lies behind this fiction needs no apology. Then as now, such love has been known to happen, and medieval love theory taught that erotic love enters the soul through the eyes (I.1096–7). Two illustrations of this scene indeed emphasize that tradition by showing the God of Love shooting an arrow of desire into the young knights' eyes.[6] But I think we can see Chaucer here seeking to reinforce those conventions with another sort of psychological truth – perhaps because there is something disproportionate, even potentially comic, about this event as a cause of everything that will follow. Love at first sight by two men for the same woman at exactly the same time makes a somewhat distant claim to credibility, as does the later moment when they stand ankle-deep in blood fighting over her, without Emelye even knowing they exist. Chaucer allows for all that is ridiculous in the situation through Theseus's response: 'Now looketh, is nat that an heigh folye? / Who may been a fool, but if he love?' (I.1798). But beneath their apparently hopeless passion, Chaucer shows a deeper movement of the spirit as well – a compulsion not comic, arbitrary, or trivial. The two young knights fall in love with Emelye for her beauty, unmistakably, but for the beauty of her freedom most of all. They cannot describe her – for they cannot see her – apart from the liberty and ease of her movement. From within prison they fall in love with a creature who seems to incarnate a condition the exact opposite of their own.

Indeed, we are made to see this gratuitous decision to love – this act of pure will – as their only available expression of something within them still free, not limited by prison walls, leg-irons, or exile.[7] The affirmation of some freedom, no matter how tenuous, is essential to their survival as fully human beings. In the words of Arcite, returned from exile in the disguise of a servant, as he raises his sword against Palamon in the grove:

> 'What, verray fool, thynk wel that love is free,
> And I wol love hire maugree* al thy myght!'   *despite
> (I.1606)

Their prison decision to love, and if necessary to die in affirmation of that love, enacts, in a way that becomes important later in the tale, a woefully distorted version of a truth taught by Lady Philosophy to Boethius in another prison: the fact that the mind and spirit can be free, even if the body is in chains. Being young knights, not philosophers, they choose to make their ultimate commitment to Emelye. But that decision is informed by values not limited to its choice of object alone, affirming both the freedom of the heart's affections, in despite of circumstance, and the power of man's will over his animal instinct merely to survive, on any terms at all. Central to man's nature as it is conceived in this poem are his need to seek freedom and his need to seek love. Palamon and Arcite in prison, looking out upon Emelye in the garden, blend these two compulsions into a single 'entente.' It is only in retrospect that we realize Emelye in her 'romynge' is, in subtler, less apparent ways, as constrained as they.

Thus the way the two knights fall in love in this tale is far more deeply rooted in its physical setting than is the version offered by the *Teseida*, and it prepares us for even more complex manipulations of the image to come. What has been to this point essentially a poetry of stasis, permitting only the barest minimum of physical movement within a formal architectural tableau, suddenly becomes animated, opening out into a realm of contingency and change. Perotheus obtains Arcite's freedom, Palamon escapes, and the opening icon of the prison/garden – now left behind as a literal place, but lodged in our memory as a mental image – is redefined through a series of metaphors and used to illuminate the significance of the action in new and deeper ways.

Released 'frely to goon wher that hym liste over al' (I.1207), Arcite feels no joy. He is in a world turned ' up-so-doun,' in which words and the things to which they point are perversely, if poignantly, reassessed:

> He seyde, 'Allas that day that I was born!
> Now is my prisoun worse than biforn;
> Now is me shape* eternally to dwelle   *it is my destiny
> Noght in purgatorie, but in helle.
> Allas, that evere knew I Perotheus!
> For elles hadde I dwelled with Theseus,
> Yfetered in his prisoun everemo.
> Thanne hadde I been in blisse, and nat in wo.
> Oonly the sighte of hire whom that I serve,
> Though that I nevere hir grace may deserve,
> Wolde han suffised right ynough for me.
> O deere cosyn Palamon,' quod he,
> 'Thyn is the victorie of this aventure.
> Ful blisfully in prison maistow dure,* –   *you can live
> In prison? certes nay,* but in paradys!   *certainly not
> Wel hath Fortune yturned thee the dys.'
>   (I.1123)

The Canterbury Tales: Critical Extracts

This extravagant reversal of values, in which freedom has become prison and prison freedom, yields a rueful sort of comedy, but the larger interest is psychological and fully serious. The way the young knights choose to assert their freedom from within the literal prison – electing to love another human being totally, making their entire happiness contingent upon someone other than themselves – is here revealed to be its own kind of bondage, a *prison amoureuse* at once bitter and sweet, painful but preferred. So cruelly perplexing is this new imprisonment that when they next meet (in a wooded grove), the encounter is described in language that recalls their former incarceration: Palamon hides in a bush, while Arcite 'rometh up and doun' (I.1515). Even outside the prison tower, their experience is characterized as captivity and constraint.

Notes

*In order to distinguish between Chaucer's characters and those of Boccaccio's poem (whether in his original text, the paintings that illustrate its medieval French translation, or McCoy's modern English translation) I refer to Boccaccio's characters by their Italian names: Teseo, Palemone, Arcita, Emilia.

1 I do not mean by this description to deny that the narrator is sometimes amused by some part of his material, especially in his representation of the young knights as lovers and philosophers. As Theseus says within the tale, 'Who may been a fool, but if he love?' (1.1799). And I do not deny that 'what passes for tragedy in the chivalric view of things can be at times funny, at times nasty' when seen from other perspectives (David, *Strumpet Muse*, p. 87). The tale is, after all, lengthy and capacious; it is not made less serious as a work of art by regarding human experience from a number of points of view, whatever occasional problems in the management of tone may arise. (I think there are a few.) But I do not think the larger purpose and dominant effect of this poem is comic (*pace* Neuse, 'The Knight: The First Mover in Chaucer's Human Comedy'), or that it is meant to expose its teller as a mercenary killer paying inept lip service to chivalric values he neither understands nor in his own life serves. Jones, *Chaucer's Knight*, argues the latter view in a book-length study that, for all its learned information, seems to me to misread convention and misjudge tone at many crucial junctures. Two early reviews of Jones's book raise the necessary objections: see Burrow, 'The Imparfit Knight,' and that by David Aers. That Chaucer refers to a poem on Palamon and Arcite as among his works written prior to *The Canterbury Tales* (*LGW*, [F] 420–1) ought perhaps to dissuade us from assuming too intimate a connection between the tale and its pilgrim-teller; it ought even more to prevent us from making that teller the hidden subject of the tale and its only coherent explanation.... Benson and Leyerle, eds, *Chivalric Literature*, argue against the prevailing view that the later Middle Ages was a period of decline in chivalry; Leyerle's concluding essay provides an elegant summary.

The Canterbury Tales: Critical Extracts

2   Boccaccio, *Teseida delle nozze d'Emilia*, III, v. 11: 'Arcita si levò, ch'era in prigione / allato al giardino amoroso.' The *Teseida* has been translated by McCoy as *The Book of Theseus*, including most of Boccaccio's own glosses (*Chiose*) to the text; throughout this chapter I quote McCoy's translation, sometimes slightly modified. Havely, *Chaucer's Boccaccio*, appeared after this chapter was in its final form; pp. 103–52 translate those parts of the *Teseida* that correspond most closely to Chaucer's poem, with linking summaries of the rest. Pratt, 'Chaucer's Use of the *Teseida*,' remains a study of fundamental interest and importance; see also his chapter on *The Knight's Tale* in Bryan and Dempster, eds, *Sources and Analogues*. Wilson, '*The Knight's Tale* and the *Teseida* Again,' assesses the larger literary identities of the two works.

3   Plate 6: Oxford, Bodley MS. Douce 371, fol. 40v. shows the tradition at its simplest. For a more elaborate version, see Valencia, Bibl. de la Universidad MS. 387, fol. 42 v (French, ca. 1420); it has been reproduced by Fleming, '*Roman de la Rose*,' fig. 31. For the text, see Dahlberg's translation, *Romance of the Rose*, pp. 121–2, of ll. 6049–144 of Jean de Meun's poem; no Middle English translation of this part of the poem has survived. Jean's House of Fortune is based upon that of Alain de Lille in the *Anticlaudianus*, Bk. VIII, which Chaucer also knew at first hand; see the translation by Sheridan, p. 189. Lydgate, 'A Mumming at London,' *Minor Poems*, II, 683 (40–58), paraphrases Jean's description, and attributes it to him; the ruined portion of the house is called 'þat doungeoun' (l. 47). Chrétien de Troyes' *Cligés* also links a prison tower and garden in complex, emblematic ways; see the edition by Micha, p. 185 (6079) to the end, or, in translation, Chrétien de Troyes, *Arthurian Romances*, pp. 171–9. Gottfried von Strassburg, *Tristan*, pp. 261–6, also uses a bipartite setting and includes explicit commentary on its meaning. Panofsky, *Early Netherlandish Painting*, I, ch. 5, brilliantly interprets certain architectural juxtapositions in the visual arts as vehicles of symbolic meaning. For interesting speculations on Chaucer's use of open and closed spaces, see Joseph, 'Chaucerian "Game" – "Earnest."'

4   ... Vienna, Natl. Lib. MS. 2617, fol. 53; the manuscript has sixteen miniatures, half of them by the anonymous master, half by a less talented hand. On this MS., see Chmelarz, 'Eine Französische Bilderhandschrift'; his 15 plates reproduce all the illuminations, with the historiated initial on fol. 17v placed at the beginning of his own text. Six of the illuminations were reproduced in fine color facsimile under the title of an associated MS., René d'Anjou, *Livre du Cuer d'Amours espris*, III, pls XIX–XXIV, a facsimile unfortunately very rare. The present picture may be seen in color in Brewer, *Chaucer and His World*, opp. p. 17 ...

5   On Mariotto di Nardo (active 1394–1431), see Berenson, *Italian Pictures of the Renaissance*, I, 129–33; he reproduces this tray, which would have been used to offer gifts at a marriage or a birth, as pl. 527. Berenson did not recognize its narrative subject, labeling it simply '*Desco da Nozze*: Garden of Love.' Now in the Staatsgalerie, Stuttgart, it has been recently published (and correctly identified) by Watson, *The Garden of Love*, pp. 73–4, and pl. 60. The Florentine drawing is from the Gerolamini MS. described above; see Degenhart and Schmitt, *Corpus der Italienischen Zeichnungen*, fig. 290a (fol. 31).

6   Cupid shoots his arrows in the Florentine drawing described above, and in an interesting sixteenth-century woodcut reproduced by Crisp, *Mediaeval Gardens*, I,

fig. 108, where it is described as an illustration to Panfillo [Pamillo] Sasso's *Strambotii*, without further bibliographical reference. Crisp was an amateur, in the old-fashioned sense of the word, and his book, though vast and useful, is not scholarly. I have searched through editions of the *Strambotii*, published in various cities in 1501, 1506, and 1511, and have not succeeded in finding this woodcut; the woodcuts vary, however, and it seems likely that the reference, though incomplete, could be proved correct. Crisp did not know that the scene derives ultimately from the *Teseida*, illustrating Bk. III, vv. 15–17: 'Arcita said: "O Palemone, do you see what I behold in those beautiful immortal eyes?...I see in them the one who wounded the father of Phaeton because of Daphne....In his hands he holds two golden arrows and now he is placing one on his bowstring as he looks at no one else but me."...Then Palemone, utterly astonished, cried out, "Alas, the other has wounded me."'

7   In the *Teseida*, the way the young knights fall in love is developed less interestingly, though the character of Emilia is, in compensation, richer and more fully detailed. (Like Creseida in the *Filostrato*, she is to be associated with the woman Boccaccio loves, and to whom he dedicates the poem....) When Palemone sees her and cries 'Alas!' (*Omè!*), she looks up at the window, realizes what that cry signifies, and is torn between her virginal modesty and her vanity. (The latter is said to be innate in women, who delight in having their beauty seen.) From that time forward, she adorns herself the more carefully when she goes into the garden; and whenever she knows she is looked upon, she sings most beautifully and walks with slow, graceful steps (III, vv. 17–19, 28–30). Chaucer kept none of this material.

Fabliau, Confession, Satire

W. A. Davenport

In the previous extract we saw Chaucer as romancier, telling a tale of the most elevated kind about high idealism and chivalry. In the realism of the depiction of arms and the tournament, and the engagement with specifically medieval notions of chivalry, courtliness and philosophy, the tale is less remote than it may first seem. Its teller, the Knight, though he is very much the ideal type of the first estate, the aristocracy, is also realized vividly through the details of the actual historical battles in which he has fought. Yet the Knight and his tale still belong to the stuff of high romance. In the following extract Davenport examines a very different strand of Chaucer's writing, that of commonplace tales and moral satires. This is in many ways a less familiar Chaucer, neither the voice of Kittredge's great human comedy, nor the detached, amused ironist mainly concerned with literary games. Rather, it is a moral voice, similar to that heard at the end of Troilus and Criseyde, *in the*

The Canterbury Tales: Critical Extracts

translation of Boethius, *in the philosophical questioning of the* Knight's Tale, *and in the* Retractions. *This voice, however, is engaged not only with philosophical ideas and ideals, but also with the corruption of the everyday world and the failure of morality in the world; flawed human nature also affords the possibility for comedy and satire. Alongside the romances, the* Canterbury Tales *contains a series of religious tales which engage with the ideal, a number of comic tales or* fabliaux, *and more serious expositions of sin such as the* Canon's Yeoman's Tale *and* Parson's Tale.

Davenport begins by comparing Chaucer to his contemporary Gower, often considered the more 'moral' writer, but in many ways offering a less direct representation of the disintegrating present in his work, Confessio Amantis. *Gower presents a social critique in his* Prologue *but then turns to classical legend to treat the experience and learning of the Lover. Chaucer, by contrast, offers a whole series of vignettes of the 'real' world through his frame narrative, the links between tales, and some of the tales themselves. Davenport by no means argues for the naturalistic or novelistic Chaucer, but rather points to the range of tales, which include a portrayal of the imperfect temporal world as well as that of high romance, just as, as Cooper emphasized, the pilgrims include a range of flawed and ideal types. This balance reflects the medieval view of human nature as constructed of warring vices and virtues. The worldly, corrupt impulse is most evident in the tales that can seem most light-hearted, the plots of which depend on deceit, violence, greed and sexual desire. While Chaucer is master of the comic form, many of the actions of his* fabliaux *live out precisely the human failings so severely condemned in the Parson's sermon. The everyday world is amusing but rarely attractive – though, as Davenport demonstrates, Chaucer is skilled in ambiguity and subtle shifts in tone. Thus the ending of the* Reeve's Tale *has a poignant romance quality, and Alisoun of the* Miller's Tale *remains one of the most attractive of Chaucerian characters in her animal vitality.*

In his translation of the fabliau *from an oral, low form almost never used in English writing into sophisticated literary art, and more generally, Chaucer also draws on the popular genre of moral satire. Davenport describes the formative role of confession in the most celebrated medieval moral satire, the alliterative poem* Piers Plowman, *and compares this to the* Parson's Tale, *which contains a series of vivid disquisitions against various sins. He suggests that Chaucer's voice may be heard in some of the Parson's heated condemnations of false swearing, magic, vanity and fine clothes, for these are themes to which the tales often return (though frequently humorously, as in the description of the Wife of Bath's red stockings and fine clothes). The Parson's voice embodies the anti-courtly strain typical of some medieval literature and demonstrates Chaucer's capacity for sharp criticism and ruthless exposition of moral failings. Davenport gives a series of examples of Chaucer's use of the attack on the 'abuses of the age' that characterizes moral satire, and of the confessional mode. Davenport argues that although Chaucer never* becomes a didactic writer and is certainly not to be equated with the Parson, a satirical aim links the exempla and fabliaux. The comic tales form a carnivalesque[1] version of the moral ones, but in both there is an underlying 'sentence' regarding the corruptions of the secular world.

Notes

1   The notion of carnival is adopted by Mikhail Bakhtin to convey the dialogic nature of literature, where a comic voice may mock or subvert the voice of authority.

W. A. Davenport, '*Fabliau*, Confession, Satire' in *Chaucer and His English Contemporaries: Prologue and Tale in 'The Canterbury Tales'*. Macmillan, Basingstoke, 1998.

Gower committed himself in *Confessio Amantis* to explore for his readers not only the instructive examples of the past, which meant taking from books the narratives of 'the world that whilom tok / Long tyme in olde daies passed', but also the troubling evidence of 'The world which neweth every dai'. What Gower had in the forefront of his mind was the disintegration, as he saw it, of the stability of the realm and the old social certainties, and his analysis of the ills of the modern world occupies him in his Prologue, but the narrative strategy which he chose for the story of his poem meant that the main evidence of the everyday world which he expresses is the first-person account of the lover's experience, what it actually is like to live through the daily anxieties of the attendant and aspiring suitor. The illustrative examples of good and bad behaviour are mostly classical, though Gower ingeniously mixes material from different sources, but the point to which the narrator repeatedly returns, is the present behaviour of the lover, the probing of his sensibility and self-awareness, seen both from the lover's own embarrassed, self-deprecating standpoint and from the confessor's kindly but ironically detached sense of Amans's weaknesses. The effects of realism and of comedy, and ultimately anticlimax, which Gower develops in the lengthy sections dealing with Amans's responses to Genius, make them the most intimate and attractive parts of his narrative, and the places where he gives substance to his claim that the human being's divisions are the microcosm of the rifts in the body politic. Gower's view of 'the modern world' is given some sense of actuality through the expression of the pressures within the particular sphere of experience available to his central character, but this is mainly an account of an inner world, the lover's sense of his existence rather than an observer's view of it.

Chaucer's frame story is more obviously concerned with the outer world, a set of contemporary characters, through which the social world is directly represented. Once the stories begin, the world of the pilgrimage becomes the point of reference to which some stories refer more closely than do others. The 'modern world' of Chaucer's poem lacks continuity, but the life expressed in the link passages is extended into some (by no means into all) of the tales. This is done in a variety of ways. The most familiar, or rather the one most often assumed by readers, is by making tales express the experience of the supposed narrator; the device is only identifiable in a limited number of tales, and there are quite a number where one could change the name of the teller without any disturbance to the sense – indeed there are one or two, such as *The Shipman's Tale*, where Chaucer clearly did. Equally obvious is the development of quarrels among the pilgrims (Miller / Reeve, Friar / Summoner) which are then extended into the tales they tell. Less clear-cut in its working is the more general device of using aspects of contemporary life as the actual material of the narrative. The tales of Miller, Reeve, Cook and Summoner are set respectively in Oxford, Cambridge, London and Yorkshire, and so happen against a more knowable background of social activity than stories of ancient Athens, Rome or Brittany, let alone the vague Arthurian world of the Wife of Bath or the Squire's Tartary. Other tales are less specific but are placed in a contemporary rural England (Nun's Priest, Friar), the suburbs of a town (Canon's Yeoman), or the not too distant France (Shipman) or Flanders (Pardoner and, jokingly, *Sir Thopas*). From this mixture of tales of here and now, and tales of long ago and far away, Chaucer creates a similar span to the one envisaged by Gower, though one where the divisions are more apparent.

For Chaucer the question was also one of genre: some kinds of narrative were not aptly concerned with contemporary affairs nor placed locally. It seems not to have been a possibility for romance in his eyes, and to set *Sir Thopas* in Flanders is in itself an indication of absurdity. Tales of love, adventure and great events were 'storial'. Though some romances of the period, such as *Gamelyn* or *Sir Degrevant*... manage to spice folk-tale narratives of the recovery of lost fortune with observations on the ways of present-day lords, brothers, neighbours, clerics, judges, stewards, Chaucer does this only to a minor degree. For Chaucer as story-teller the commonplace world is the place for commonplace acts, even if strung together by fantastic, absurd, exaggerated motives and sequences: lusts, thefts, deceits and out-wittings are detectable in many types of tale, but those of the contemporary world are mainly for momentary satisfactions, immediate gratification rather than winning a place in society, defining a role in life or achieving a major ambition. So for a handful of his non-gentle narrators Chaucer invents the 'cherles tale' as a loose classification for those stories of sex, greed and tricks which seem to have become detached from the moral theme which authenticates the *exemplum*. These are added to his various forensic tales and his confessional prologues as part of his way of handling the 'world that neweth every day'.

It is well known that Chaucer seems to be the first English writer, apart from the anonymous author of the incomplete *Dame Sirith* [thirteenth-century], to give literary expression to those comic, often scurrilous, stories of middle- and low-class life usually known as *fabliaux*.[1] And he is, as far as one can tell, seldom in these stories simply adapting, let alone translating, a single, known source. Versions of *The Reeve's Tale* and *The Shipman's Tale* occur in Boccaccio's *Decameron* and are the main evidence suggesting that Chaucer did know the Italian work, though his versions are not exactly like Boccaccio's. For the rest there are no more than general analogues and similarities, in Flemish, Italian and German for *The Miller's Tale*, in Latin and German for *The Friar's Tale*, in French for *The Summoner's Tale*, and in various places for the medley of *The Merchant's Tale*. Something similar may be said of some other types of tale dealing with 'modern' life: the story told in *The Pardoner's Tale* is widespread, but there is no one obvious direct source, and there is no known source for the narrative parts of *The Canon's Yeoman's Tale*. This uncertainty about origins suggests that Chaucer's tales of contemporary life were versions of anecdotes and tales in general circulation; that is, literary versions of the oral and improvisatory, retaining their informality but made 'textual'.

Certainly his naming 'cherles tales' as a category in *The Canterbury Tales* (apart from inviting identification of his stories with the idle tales of the tavern condemned by Langland and the preachers of the period) suggests special judgement of some sort. One might argue that by being dismissive and bidding those who do not like smut to turn over the page Chaucer suggests a kind of exemption from criticism (the cynical reader might see it as a way of actually directing the attention of potential readers to the most titillating bits). On the other hand, the labelling does downgrade the tales and raises critical questions which, perhaps because of the incompleteness of the work, Chaucer does not resolve: how can one compare, even in such broad terms as those of *sentence* and *solas*, tales which appeal to such widely differing tastes? Chaucer seems to claim, in the case of *The Miller's Tale*, that laughter unifies all classes: nobody but the irascible Reeve is offended by the story and he is annoyed not because of the smutty bits but on behalf of aggrieved carpenters. However, though many readers may defend the tale as essentially wholesome and life-enhancing, and the unpunished Alisoun as some kind of free spirit allowed to giggle 'Tehee!' with impunity, the conjunction with *The Reeve's Tale* is a reminder that *fabliau* tales are usually rather callous in their humour, and that most of the stories in *The Canterbury Tales* that are concerned with contemporary life have, in fact, some element of nastiness in them. It is not difficult from these tales to see Chaucer's view of the world in his own day as a violent, brutal one and to identify the aggressive quality even in the jokes.

The Canterbury Tales: Critical Extracts

The place in medieval writing where that world is most often treated is in vernacular sermon literature: to look at the way of the world is to enumerate the 'abuses of the age' and to classify them as the workings of the seven deadly sins or of the social ambitions and follies to which a human being's estate made him or her liable. Scornful exposure of vice and folly, invective against appetite, indulgence and self-gratification, and exhortation towards restraint, moderation and self-denial are the company that examination of current behaviour usually keeps. As we have seen above, the use of the *exemplum* in confessional manuals and sermons is a main type of narrative in Middle English. Confession in itself has a strong influence on the literary forms and their procedures in the period. John Burrow pointed out many years ago the importance of confession and of confessors in Ricardian poetry, and the ways in which Chaucer's poor Parson, Langland's Repentance, the *Gawain*-Poet's Sir Bertilak and Gower's Genius, all, in their different ways, served 'to confront the reader with a knowledge of human weakness formed in the confessional'.[2] As important as the taste for psychological analysis which this indicates in the narratives of the period, is the inevitable engagement with pictures of contemporary social activity and of individual actions, motives and processes of thought which this interest in confession necessitated for writers. In Chaucer's time it is in *Piers Plowman* clearly that this material is most powerfully used as the basis of narrative. Allegorical scenes dramatizing the working of sin in private and in public life are scattered through the poem, but the confessional strategy is concentrated into Passus V (B-Text) where each of the Seven Deadly Sins in turn provides a first-person review of how the sin affects human behaviour. Some are quite brief, giving only a quick identification of the vice, but most are detailed monologues which build up a series of scenes and actions. Langland turns lists of transgressions into biographical sequences, so that confession produces accounts of composite careers of vice. At the same time the device of allegory creates from these self-examinations archetypal caricatures: allegorical sins cannot change, unless they get rid of one name and earn another; the personification of the sinful state is fixed in an endless repetition of the typifying actions and thus from hopeless self-exposure bitter comedy results. The confession of Gluttony is presented as a narrative: going to confess is itself a hazardous journey to the church past the tavern, and Glutton's will is too weak for him to pass by the good ale and hot spices offered by Betty the ale-wife. All Glutton's mates are gathered together on the benches within, and a roll-call of trades and of tavern-haunters follows:

Cesse the *Souteresse* sat on the benche,	*Shoemaker*
Watte the *Warner* and his wif bothe,	*warren-keeper*
Tymme the Tynkere and tweyne of his knayves,	
Hikke the *Hakeneyman* and Hugh the *Nedlere*,	*horse-hirer, needle-maker*

255

The Canterbury Tales: Critical Extracts

> Clarice *of Cokkeslane* and the Clerk of the chirche, *a whore*
> Sire Piers *of Pridie* and Pernele of Flaundres, *a priest*
> Dawe the Dykere, and a dozeyne othere –
> A *Ribibour*, a *Ratoner*, a *Rakere* of Chepe, *fiddler, rat-catcher, scavenger*
> A *Ropere*, a *Redyngkyng*, and Rose the Dysshere, *ropemaker, master thatcher(?)*
> Godefray of Garlekhithe and Griffyn the *Walshe*, *Welshman*
> And of *upholderes* an heep, erly by the morwe, *old-clothes men*
> Geve Gloton with glad chere good ale to *hanselle*. *as a treat*
> (*PPl*, V, 308–19)

Glutton's indulgence is traced in all its grossness and in all its stages, from the laughter of the company and 'Lat go the cuppe!' to the violent revenges of overstrained bladder and bowels, the drunken stagger like a blind minstrel's dog 'som tyme aside and som tyme arere', pitching headlong and vomiting, being put to bed for a two-day sleep and the regrets of waking, together with the reproaches of his wife; only then does Glutton confess to sins of the tongue – blasphemy as well as wasteful eating and drinking, and including the incidental temptations:

> For love of tales in tavernes into drynke the moore I dyved.
> (*PPl*, V, 377)

However, as is inevitable for these personifications of sin, the promise of abstinence is accompanied by expression of loathing of it.

Like Gower and Langland, Chaucer could produce adequate vehemence for the enumeration and the condemnation of the varieties of sin, but his definitions of the seven sins in *The Parson's Tale* and of their sub-types and the remedies against them are, for the most part, in general moral terms, with much biblical reference, especially to the *Wisdom* of Solomon, and not specific to the forms of sin of his own day. The odd flicker of pungent expression indicates special areas of strong feeling and it is interesting that, where Langland is particularly vivid in illustrating Gluttony and Envy, Sloth and Avarice, Chaucer sounds especially aroused on the subjects of Pride and Anger. In the latter case, apart from noting among the items of interest his expression of the period's loathing of abortion and contraception as aspects of homicide, one cannot fail to observe the rich scorn for that aspect of swearing associated with the mumbo-jumbo of fortune-tellers and magicians, condemned for:

> horrible sweryng of adjuracioun [exorcism] and conjuracioun [conjuring up spirits], / as doon thise false enchauntours or nigromanciens in bacyns ful of water, or in a bright swerd, in a cercle, or in a fir, or in a shulder-boon of a sheep... (*CT*, X, 603)

Condemned too are those who:

> bileeven on divynailes [divinations], as by flight or by noyse of briddes, or of beestes, or by sort, by nigromancie, by dremes, by chirkynge [creaking] of dores or crakkynge of houses, by gnawynge of rattes and swich maner wrecchednesse. (*CT*, X, 605)

He is forthright too on the anger of those who reproach others by using abusive physical terms: 'as mesel', 'croked harlot' (624), or 'if he repreve hym uncharitably of synne as "thou holour", "thou dronkelewe harlot" and so forth'. Even here Langland is more pointed as he illustrates the destructive power of Wrath by imagining the nuns in a convent jealously sniping at one another:

> Til 'Thow *lixt*' and 'Thow lixt' lopen out at ones, *lie*
> And either hitte other under the cheke.
> (*PPl*, V, 161–2)

The echoes of the condemnation of swearing in *The Pardoner's Tale* are even clearer in the case of Gluttony, where ... Chaucer uses almost the same words in defining the sin and in quoting St Paul in support, as are used as basis for the Pardoner's purple, rhetorical version. The most striking interpretation of sin in terms of the manifestations of contemporary life are found in that aspect of Pride concerned with vanity and outward display. From Chaucer's eloquence on this topic one might conclude that extravagance of dress was the offence in contemporary life that most aroused his passions, or his sense of the absurd. Nowhere else in his work is the statement of the satirist's position of moderation quite so clearly defined as in his twofold condemnation, first of wasteful excess of clothing:

> As to the first synne, that is in superfluitee of clothynge, which that maketh it so deere, to harm of the peple; nat oonly the cost of embrowdynge, the degise endentynge [showy notching of the edges] or barrynge [adding decorative strips], owndynge [undulating stripes], palynge [vertical stripes], wyndynge [twisting patterns], or bendynge [diagonal stripes], and semblable wast of clooth in vanitee, but ther is also costlewe furrynge in hir gownes, so muche pownsonynge of chisels [punching designs with tools] to maken holes, so much daggynge [slitting] of sheres; forthwith the superfluitee in lengthe of the forseide gownes, trailynge in the dong and in the mire, on horse and eek on foote, as wel of man as of womman, that al thilke trailyng is verraily as in effect wasted, consumed, thredbare, and roten with donge, rather than it is yeven to the povre... (*CT*, X, 416–19)

The Canterbury Tales: Critical Extracts

Then, on the other side, he exposes the vice of immodest brevity of dress:

> Upon that oother side, to speken of the horrible disordinat scantnesse of clothyng, as been thise kutted sloppes [short outer coats], or haynselyns [short jackets], that thurgh hire shortnesse ne couere nat the shameful membres of man, to wikked entente. Allas, somme of hem shewen the boce [bulge] of hir shap, and the horrible swollen membres, that semeth lik the maladie of hirnia, in the wrappynge of hir hoses; and eek the buttokes of hem faren as it were the hyndre part of a she-ape in the fulle of the moone. And mooreover, the wrecched swollen membres that they shewe thurgh disgisynge [style of clothing], in departynge [splitting the colour] of hire hoses in whit and reed, semeth that half hir shameful privee membres weren flayne. (*CT*, X, 422–5)

So much for the attractiveness of parti-coloured hose, which Chaucer further castigates in other colours: black/white, white/blue, black/red, as displaying an interesting variety of venereal and other diseases. As to women's dress, he interestingly singles out those whose features make them seem 'ful chaast and debonaire' but who 'notifie in hire array of atyr likerousnesse and pride'. A further area of vain display is in the keeping of costly, thoroughbred horses and in their array:

> in to curious harneys, as in sadeles, in crouperes, peytrels [horse-collars], and bridles covered with precious clothyng, and riche barres and plates of gold and of silver. (*CT*, X, 433)

Chaucer, or at least his Parson, would, it is clear, take a strong moral line about the unnecessary vanity and display of the appearance of the Green Knight and his horse as they appeared at Camelot, which provides an interesting gloss on that scene in *Sir Gawain and the Green Knight*, so often superficially read as exposing the failings of the Arthurian court. Chaucer is writing in the voice of a plain-living, high-thinking Parson and one can identify an anti-courtly strain running through this passage in particular. In going on to condemn the 'holdynge of gret meynee' Chaucer is not far from the attacks on the pride of 'gentlery-men' and the oppressions of maintenance expressed through the mouths of the shepherds in the Towneley plays, but, within the context of *The Canterbury Tales*, the passage has more interest as a set of literary markers than as a political statement. Yet another topic full of suggestion for passages elsewhere in Chaucer and other writers of the period is the condemnation of the pride of the table, seen in:

> excesse of diverse metes and drynkes, and namely [especially] swich manere bake-metes [meat or fish pies] and dissh-metes [stews], brennynge of wilde fir

and peynted and castelled with papir, and semblable wast.... And eek in to greet preciousnesse of vessel and curiositee of mynstralcie, by whiche a man is stired the moore to delices of luxuric... (*CT*, X, 444–6)

The role in which one sees Chaucer in such passages is that of the attacker of the abuses of the age, using the form of moral complaint to categorize society's excesses and to assert a reasonable morality of restraint and frugality. It identifies a stance towards the contemporary world which it is easy to see reflected in many of the fictions within *The Canterbury Tales* which use contemporary settings.

Excess in clothing and appearance is a major theme in both *The Miller's Tale* and *The Reeve's Tale*. Absolon, the Oxford parish clerk, going through all the motions of love longing, playing his guitar yearningly under the beloved's window in the small hours, is portrayed as a precious dandy with exaggeratedly curly, fan-shaped hair-do, fashionably ornamented shoes, red hose and light blue tunic; his gleaming white surplice is seen as part of his ensemble rather than a sign of his office and, since his tripping, dancing legs and his strutting about as Herod on the mystery play's scaffold are much in evidence, the surplice presumably did not conceal much or often. Kissing Alisoun's bottom is a particular humiliation for 'this joly lovere', delicate about personal hygiene, 'squaymous of fartyng' and preparing for his night-time wooing by chewing spices, combing his hair and sucking a lozenge. This is a fuller, richer satirical exposure of folly than the character descriptions in the *General Prologue*. 'Deynous Symkyn' in *The Reeve's Tale* is a more dangerous case, but it is the picture of this 'proud and gay' miller, bristling with weaponry, cutlass in his belt, dagger in his pocket and Sheffield knife stuck in his stocking, as he sets off for church with his proud, pert wife, his red hose matching her gown, that sets up, with contemptuous, dismissive sarcasm, the target for the tale. Absolon's vanity and Symkyn's pride are the keynotes of the town life Chaucer sketches in for Oxford and Cambridge respectively, waiting to be punished by the quicker-witted student characters. Chaucer sets up a more ambiguous picture in his wonderfully vivid portrayal of Alisoun, the sexy wife of the older carpenter, John, in *The Miller's Tale*. Partly an admiring evocation of physical allure, the portrait adds greatly to the freshness and comic liveliness of the tale; with the weasel's slimness, breath of honey and apples, the colt's skittishness, the spring newness of pear-blossom, the sweet voice of the swallow, Alisoun is both a fine realization of a masculine ideal and a *tour de force* showing just how flexible and imaginative a medieval poet could be when, essentially, demonstrating the rules of rhetoric for the depiction of a person. Richness and undercutting complexity are added to the passage by touches which convey Alisoun's vanity in her appearance (the plucked eyebrows, the dramatic black and white costume, the low collar with its large brooch to direct the eye, the lacing of the shoes high up the legs) and which suggest in the final lines her possible history:

> She was a *prymerole*, a *piggesneye*,   *primrose, pig's eye (flower)*
> For any lord to leggen in his bedde,
> Or yet for any good yeman to wedde.
>   (*CT*, I, 3268–70)

We are not told that this is what had happened, but this town wife, who looks and smells like a country girl but shines as brightly as a newly minted coin, has ended up married to an honest, well-meaning and well-to-do, but stupid carpenter, and a lord's bed could have been the route by which she arrived there.

These passages of description identify the essentially satirical flavour of the *fabliaux*. Enjoyed for their farcical, slapstick endings and the robust sexual comedy, both tales go beyond the joking plot material and its tricks, games and outwittings, and certainly beyond any idea that Chaucer was writing in a 'low' style in order to provide for his ventriloquist's dummies tales which we might realistically expect such churls as the Miller and the Reeve to tell. Between the supposed brawling rivalries of such tale-tellers, with the accompanying harlotries of their stories, and the knowingness of Chaucer's sophisticated audience is a gap in which the literary and linguistic wit can reverberate. In the case of the tales of Miller and Reeve two stories of town and gown and of generation rivalry are tricked out with some of the trappings of courtly love tales.

> 'Fare weel, Malyne, sweete wight!
> The day is come; I may no lenger byde;
> But everemo, wherso I go or ryde,
> I is thyn awen clerk, swa have I *seel!*'   *good fortune*
>   (*CT*, I, 4236–9)

So Aleyn, the more enterprising of the two likely lads from the north who have successfully juggled with the placing of the beds and cradle to procure sex with the overbearing miller's daughter and wife, as he bids farewell to the daughter in a pastiche of the courtly *aube*, the dawn song of parting lovers, given a homely flavour by the touches of northern dialect (*I is*, *awen*) with which Chaucer flecks his students' speech. The scene is as uncourtly as Nicholas's display of his skill in 'deerne love' and 'solas' which consists of a quick grope in a furtive corner, but he too is given the language of the yearning lover:

The Canterbury Tales: Critical Extracts

'Lemman, love me al atones
Or I wol dyen, also God me save'.
(*CT*, I, 3280–1)

Such parodic allusion colours the sequence of role switches, as the opening relationship of 'riche gnof' and 'poure scoler', landlord and angelic, if secretive, student, turns swiftly into jealous old husband and randy young lodger, to gullible dotard and artful exploiter, to exhausted dupe and triumphant show-off, and, finally, to injured madman and scalded howler. At any moment such cartoon figures may be given a balloon of speech from any literary source:

This carpenter answerde: 'Allas, my wyf!
And shal she drenche? Allas, myn Alisoun!'
(*CT*, I, 3522–3)

Thus John, suddenly reappearing as caring husband in a moment of lyric lament. Or:

'What do ye, hony-comb, sweete Alisoun,
My faire bryd, my sweete cynamone...
I moorne as dooth a lamb after the tete.
Ywis, *lemman*, I have swich love-longynge   *sweetheart*
That lik a *turtel* trewe is my moornynge.'   *dove*
(*CT*, I, 3698–9, 3704–6)

Absolon this time, echoing the Song of Songs.

Another satirical thread from *The Parson's Tale*, the condemnation of divination and swearing, illuminates the passage where Nicholas misuses his astrological knowledge to spin a yarn for old John of the coming of the second Flood. Here casual blasphemy is merely part of the convincing rhetoric – another stylistic guise slipped on for the moment:

He seyde, 'John myn hooste, *lief* and deere,   *beloved*
Thou shalt upon thy trouthe swere me heere
That to no wight thou shalt this conseil *wreye*,   *reveal*
For it is Cristes conseil that I seye.
And if thou telle it man, thou art *forlore*;   *lost*
For this vengeaunce thou shalt han therfore,
That, if thou *wreye* me, thou shalt be *wood*.'   *betray, mad*
(*CT*, I, 3501–7)

The irony of this threat, given the ending of the story, is another bit of evidence of the highly worked quality of the tale, to add to the satirical portraits, full of innuendo, the stylistic games, the verbal repetitions (*hende* Nicholas, *joly* Absolon), the dovetailing of details (the hole in the door, the low-silled window), the interweaving of two sets of action, the careful pacing of the tale, to say nothing of the echoes of the preceding *Knight's Tale* which many critics have analysed. More expenditure of poetic craft went into this tale than most, whether or not to 'justify' the inclusion of such material is not clear; certainly this is the showpiece of the *fabliau* genre, an experimental narrative fusing together elements from other types of writing, which create perspective for it. It is as little a 'naturalistic' observation of contemporary life as *The Knight's Tale* or *The Franklin's Tale*, but it tells us something about the social tensions and the follies of the time.

The combination of experimenting with narrative expression and satirical exposure of contemporary vice and folly is most strikingly evident in the anecdotal sections of *The Canterbury Tales* – in such link passages as the Host's revelations about his wife's character, or, in a more sustained combination of journalistic casualness and intellectual design, in the most deliberately 'colloquial' pieces, *The Canon's Yeoman's Prologue and Tale* and the Wife of Bath's so-called *Prologue*. Comparison with Langland's Passus V is again instructive. Langland turns his longer confessions of sin into allegorical autobiographies, dramatized versions of the definitions of sin in such manuals as *The Parson's Tale*. Coveitise works his way through a career of cheating, fraud and money-fiddling, from apprenticeship among tricksters at fairs to working as a draper and setting up his wife as weaver and brewer; then he turns to coin-clipping, money-lending and exploiting the opportunities given to estate-agent and banker's courier. Sloth is a composite portrait, beginning with the idle wastrel who knows nothing but rhymes of Robin Hood and the sort of stories millers and reeves tell:

> I am ocupied eche day, halyday and oother,
> With ydel tales at the ale and outherwhile in chirches;
> Goddes peyne and his passion, *pure selde* thenke I on it;   *very seldom*
> I visited nevere feble men ne fettred folk in *puttes*;   *prisons*
> I have levere here an harlotrye or a somer game of *souteres*,   *shoemakers*
> Or *lesynges* to laughen of and bilye my neghebores   *lies*
> Than al that evere Marc made, Matthew, Iohan and Lucas.
> And vigilies and fastyng dayes – al thise late I passe,
> And ligge abedde in Lenten and my lemman in myne armes
> Til matyns and masse be do...
> (*PPl*, V, 403–12)

Then he is a middle-aged priest, ignorant and neglectful, lured to action only by profit, letting the very food in his possession rot. Langland does not turn his images into the story of an individual life, but his sequence provides the stages which by implication include narratives whose details we can fill in for ourselves. I mentioned above other narrative features such as short dramatized scenes: Envy eying his neighbours in church, Glutton with his cronies in the tavern, engaging in noisy games and guzzling, until he explodes at all openings and has to be lugged home to bed. Not all readers of *Piers Plowman* have felt that these satirical vignettes actually fit Langland's overall purpose; Malcolm Godden, for instance, sees Langland as discovering in such passages 'an essential colourful grotesqueness in humanity' which is resistant to his own idealism.[3] Yet, in some ways, the section of grotesque vividness in Passus V is the most powerful moral writing in the whole poem, providing the images through which we can identify the working of sin in ourselves and in our society.

It is out of such didactic literary forms that Chaucer created *The Canon's Yeoman's Prologue and Tale*, where catechism and confessional revelation gradually turn into a demonstrative narrative, and finally into intellectual condemnation. The subject is an aspect of covetousness, illustrated through the pseudo-science of alchemy. In one respect it is a translation into fiction of the passages in *The Parson's Tale* which condemn the 'false enchaunters' engaged in divination as much as the sin of covetousness, but Chaucer integrates the moral material unusually closely into its fictional circumstances. It is the only story which grows entirely out of the dramatic material of the frame-story of *The Canterbury Tales*. Chaucer has developed some threads of dramatic interchange between the tellers and the content of their tales: the Miller's story of a carpenter's humiliation stings the bitter Reeve, also a carpenter, into a story of a proud miller humbled; Summoner and Friar demonstrate their mutual loathing by telling stories which expose the viciousness of the other's profession. This is one of the strategies Chaucer used to create variety of effect within the tale series and to add verisimilitude to the tale-telling process. But in the case of *The Canon's Yeoman's Tale* the story both develops out of the dramatic incident of the incursion into the pilgrimage of the self-important Canon and his attendant, and takes the Canon and his particular brand of villainy as its subject; here it is not a question of similarities but of actual biographical exposure. Chaucer begins with the Host's observant and inquisitive probing of the Canon's life, as a result of which, even while his master is still present, the yeoman begins to betray the confidence trickster's assumed social position and to expose their seedy, hand-to-mouth existence in the back streets of some town. The simple servant's ingenuousness moves unobtrusively to the detached observer's account of the fantastic life of obsessive chemical greed, full of the technical language of the trade, building up to a climax in the demonic scenes of the Canon and his confrères blowing up the fire and darting back from violently exploding metals:

263

> And somme are scatered al the floore aboute,
> Somme lepe into the roof. Withouten doute,
> Though that the feend noght in oure sighte hym shewe,
> I trowe he with us be, that like shrewe!
> In helle, where that he is lord and sire,
> Nis ther moore wo, ne moore rancour ne ire.
> (*CT*, VIII, 914–19)

Only then does the tale (in the Pars Secunda) move into fiction, but it does not move far, for the second canon of this anecdote ('This chanon was my lord, ye wolden weene? / Sire hoost, in feith ... / It was another') is simply an extension of the first, as the story is an enlargement of the colloquial interchange with which it began into an exemplary tale, and finally into moral and philosophical condemnation of the blasphemy of the attempt to 'multiplie' and change the elements that God ordained. The gradual acquisition of wit and wisdom by the narrating voice, as the tale moves from dialogue to chronicle to rhetorical demonstration, is the clearest illustration of Chaucer's inventing the narrator to fulfil the needs of the material, rather than the reverse: we could hardly forecast that this simple yeoman would end up quoting Hermes Trismegistus or debating the wisdom of Plato, if we approached it from a naturalistic/dramatic point of view.

The actual social material which is expressed in the tale consists of some interesting pictures of pseudo-science (some readers have thought it drawn from Chaucer's personal experience), with all its technical jargon, and of town life at the edges of the criminal classes, with churchmen in the roles of both rogue and dupe. Another such picture, at a lower level of London life, is the main interest of the brief fragment of the supposed *Cook's Tale*, where Perkyn Revelour, epitome of the idle apprentice setting out on a rogue's progress, is pictured kicking his legs about in the Cheapside taverns, dicing in the streets, and being absorbed into the life of debauchery, while his master, regardless of his poor performance as apprentice victualler, signs the document of release in order to get rid of him; he finds his level living with a like mate, whose prostitute wife brings in the household income. Chaucer did not write enough of this for us to see what narrative or technical interest he might have created from such bleak, unpromising material; clearly he is well inside the basic stuff of 'Abuses of the Age' satire, dealing with the vices of the lecher and the tavern-haunter, the rogue on his way to Newgate. He found a more successful vehicle for the exploration of the blasphemies of tavern sins in *The Pardoner's Tale*.

The Canon's Yeoman's Tale is one demonstration of what Chaucer could do with confession as a narrative mode: from supposedly impromptu self-revelation grows an illustration of vice in action, and so the three parts of the text cleverly combine naturalistic expression of experience, vivid local colour and the authoritative voice of the satirist, labelling his specimens; the voice of the confessee gradually becomes the voice of the confessor. Some of the same stylistic devices are used by Chaucer in *The Wife of Bath's Prologue*, though here he tried to do it all in one voice; the authorities, which provide the context for the Wife's story of her own marriages, all have to be quoted at second-hand, either attributed to hearsay, or brought into the Wife's supposed sphere of knowledge by the agency of her one educated husband, Jankyn, and his collection of anti-feminist literature. The literary model for this and the Pardoner's *Prologue* is as much a literary one (the monologues of the allegorical figures in *Le Roman de la Rose*) as the confession proper.

As a cynical and comic view of contemporary marriage, the Wife's *Prologue* invites comparison with the deft but rather dreary *Shipman's Tale*, in which merchant, wife and monk exchange money and sex in a way which makes them seem one and the same. The Wife of Bath's treatment of her first three, rich, old husbands is conceived in a similar spirit:

'I wolde no longer in the bed abyde,
If that I felte his arm over my syde,
Til he had *maad his raunson* unto me;   *paid his due*
Thanne wolde I suffre hym do his *nycetee*.   *foolishness*
And therfore every man this tale I telle,
Wynne whoso may, for al is for to selle;
With empty hand men may none haukes lure.'
                                        (*CT*, III, 409–15)

Not only does the textual evidence suggest that *The Shipman's Tale* may have been first written with the Wife of Bath as teller, but there is clearly continuity of thought between the two: hard luck, says the narrator, on the husband who has a party-loving wife; the feasts and dances are mere transitory pleasure which passes 'as dooth a shadowe upon the wal', but they still have to be paid for:

The *sely* housbonde, algate he moot paye.   *poor*
He moot us clothe, and he moot us arraye,
Al for his owene worshipe richely,
In which array we daunce jolily.
                                        (*CT*, VII, 11–14)

Chaucer takes the subject no further in *The Shipman's Tale* than the achievement of a balance: the monk has had his night's pleasure and it has cost him nothing, the wife has the money to pay her clothes bills at the cost of a bit of adultery and a few fibs, the merchant would probably have had to pay the bills anyway but has to accept the settlement of perpetual credit in the form of the 'joly body' of his wife. In the Wife of Bath's longer version Chaucer develops an extended plot beyond the first three marriages, in which the Wife's commercial instincts and ready play-acting enable her to tyrannize over her panting old sex slaves, by showing her also in the role of resentful victim, first of the fourth husband's adulteries and then of her fifth, younger, husband's infuriating mixture of attractive virility and teasing expertise in anti-feminist rhetoric. The truce eventually reached at the cost of a burned book, deafness, a few bruises and the husband's acceptance of the wife's rule, is, in its way, as cynical as the rest of the tale, but it does provoke the frivolous thought that perhaps Amans, in *Confessio Amantis*, despite his old age, could have found some happiness by getting Genius' book burnt too.

Chaucer is most obviously taking on the role of satirist when he uses the preacher's voice, with the licence that goes with it to express moral *sentence* explicitly. We have seen some examples from *The Parson's Tale* of his taking on the voice without apparent irony, and compiling a non-fictional discourse which has both the exhortations to penitence and the definitions (with some illustration) of the sins and their sub-types; the satirical mode that accompanies the sermon manner is that of scornful invective against the grotesque forms which sin can take. Elsewhere in *The Canterbury Tales* the preacher's role is used with various degrees of irony, as was demonstrated in the previous section. The Pardoner begins in confessional mode. Based on the hypocritical Faux Semblant in *Le Roman de la Rose*, this long-haired, androgynous figure expresses no penitence but reveals his own sin. His preaching on the theme of covetousness is motivated by greed for money and not in the least by the desire to save souls, and all of his considerable arts as a preacher are devoted to making his audience open up their purses and give.

> Of avarice and of swich cursednesse
> Is al my prechyng, for to make hem free
> To *yeven* hir pens, and *namely* unto me.   *give, particularly*
> For myn entente is not but for to wynne,
> And nothyng for correccioun of synne!
> (*CT*, VI, 400–4)

So we are given a clear guide as to purpose and method (the use of old stories to stick in the audience's mind, flavoured with some bits of Latin, and supported by a few impressive-looking documents and supposed relics), before the tale itself: a sermon in a high rhetorical mode, with much apostrophe and violent imagery, with its *exemplum*. Insofar as it provides a comparison in rhetorical method for *The Parson's Tale*, it makes it difficult for us to read that later tale in the Canterbury series in complete innocence. The Parson is less showy, less meretricious, in his use of language, but less interesting in his bookish classifications and enumerations, thorough but laborious; from the point of view of the pilgrimage's own main literary critic, the Host, the discourse probably does not meet an audience's requirements. He instructs the Parson thus:

> 'Sey what yow list, and we wol gladly heere.'
> And with that word he seyde in this manere:
> 'Telleth,' quod he, 'youre meditacioun
> But hasteth yow – the sonne wole adoun –
> Beth fructuous, and that in litel space,
> And to do wel God sende yow his grace!'
>
> (*CT*, X, last few lines of *The Parson's Prologue* as they appear in the MSS., though modern editions usually reorder the lines)

Certainly he fails the 'litel space' criterion and his presentation of the sins has a good deal less impact than Chaucer gives to the Pardoner, though the Parson's explanations are clearer. Of course, it is the same Host who rejects the Pardoner's rhetoric with such vehemence at the end of his tale, when the Pardoner pushes his luck, too confident that he will again have worked the old trick on his audience, which gives us our indicator, if we need it.

Something closer to modern senses of satire is identifiable in the pairing of the *Friar's Tale* and *Summoner's Tale*. In their mutual exposure of professional vice, the pair create an effect of balance, one prejudice being countered by the other; if summoners are exposed as cruel predators, extorting money by terrorizing the weak, then friars are revealed as hypocritical liars, winning money by flattery, oily sycophancy and false holiness; one is as likely to be true as the other. The Friar shows, by nice verbal distinctions, that the Devil has a greater sense of fairness than a summoner; the Summoner demonstrates by anal humour, puns and quibbles the utter worthlessness of the friar. In both tales there exists a finicky, academic element that points the humour, especially striking in the parody of theological debate about substance and the incorporeal (the kind of argument often typified by the idea of debate about how many angels could stand on the point of a pin) provided by the discussion of how to divide a fart up into equal shares for all the friars; this could be linked to a flavour of mock intellectualism identifiable in all the *fabliaux*.

'Sentence' does often consist of the identification and castigation of folly and vice and the satirical aim links *exemplum* and *fabliau*. These two literary forms are close together in several respects and might be seen as different adaptations of similar story material. Nykrog pointed to the moral generalizations that are part and parcel of many French *fabliaux*[4] and Burrow

267

observes that *exemplum* and *fabliau* both 'portray the same world of ordinary people'.[5] Differences between them may suggest that they come from two different sides of a religious/secular divide, but the difference is often a matter of emphasis rather than of kind. Though some of the stories told in *The Canterbury Tales* are clearly identified with a genre, there is a sense of common currency of tale material shared by many which crosses the boundaries of genre. Chaucer sets a number of variables at work when he embarks on the business of exploring the 'tale': one of them is testing the nature and extent of exemplification, how far tales prove points, whether the voice that utters them changes the nature of their truth, how far they are to be taken seriously.

Chaucer's own strategy (apart from the 'cherles tale' label) is to develop a running theme of the pairing of and the distinction between 'ernest' and 'game'. To distinguish between them is to avoid making inappropriate judgements:

> '... men shal nat maken ernest of game.'
> (*CT*, I, 3186)

The tale-telling competition is itself a game with its own rules, and tale-tellers are exhorted to conform, as when the Host bids the Clerk avoid bookishness:

> 'It is no tyme for to studien heere.
> Telle us some myrie tale, by youre fey!
> For what man that is entred in a pley,
> He nedes moot unto the pley assente.'
> (*CT*, IV, 8-11)

Some modern critics have linked this to Bakhtin's theory of carnival, which sees medieval life and literature as expressive of two coexistent aspects of the world, the serious and the laughing;[6] carnival images often parody the serious forms and celebrate the values of the body rather than the spirit.

Here is another instance of the poet's being able to enter into both aspects of moral dialogue. Like Gower and like Langland, Chaucer creates a sense of depth and truth by being able to think both from the view of the preacher and the preached to; the role of the one confessing may be analytical or distressed, flaunting or re-enacting earlier error, while the voice of the confessor may be humane or censorious, scathing, judgemental and admonitory. While Chaucer's *fabliaux* and other stories of contemporary life may, as types of narrative, show an experimental, adventurous aspect in his building up the fictional variety within *The Canterbury Tales*, the actual material of these tales overlaps at many points the interest in the moral standards of contemporary public and private life which occurs in other English writing of the period.

The actual plots may have their analogues in continental comic tales, but the subjects they include and the scenes they use open the way to the inclusion in the fiction of both social observation and an exploration of possible narratorial stances towards both contemporary morality and contemporary moralists.

Notes

1. See P. Nykrog, *Les Fabliaux: Étude d'histoire littéraire et de stylistique médiévale*, Copenhagen, 1957; John Hines, *The Fabliau in English*, London, 1993.
2. Burrow *RP*, p. 106.
3. Malcolm Godden, *The Making of 'Piers Plowman'*, London, 1990, p. 43.
4. P. Nykrog, *Les Fabliaux*, cited in note 1 above.
5. J. A. Burrow, *Medieval Writers and their Work*, Oxford, 1982, p. 84.
6. See Steve Ellis, *Geoffrey Chaucer*, Writers and their Work Series, Plymouth, 1996, pp. 43–6.

Gems of Chastity

Ian Bishop

Ian Bishop's study offers a useful introduction to theme and narrative structure of the Canterbury Tales. *In this chapter he considers the topic of children in the* Prioress's Tale *and* Physician's Tale, *contrasting the lyric, naturalistic quality of the former with the rhetorical, sometimes strained tone of the latter, and comparing both to the* Second Nun's Tale. *All three take as their poetic nucleus the theme of chastity, a subject common in medieval religious writing and one that demonstrates clearly the differences between the medieval and modern mindset. Chaucer experiments in each tale with a different genre of religious writing: saint's life, miracle tale and classical moral tale. While their various treatments of chastity and related topics such as virginity, sainthood, martyrdom and miracle contribute to the general debate of the* Canterbury Tales, *the individual stories also represent masterful instances of their kind. Bishop sees the* Second Nun's Tale *and* Physician's Tale *as less successful than the* Prioress's Tale, *although this is debatable. The* Second Nun's Tale, *for example, retells the familiar story of St Cecilia's life and martyrdom with great art: the tale is unified by a vivid series of imagistic oppositions (the colours red and white, the images of sight and blindness, dream and reality) and Cecilia becomes a remarkable voice of authority and argument. The* Physician's Tale, *by contrast, works through the shock of Virginia's murder by her father in order to preserve her from rape. The story is troubling in that it is situated in a pagan universe: Virginia's life appears to follow the pattern of the Christian virgin martyr and yet the context disallows sainthood and the promise of eternal life. The story portrays a mechanistic universe which in some ways resembles that of the* Knight's Tale.

The Prioress's Tale *is the most optimistic of the three tales of chastity, although it too is disturbing. Critics have frequently condemned the worldly Prioress, whose potentially secular nature is epitomized by the ambiguous words of her brooch, 'amor vincit omnia' (love conquers all), as well as by her lap dogs fed on white bread. Bishop's humanist, relaxed analysis explores effectively how differently this violent and anti-Semitic tale would have been read in the Middle Ages and how notable its affective naturalism is, by contrast to the 'sentence' and high rhetoric of the* Physician's Tale. *He employs the notion of affective piety, so powerful in medieval religion: devotional texts and medieval art frequently and overtly played on the emotions by, for example, graphically portraying Christ's wounding or the martyrdom of the saints in order to provoke feelings of pity, awe, and more profound piety. For the mystics, visionary experience was often the result of contemplation of an image such as Christ's blood or tears, or the Virgin's grief. What seems strange to us, the image of violent death of a child, forms part of this affective process, and is chosen by both the Prioress and the Physician in order to move their audiences. Bishop notes how common such sentimentality was even in the Victorian period, whereas it can seem extreme and bathetic to the contemporary reader.*

Bishop discusses medieval attitudes to children to argue that they were seen as natural emblems of chastity. He considers the equation of innocence with grace, and links the Prioress's Tale *to the feast of the Holy Innocents, the boy-children killed by Herod, while he associates the Virginia story with the actual death of Edward III's daughter. This kind of contextualization is especially useful in considering tales that are apparently remote and extreme. Whereas the* Physician's Tale *employs a process of formal rhetoric and 'sentence', the Prioress is striking in her realism – again a factor we do not readily associate with the excesses of the tale. Bishop explores the use of factual precision in the portrayal of the school, the boy's behaviour and unconsciousness, and his relation with other boys: the tale thus differs from traditional stories of the precocious child martyr. Bishop discusses too the difficulty for the modern reader of the story's anti-Semitism, and places this sensitively in the context of the expulsion of the Jews from England and medieval attitudes to pagans; for Bishop, the story is less specifically about Judaism than about the threat of evil to Christianity and its punishment by divine Providence. The Prioress's story is violent, sometimes uneasy, but like stories of the virgin martyrs finally optimistic in its demonstration of the celestial. Whatever the Prioress's apparent worldliness, the narrative assigned to her recalls the ultimate end of the pilgrimage, the tomb of a different kind of martyr, Thomas à Becket of Canterbury.*

The Canterbury Tales: Critical Extracts

Ian Bishop, 'Gems of Chastity' in *The Narrative Art of the 'Canterbury Tales': A Critical Study of the Major Poems*. London, Dent, 1988.

Children are among the least fortunate of mortals in the *Tales*. Four of them have speaking parts; and, of these, there is only one who is not murdered. Even this child – the serving-boy in the Pardoner's Tale – is introduced somewhat ominously to warn against the activities of the 'privee theef, men clepeth Deeth'. As for the others: the seven-year-old schoolboy in the Prioress's Tale has his throat cut by Jews, the three-year-old son of Hugelyn in the Monk's Tale is starved to death along with his father and brothers, the fourteen-year-old Virginia in the Physician's Tale is decapitated by her father in order to save her from a fate worse than death.... This chapter is concerned with the stories of the other two innocent victims, but more especially with the Prioress's Tale.

The obvious companion piece to the Prioress's Tale is that told by her own companion, the Second Nun. Apart from the Man of Law's Tale concerning Custance (which hovers between the genres of saint's legend and romance), these are the only tales of 'hoolynesse' in the compilation. They are both examples of 'affective piety' – attempts to edify the hearer by appealing to the emotions rather than to the intellect.[1] The Second Nun's Tale is indeed a saint's legend; the Prioress's Tale belongs to another well-established genre, the 'Miracle of the Virgin'. The Legend of St Cecilia was written before the compilation of the *Tales* and later incorporated as the Second Nun's Tale. It is not, in my opinion, one of Chaucer's more successful poems. Nor do I regard the Physician's Tale as particularly successful. But this tale, set in the legendary period of Roman history, will serve as a foil to set off some of the more positive qualities of the Prioress's Tale.

The Prioress prefaces her narrative with an Invocation to Mary, composed in an elevated style that draws upon Dante for much of its sentiment and diction. Nevertheless, its dominant note is one of humility. It begins by citing the Psalm verse, 'Out of the mouths of babes and sucklings hast Thou perfected praise, O Lord', and concludes with the speaker's likening herself to an infant – in the etymological sense of 'a child... That kan unnethes [scarcely] any word expresse'. So she beseeches Mary: 'Gydeth my song that I shal of yow seye' (VII, 487). The designation 'song' is appropriate enough for this brief and pathetic narrative, as there is an almost lyrical quality about its use of the 'rhyme royal' stanza. Moreover, this 'song' is a song about a song: the Marian antiphon *Alma Redemptoris Mater*, which the schoolboy determines to master because it is 'maked in *reverence* / Of Cristes mooder' (VII, 537–8; my italics) and sings it 'wel and boldely' on his way to and from school.[2] Unfortunately, his route traverses the Jewish quarter, and Satan (we are told) incited the Jews to feel resentment against the singing, within their territory, of something whose 'sentence [subject] / ... is agayn youre lawes

271

reverence' (563–4; my italics). So they hire a cut-throat to murder the child and dispose of his corpse in a privy 'Where as thise Jewes purgen hire entraille'. It is in this unsavoury environment that the miracle occurs. The child's whereabouts are revealed by his continuing to sing the Marian antiphon, even though 'with throte ykorven [he] lay upright':

> He *Alma redemptoris* gan to synge
> So loude that al the place gan to rynge.
> (VII, 612–13)

Nor is this repulsive place his final auditorium. For the Prioress (cf. 'quod she' at VII, 581) has already affirmed that this 'martir, sowded to virginitee' has now joined a choir where he may sing in perpetuity:

> Now maystow syngen, folwynge evere in oon*   *always
> The white Lamb celestial – quod she –
> Of which the grete evaungelist, Seint John,
> In Pathmos* wroot, which seith that they that goon   *Patmos
> Biforn this Lamb, and synge a song al newe...
> (VII, 580–4)

This example of 'affective piety' certainly moves the pilgrim audience (VII, 691). But the first reaction of a twentieth-century reader may well be to regard it as sentimental, mawkish, superstitious, credulous and – in view of its attitude towards the Jews – bigoted.[3] His second reaction may be to wonder whether Chaucer is not being ironical; whether he is not satirizing effusions of 'affective piety' of the kind that might well appeal to the 'conscience and tendre herte' of the Prioress of the General Prologue – the murdered 'clergeon' now being substituted for the hurt animals. Still another reaction may be experienced when one remembers that the author of 'Lucy Gray', and principal contributor to *Lyrical Ballads*, was moved to modernize Chaucer's 'song'. Wordsworth's prefatory remark about the 'fierce bigotry of the Prioress' is often remembered. But we should also recall the way in which his sentence continues:

> The fierce bigotry of the Prioress forms a fine background for her tenderhearted sympathies with the Mother and Child; and the mode in which the story is told amply atones for the extravagance of the miracle.

The mode in which the story is told is indeed remarkable. Whatever may be urged against it, the Prioress's Tale remains one of the most memorable of the Canterbury series.

That is more than can be said for Chaucer's other story of child murder, the Physician's Tale. In fact, this tale, derived ultimately from Livy's history of Rome, has a much more interesting plot than that of the miracle of the Virgin. Virginius had brought up his only child in accordance with the austere and decent standards of conduct so much admired in the early republicans by later generations of moralists. Her beauty was noticed by the corrupt and lecherous justice, Appius, who contrives, by abusing his judicial power and by an outrageous perversion of the law, to obtain the girl as his ward. Her father, in order to save his beloved daughter from becoming the slave to Appius's lust, kills her. The dilemma in which Virginius finds himself is even more acute than that of Isabella in *Measure for Measure*: it is 'tragic' by any definition of the term. Yet the Physician's Tale never realizes its tragic potentiality. How is it that it fails to come to life, whereas the Prioress's Tale is so vivid?

Before pursuing further this critical question, it is necessary to consider a difference between medieval and modern attitudes towards children that affects our appreciation of both tales. Child murder is not the only feature that the narratives have in common. The phrase 'gemme of chastitee' is applied to both child victims. Virginius addresses his daughter with this phrase as he is about to kill her (VI, 223). The 'clergeon' [boy] is so described at VII, 609, where he is also called 'this emeraude / And eek of martirdom the ruby bright'. Such a way of regarding children may strike us as rather precious. It also occurs in *Pearl*, where the dominant image, when applied to the child who died before she was two years old, includes chastity among its multiple significations. It is largely on account of his chastity that the image of the pearl is associated with the hero of another poem in the same MS: *Sir Gawain and the Green Knight*. During the denouement Bertilak says that, just as a pearl is of greater value than the white pea, so is Gawain worth more than other knights:

'As perle bi the quite* pese is of prys more,   *white
So is Gawayn, in god fayth, bi other gay knyghtes.'
(2364–5)

The commendation is well deserved, since the hero has thrice resisted pressing temptations to commit adultery. But it may seem to us that a baby and a boy of seven hardly deserve to be praised for what they cannot possibly have earned. The medieval attitude was different: its rationale is set out in the course of the debate in *Pearl*. The dreamer objects to the maiden's being made a queen in heaven, when she died so young that she was incapable of either pleasing God or praying to Him, being ignorant even of the Paternoster and Creed, the very rudiments of religious instruction. He asks:

> 'What more honour moghte* he acheve   *might
> That hade endured in worlde stronge,
> And lyved in penaunce hys lyves longe,
> Wyth bodyly bale* hym blysse to byye?'*   *suffering   *buy
> (475–8)

The maiden argues that, on the contrary, the longer one lives on Earth, the more opportunity one has for committing sin. Admittedly, it is possible for the sinner to repent and to be restored to a state of Grace through God's mercy. But the innocent child, who has never fallen out of the state of Grace bestowed in baptism, is guaranteed salvation (665–8, 684). Chastity, like innocence, was a quality that God prized for its own sake, whether one had striven for it or not.

The 'litel clergeon', having only just attained his first climacteric, was still officially 'within degree of innocence'.[4] So, on the several occasions when the Prioress calls him an 'innocent', the term has something of a technical sense. He is also associated with the Holy Innocents, the children of two years and under, whom Herod ordered to be slain (Matt. 2: 16–18).[5] At VII, 574, the Jews are apostrophized as 'cursed folk of Herodes al newe', and at 627 the child's mother is called 'This newe Rachel' – where she is compared, by implication, with the mothers of the Innocents (cf. Matt. 2: 18). We have remarked how, after death, he joins the choir of (male) Virgins, who follow the Lamb (Rev. 14: 3–4). It was believed that the Holy Innocents too formed part of that procession. Whereas the Gospel for the Mass for Holy Innocents' Day (28 December) consists of the passage from Matthew that describes their massacre, the Epistle consists of the account of the procession from Revelation. The Holy Innocents were regarded as having been baptized in their own blood, and were celebrated as the first Christian martyrs, even though they did not seek martyrdom. On the same principle, the 'litel clergeon' is not only a 'gemme of chastitee' but also 'of martirdom the ruby bright'. The child in *Pearl*, though no martyr, is also associated with the children 'a bimatu et infra' ('of two years and under') whom Herod ordered to be slain. The association is made by implication when the dreamer says to the maiden 'Thou lyfed not two yer in oure thede [country]' (483); it is also implied by including her in the procession of the hundred and forty-four thousand Virgins who follow the Lamb (though here the virgins are female, unlike those in Revelation).

Virginia, that other 'gemme of chastitee', is in a somewhat different position, not only because she is a pagan, but also because she has already attained her second climacteric. She is old enough to have taken deliberate measures to maintain her chastity:

> And *of hir owene vertu, unconstreyned,*
> She hath ful ofte tyme syk hire feyned,
> For that she wolde fleen the compaignye
> Where likly was to treten* of folye,   *speak
> As is at feestes, revels, and at daunces,
> That been occasions of daliaunces.
> (VI, 61–6, my italics)

She is prepared to tell a 'white lie' in order to be virtuous. Christians are, of course, required not only to resist temptation, but to avoid 'the occasion of sin'. The behaviour of this pagan girl would have won the approval of any medieval (or Victorian) father.[6] She has none of the forwardness that modern teenagers are supposed to delight in. Though she was as 'wis as Pallas', she never spoke out of turn. Nor did she employ 'countrefeted termes...to seme wys' (51–2) – in other words, she used no 'wise-cracks' or vogue expressions in order to appear a sophisticated little madam. In commenting (rather ponderously) on the vices she shuns, the narrator never forgets that she is still a child:

> Swich thynges maken children for to be
> To soone rype and boold, as men may se,
> Which is ful perilous, and hath been yoore.*   *always
> For al to soone may she lerne loore
> Of booldnesse, whan she woxen* is a wyf.   *grown
> (VI, 67–71)

(i.e. '...when she has grown up to be a woman'). These remarks lead on naturally to the two apostrophes, to governesses and parents respectively. 'Maistresses' of lords' daughters are reminded of their solemn responsibility for their charges. Indeed, their accountability is seen as similar to that of baptismal sponsors:[7]

> Looke well that ye unto no vice assente,
> Lest ye be dampned for youre wikke entente.
> (VI, 87–8)

The apostrophe concludes:

> Of alle tresons sovereyn pestilence
> Is whan a wight bitrayseth innocence.
> (VI, 91–2)

The story that follows, however, is not about Innocence betrayed by a tutor, but – even worse – by a judge. We are told that Virginia 'So kepte hirself hir neded no maistresse' (106). Nevertheless, the tone of the passage shows that she is thought of as still being virtually 'within degree of innocence' – no less than the child in *Pearl* or the 'litel clergeon'.

It was not unprecedented for a girl of such an age to be regarded in this way in fourteenth-century England. In chapter 2, I referred to letters of Edward III concerning the death of his fifteen-year-old daughter, Joan. In them, the King gives thanks that God has snatched his daughter away from the miseries of this deceitful world, when 'puram et immaculatam, in annis Innocentiae suae' (pure and spotless, *in the years of her innocence*). He has deigned to call her to Heaven, where, joined to the Heavenly Spouse, 'in Choro Virginum perpetuo regnatura' (she will reign for ever in the choir of Virgins).[8] These are the very sentiments expressed in *Pearl* and the Prioress's Tale. Unfortunately, Virginia, as a pagan, can fall back only upon the rather negative *solacium*: 'Blissed be God, that I shal dye a mayde!' (248).

To return to 'the mode in which the story is told'; that of the Physician's Tale is deliberately sententious. Of the tales that employ formal rhetoric with serious intent, the Physician's has the highest proportion of 'amplification' to narrative. Virginia is introduced by means of a formal *descriptio*; and we have already remarked how it is rigidly divided into *effictio* and *notatio*.[9] Moreover, we observed that this *effictio* expands the customary allusion to Nature into a prosopopoeia, in which the goddess steps on to the stage and pronounces her own panegyric of the girl's physical beauty. The proper function of 'amplification' is to make a narrative more significant, or to 'slant' it in a particular direction, rather than merely to fill out its bulk. Such is indeed the purpose of Nature's oration here. She first makes the standard boast that her creations are superior to anything that even the finest human artists can produce. But the idea is expressed in a particularly telling way:

> 'Thus kan I forme and peynte a creature,
> Whan that me list;* who kan me countrefete? *please
> Pigmalion noght, though he ay forge and bete,
> Or grave,* or peynte; for I dar wel seyn, *engrave
> Apelles,* Zanzis,* sholde werche in veyn *legendary artists
> Outher to grave, or peynte, or forge, or bete,
> If they presumed me to countrefete.'
> (VI, 12–18)

The repetition of the slow procession of mostly monosyllabic verbs conveys a vivid impression of the artists laboriously plodding in an attempt to catch up with the demiurge whose creations they vainly try to imitate.

In the second part of her speech Nature declares herself to be the 'vicaire general' to God, the 'formere principal',[10] and she says of Virginia: 'I made hire to the worshipe of my lord' (26). The effect of this passage is to cause the lustful designs of Appius to appear, not only humanly atrocious, but as an act of sacrilege against God's prized creation. It is therefore appropriate that it should be 'the feend' (130) who suggests to the wicked judge the legal trick by which he may gain the wardship of the girl.

The portrait of Virginia's beauty (30–8) is a not very imaginative exercise in periphrasis, and the succeeding *notatio* is (as we have seen)[11] largely a study in writing variations on a basic epithet. At VI, 72, the sententious conclusion of the *descriptio* leads into the two admonitory apostrophes, each supported by its own *exemplum*. 'Maistresses' are informed that they have been engaged for one of two reasons: either because they are virtuous, or for the opposite reason – that they are all too familiar with 'the olde daunce' (79). Chaucer applies this phrase also to the Wife of Bath and her knowledge of amorous dalliance (I, 476). The momentary bringing together of these two disparate worlds is the first hint of a threat to Virginia's sheltered upbringing. Chaucer is probably here thinking of the duenna in the *Roman de la Rose* (called 'Vekke' in the ME translation) – which is, in fact, his most immediate source for the story of Appius and Virginia. The 'Vekke' is appointed as Bialacoil's gaoler after the lover's first, unsuccessful attempt to obtain the rosebud. She is appointed precisely because she knows the tricks of the trade. As Chaucer's *exemplum* observes, former poachers often make the best game-keepers:

> A theef of venysoun, that hath forlaft*   *abandoned
> His likerousnesse,* and al his olde craft,   *lechery
> Kan kepe a forest best of any man.
> (VI, 83–5)

(There is hardly any need to draw attention to the sexual overtones of both vocabulary and imagery in these lines.) In Jean de Meun's poem the 'Vekke' notoriously betrays her trust;[12] so it is as well that Virginia 'so kepte hirself' that she needed no such keeper. The threat to innocence is increased in the image that supports the apostrophe to the parents of less privileged children. The apostrophe itself merely gives the conventional – and irrelevant – medieval admonition of 'spare the rod, and spoil the child'. But the supporting *exemplum* envisages the wolf worrying the charges of a 'shepherde softe and necligent'.

The narrator self-consciously concludes this apostrophe with the comment:

> Suffiseth oon ensample now as heere,
> For I moot turne agayn to my matere.
> (VI, 103–4)

It does indeed look as if the narrative is about to be resumed, but it is a false dawn: what is resumed is the *notatio*, which even includes a formal personification of Envy. The narrator calls this personification a 'descripcioun', and attributes it to an anonymous 'doctour' (who has been identified as St Augustine).[13]

When the story eventually gets under way at VI, 118, its narration is not particularly well managed. The manner in which Appius brushes aside Virginius's plea is too blatant to be credible; and the speed with which 'a thousand peple in thraste' to denounce the notoriously (cf. VI, 262–6) corrupt judge, after Virginia has been decapitated, merely makes the reader wonder why they had not acted earlier. The scene between father and daughter certainly has some moments of pathos. But why does Virginius address her as 'endere of my lyf' (218)? When the dying Arcite addresses this conventional, amatory phrase to Emelye (I, 2776) it has a poignantly literal meaning; but it is inept to put it into Virginius's mouth when it is he who is about to end his daughter's life. In his *Ars Versificatoria*, Matthew of Vendôme [thirteenth-century] had recommended five possible ways of ending a poem. One was 'per recapitulationem sententiae' – a summary of the work's moral 'sentence.'[14] The tale concludes with ten lines of sententious epilogue, whose import is neatly encapsulated in the chiasmic final line: 'Forsaketh synne, er synne yow forsake.' But this moral is both misplaced and tactless; for it seems to imply that the reader will have identified himself with the villain of the story! Perhaps the explanation for its presence is to be found in the tale's immediate source. In the *Roman de la Rose*, Jean de Meun introduces the story as an *exemplum* into a discussion about corrupt judges.[15] Chaucer has shifted the interest of the story from Appius to Virginia, but has nevertheless concluded with a *sentence* that would have been more appropriate in his source. A slightly more apt moral is afterwards extracted by the Host, who is deeply roused by the tale (VI, 287–300). The moral focus of the tale itself remains blurred; and, despite certain local felicities, the whole suffers too obviously from having been subjected to the 'process' of applied 'amplification'.[16]

It would be untrue to say that there is no rhetoric in the Prioress's Tale; but rhetorical devices do not obtrude themselves as they do in the Physician's. The 'clergeon' may be destined for sainthood; but he is not introduced by way of an idealized description; instead, he is shown in his first term at school. The first two stanzas tell us, with the factual precision and economy of a well-organized *fabliau*, all that we need to know about the location of the school. Almost immediately a slight discrepancy between the 'tale' and its 'teller' is noticeable. The Prioress's tone is sentimental as well as devout. She refers to the boy as 'litel child', 'litel sone' and 'litel clergeon' – where the substantive is itself already a diminutive form. This even colours his environment: he attends 'a litel scole', where he learns from 'his litel book'. The Prioress is immediately reminded of 'Seint Nicholas' (514), to whose legend she had already alluded in her Prologue, when she described how infants 'on the brest soukynge' had praised the Virgin (VII, 458–9). At 538, she continues to groom the boy for sainthood by calling him 'this innocent', thereby invoking the various, highly charged connotations of that term which we have already considered.

The discrepancy resides in the fact that the small boy himself is no sentimentalist; nor is there any evidence of his displaying abnormal piety. In fact, the Christian school is 'litel' in quite an objective sense, since more than one class has evidently to be accommodated in a single room. It is this arrangement that enables the boy to overhear the children in the higher class sing *Alma Redemptoris Mater*. He has its first verse by rote before he knows that it is addressed to Mary. Evidently he is first attracted by the tune and by the same impulse which caused my seven-year-old daughter to find her elder sister's prescribed piano pieces more interesting than her own. He is no Peter Pan, and has no wish to remain for ever in the infants' class with his 'litel book'; he wants to be doing what the bigger boys are doing. He beseeches an older boy to translate the song for him 'Ful often tyme upon his knowes bare' (529). This may sound exaggerated to us. But 'on his bare knees' was a stock phrase; and the action itself would not be thought unusual in an age when formal gestures were common, and when, for example, servants might be expected to kneel to offer a cup to their master.[17] Schoolboys are notorious sticklers for 'class'-distinctions. The reason for the older boy's initial reluctance to grant this request is soon apparent. He declares: 'This song, *I have herd seye*, / Was maked of our blisful Lady free' (my italics). And he concludes with the archetypal schoolboy confession: 'I lerne song, I kan but small grammere' (i.e. 'Latin') – incomparably less than the 'small Latin' with which Ben Jonson credited Shakespeare.

As soon as he hears what the song is about, the younger boy's eagerness to learn it all is redoubled. But even this is not necessarily a symptom of unusual piety. We have already been informed that it was his own widowed mother who taught him to reverence the image of the Virgin when he passed a wayside shrine (505). His desire to master the antiphon 'er Cristemasse be went' may be as much motivated by a desire to please his own mother as Christ's. In the mind of a seven-year-old the distinction would, in any case, be somewhat blurred: the latter would be seen by him as just a sublimation of the former. His singing of the anthem aloud in the street is an entirely unselfconscious act: he was unaware that it would offend the Jews. Nor was he aware that it would one day disconcert the Philistines. No doubt most passers-by in a modern English street would be embarrassed if they encountered a child singing 'wel and boldely' a hymn he had just learnt at school; in Italy, on the other hand, it would seem perfectly natural. There is no evidence that the 'clergeon' sought martyrdom deliberately, as did that other seven-year-old who sings a snatch of church music as he is about to be killed: the Saint Kenelm of the *South English Legendary*.[18] The boy king is warned of his death in a dream, which his nurse correctly interprets for him. Nevertheless, he allows his treacherous 'maister', Askebert, to conduct him alone to the Forest of Clent. When Askebert makes his first attempt to slay him, the boy calmly informs him that he is wasting his time, since his martyrdom is ordained to take place in another spot. When they reach the destined place, he asks his 'maister', Askebert, 'wel mildeliche', why he does not 'get on with it at once',[19] and sings from the *Te Deum* the appropriate verse: 'The faire compaygnie of martyrs, Louerd, herieth [Thee].' Chaucer was familiar with the legend. In the Nun's Priest's Tale, Chauntecleer cites it as an *exemplum* to support his argument about the prophetic nature of dreams. He remarks of Kenelm:

> ...but he nas but seven yeer oold,
> And therfore litel tale hath he toold
> Of any dreem, so hooly was his herte.
> (VII, 3117–19)

There is no suggestion that the 'litel clergeon' wishes likewise to join prematurely 'the glorious army of martyrs'. Nevertheless, this lack of conscious intent would not (as we have seen) have prevented him, any more than the Holy Innocents, from entering that company.

If the Prioress seems a little too 'enthusiastic' in her representation of the 'innocent', what shall we think of her attitude towards the Jews?[20] Stories about the ritual murder of Christian boys by Jews were common enough at the time.[21] Is Chaucer implicitly criticizing the intelligence of this nun for accepting such a tale credulously and uncritically? At least the tale's 'fierce bigotry' could not have done any immediate harm, as Edward I had imposed his 'final solution' to 'the Jewish problem' as long ago as 1290, when all Jews were expelled from England (and were not officially permitted to return until the time of Cromwell). The opening stanza places the action in remote 'Asye', but the final stanza brings it home by invoking the boy, Hugh of Lincoln, 'slayn also / With cursed Jewes... but a litel while ago'. In fact, the event was supposed to have taken place in 1255. It is unlikely, however, that the narrator's prime intention here was to be inflammatory. It was customary for a pious work to conclude with a prayer, and especially an invocation to an appropriate saint. Hugh of Lincoln was the obvious choice from among the 'innocents'.

Nevertheless, it is impossible to overlook the epithet 'cursed', which is here applied to the Jews not for the first time in the tale. Nor can one disregard the description of Satan prefatory to his incitement of the Jews to conspire against the singer of (what was for them) blasphemy:

> Our firste foo, the serpent Sathanas,
> That hath in Jues herte his waspes nest,
> Up swal, and seide, 'O Hebrayk* peple, allas!...'   *Hebrew
> (VII, 558–60)

Is the mixed metaphor meant to betray the confusion of an over-emotional narrator? It might be thought that the narrator dwells with too obvious satisfaction upon the punishment of the perpetrators of the murder (628–34). But at least the punishment is just. The stanza concludes by declaring that the Provost 'heng hem by the lawe'; and the narrator comments 'Yvele shal have that yvele wol deserve'. The Jews are punished according to the Mosaic law which they would themselves recognize. It also happened to be, in effect, the civil law of the Middle Ages. Christians would have been treated in the same way. The treatment of the perpetrators of this hideous child-murder is similar to that of those accused of murdering the traveller, in the anecdote inserted into the Nun's Priest's Tale (cf. VII, 3058–62).

Finally, we return to 'this newe Rachel' at the end of the preceding stanza. The liturgical reason for bestowing this title upon the child's mother has already been considered. Nevertheless, it may seem tactless, in the context, to associate her with the wife of Jacob (also called 'Israel') and mother of the Jewish race. Against this, however, should be remembered the fact that, in Chaucer's day, Rachel was regarded as a 'type' of that later Jewess, the Virgin Mary.[22] It is also easy to forget that the Holy Innocents were Jews. It is important to notice that the hostility towards the Jews in this tale is religious rather than racial. In the Asian city, where the action is set, the villains might just as well have been Muslims. The attitude of the Jews towards the 'clergeon' and his song is not unlike that of the Sultana towards Custance and her 'fontful water' in the Man of Law's Tale (II, 357). It is impossible that our reading of this tale should be unaffected by our memory of the Nazis' murder of six million children, women and men, because they were born of Jewish stock. The memory of that unspeakable atrocity should prevent us from feeling self-righteous and smug when reading a story of 'medieval barbarity'. But the nearest modern analogy to the situation in the tale strikes much nearer home than the Third Reich. If a Roman Catholic boy were to walk through a Protestant area of Belfast singing a Marian antiphon, it is not impossible that members of some extreme Protestant organization might behave as the Jews do in the tale; and the same might equally well happen – *mutatis mutandis* – to a Protestant child. The 'conscience and tendre herte' of a devout nun, on hearing of such an atrocity, might well react in the way that the sensibility of the Prioress does. Certainly the narrator of this tale is partisan; but she belongs to the same party as Chaucer, who also had a special devotion to the Virgin. The 'mode in which the story is told' enables us to enter into the mind of a teller who is sincerely affected by a work of 'affective piety'. At the same time (as so often happens when reading Chaucer), we are left wondering whether the apparent inconsistencies in the tale may not have been 'planted' in order to encourage us to take a detached, critical view of the narrative and the genre to which it belongs.

Notes

1. On 'affective' devotion, see Douglas Gray, *Themes and Images in the Medieval English Religious Lyric* (London, 1972), pp. 18 ff.
2. Cf. the rubric in Hengwrt MS.: 'Here beginneth the Prioresse Tale of Alma Redemptoris Mater' (N. F. Blake, ed. cit., p. 474).
3. See Florence H. Ridley, *The Prioress and the Critics* (University of California, Berkeley, 1965).
4. The phrase comes from Mirk's *Festial*: see I. Bishop, *Pearl in its Setting*, pp. 109 and 116.
5. See Marie P. Hamilton, 'Echoes of Childermas in the Tale of the Prioress', in E. Wagenknecht (ed.), *Chaucer: Modern Essays in Criticism* (New York, 1959), pp. 88–97. Also *Pearl in its Setting*, ch. 7.
6. On medieval education of girls of good family, see N. Orme, 'Chaucer and Education', *ChR*, 16 (1981–2), pp. 38–59, esp. p. 45....
7. On the responsibilities of baptismal sponsors, see *Piers Plowman*, B, ix, 75–9 (ed. Schmidt, p. 94). For an example of a treacherous 'maister' who had charge of the education of a royal minor, see the legend of St Kenelm....
8. See... I. Bishop, '*Solacia* in *Pearl* and in Letters of Edward III Concerning the Death of his Daughter, Joan', *N & Q*, 229 (December 1984), pp. 454–6.
9. See ch. 3, pp. 63–4 [of *The Narrative Art of the 'Canterbury Tales'*]
10. For similar characterization of Nature in *PoF*, see ch. 2, p. 31. [ibid.].
11. Ch. 3, pp. 63–4 [ibid.].
12. *Roman de la Rose*, lines 12541–14546.
13. See Robinson's note on VI, 117.
14. As noted by C. S. Lewis, *The Discarded Image*, p. 195.
15. *Roman de la Rose*, lines 5589–794.
16. For a somewhat different explanation of the tale's failure, see Sheila Delany, 'Politics and the Paralysis of Poetic Imagination in The Physician's Tale', *SAC*, 3 (1981), pp. 47–60. Also N. Coghill, 'Chaucer's Narrative Art' in D. S. Brewer (ed.), *Chaucer and Chaucerians* (London and Edinburgh, 1966), pp. 126–8.
17. Cf. *Piers Plowman*, B, x, 307–8 (ed. Schmidt, p. 111).
18. The best edition of this particular legend is in J. A. W. Bennett and G. V. Smithers (eds), *Early Middle English Verse and Prose* (Oxford, 1968), pp. 96–107.

19 Ibid., p. 101, line 104.
20 For a well-informed and well-balanced discussion of this controversial matter, see A. B. Friedman, 'The Prioress's Tale and Chaucer's Anti-Semitism', *ChR*, 9 (1974), pp. 118–29 – in addition to Ridley (see n. 3 above).
21 See N. Cohn, *The Pursuit of the Millennium* (London, 1957), esp. p. 72.
22 Cf. the lyric attrib. William of Shoreham, No. 32 (lines 53–4), in Carleton Brown (ed.), rev. G. V. Smithers, *Religious Lyrics of the XIVth Century* (Oxford, 1952).

Anti-feminism

Jill Mann

In a very different context, Jill Mann addresses the same question as Ian Bishop, though she is more explicit: how can we not expect Chaucer to use the language of his day? While Mann's concern is Chaucer's 'masculine' language and the constraints it places on women, it is equally the case that Chaucer could not but employ the religious language of his day, which can carry assumptions or implications as alien to many contemporary readers as implications about sexual hierarchies. Rather than demanding of Chaucer a new language as many – particularly feminist – critics have, we need to consider precisely how Chaucer employs the terms of his own times, often, as Bishop shows, to question and rewrite cultural assumption – as, for instance, in the small but telling gesture of alluding to the mother of the boy in the Prioress's Tale *by the Jewish name, Rachel. More dramatic but not dissimilar is Chaucer's rewriting of anti-feminist terms in the* Wife of Bath's Prologue. *Of all Chaucer's creations, the Wife is the most three-dimensional and, as we have seen, has inspired the most critical discussion, which often lends her autonomy in a startling way. It is both ironic and a testimony to Chaucer's literary art that the Wife should seem the most 'real' of the pilgrims, for in fact she is the most literary, constructed out of the stereotypical traits attributed to women by anti-feminist writers such as St Jerome.*

It is crucial to understand medieval misogyny in the context of medieval thought more generally: women were viewed as different by nature from men. According to the better-known account of Creation in the Book of Genesis, Adam was created when God breathed life into the dust of the ground, whereas Eve was formed from Adam's rib and identified from the start as his possession: the woman was associated definitively with the body and, appropriately, was the bearer of children, while the man was linked to rationality and the soul, and seen as having the right to rule women. The woman's frailty was proven by her role in the Fall: singled out as the weaker vessel by Satan, she took of the fruit of the Tree of Knowledge, 'and did eat, and gave also unto her husband with her; and he did eat' (Genesis 3: 6). Because the Fall resulted in the first act of lust, the woman was connected with sexual temptation: St Paul's epistles repeatedly warn against women as frail, tempting and inferior, the 'second sex'; later, St Jerome condemned the natural provocativeness of women, writing of the woman's insatiable capacity for lust, and there is a plethora of other damning clerical writings against women. The model of Eve, the fallen lustful woman, was opposed by Mary, the Second Eve. Crucial to Mary's perfection was her virginity: she had conceived without participating in a sexual act, so that she remained unpolluted, immaculate. Those who elected to follow her by leading the celibate religious life were viewed as empowered by sloughing off the taint of the lustful body. Although it was recognized that not all could pursue this life, there was no doubt that virgins were at the top of the hierarchy of chastity, with widows next, and chaste wives lowest. Women were polarized, Eve at one pole and Mary at the other. The virtuous, rewarded woman tended also to be the passive, suffering, virgin saint — often a martyr, since only the dead virgin was totally free from the threat of the body. It is with this tradition that the religious tales engage, and it is interesting that Chaucer's saint's life, the* Second Nun's Tale, *portrays an unusually active female saint. His* Legend of Good Women, *by contrast, presents the passive model of female virtue.*

The Wife of Bath's Prologue *engages directly with the limits of female stereotypes, in particular the problematic nexus of virginity, passivity and virtue. It is by using these stereotypes, rather than attempting to convey 'how women feel', that Chaucer addresses 'the problem of speaking in the voice of a woman'. This is a complex manoeuvre that works by setting the speaker, the Wife, against her speech, which voices the conventional arguments of clerical thinkers.* The Prologue *works subversively, as the Wife of Bath sets up her own 'experience' against the 'authority' of the clerks — to become herself another kind of authority. Mann explores how Chaucer rewrites the sources for each part of the* Prologue, *such as St Jerome's treatise on virginity, and considers the 'book of wikked wyves', the anti-feminist miscellany that the Wife's fifth husband owns. Mann's examination is scholarly, acute regarding medieval literary tradition and Chaucer's use of sources, but also attuned to contemporary theoretical issues, particularly the feminist agenda. Mann presents the Wife as practising an alternative process of exegesis — one that undoubtedly would have shocked the saintly Jerome, and still has the capacity to provide extraordinary amusement. We are made uneasily aware of how persuasively authorities can be twisted to fit individual biases. The Wife turns Jerome's arguments inside out, but also employs anti-feminist commonplaces to create the speeches of her five husbands. Mann demonstrates the ambiguity of the work: in the final part of the* Prologue *the Wife herself enacts anti-feminist stereotypes even while she objects to them. It is for this reason in particular that a number of critics, most notably Elaine Tuttle Hansen, argue against the conventional view of Chaucer as 'womanis frend'. Mann, by contrast, pays careful attention to Chaucer's use of literary sources and conventions, and his rewriting of anti-feminism*, *to show precisely his awareness of 'the prison house of masculine language'*, *and she considers too the reconciliation suggested at the end of the* Prologue. *What is striking is not that Chaucer cannot step wholly outside the thought-world of his age, but how imaginatively and radically he can approach and question it. In the* Wife of Bath's Tale, *which Mann goes on to consider, we are offered a different perspective on what it is that women 'moost desiren' and a complex discussion of sovereignty and* gentillesse. *At the same time we are left with an uneasy conclusion that reflects the ambiguity of the Wife as fictional creation: a rapist gains a beautiful young wife. The tale sustains and develops the emphases of the* Prologue, *but also responds to the 'experience' of the Wife with the fantasy of romance, to offer a fluid wish-fulfilment world where nothing is ever quite what it seems.*

Jill Mann, from 'Anti-feminism' in *Geoffrey Chaucer*. Harvester Wheatsheaf, New York, 1991.

With the Wife of Bath Chaucer sets himself a new problem: the problem of speaking in the voice of a woman. How is he to achieve some kind of authenticity without incurring the charge of male ventriloquism? How is the woman who has been spoken *about* for centuries to be represented as speaking for herself? Chaucer's way of dealing with this problem is to meet it head on: what comes out of the Wife's mouth is not a naive attempt at an unprejudiced representation of 'how women feel', but rather the most extensive and unadulterated body of traditional anti-feminist commonplace in the whole of the *Canterbury Tales*. Chaucer renounces the attempt to invent radically new material; he does not even juxtapose with the anti-feminist stereotypes any of the contrasting stereotypes which would counteract their effect. He does not, that is, take the easy and obvious way out by having the Wife, like Jean de Meun's La Vieille (her most obvious literary ancestor), justify herself by reference to Ovid's abandoned heroines – Dido, Phyllis, Ariadne – or by an appeal to examples of good women – Penelope, Alcestis, Griselda. Instead, he plots speaker against speech, in the paradoxical mode of the Abelard–Heloise correspondence, by giving the anti-feminist material to the Wife, and the tale of Griselda, supreme example of the good woman, to the Clerk, representative of the class whom the Wife accuses of never having anything favourable to say about the female sex. The anti-feminist material appears in different guise in each of the Prologue's three main sections: Jerome's arguments in favour of virginity form the basis of the first part; the second part dramatizes Theophrastus's account of female vices into the Wife's account of how she scolded her husbands; and the third part reproduces the sample miscellany of anti-feminist proverbs and anecdotes contained in Jankin's 'book of wikked wyves'. Jerome has the starring role as arch-representative of anti-feminist writing, but the *Epistola Valerii*, the *Romance of the Rose*, Deschamps's *Miroir de Mariage*, Matheolus's *Lamentations* and the Solomonic proverbs provide a strong supporting cast.

The prominence of this traditional anti-feminist material finds its justification in the fact that the Wife of Bath is locked into a continuing struggle not so much with men as with their stereotypes of her sex – or, as she would put it, with 'auctoritee' (Hanning, 1985, 16–18). In her final quarrel with Jankin, it is not the man she goes for, but the book. The motivating force behind the first part of her Prologue, which subverts Jerome's arguments against multiple marriage without ever actually naming him, becomes clear in her account of the contents of this book, in which Jerome figures as arch-representative of the clerical anti-feminism embodied in Jankin himself.

> He hadde a book that gladly, nyght and day,
> For his desport he wolde rede alway;
> He cleped it Valerie and Theofraste,
> At which book he lough* alwey ful faste. *laughed
> And eek ther was somtyme a clerk at Rome,
> A cardinal, that highte Seint Jerome,
> That made a book agayn Jovinian...
> And alle thise were bounden in o volume.
> And every nyght and day was his custume,
> Whan he hadde leyser and vacacioun* *spare time
> From oother worldly occupacioun,
> To reden on this book of wikked wyves.
> He knew of hem mo legendes and lyves
> Than been of goode wyves in the Bible.
> For trusteth wel, it is an impossible
> That any clerk wol speke good of wyves,
> But if it be of hooly seintes lyves,
> Ne of noon oother womman never the mo.
> Who peyntede the leon, tel me who?
> By God, if wommen hadde writen stories,
> As clerkes han withinne hire oratories,* *chapels
> They wolde han writen of men moore wikkednesse
> Than al the mark of Adam* may redresse. *male sex
> (669–75, 681–96)

'Who painted the lion?' The Wife is referring to the well-known fable which relates how a lion and a man argued over which of them was superior to the other.[1] When the man attempted to prove his case by pointing to a picture of a man overcoming a lion, the lion asked who painted the picture, and on receiving the obvious reply – 'A man' – commented that if lions could paint, then the picture would be very different. Women, for the Wife of Bath, are in the same position as the lion: they are powerless to correct the distorted image of themselves produced by clerical misogynists and given all the weight of bookish authority.[2] The Wife's concern is to strip off the impersonal disguise of 'auctoritee' and to reveal the biased individual behind the mask.

As David Aers has noted, there is no essential difference between the Wife of Bath's manipulation of 'auctoritees' and that of the clerics she attacks; 'the standard practices of medieval exegesis included the sustained pulverization and fragmentation of Biblical texts, the utter dissolution of their existential and historical meanings, and the imposition of pre-determined dogmatic propositions' (1980, 86; cf. Donaldson, 1977, 5–7). The battle between Jovinian and Jerome is a battle for possession of biblical texts, which each in turn selects, interprets and synthesizes in the construction of his own argument. Each appeals to the biblical texts as fixed and unalterable reference-points, investing the argument with impersonal authority,[3] yet each interprets them according to his own bias, using them as fluid elements in a personal discourse. 'Authority has a waxen nose: that is, it can be turned in either direction' ('Auctoritas cereum habet nasum: id est, in diversum potest flecti sensum'), as Alan of Lille sagely observes.[4] For Jovinian, God's command to 'increase and multiply' is to be taken literally; for Jerome, it must be read in the light of Paul's recommendations of virginity. Marriage is to be praised, but virginity is to be preferred (*Adv. Jov.* I.2, I.16). The Wife of Bath's contribution to the debate makes fluidity even more fluid by virtue of the simple but confusing fact that it draws on both disputants at once: if, like Jovinian, she clings to the literal 'text' of God's command to 'wexe and multiplye' (28–9), she is equally happy to appropriate Jerome. She serenely grants the superiority he claims for virginity, repeating his metaphor of the different vessels in a lord's household – some of gold, some of wood – whose equal serviceableness but differing dignity is representative of the relationship between virginity and marriage (91–104; cf. *Adv. Jov.* I. 3, I.8). But the *affective* power of the metaphor disappears under the Wife's cheerful renunciation of spiritual ambition. Jerome's arguments merge with her own purposes; rebellion speaks with the voice of orthodoxy.

If the Wife asserts her 'experience' against written 'auctoritee', she does not therefore abandon the verbal world, but rather adapts its techniques to her own ends. Jerome's triple comparison of virginity, marriage and lechery to wheat-bread, barley-bread and dung (*Adv. Jov.* I.7) opens up alarmingly to new meaning as the Wife subjects it to the same sort of close reading as the exegetes apply to biblical texts.

I nyl* envye no virginitee.	*will not
Lat hem be breed of pured* whete-seed,	*refined
And lat us wyves hoten* barly-breed;	* be called

And yet with barly-breed, Mark telle kan,
Oure Lord Jhesu refresshed many a man.
(142–6)

The comparison loses its original meaning under the pressure of lateral thinking: function is substituted for hierarchical ranking. Yet the ingenuity practised here is close kin to that evident in the way Jerome finally disposes of the command to 'increase and multiply and fill the earth' by focusing on the word 'earth': 'marriage fills the earth, virginity fills heaven' (I.16). The comic play of the Wife's arguments is thus ballasted with a serious point: the stability of words lasts only as long as does the assent to the authority that fixes their meaning (Mann, 1974; Aers, 1980, 93–9).[5] The Wife sets herself up as a new 'authority' (and is meekly accepted as such by the Pardoner: 164–87): male discourse passes into female control.

The first part of the Prologue thus prepares for the second, in which the Wife relates how she cowed her first three husbands into submission by her lengthy tirades against them. The source-material of this whole long section (235–394) is, as I noted earlier, Jerome's citation of Theophrastus's *Golden Book*, but it also incorporates material from the *Epistola Valerii* and the vernacular texts that draw on the Theophrastan material, in particular the *Romance of the Rose* and Deschamps's *Miroir de Mariage*. But it is not only the source-material that links these latter texts to Chaucer's, it is also their common exploitation of the dialogic potential of that source-material, and their elaboration of it into ironies of different kinds (cf. Muscatine, 1957, 210–11). I shall deal with the *Miroir* first, although chronologically it is the later of the two, because its ironies are simpler in structure. They arise from the frequent use of quoted speech in the long letter from Repertoire de Science to Franc Vouloirs which occupies the bulk of the work. There is, as we might expect, a chorus of male voices reporting the faults of their wives; but we also hear a great deal from the wives themselves. First a typical wife outlines all the expensive things she needs to keep her happy: clothes, jewels, luxurious furnishings, household goods, spices and cooking materials. This is Theophrastus's third-person account of female needs, cast in first-person form (*Adv. Jov.* I.47). A little later, we find her outlining her husband's faults:

'By our Lady, such-and-such a woman is publicly respected, well-dressed and well turned-out, while I, wretched creature, am poor and despised by everybody! But I see well what's at the bottom of it: you've got your eye on our neighbour when she comes to call, I can see it, because you care nothing for me. You flirt with our maid; what did you bring her back from market the other day? Unlucky was the day you married me! I have neither husband nor lover.' (1594–1608)

This speech exactly reproduces Theophrastus's example of female nagging:

> '*That* woman is better dressed when she goes out; she is respected by everyone, while I, wretched creature, am despised among women. Why were you eyeing our neighbour? What were you saying to our maid? What did you bring back from market? *I* am not allowed a male friend or acquaintance.' (*Adv. Jov.* I.47)

For Repertoire de Science, as for Theophrastus, it is not necessary to demonstrate the lack of truth in these complaints: the mere voicing of them is sufficient evidence of female troublesomeness. Yet the irony by which the speeches of women attacking men are made an essential part of a male attack on women remains open to perception by the reader.

In Jean de Meun, this use of speeches-within-speeches to create a polyphonic utterance is much more complicated: the Theophrastan material forms part of a whole system of utterances working ironically against each other. Its outer framework is the speech of the lover's friend, Amis, who is warning him of the incompatibility of love and 'seigneurie' ('lordship'); to illustrate his point he invents a long speech by a jealous husband (Le Jaloux), the kind of man who wants 'mestrise' over his wife, as an example of what *not* to do (8437–9330). Le Jaloux nags his wife about her infidelities and extravagances, and recapitulates Theophrastus's warnings against women, regretting that he did not listen to them. Yet just as Jerome paradoxically precedes his quotation of Theophrastus with the exemplary stories of good women, so Le Jaloux is imperceptibly led into recounting the stories of Penelope and Lucretia. Embedded in his recital of the wrongs women inflict on men, we find clear examples of the wrongs men do to women. Le Jaloux retrieves himself by retreating to his Theophrastan material and reinforcing it from the *Epistola Valerii*, but he runs into trouble again when he tries to use Heloise's *dissuasio* as further support. For here his approval of the subject-matter forces him into admiration for the woman speaker, and he can pursue his anti-feminist line only by claiming that 'no such woman has lived since' (8795–6), and that her learning enabled her to rise above the limitations of her sex.

But it is not only in its testimony to the selflessness of its author that Heloise's *dissuasio* undermines Le Jaloux's tirade: it is also in the fact that it harmonizes perfectly with the outer framing speech of Amis. For Le Jaloux fuses with Abelard's account of Heloise's dissuasion her own later comments on it in the *Letters*:

> God knows I never sought anything in you except yourself; I wanted simply you, nothing of yours. I looked for no marriage-bond, no marriage portion, and it

The Canterbury Tales: Critical Extracts

was not my own pleasures and wishes I sought to gratify, as you well know, but yours. The name of wife may seem more sacred or more binding, but sweeter for me will always be the word mistress, or, if you will permit me, that of concubine or whore... [In the *Historia Calamitatum*] you thought fit to set out some of the reasons I gave in trying to dissuade you from binding us together in an ill-starred marriage. But you kept silent about most of my arguments for preferring love to wedlock and freedom to chains. God is my witness that if Augustus, Emperor of the whole world, thought fit to honour me with marriage and conferred all the earth on me to possess for ever, it would be dearer and more honourable to me to be called not his Empress but your whore. (trans. Radice, 114)

Le Jaloux incorporates this passage into his account of the *dissuasio*:

She asked him to love her but to claim no right over her except that freely granted by grace ['de grace et de franchise'], without lordship or mastery ['sanz seigneurie et sanz mestrise'], so that he could study without any ties, be his own person, quite free, and that she might devote herself to study, being not devoid of learning... It is written in so many words in the letters she sent him even after she was abbess, if anyone wants to search through their pages: 'If the emperor of Rome, to whom all men are subject, condescended to wish to take me to wife and make me mistress of the world, I would rather' she said, '– and I call God to witness – be called your whore than his crowned empress.' (8747–54, 8783–94)

Heloise's rejection of 'seigneurie' and 'mestrise' accords, not with the speech of Le Jaloux, who is their arch-representative, but with the outer speech of Amis, who like her prizes 'grace' and 'franchise' (cf. Dronke [1975] 1984, 383–4; Kelly, 1975, 44–6). The voice of 'franchise' speaks not only outside the voice of 'mestrise', but also within it, though Le Jaloux himself is deaf to it. Monologue becomes concealed dialogue; speech works against speaker.

Chaucer's own counterpointing of speech and speaker in the *Wife of Bath's Prologue* probably owes a general debt to both these instances, but it goes beyond both of them in complexity. The Wife's tirade against her husbands begins in a quite unsurprising way as a reprise of the Theophrastan sample of female nagging:

'Sire olde kaynard,* is this thyn array?	*dotard
Why is my neighebores wyf so gay?	
She is honoured overal ther* she gooth;	*everywhere
I sitte at hoom; I have no thrifty clooth.*	*serviceable clothing
What dostow at my neighebores hous?	
Is she so fair? Artow so amorous?	

What rowne* ye with oure mayde? Benedicite!   *whisper
Sire olde lecchour, lat thy japes be!
And if I have a gossib or a freend,
Withouten gilt, thou chidest as a feend,
If that I walke or pleye unto his hous!'
(235–45)

At this point, however, Theophrastus reverts to a third-person account of female vices, and one would expect the Wife therefore to drum up further examples of male failings from other sources. Instead, she continues to follow the Theophrastan model, this time passing off his anti-feminist observations as quotations of what her husbands had said to her when drunk. Her phraseology often echoes the expansions of Theophrastan material in Jean de Meun or Deschamps or Matheolus's *Lamentations*, but comparison with the original is the most succinct way of indicating the close relations between the Wife's speech and this traditional material.

Theophrastus: 'To support a poor wife is hard work; to put up with a rich one, is torment.'

The Wife: 'Thou seist to me it is a greet meschief
To wedde a povre womman, for costage;
And if that she be riche, of heigh parage,
Thanne seistow that it is a tormentrie
To suffre hire pride and hire malencolie.'
(248–52)

Theophrastus: In addition, there is no choice in the case of a wife: she must be taken as she is. Whether she is bad-tempered, stupid, deformed, proud, has bad breath – whatever her fault, we find out after marriage. A horse, an ass, an ox, a dog, even the basest slaves, clothes, kettles, wooden stools, cups, and earthenware jugs, are all tried out first and then bought; only a wife is not displayed before she is wed, lest she fail to give satisfaction.

The Wife: 'Thou seist that oxen, asses, hors, and houndes,
They been assayed at diverse stoundes;
Bacyns, lavours, er that men hem bye,
Spoones and stooles, and al swich housbondrye,
And so been pottes, clothes, and array;
But folk of wyves maken noon assay,
Til they be wedded – olde dotard shrewe!–
And thanne, seistow, we wol oure vices shewe.'
(285–92)

Multiplying examples would only repeat the point. When the Wife has exhausted Theophrastus, she moves on to the rest of Jerome's text, and supplements it with snippets from his vernacular imitators. The exact source is not important; what matters is that her long speech is almost entirely made up of the commonplaces of anti-feminist tradition, presented as what her husbands allegedly said to her. This is emphasized by the obsessive repetition in varied forms of the phrase 'thou seyst' ('seistow', 'thou seydest'); it recurs twenty-five times in all in nearly a hundred and fifty lines. Almost all the Wife's tirade against her husbands, apart from the first twelve lines, is reported speech – nothing other than what *they* are supposed to have said to *her*. Male attacks on women become the very substance of a female attack on men. The Wife uses anti-feminist satire as a blunt instrument with which to beat her husbands into submission (Murtaugh, 1971, 476; cf. Knapp, 1986, 391).

There is no evidence, of course, that these particular husbands ever did say any of the things the Wife puts into their mouths; her triumphant conclusion – 'And al was fals' (382) – acknowledges this. But by the same token, there is no real evidence that the Wife actually did the things that are alleged of women. The Wife's speech is performative rather than constative; it does not document the realities of an individual marital relationship (as is already evident from the fact that it is addressed indifferently to *three* husbands). The Wife's constant use of the plural – 'we wyves', 'us', 'oure' – dissolves her individual situation into a general female experience, and acts as a constant reminder of the anti-feminist commonplaces on which she draws. No matter that these particular husbands never made these accusations, their hackneyed character is evidence in itself that plenty of other men did.

The double structure of the Wife's tirade, like the double structure of the encomium on marriage in the *Merchant's Tale*, thus turns out to be the most important thing about it. Within the speech of the Wife bullying her husbands, we can hear the speeches of countless husbands bullying their wives. Her tirade thus functions simultaneously as a demonstration of female bullying and a witness to masculine oppression. What is more, it suggests that female bullying and masculine oppression have a strangely symbiotic relationship: each feeds off the other. The Wife uses the traditional masculine attacks on her sex as a way of legitimizing her own tirade; her husbands (or male readers) could equally well appeal to her scolding as evidence of the contumaciousness of women.

The double structure of the Wife's speech thus has a meaning of far wider import than its role in the Wife's individual experience. And yet it plays a crucial role in creating our sense of the Wife as a living individual. For what it demonstrates is her *interaction* with the stereotypes of her sex, and it is in this interaction that we feel the three-dimensional reality of her existence.

That is, she does not live in the insulated laboratory world of literature, where she is no more than a literary object, unconscious of the interpretations foisted upon her; she is conceived as a woman who lives in the real world, in full awareness of the anti-feminist literature that purports to describe and criticize her behaviour, and she has an attitude to *it* just as it has an attitude to her. On a previous occasion I have commented on a similar example of individual interaction with class satire in the *General Prologue*, where we are told that the Monk doesn't give a 'pulled hen' for the proverb that declares a monk out of his cloister to be like a fish out of water. In other satirists, we find the proverb used to comment on monks; only in Chaucer does the Monk comment on the proverb (Mann, 1973, 31). Neither the Monk nor the Wife of Bath simply *is*; they are also conscious of what others suppose them to be, and their own individuality has to work itself out through this consciousness.

In the last section of the Wife's *Prologue*, however, the anti-feminist stereotypes reassert their power over the woman's life, as she is forced to listen to her husband's endless readings from his 'book of wikked wyves'. Like the wife of Le Jaloux, she is forced to listen to a catalogue of female vices, but here the emphasis is on the book as source of and authority for this anti-feminist attack. Lee Patterson sees the Wife's attempt to put an end to this torment by tearing three pages out of Jankin's book as a gallant bid for feminine freedom which is nevertheless doomed to failure: although 'in the [Wife's] Prologue clerical antifeminism is appropriated by a woman's voice in order to articulate feminist truths', nevertheless the Wife 'remains confined within the prison house of masculine language; she brilliantly rearranges and deforms her authorities to enable them to disclose new areas of experience, but she remains dependent on them for her voice' (1983, 682; cf. Gottfried, 1984–5). There is a great deal of truth in this comment – as I suggested earlier, Chaucer could not invent a new 'female language', and sensibly did not try to do so – but I think it fails to take account of the degree to which the Wife's *Prologue* is designed precisely to make the reader conscious of the confining nature of 'the prison house of masculine language'. The Wife's tirade to her old husbands, with its repeated 'thou seyest', is the first step to this end, yet it remains open to a male reading as well as a female one. Just as the marriage encomium in the *Merchant's Tale* can be read from either a male or a female point of view, so in the Wife's speech to her old husbands we can listen to the female nagging of its frame or the male nagging of its content, as our bias leads us. But when she recounts Jankin's readings from his anti-feminist book, there is no choice and no escape: we listen to these readings in the Wife's position – that is, *as a woman*. The repeated phrases here are 'Tho redde he me', 'tolde he me', 'he tolde me eek', all emphasizing the presence of the listening woman.

>   'Tho redde he me how Sampson* loste his heres: *first of a list of men
>   Slepynge, his lemman* kitte it with hire sheres;   betrayed by women
>   Thurgh which treson loste he bothe his yen.*   *sweetheart
>   Tho redde he me, if that I shal nat lyen,   *eyes
>   Of Hercules and of his Dianyre,
>   That caused hym to sette hymself afyre...
>   He tolde me eek for what occasioun
>   Amphiorax at Thebes loste his lyf...
>   Of Lyvia tolde he me, and of Lucye...
>   Thanne tolde he me how oon Latumyus
>   Compleyned unto his felawe Arrius.'
>   (721–6, 740–1, 747, 757–8)

In this string of narrative *exempla* and proverbs, second-person invective disguises itself as third-person statement; phrases such as 'a womman', 'an angry wyf', claim the authority of impersonal generalization, but they mean '*you*', as their effect on the Wife indicates.

>   'Bet is,' quod he, 'thyn habitacioun
>   Be with a leon or a foul dragoun,
>   Than with a womman usynge for to* chyde.   *accustomed to
>   Bet is,' quod he, 'hye in the roof abyde,
>   Than with an angry wyf doun in the hous;
>   They been so wikked and contrarious,
>   They haten that hir housbondes loven ay.'
>   He seyde, 'A womman cast hir shame away,
>   Whan she cast of hir smok'; and forthermo,
>   'A fair womman, but she be chaast also,
>   Is lyk a gold ryng in a sowes nose.'
>   Who wolde wene, or who wolde suppose,
>   The wo that in myn herte was, and pyne?
>   (775–87)

With her three old husbands, the Wife was in control, manipulating antifeminist satire to serve her own ends; here she is reduced to its helpless object. The point about this passage is that it forces us to *experience* the 'prison house of masculine language'; vain attempts to fantasize about life outside the prison walls are beside the point until the key is turned.

Chaucer's master-stroke in demonstrating the absoluteness of this confinement is his dramatization of the fact that the more vigorously the Wife asserts herself in opposition to traditional anti-feminism, the more she conforms to its stereotyped image of her. As she gleefully uses it to berate her old husbands, she appears before us as its typical representative: rebellious, nagging, domineering. Similarly, Jankin's stream of anti-feminist abuse succeeds in *provoking* a violent outburst of the anger which anti-feminist satire insists is a particular failing of women. In both cases anti-feminist literature becomes a dynamic element in the very situations it purports to observe dispassionately from the outside. Jerome might well protest that what he meant by his work was simply to defend virginity, but such protests would be futile; the meaning of his work is fixed in the 'gloss' his male readers bring to it.

If, therefore, the *Wife of Bath's Prologue* is largely constructed of anti-feminist satire, this in no way implies Chaucer's endorsement of it. A lesser writer than Chaucer might have attempted to ignore the anti-feminist stereotypes, to imagine a female experience as yet unrecorded in literature. But the attempt to escape stereotypes – as Chaucer must have known – leads only to different stereotypes, created in the mirror-image of their predecessors, as the Ovidian heroines reverse the picture of the shrew. The process is evident in the way that feminism has rejected the old stereotypes, only to lend its energies to the identification of 'role-models', which are, as Christopher Ricks points out, merely stereotypes you approve of (1988, 118). Ricks's further remarks on the place of stereotypes in art are highly pertinent to what I have been arguing about their role in the *Wife of Bath's Prologue*:

> It is true that art, being fine, cannot be simply crude, but it would not follow from this that stereotypes should not have a place in art in their crude state, since there is no reason why the stereotyping should not itself then be 'placed' by the work of art, contemplated with 'a suspicious and interrogating eye' and understood. This would not be the same as making the state of the stereotype itself uncrude, but would be the provision of an uncrude setting, context, or ethos. This would be to engage something intrinsic not only to the stereotyped character but also to our own ways with stereotypes. (118–19)

Writing the truth of woman's existence, in the *Wife of Bath's Prologue*, means not turning one's back on stereotypes, but accepting that their existence is the centrally important and interesting fact to be confronted. It means acknowledging the power they exert even as they are resisted, because they will define the form of the resistance (Hanning, 1985, 19). Chaucer could not plumb the unrecorded secrets of woman's existence, but he *could* anatomize the literary stereotypes which set the terms in which male–female relationships were played out, and he could question the male writer's role as the 'auctoritee' that supports them. And he could, in the Wife of Bath, give us the imagined representation of an individual engagement with these stereotypes and their absorption into an individual life.

The *Wife of Bath's Prologue* does not, however, end in this state of unresolved hostility. The quarrel that breaks out when the Wife attacks Jankin's book ends in his capitulation and the establishment of marital harmony. The suspicion of sentimentality in this unexpected 'happy ending' is hard to avoid, and it is worth quoting the passage in its entirety so that the mechanisms by which the final accord is reached can be seen in detail.

> And whan I saugh he wolde nevere fyne*   *cease
> To reden on this cursed book al nyght,
> Al sodeynly thre leves have I plyght
> Out of his book, right as he radde, and eke
> I with my fest so took hym on the cheke
> That in oure fyr he fil bakward adoun.
> And he up stirte as dooth a wood leoun,
> And with his fest he smoot me on the heed
> That in the floor I lay as I were deed.
> And whan he saugh how stille that I lay,
> He was agast and wolde han fled his way,
> Til atte laste out of my swogh* I breyde.*   *swoon   *woke
> 'O! hastow slayn me, false theef?' I seyde,
> 'And for my land thus hastow mordred me?
> Er I be deed, yet wol I kisse thee.'
> And neer he cam, and kneled faire adoun,
> And seyde, 'Deere suster Alisoun,
> As help me God, I shal thee nevere smyte!
> That I have doon, it is thyself to wyte.*   *blame
> Foryeve it me, and that I thee biseke!'
> And yet eftsoones* I hitte hym on the cheke,   *immediately
> And seyde, 'Theef, thus muchel am I wreke,*   *avenged
> Now wol I dye, I may no lenger speke.'
> But atte laste, with muchel care and wo,
> We fille acorded by us selven two.
> He yaf me al the bridel in myn hond,
> To han the governance of hous and lond,
> And of his tonge, and of his hond also;
> And made hym brenne his book anon right tho.
> And whan that I hadde geten unto me,
> By maistrie, al the soveraynetee,
> And that he seyde, 'Myn owene trewe wyf,
> Do as thee lust the terme of al thy lyf;
> Keep thyn honour, and keep eek myn estaat'-
> After that day we hadden never debaat.

> God help me so, I was to hym as kynde
> As any wyf from Denmark unto Ynde,
> And also trewe, and so was he to me.
> (788–825)

The first observation to be made about this quarrel is that it is completely convincing *as* a quarrel, and what makes it so is its sense of emotional flux, which manifests itself as a constant modulation between aggression and pathos. Finding herself prone on the floor, the Wife abandons belligerence for plaintiveness; she seizes the chance to exercise the moral superiority of the obvious victim, which Jankin, aghast at the effects of his own violence, is obliged to recognize. But he cannot resist inserting into his apology the defence that she has brought his attack upon herself ('it is thyself to wyte'). In retaliation the Wife briefly reasserts her rights in the quarrel by means of the token blow on the cheek which acts as an emblematic form of vengeance ('thus muchel am I wreke'), although immediately indicating her reluctance to revive hostilities by lapsing back into pathos ('Now wol I dye').

The same alternation of assertiveness and conciliation marks the resolution of the quarrel between Pluto and Proserpina in the *Merchant's Tale*. Proserpina's long harangue having worn Pluto into submission, he nevertheless feels obliged to salvage some remnants of his dignity by asserting that his original decree shall stand:

> 'Dame,' quod this Pluto, 'be no lenger wrooth;
> I yeve it up! But sith I swoor myn ooth
> That I wolde graunten hym his sighte ageyn,
> My word shal stonde, I warne yow certeyn.
> I am a kyng; it sit* me noght to lye.' *befits
> (2311–15)

Proserpina responds with a matching assertion of her own dignity and a reaffirmation of her determination to nullify Pluto's decree by her own assistance to May:

> 'And I,' quod she, 'a queene of Fayerye!
> Hir answere shal she have, I undertake.'
> (2316–17)

But honour thus satisfied, she shows that she too knows the advantages of appeasement:

'Lat us namoore wordes heerof make;
For sothe, I wol no lenger yow contrarie.'
(2318–19)

Like the quarrel between Jankin and the Wife of Bath, this quarrel shows an instinctive oscillation between self-vindication and placatory assuagement. Mutual peace is achieved by a delicate process of attunement which calibrates defence of one's own wounded feelings with an acknowledgement of the other's peaceable overtures.

The second notable thing about the quarrel between the Wife of Bath and Jankin is that the Wife's victory is won not by aggression but by pathos. It is her plaintive speech of martyred affection – 'Er I be deed, yet wol I kisse thee' – that opens the way for Jankin's apology and acknowledgement of answering affection. Sentimentality is again excluded by the comic aspects of this plangency; not only is she clearly milking the pathos for all it is worth, she is also sufficiently in command of her wits to increase the moral superiority she has already won by reminding Jankin of the material benefits that her death will bring him. But the knowingness behind the pathos simply reinforces the point: the power of the underdog is real enough to be exploited by a good tactician. And what is acted – even what is over-acted – can nevertheless correspond to a real feeling: the extremity of the situation allows the Wife and Jankin the relief of abandoning confrontation for their own version of tenderness.

It is this relief that makes Jankin's final surrender into something other than a simple example of triumph for the shrew. His surrender of 'maistrye' is met by the Wife's subsequent fidelity and kindness. We may be tempted to write this off as a travestied version of marital harmony which goes against all medieval orthodoxy on the rightful and necessary ascendancy of the husband. Yet if this is a comic version of marital happiness, it is not *ipso facto* a travesty: elsewhere in Chaucer's works, we find the same surrender of masculine 'maistrye' presented in all seriousness as the foundation on which conjugal harmony is built.

Notes

1 The fable is number 24 in Avianus's collection (though here it is a sculpted tombstone rather than a painting that is in question), and also appears, for example, in the *Romulus Vulgaris* and the *Romulus Nilantinus* (ed. Hervieux, 2^2: 231, 544), in Marie de France's *Fables* (no. 37) and their Latin derivative (ed. Hervieux, 2^2: 623–4).
2 For evidence of clerical anti-feminism in medieval Oxford, see Pratt (1962).

3 *Adv. Jov.* I.4: 'adversus singulas propositiones ejus, Scripturarum vel maxime nitor testimoniis: ne querulus garriat, se eloquentia magis quam veritate superatum'.
4 'De Fide Catholica' I.xxx (*PL* 210, col. 333).
5 The struggle for control of the text extends itself into the marginalia that accompany the *Wife of Bath's Prologue* in the manuscripts; see Caie (1975–6), answered by Schibanoff (1988).

The Franklin's Tale

Angela Jane Weisl

Among the group of romances in the Canterbury Tales *the* Wife of Bath's Tale *and the* Franklin's Tale *fall into a romance sub-genre, that of the Breton lay. This genre originated with the* lais *of Marie de France, short courtly tales of intense emotion that retold the oral stories of the Bretons in literary form. Marie was especially concerned with issues of love and* gentillesse, *and with the woman's voice. Both Chaucer's Breton lays continue this emphasis while using the traditional matter of chivalric romance. In this extract, Angela Jane Weisl considers the emotional and literary structure of the* Franklin's Tale *and examines the way that as a romance it writes Dorigen out of an active role. The early critic Kittredge viewed the story as offering the ideal response to the variously flawed views of the other tales in the 'Marriage Group', by presenting a model of mutual love and equal sovereignty in marriage. The Franklin states at the start the need for freedom in love: 'Love wol not been constreyned by maistrye' (764), and tells how Arveragus adapts the traditional male role of 'servant in love, and lord in marriage' (793), becoming lord in name only.*

Weisl suggests that the Franklin's Tale *is more problematic than its apparent insistence on the ideals of marital* trouthe *and equality implies. Her argument follows that of critics such as Susan Crane in presenting the tale as a 'male game that disenfranchises its female characters'. It seems to have a happy ending, but it is one in which the heroine, Dorigen, is largely ignored. In the first part of her chapter, Weisl has explored the genre of the story, comparing it with Marie de France's* lais. *She notes the difficulty of phrasing the contract between Dorigen and Arveragus, and the static nature of Dorigen's role: while Arveragus departs to pursue chivalric honour, Dorigen can only enter into romance games or lament to while away the time; when Aurelius asks for her love, she responds in a game-like manner, ensnared by romance convention. In this extract, Weisl compares Dorigen's approach, which depends on the notion of literal truth, to that of the clerk, who creates the illusion of the disappearance of the rocks. Such male 'magic' is exclusive, dependent on learning and the debate tradition from which women are excluded.*

Weisl explores how, when the rocks seem to have disappeared, Dorigen is brought into a public arena where she no longer possesses the romance heroine's power to command, but instead is subject to the contract to which she has given her word. Weisl's discussion of Dorigen's long lament, often criticized as ridiculous, is sympathetic: she describes persuasively how Dorigen's examples, even when far-fetched, portray her as valued by men on account of her chaste body; dishonour of the body is thus worse than death. In being sent to fulfil her word, she is sent into a male world where women's bodies are objects of exchange and where the power of words belongs to men. Romance is reversed and the setting changes from summer to winter. Even when Aurelius is moved to forgiveness, it is Arveragus's honour that effects this, and Dorigen appears the least free in the final instance. It is difficult not to see her as the object, freed only through male actions and emotions, rather than through her own honour and desire. The tale uneasily opposes different kinds of trouthe: *the word and the marital bond.*

Weisl's analysis, although carefully contextualized to take account of literary history and convention, is on the whole a feminist one; the tale may also be seen in more philosophical terms, as being about the impossibility of absolute morality. Moral principles become untenable when taken to extremes: adherence to the promise, which is upheld as the highest honour, threatens marital honour. Yet at the same time the tale is optimistic, for the choice to pursue impossible honour is rewarded: God intervenes, as he did to save Isaac from sacrifice. We are made aware of the human need for flexibility, grace and forgiveness, but also left to wonder what happens when a benign God does not step in (as in the Knight's Tale*). How tenable is absolute morality then? Such are the moral conundrums Chaucer sets us.*

Angela Jane Weisl, from 'The Franklin's Tale' in 'Public Authority and Private Power' in *Conquering the Reign of Femeny: Gender and Genre in Chaucer's Romance.* D. S. Brewer, Cambridge, 1995.

That clerks are often situated in opposition to women is also nothing new. In the *Wife of Bath's Prologue* we are reminded that 'it is an impossible / That any clerk wol speke good of wyves / But [Unless] if it be of hooly seintes lyves, / Ne of noon other womman never the mo' (III 689–91) and 'no womman of no clerk is preysed' (III 706). It is also clear from the Wife's pronouncements that clerks write the books of 'wykked wyves' as well as read them. Furthermore, the *Clerk's Tale* presents an ambiguous example; it praises Griselda for her obedience to her lord in all things; even before the Clerk's exegesis tells us to read it as such, the poem seems more like a 'holy seintes lyve' than an encomium to women in marriage. Griselda is valued for her submission to her husband, a value that Dorigen's and Arveragus's marriage contract seemingly voids; thus, this clerkly voice opposes Dorigen's position before she even makes her deal with Aurelius. Dorigen, in fact, perceives clerkly discourse as different from her own, much as Marie de France does in her Prologue. In the black rocks speech she says, 'I woot wel clerkes wol seyn as hem leste [please], / By argumentz, that al is for the beste, / Though I ne kan the causes nat yknowe' (V 885–7). While clerks can create reasons to show that the terrible danger and destruction that she fears are 'for the beste,' these rationalizations are foreign to Dorigen, who finds the rocks to be 'werk unresonable' (V 872). Crane's formulation of Dorigen's separation from masculine, clerkly discourse despite its role in defining her is particularly salient:

> Dorigen's sense of isolation from intellectual argument defines her femininity along the axis of clerical writing, just as her beauty, emotion, and dependence on Arveragus define her in courtly terms. Heroines of romance can be intelligent and well-educated, but clerical writing in sermons, estates literature, and satires emphasizes that irrationality is characteristically feminine, and reason masculine. Thus much knowledge is difficult of access for women. Dorigen is aware of the importance of clerical teaching to her own life – it could alleviate her concern about the rocks and reconcile her to suicide – but she finds herself unwilling to follow its learned precepts. As with the status in romance, she experiences a difference that is already asserted in clerical texts. ('Franklin' 247)

When Dorigen says, 'To clerkes lete I al disputison [disputation]' (V 890) she makes even clearer her separation from their discourse, which she makes sound illusory and profoundly foreign to the reality she encounters. While she sees the black, jagged, dangerous rocks, the clerks turn them into something much less tangible and therefore much less physical – a subject for debate. Because this method of argument is unavailable to her, she is unable to imagine the disappearance of the rocks, and when they do seem to disappear, she is unable to see through the illusion.

What is ironic here is, of course, that the clerks are right; leaving the rocks where they are is 'for the beste'; it is their disappearence that causes the trouble. For the illusion does not help Arveragus to return home safely – it is unable to do so by its very nature; he arrives several lines before Aurelius rises from his lamenting to go find the clerk in the first place. The rocks are still there when Arveragus returns, everything seems to be all right, and Dorigen and Arveragus are reunited 'in joye and blisse' (V 1099). It is, by the tale's calculation, 'two yeer and moore' later that the rock-trick takes place. It is also no longer May; instead it is midwinter, shortly after Christmas time, when Aurelius finds Dorigen in the temple. Although Aurelius begins to address her in the courtly mode, calling her 'My righte lady,.../ Whom I moost drede and love as best kan, / And lothest were of al this world displese' (V 1311–13), the context is wrong and his words do not ring true. His desire not to displease her is soon replaced by a subtle threat:

> Ye sle me giltlees for verry peyne.
> But of my deeth thogh that ye have no routhe,
> Avyseth yow er that ye breke youre trouthe.
> Repenteth yow, for thilke God above,
> Er ye me sleen by cause that I yow love.
> (V 1318–22)

'Love me or I will die' is a common plaint of the courtly lover, but by making it in a public place, rather than the walled garden of romance, and by alluding to Dorigen's 'trouthe,' Aurelius takes a private game and makes it a public contract. Indeed, the tale shifts here from the interior spaces of the romance that allowed Dorigen's and Arveragus's equal marriage but required Dorigen's agreement with Aurelius, to the public arena of contractual obligation, truth, and honor – male standards that knights in romance have to uphold. Once the conditions of romance are removed, there is no possibility for Dorigen's autonomy; Aurelius's allusion to her power over him is merely a rhetorical convention devoid of any real meaning. His reference to her 'trouthe' and his reminder that she 'have youre beheste in mynde' (V 1335) show her that he feels she is contractually obligated to him. Dorigen is dismayed; she 'wende [thought] nevere han come in swich a trappe' (V 1341). That she 'wende nevere by possibilitee, / That swich a monstre or merveille myghte be!' (V 1344–5) is no longer important; Aurelius has turned her game, which she herself called a 'follie' in the garden scene, from a private, courtly exchange to one that Dorigen is publicly required to fulfill. That the rock trick is indeed a 'monstre' and a 'merveille,' an illusion being foisted upon her which goes, as she says, 'agayns the proces of nature' (V 1345) is not in itself the point; she is indeed caught in a trap between the private and public worlds of the tale, between the conventions of romance and the 'reality' of the outside (including her marriage) in which she is forced to function.

Once forced into this public context, Dorigen is transformed into the passive woman. She begins to lose her autonomy even before Arveragus takes it away. Her recital of tragedies, while excessive and perhaps comic, shows her sense of being dishonored at the hands of men; the women to whom she compares herself all commit suicide either to avoid rape or because they have been raped. Although the exempla in this *Legend of Dead Women* do not really apply to Dorigen's situation, it is clear that she fears 'to been defouled with mannes foul delit' (V 1396); she says, 'I wol conclude that it is bet for me / To sleen myself than been defouled thus' (V 1422–3). It is the only way she sees to be 'trewe unto Arveragus' (V 1424), since, as Dinshaw points out, Dorigen's only truth is 'truth in love,' a constituted function within the structure of patriarchal society, in which her desires must conform to those of the men who possess her (Dinshaw 7). Ironically, romance conventions are more able to accommodate her adultery than her fidelity, since her relationship with Aurelius follows the genre's expectations. Because she is essentially possessed by two different men with two different sets of desires, Dorigen is destined to be unfaithful to one or the other. Like Criseyde, she is judged by this alone. But here, her sense of fidelity, of being a faithful wife, is in conflict with the masculine notion of truth, a public keeping of one's word.

When Arveragus tells Dorigen that 'Trouthe is the hyeste thyng that man may kepe' (V 1479) he is not talking about the same fidelity (to one's word, promise, and values) that she is. Like Aurelius, Arveragus focuses on the public here, and in doing so, seizes the role that was merely supposed to be an illusion, his lordship over her. Dorigen merely tells him the reason for her despair; she does not even ask for advice, but Arveragus responds with an order. Once out of the romance context, the *name of soveraynetee* that he held over her 'for shame of his degree' (V 751–2) all too easily becomes a reality. The answer to David's question, 'Which truth should Dorigen keep?' (187) is clear; she has no choice but to keep Arveragus's. While Dorigen unwittingly breaks her truth in love through her 'promise' to Aurelius, Arveragus wittingly breaks the truth of their marriage contract, substituting the public power he held only in name for the more equal relations they had before. Martin notes that Arveragus gives Dorigen 'a truth and honor' (V 128) outside marital relationships in the public world of contracts, which she says makes Dorigen 'a person outside her relationship with Arveragus and Aurelius's fantasies about her' (128–9). While it is certainly appealing to read the lines this way, since they allow Dorigen to maintain some of her autonomy, Arveragus's threat:'..."I yow forbede, up peyne of deeth, / That never, whil thee lasteth lyf ne breeth, / To no wight telle thou of this aventure –"' (V 1481–3) again imposes his will over hers, and denies all the other bonds of the tale: Dorigen's and his marriage contract, her agreement with Aurelius, Aurelius's false claim, and her own sense of honor and fidelity, which require her to remain faithful to her husband (Aers, *Chaucer* 88). Arveragus has ceased to recognize their equal marriage; at this point in the tale Dorigen's desires are not consulted any more than Emelye's are in the *Knight's Tale*. In this crisis, Arveragus denies Dorigen's subjectivity and desires; 'she stands before his judgment deprived of voice' (Aers, *Chaucer* 89). To have a voice in romance is to be male, and a woman cannot be a man. Arveragus even orders her to 'make no countenance of hevynesse' (V 1485); he attempts to deny her even her sorrow, upholding his public sovereignty over everything else, since his reputation is the highest thing he can keep in an honor-based culture. Being cuckolded is, for Arveragus, the real tragedy. By forcing her to follow his plan, Arveragus ironically reverses the traditional courtly threat, rather than saying, as Aurelius often does, 'give in to me or I'll die,' he makes the danger much more apparent, saying, 'give in to me or you'll die.' But he also removes the one context in which Dorigen maintained any power. As a romance heroine she maintained a kind of autonomy, at least in the private spaces of love; once the poem makes the public concerns of men into Dorigen's, she becomes a silent object of exchange.

This transformation of the lady takes away the trappings of romance, most notably the woman's ostensible power and voice. Dorigen's meeting with Aurelius takes place in winter on a public street, 'Amydde the toun, right in the quykkest strete' (V 1502), not in the May garden of romance, in what Martin calls 'one of the least romantic trysts in literature' (122). It is not Dorigen's sorrow that moves Aurelius to *gentilesse*; rather, it is Arveragus's great *gentilesse* that causes him to give up his claim. Dorigen remains a commodity of male exchange. Just as Arveragus has sent her to Aurelius, he now sends her back again. When he addresses her, it is as a vehicle that will transport his words, which he tells her to 'seyth to youre lord Arveragus' (V 1526). When he does speak to her directly he calls her 'the trewest and the beste wyf / That evere yet I knew in al my lyf' (V 1539–40) – since it is in her role of wife that Arveragus has the 'lordshipe' and she is his 'servant,' even in the contract at the beginning, it is clear that Dorigen's days as a lady with independent power and authority are over. By supporting what would be legally and for the most part socially the case in Chaucer's England, the Franklin seems to create an argument for a morality that supports the social *status quo*.

Indeed, the concluding description of Dorigen's and Arveragus's relationship provides a different picture of marriage than that with which the tale began:

> Arveragus and Dorigen his wyf
> In soveryn blisse leden forth hir lyf.
> Nevere eft ne was ther angre hem bitweene.
> He cherisseth hire as though she were a queene,
> And she was to hym trewe for everemoore.
>   (V 1551–5)

The structure of this formulation shows how deeply their relationship has changed. Arveragus's primacy is asserted, and Dorigen, defined entirely through her relationship to him, maintains only the role of wife (inferior); she is no longer his lady (superior) or his love (equal). He cherishes her like a queen, but that does not give her any autonomy or power, as Crane points out:

'She is loved and honored as a reflection of her lover's desires and ideals – not as an autonomous person' (249). The truth she wanted to maintain in the first place, that is her faithfulness to Arveragus, is all she has left, but it has been won at a great cost. This is 'resolution without regeneration,' which highlights the imposed and arbitrary nature of the ending still to come (Aers, *Chaucer* 90–1). Chaucer's description of Dorigen's and Arveragus's relationship and the evaluation of *gentilesse* that follows are both evasions of the problems the text itself has created.

The rest of the tale is a male exchange concerned with male *gentilesse*, an exchange that begins with Aurelius's desire to prove that 'thus kan a squier doon a gentil dede / As wel as kan a knyght' (V 1543–4). The Franklin has proved that he can tell a romance 'as wel as kan a knyght' with all its conventional hierarchies preserved; Dorigen and Emelye end up much the same way. The Franklin's question, 'Which was the mooste fre, as thynketh yow?' (V 1622) has one clear answer; Dorigen is not *fre* at all. She has escaped from the trap of her two promises only to be marginalized by her genre. When Paul Olsson says:

> His (the Franklin's) tale celebrates a group of people who can act decisively without imposing tyranny or sorrow, who eliminate suffering and evil through tolerance, a generosity, and an insouciance that fulfill the dream of Epicurus in Dante's *Convivio*, namely delight without pain. (267–8)

he fails to notice the tyranny imposed on Dorigen by Arveragus, whose generosity has been greater to another man than it has been to his wife.[1] This tyranny is easy to miss, in part, at least, because Dorigen is not even involved at the end of the tale. Although all is seemingly well at the end of the tale, as Crane notes, all is not well in romance for those whom the genre disenfranchises ('Franklin' 245).

Dorigen is controlled both by the romance genre and clerkly authority; she is powerless to resist her destiny within the confines of the genre's limits. Like the *Wife of Bath's Tale*, the *Franklin's Tale* considers issues of women's autonomy and power, yet the egalitarian vision it proposes runs into trouble in the romance context. The genre cannot accommodate women's sovereignty except in the very private context of love service; once tested outside the romance garden, it collapses, and patriachal authority reasserts itself. It cannot, finally, uphold an equal marriage either; what Dorigen gets at the end of the tale is what Emelye gets, what the Loathly-Lady-turned-heroine gets. By continuing the tale beyond its initial 'happily ever after' ending, Chaucer is forced to allow romance convention to assert itself. At the end of this tale, the status quo, which Dorigen and Arveragus's marriage has disturbed as much as Aurelius's trick has, reclaims its ground. Dorigen's greatest fault is that she cannot see that her equal marriage was as illusory as the rocks' disappearance. In both cases she is manipulated by men, by her genre, and by the society in which she functions.

For all its being set in Brittany, the fictional, mythic *lai* world, the *Franklin's Tale* ultimately functions in the public arena of truth, honor, and contractual obligation, a masculine world in which Dorigen cannot maintain the autonomy given to her in the compressed *lai* at the beginning of the tale. We are again reminded that for all the seeming possibility of female desire and concern being approached within the romance, the genre is finally about men and their desires. Marie's *lais*, although they take women's concerns into account, are primarily about the men for whom they are named.[2] The *gentilesse* with which the *Franklin's Tale* ends is a traditional romance value given great importance in Marie's and the Middle English Breton *lais*, but it is also a primarily male concern. By constraining Dorigen at its end – she never has the opportunity to be *fre* – the *Franklin's Tale* shows the romance's position as an inherently male game. The romance's borders can be tested by new configurations of power – Dorigen's and Arveragus's equal marriage or the female authority of the *Wife of Bath's Tale* – but they ultimately reassert themselves and require male dominance and female submission. For all their attempts to change the romance genre's terms, Dorigen and the Loathly Lady are finally defined by the confluence of their gender and their genre. There are no stories to tell about autonomous women with desires of their own in a romance context; to alter the woman's role into something close to the masculine is to doom the romance to failure. As powerless objects in a courtly, male game, women are ultimately unable either to escape or resist the *maistrye* imposed on them by the narrative necessity of the romance plot.

Notes

1 Alfred David notes that no one is really *fre* in the tale since each man [*nota bene*] gives up something that doesn't really belong to him in the first place. Arveragus places Dorigen's word to Aurelius above their love, giving her up as if he had sovereignty over her and she is his property, while Aurelius extracts a false promise and the Clerk charges for what is only an illusion (189).
2 *Le Fresne* is the only one of Marie's *lais* that is named for the woman; indeed, Fresne is one of the few named women in the entire collection. Although many men remain unnamed, they are fewer in number than the women.

'Glose/Bele chose': The Wife of Bath and Her Glossators
Eunuch Hermeneutics

Carolyn Dinshaw

These two extracts from Carolyn Dinshaw's Chaucer's Sexual Poetics *exemplify a more radical theoretical approach to the* Canterbury Tales. *Dinshaw combines scholarship and an acute awareness of the medieval thought world with an explicitly feminist agenda: to reveal Chaucer's construction of gender, but also to offer readings that sometimes go 'against the grain' in order to emphasize figures at the margins, women and homosexuals. Dinshaw draws on the work of French feminists, in particular Luce Irigaray, who rewrite the psychoanalytic approach of Jacques Lacan from a feminist viewpoint.[1] Essential to Irigaray's thought is the notion of Woman as Other within a patriarchal universe where language is male, and women permanently excluded from it at a fundamental level. In many ways such thought is appropriate to the medieval period, when views of women were fixed, based on what were believed to be essential differences in nature; for anti-feminist thinkers, women certainly represented a threatening Other. It is perhaps surprising that such a view should still seem justified in the modern period: biological determinism is one of the difficulties inherent in some radical feminist thought (by contrast, for example, to the liberal humanism of Jill Mann's feminist readings).*

This ideological stance, however, allows Dinshaw an interesting, sometimes provocative perspective on medieval writings. Her readings tend to be most persuasive when she is discussing tales that in some way confront patriarchy and the 'patriarchal hermeneutic' (that is, defining truth in terms of a set of binary oppositions that place men at the centre and women as Other). She moves beyond an engagement with the nature of the patriarchal 'prison house' to explore how Chaucer may challenge this. It is possible, as Mann argues, to see Chaucer's perspective as remarkably modern, in that a prologue and tale such as the Wife of Bath's *can be read sympathetically from so radical a viewpoint.*

In her analysis of the Wife of Bath's Prologue *Dinshaw explores the clerical practice of 'glossing' (explicating through marginal glosses) instanced by the Wife: Dinshaw's reading places the man as the glossator, the woman as text, associated with the body and with matter, to be moulded and controlled. Whereas the* Man of Law's Tale *is about control of the woman's body, in the* Wife of Bath's Prologue *the body is set up against clerical teaching from the Wife's first interruption. Dinshaw considers the Wife's extravagant clothing, which draws attention to her presence and challenges the marginalization of Woman as Other; in the same way,*

The Canterbury Tales: Critical Extracts

the Wife borrows and adapts patriarchal discourse. Dinshaw argues that the Wife does not desire to subvert so much as to reform patriarchal discourse, to make the body into something pleasing and 'of valuable signification'. She also sees the Wife as peculiarly compelling even for Chaucer, in that she represents a male fantasy

Plate 8 The Pardoner, from *The Ellesmere Chaucer*. The Art Archive/Victoria and Albert Museum, London.

of reform and a proto-feminist mode of reading and living. Dinshaw is radically more positive in her reading of the Wife than is Mann, who takes further into account the literary conventions with which the Wife is constructed. Both, however, demonstrate Chaucer's extraordinary ability to move beyond conventional notions of gender.

In considering the Pardoner, Dinshaw applies a variant of gender theory – queer theory – and again achieves an interesting and provocative reading.[2] This argument is more tangential than the last, building on slighter evidence in the text and slipping further into the problematic tendency, so evident in earlier Chaucer criticism, of treating the characters as real. Dinshaw gives the Pardoner a complex fictional life and role in the Tales that is not as substantially borne out as the Wife's is, although, like the Wife, the Pardoner has a unique, self-revelatory prologue. Dinshaw's interest is not in the corrupt practices expounded in this, but in the Pardoner's otherness: accused of being a homosexual or a eunuch by Harry Bailly, he, like women, occupies a kind of 'outside' space. He is either literally or figuratively 'not a man'. Again, Dinshaw considers clothing, to suggest an absence, literal or figurative, beneath the veiled person of the Pardoner. Her view of the Pardoner as 'tormented' is debatable, but she offers an interesting analysis of how he is cut off from the signification of language and its wholeness, just as his physical person is portrayed as in some sense fragmented. Meaning for the Pardoner is situated in the greed he can never satisfy, in the objects that surround him that he knows to be false: Dinshaw analyses these in terms of fetishism. The Pardoner becomes a marginal figure, who confounds boundaries of gender and meaning and hence allows both pilgrims and reader to question the nature of Truth itself. Dinshaw's readings are plausible in so far as she remains attuned to the nature of medieval thought while employing contemporary theory. Such approaches reveal a Chaucer made new for the present: it can, however, be challenging to reconcile this new Chaucer with the writer of the fourteenth century.

Notes

1 Lacan argued that the unconscious was structured like a language, and that language was phallocentric, depending on the law of the father; feminist psychoanalytic thinkers such as Julia Kristeva and Luce Irigaray have developed the idea of the woman as displaced within this realm.

2 See also Dinshaw's study, *Getting Medieval: Sexualities and Communities, Pre- and Postmodern* (Duke University Press, Durham, NC, 1999).

Carolyn Dinshaw, from '"Glose/Bele chose": The Wife of Bath and Her Glossators' and 'Eunuch Hermeneutics' in *Chaucer's Sexual Poetics*. University of Wisconsin Press, Madison, 1989.

'Glose/bele chose': The Wife of Bath and Her Glossators

The Man of Law has just concluded his tale of Constance, reuniting father and daughter in one big ideological embrace, and it has pleased that manliest of men, Harry Bailly. The Host's delight in this tale, expressed in the Epilogue of the *Man of Law's Tale*, comes as no surprise: as we've seen, the Man of Law's *vita* of Constance – like Chaucer's 'Seintes Legende of Cupide' that the Man of Law mentions in his Introduction – has represented its heroine as a will-less blank and has thus controlled the threat that an independent female 'corage' would pose to patriarchy. Such control of the 'sleightes and subtilitees' of women (as he will put it later, in response to the *Merchant's Tale* [4: 2421]) is immensely appealing to the henpecked Harry; impressed by the Man of Law's performance, he stands up in his stirrups and calls out: 'Goode men, herkeneth everych on!' He then asks another one of 'ye lerned men in lore,' the Parson, to tell a tale. But the prospect of a suffocating sermon, especially after the Man of Law's tale, is too much for the Wife of Bath. Out of this company of 'goode men' the voice of the woman bursts: 'Nay, by my fader soule, that schal he nat! ... He schal no gospel glosen [gloss] here ne teche.' Instead, 'My joly body schal a tale telle,' a tale having nothing to do with 'philosophie, / Ne phislyas [cases], ne termes queinte of lawe.'[1] The Wife opposes her tale to the 'lerned men's' lore: it is her 'joly body' against their oppressive teaching and glossing.

The Wife – a clothier, dealer in *textus* – continues in her Prologue to oppose herself to glosses. 'Men may devyne and *glosen*, up and doun' (3: 26; my emphasis) about how many men one may have in marriage, but the Wife knows that God bade us to increase and multiply: 'That gentil *text* kan *I* wel understonde.' In this endlink to the *Man of Law's Tale* and beginning of the *Wife of Bath's Prologue*, woman is associated with the body and the text – as in the Pauline exegetical assimilation of literality and carnality to femininity ... – and is opposed to the gloss, written by men, learned, anti-pleasure, and anti-body.

Indeed, outfitted in her ostentatious garb – thick kerchiefs, fine stockings, new shoes, huge hat – and emphasizing that those 'gaye scarlet gytes' are well used, the Wife of Bath herself is an embodiment of the letter of the text as Jerome has imaged it in his paradigm of proper reading: like the alien woman of Deuteronomy 21, she is a woman whose clothed appearance is centrally significant. But unlike that new bride, she retains her costume (which she intends, I argue, to be alluring, however overwhelming and repellent others might find it), revels in her seductive person and adornment: *her* hair isn't shaved, *her* nails aren't pared.[2] Unlike that silent bride – and unlike her virtually mute relations, the passive feminine bodies manipulated by the narrator of the *Legend of Good Women* and Constance in the *Man of Law's Tale* – the Wife speaks: whereas that alien captive is passed between men at war, her desire conforming to the desire of the men in possession of her, the Wife makes her autonomous desire the very motive and theme of her performance.[3] And if Jerome's paradigm – a forerunner of Lévi-Strauss's patriarchal paradigm, just as we have seen the *Man of Law's Tale* to be – runs on the assumption that all women are functionally interchangeable (an assumption on which Pandarus and Troilus operate as well), the Wife of Bath would seem to regard *men* as virtually interchangeable: 'Yblessed be God that I have wedded fyve! / Welcome the sixte, whan that evere he shal,' she declares (44–5), and elaborates:

> I ne loved nevere by no discrecioun,*   *moderation
> But evere folwede myn appetit,
> Al were he short, or long, or blak, or whit;
> I took no kep, so that he liked me,
> How poore he was, ne eek of what degree.
> (622–6)

The Wife of Bath, in fact, articulates, makes visible, exactly what that patriarchal hermeneutic necessarily excludes, necessarily keeps invisible. She represents what the ideology of that model – an ideology incarnated, as we've seen, by the Man of Law – can't say, can't acknowledge, or acknowledges only by devalorizing and stigmatizing as Other: she represents independent feminine will and desire, the literal body of the text that itself has signifying value and leads to the spirit without its necessarily being devalued or destroyed in the process.[4] The woman traded must be silent; the Wife talks. The woman's desire must be merely mimetic; the Wife chronicles her own busy 'purveiance / Of mariage' (570–1). The gloss undertakes to speak (for) the text; the Wife maintains that the literal text – her body – can speak for itself. If the Man of Law must energetically suppress the feminine, the Wife vociferously speaks as that Other created and excluded by patriarchal ideology, and in this way she reveals the very workings of this ideology. Most penetratingly, as her *Tale* suggests in its narrative focus on a rapist, if the patriarchal economy of the trade of women proceeds without woman's necessary acquiescence, it is always potentially performing a rape. (The rape is, in fact, Chaucer's own innovation to the traditional stories that inform this tale, a deliberate alteration that argues for its significance in the whole of the Wife's performance.)[5]

We might say, then, that the Wife is everything the Man of Law can't say, everything Criseyde, everything Philomela might have said, given the chance. She makes audible precisely what patriarchal discourse would keep silent, reveals the exclusion and devalorization that patriarchal discourse performs. Speaking as the excluded Other, she explicitly and affirmatively assumes the place that patriarchal discourse accords the feminine. Far from being trapped within the 'prison house' of anti-feminist discourse, the Wife of Bath, I argue, 'convert[s] a form of subordination into an affirmation,' to adapt Luce Irigaray's words here; she *mimics* the operations of patriarchal discourse. As Irigaray has characterized it, such mimesis functions to reveal those operations, to begin to make a place for the feminine:

> There is, in an initial phase, perhaps only one 'path,' the one historically assigned to the feminine: that of *mimicry*. One must assume the feminine role deliberately. Which means already to convert a form of subordination into an affirmation, and thus to begin to thwart it.... To play with mimesis is thus, for a woman, to try to recover the place of her exploitation by discourse, without allowing herself to be simply reduced to it. It means to resubmit herself – inasmuch as she is on the side of the 'perceptible,' of 'matter' – to 'ideas,' in particular to ideas about herself, that are elaborated in/by a masculine logic, but so as to make 'visible,' by an effect of playful repetition, what was supposed to remain invisible: the cover-up of a possible operation of the feminine in language.[6]

Irigaray's own project of mimesis is immense – it intends the thwarting of all patriarchal discourse – and I cannot engage here the complex context in which she develops the idea. Such a concept of mimesis is in itself, however, very powerful: it seems to me strikingly useful to the analysis of the Wife of Bath's performance, a performance that is at once enormously affirmative and adversative. But the Wife is also crucially unlike the woman Irigaray describes here; she 'plays with mimesis,' mimics patriarchal discourse ('Myn entente nys but for to pleye,' she maintains [192]), not in order to 'thwart' it altogether, to subvert it entirely, but to *reform* it, to keep it in place while making it accommodate feminine desire. What the Wife imagines in her *Prologue* and *Tale* is a way in which such patriarchal hermeneutics as imagined by Jerome, Macrobius, and Richard of Bury can be deployed to the satisfaction of everyone under patriarchy, according a place of active signification to both masculine and feminine: clerk and wife, gloss and text, spirit and letter, 'matter' and 'ideas' (Irigaray mentions the Aristotelian terms I've discussed in my Introduction). What would be necessary to the satisfying formulation of sexualized hermeneutics is, in fact, inherent in that Hieronymian image itself, an understanding of the feminine not as only the distracting veil but the fecund body, not as merely something to be turned away from, gotten rid of, passed through, but as something that is, in itself, at once a locus of pleasure *and* a locus of valuable signification. The Wife thus articulates the happy possibility of reforming the patriarchal and fundamentally misogynistic hermeneutic based on the economy of possession, of traffic in texts-as-women, to make it accommodate the feminine – woman's independent will and the signifying value of the letter.

The Wife of Bath, in fact, would seem to be Chaucer's favorite character, and the reasons for this become clearer and clearer. As Robert A. Pratt has put it in his analysis of Chaucer's evolving idea of the Wife, from her early characterization as teller of the *Shipman's Tale* to her fully fleshed-out form as we know it now,

> She appears to have interested Chaucer more, to have stimulated his imagination and creative power more fully and over a longer period, than any other of his characters.[7]

She pops up again and again: apparently irrepressible, she bursts out of even the confines of her 'fictive universe,' the *Canterbury Tales* – where she provokes the excited interjections of Pardoner and Friar and is deferred to as a certain kind of authority by both Clerk and Merchant – to be cited in Chaucer's own voice in 'Lenvoy de Chaucer a Bukton.'[8] The Wife is a source of delight for this male author precisely because through her he is able to reform and still to participate in patriarchal discourse; he recuperates the feminine *within* the solid structure of that discourse.

This is a male fantasy, of course. And when we consider that such desire for the reform – not the overturning – of patriarchy is represented as a woman's desire, it is even more apparent that this is a masculine dream. Granted that it is indeed such a fantasy, we might remark that it is not a bad one, after all; it is not exploitative of the feminine for purely masculine gratification. Through the Wife, Chaucer imagines the possibility of a masculine reading that is not anti-feminist, that does acknowledge, in good faith, feminine desire; and further, he represents the struggle and violence to the feminine that accompany the articulation of this fantasy. Through the Wife, then, Chaucer recuperates the sexualized hermeneutic that he recognizes as both pervasive in the medieval literary imagination and manifestly flawed. He has shown its limits in *Troilus and Criseyde*, the *Legend of Good Women*, and the *Man of Law's Tale*, has shown the toll thereby taken on the feminine; he continues, in the *Wife of Bath's Prologue* and *Tale*, to register the toll taken on the feminine corpus in even the imagining of patriarchy's reform. The Wife expresses a dream of masculine reading that is not anti-feminist and a feminine relation to the condition of being read that is not anti-masculinist – but she does so after having been bruised and battered, permanently injured by that clerk Jankyn, in their concussive renovation of patriarchal discourse.

Eunuch Hermeneutics

Very early in her *Prologue*, just as she is warming to her theme, the Wife of Bath is interrupted by the Pardoner. He initially bristles at her images of 'tribulacion in mariage' (3: 173), but after she orders him to hear her out, he in fact urges him to teach him the tricks of her trade. It might seem that there couldn't be a more unlikely pair: the Wife, flamboyantly arrayed and ostentatiously heterosexual, 'carping' and in good fellowship with the company, and the Pardoner, that defective man, who makes the 'gentils' cry out even before he begins his tale. But characters are never only coincidentally brought together in Chaucer's works, and similarities between these two become apparent even on the surface level of apparel: once again, we find that clothing is an important index of broader significance in Chaucer's poetics. The Pardoner is as clothes-conscious as is the Wife of Bath in her intentionally alluring 'hosen...of fyn scarlet reed' (1: 456): wearing no hood, with only a cap, 'Hym thoughte he rood al of the newe jet [fashion]' (1: 682). If, as I have suggested, the Wife of Bath is an incarnation of the seductive letter of the text, we might ask what hermeneutic significance this Pardoner, styled *à la mode*, carries. What would we find if those clothes were stripped?

Not a female body, beautiful and fertile, needing protection from the gaze of the uninitiated, as in the traditional image of the allegorical text we've seen in writers from Macrobius to Richard of Bury. But underneath those clothes we might not find a whole male body either. The narrator of the *General Prologue* apparently does not know *what* the Pardoner is: 'I trowe he were a geldyng or a mare' (1: 691) is his notorious speculation.[9] Clear and straightforward gender categories of masculine and feminine – categories, as I have suggested throughout this book, fundamental to the social discourse of the Canterbury pilgrimage – apparently do not apply.

The patriarchal hermeneutic I have been describing – the passage of a woman between men and her stripping, reclothing, marriage, and domestication – is a *heterosexual* hermeneutic as well; it has as a goal the increase and multiplication of a univocal truth.[10] But the Pardoner, that sexually peculiar figure, problematizes all these terms and procedures. For one thing, he does not allow himself to be stripped and revealed, as it were: he won't allow himself to be known, won't reveal his intentions, his meaning, his truth. He expends much energy on keeping a veil on, on keeping himself screened from the gaze of others. He attempts to create a screen, first of all, via the self-conscious style of his clothes, a screening the narrator senses. The Pardoner is the only pilgrim in the General Prologue whose own sartorial intentions – his will to dress – are reported by the narrator: 'Hym thoughte he rood al of the newe jet.' Some critics have suggested, further, that the Pardoner's insistent profession of his own avarice works to screen a sin or condition judged to be more heinous. Robert Burlin, for example, supposes that the Pardoner obscures his sexual peculiarity from his audience's view with his 'cynical revelations' of greed, while Lee Patterson suggests that 'the very excess of the Pardoner's revelations' itself hides him from his hearers.[11] In that busy process of screening, the Pardoner might be seen to pick up roles offered by others around him, as critics have pointed out again and again: he seems in fact to play at homosexual display as the Summoner joins him in his love song, 'Com hider, love, to me' (1: 672); he plays at heterosexuality, imagining stepping into the place the Wife of Bath delineates for husbands; he advertises the kind of corruption the 'gentils' seem to expect from pardoners, boasting of loose tricks with 'wenches' in every town *after* those 'gentils' have insisted they won't listen to any 'ribaudye' (6: 324).

By keeping that veil on, the Pardoner generates the desire to know – 'I trowe...,' imagines the narrator – and then plays off it, indeed appearing to satisfy it excessively.[12] But no one really knows what the Pardoner is, neither the narrator nor later interpreters of his performance; his clothes do not necessarily promise a beautiful, fecund, normal, or even identifiable body beneath.[13] Put in hermeneutic terms, the Pardoner's clothed body suggests that the existence of the letter of the text does not at all ensure the existence of a spirit, a truth beneath it. In fact, the Pardoner opens out another – unnerving – possible hermeneutic significance of the image of the body swaddled in veils: there is perhaps *nothing* underneath those cloaks of representation. There might be nothing but veils and letters covering a fundamental absence, a radical lack of meaning or truth.[14]

The Pardoner is, after all, a 'geldyng or a mare'; he is identified, that is, in terms of an absence of something: either male sexual organs (he is a gelding, a castrated horse) or masculine gender identification (he is a mare, a female horse).[15] The context rendering this identification significant is, of course, patriarchal, heterosexual, fundamentally androcentric; the Pardoner can be distinctly identified in terms of such lack because masculinity – located in these attributes – defines identity and power in the culture. As we've seen in the *Man of Law's Tale*, the crucial distinction in patriarchal culture between man and woman is really between man and not-man; if the Pardoner is a eunuch, as the widely accepted critical gloss of 'geldyng' goes, he is a man who, significantly, is not a man (he is a not-man); but if he is an effeminate male, as a gloss of 'mare' has it, he is womanish but not a woman (a not-woman or, better, a not-not-man).[16] If he is neither man nor not-man, his identity is constituted by a negation of, or alienation from, the Same *and* the Other in androcentric culture.

Further, if the Pardoner is taken to be an effeminate homosexual, as another gloss of 'mare' goes, he is, in the normative terms of patriarchal, heterosexual culture, a man who puts himself in the 'feminine' position in homosexual intercourse.[17] He would thus bodily enact what I have suggested...the Clerk and Chaucer imaginatively do: as men who put themselves in the woman's place, they see things from the woman's point of view. For those male figures, such a 'feminine' position yields opportunity, a valorization of what is devalued in patriarchal culture, a speaking of and for what is silenced; but for the Pardoner, such a position yields not opportunity but torment. In his lacking being he reifies the disturbing suggestion that there is no guarantee of meaning, realizes the unsettling possibility that there is no fullness and plenitude of signification underneath the wraps of the letter. If, as we've seen in the *Clerk's Tale*, a 'feminine' poetic strategy provides a positive, fruitful alternative to oppressive, power-asymmetrical patriarchal discourse, the Pardoner's strategy, I suggest, would threaten an end to reading and telling tales altogether.

The Pardoner is defined by absence – he's a not-man or not even that – and it is in this fundamental sense that I shall take him to be a eunuch, a figurative one if not in fact a literal one as well. His sense of his own lack informs his social behavior, his interactions with others; his incompleteness, moreover, informs the very thematics and narrative strategies of his *Tale*. Most tellingly, it represents his view of the nature of language itself. As we shall see, it is not only modern theorists who analyze language as radically fragmentary: medieval thinkers too were preoccupied with a sense of the fundamental incompleteness of human language. The Pardoner enunciates a strategy of using language in a postlapsarian world, cut off from primary wholeness and unity: he acts according to what I call a hermeneutics of the partial, or, for short, eunuch hermeneutics.[18] The hermeneutic I have identified as heterosexual discards the surface of the text, the letter and its wanton seductions, for the uncovered truth, but the eunuch suggests that the passage between the letter and any sentence within is not so smooth, is not guaranteed. Indeed, the Pardoner disrupts altogether the hierarchy of values placed on the letter and the spirit. His hermeneutic is motivated in fact by a fundamental *refusal* to know; it is informed, I shall suggest, by a logic of fetishism.

As we shall see, the Pardoner surrounds himself with objects – relics; sealed documents; even words, regarded as objects – which he substitutes for his own lacking wholeness. But these objects, used thus as fetishes, are themselves fragments and can't properly fill the lack that hollows the Pardoner's being. Robert P. Miller has demonstrated that eunuchry was used in the Christian exegetical tradition as a powerful figure for the spiritual condition of radical wanting, radical desire, that is *cupiditas*. I propose to analyze eunuchry as a figure as well but shall concentrate on its psychological valence: the substitute objects the Pardoner adopts can't convert his bottomless *cupiditas* into *caritas*, a state of oneness, plenitude, fullness.[19] Nevertheless, even though the

Pardoner *knows* that his relics, documents, words are defective substitutes – they are fakes, and he tells us so – he holds on to the fetishistic belief that they can make him whole, part of the body of pilgrims, and of the larger body of Christians. If we express this in terms of the problematics of interpretation, we can say that the eunuch's hermeneutics proceeds by double affirmations, double truths, the incompatible positions of recognition and disavowal, knowledge and belief.

Chaucer's initial juxtaposition of the Pardoner with the Wife of Bath in the interruption in her *Prologue* introduces a perspective utterly outside patriarchal discourse and suggests a potential unsettling of its hermeneutic enterprise altogether. The *Pardoner's Prologue* and *Tale* further problematize the assumptions and procedures of that patriarchal project. As we've seen, the relative stability, significance, and value of the letter and the spirit, on the one hand, and the culture's construction of gender, its establishment of unambiguous gender distinctions and hierarchy, and its prohibition of transgressive sexual relations, on the other, are interdependent. The Wife of Bath, speaking as an incarnation of literality, carnality, and femininity from within a patriarchal paradigm, dreams of a renovation of oppressive patriarchal discourse: she dreams of an ideal relationship between wife and husband, text and gloss, letter and spirit. But that dream of recuperation, as she and the Clerk show, is idealistic indeed; the discourse, as they know it, depends on a turning away from the body and experience of woman, and thus the Wife's dream remains a dream. The Pardoner in his person deepens this critique of patriarchal, androcentric discourse; he in fact shows the inadequacy of the very categories – masculine/feminine, letter/spirit, literal/figurative – by which it proceeds. He confounds the idea of an easy passage between clothes and the body, the surface and the meaning, the letter and the spirit, and deconstructs the neat, reassuring discovery procedures of interpretation we have seen figured among the Canterbury pilgrims. He is a paradoxical figure of wily cynicism and plangent desire, as we'll see, and his performance threatens to derail (so to speak) this pilgrimage to Truth, 'compounding' as it does verity with falsehood, 'fals' with 'soth' (*House of Fame*, 1029).

But the Pardoner does not, in fact, end the pilgrimage. Instead, his performance urges his audience to think further, in ways entirely outside established social categories. I shall suggest at last that Chaucer, through the Pardoner – that figure utterly different from the other men and women, that figure entirely out of their bounds, that figure of fundamental, radical absence – leads his listeners to contemplate another being entirely out of their bounds: this one, however, of absolute Presence.

The Canterbury Tales: Critical Extracts

Notes

1 The ascription of speaker to these lines is uncertain. The entire Epilogue to the *Man of Law's Tale* presents textual difficulties: it does not appear in twenty-two of the fifty-seven manuscripts of the *Canterbury Tales*, including Ellesmere, a condition that suggests to Robinson that Chaucer abandoned it in his developing plan for the *Tales*. But, as Robinson goes on to state, there is no question of its genuineness as Chaucerian. *Who* interrupts the Host at line 1178 is uncertain from the textual evidence: manuscripts ascribe the speech to the Shipman, the Squire, or the Summoner (see Robinson's summary account, in *The Works of Geoffrey Chaucer*, ed. F. N. Robinson, 2nd edn [Boston: Houghton Mifflin, 1957], pp. 696–7). I follow Robert Pratt's argument in his classic article, 'The Development of the Wife of Bath' (in *Studies in Medieval Literature in Honor of Professor Albert Croll Baugh*, ed. MacEdward Leach [Philadelphia: University of Pennsylvania Press, 1961], pp. 45–79), that the lines were originally written for the Wife of Bath in order to link the *Man of Law's Tale* to her tale (which was later reassigned to the Shipman after Chaucer wrote a new prologue and tale for her). Pratt, of course, follows the Bradshaw shift in putting the *Shipman's Tale* after this endlink (Fragment B^2), but his argument about the lines' speaker doesn't necessitate this move. (For a defense of the Ellesmere order, see E. T. Donaldson, 'The Ordering of the *Canterbury Tales*,' in *Medieval Literature and Folklore Studies: Essays in Honor of Francis Lee Utley*, ed. Jerome Mandel and Bruce A. Rosenberg [New Brunswick, NJ: Rutgers University Press, 1970], pp. 193–204.) The verbal echoes of the Man of Law's Epilogue in the *Shipman's Tale* – and in the later Wife of Bath's *Prologue* and *Tale* – are unmistakable: 'joly body,' for example, occurs at line 423 of the *Shipman's Tale*. Although the second and third editions of Robinson print 'Seyde the Shipman' at line 1179, both Fisher and Donaldson, in their editions, emend the text to make the Wife of Bath the speaker of these lines.

Lee Patterson, '"For the Wyves love of Bathe": Feminine Rhetoric and Poetic Resolution in the *Roman de la Rose* and the *Canterbury Tales*,' *Speculum* 58 (1983): 656–95, has explicated the significance of the Wife of Bath's 'joly body' in terms that prefigure my own, and makes many related points. As he puts it, 'The Wife's text...solicits both body and mind, and it requires for its explication both an erotics and a hermeneutic' (p. 658). In observing that 'the language of poetry, as enacted by the poet and received by the reader, is habitually conceived in the Middle Ages in sexual, and specifically in feminine terms' (p. 659), he suggests a structure of sexualized poetics consonant with the one I describe here, and he undertakes, as I do, to determine what the creation of the Wife means to Chaucer's masculine poetic self-definition. The Wife proposes, in Patterson's terms, a 'reading at once both literal and moral' (p. 694); but while I stress the patriarchal gratifications of such a hermeneutic, Patterson proposes a more fully subversive cultural value for it.

2 The Wife's clothing seems to have been an essential part of her character from her very beginnings as teller of the *Shipman's Tale*, as several critics, including Pratt,

have observed (see n. 1 above, on the Wife of Bath as original teller of that tale). The narrator's voice, as the *Shipman's Tale* opens, insists that husbands must clothe their wives properly, 'in which array we daunce jolily' (7: 14). The wife in the tale needs money to pay for new clothes, so she borrows from the lascivious monk John (and pays for these 'frankes' with her 'flankes' [201–2]). But clothes are absorbed into the larger economic nexus of the *Shipman's Tale*: see Gerhard Joseph, 'Chaucer's Coinage: Foreign Exchange and the Puns of the *Shipman's Tale*,' *ChauR* 17 (1983): 341–57; and Thomas Hahn, 'Money, Sexuality, Wordplay, and Context in the *Shipman's Tale*,' in *Chaucer in the Eighties*, ed. Julian N. Wasserman and Robert J. Blanch (Syracuse, NY: Syracuse University Press, 1986), pp. 235–49. As Patterson, in 'For the Wyves love of Bathe,' has also suggested, although an association of the literary and the sexual is suggested in the triple pun on 'taillying' at the end of the tale, it remains for the Wife of Bath, in her present *Prologue* and *Tale*, to develop the full hermeneutic value of her 'joly body' in her fine and showy dress.

3 It is along this continuum defined by the Hieronymian paradigm – compliant, passive, silent brides on the one end, vocal Others on the other end – that almost all the female characters of the *Canterbury Tales* can in fact be read: Alisoun of the *Miller's Tale*, May of the *Merchant's Tale*, the Prioress (a bride of Christ), and Pertelote, to name a few.

4 For an argument supporting the claim that Chaucer intends to show respect for literal reading in his creation of the Wife as literal exegete, see Lawrence Besserman, '"Glosynge Is a Glorious Thyng": Chaucer's Biblical Exegesis,' in *Chaucer and Scriptural Tradition*, ed. David Lyle Jeffrey (Ottawa: University of Ottawa Press, 1984), pp. 65–73. Besserman suggests that Chaucer's increasing respect for the letter might have derived from the contemporary, anti-fraternal movement as well as from late fourteenth-century English biblical translators. (On the issue of the literal, see also Douglas Wurtele, 'Chaucer's *Canterbury Tales* and Nicholas of Lyre's *Postillae litteralis et moralis super totam Bibliam*,' in *Chaucer and Scriptural Tradition*, pp. 89–107.) I shall discuss Chaucer's possible response to these late fourteenth-century movements in my treatment of the *Pardoner's Tale* ... agreeing with Besserman's idea but also suggesting that a good deal of anxiety about the integrity of the letter motivates that growing 'respect.' The argument about Chaucer's respect for literal exegesis goes counter to D. W. Robertson's famous pronouncements about the Wife in *A Preface to Chaucer* (Princeton, NJ: Princeton University Press, 1962), pp. 317–31. For more recent articulations of a basically Robertsonian position, see Graham D. Caie, 'The Significance of the Early Chaucer Manuscript Glosses (with Special Reference to the *Wife of Bath's Prologue*),' *ChauR* 10 (1976): 350–60; and Sarah Disbrow, 'The Wife of Bath's Old Wives' Tale,' *SAC* 8 (1986): 59–71.

5 The exact source of the *Wife of Bath's Tale* is unknown, but of the known analogues (including *The Marriage of Sir Gawain*, *The Wedding of Sir Gawen and Dame Ragnell*, and the *Tale of Florent* in Gower's *Confessio amantis*), none includes a rape. For a summary of possible narrative sources of the rape, see the *Riverside Chaucer*, 872–3; and see, for contrast to my discussion, Bernard F. Huppé's 'Rape

and Woman's Sovereignty in the *Wife of Bath's Tale*' (*Modern Language Notes* 63 [1948]: 378–81), for an analysis of the rape as an 'indication of the structural perfection' (p. 378) of the tale.
6 Luce Irigaray, *This Sex Which Is Not One*, trans. Catherine Porter (Ithaca, NY: Cornell University Press, 1985), p. 76. For an expression of the view that the Wife of Bath is 'confined within the prison house of masculine language,' see Patterson, p. 682; see also Hope Phyllis Weissman, 'Antifeminism and Chaucer's Characterization of Women,' in *Geoffrey Chaucer*, ed. George D. Economou (New York: McGraw-Hill, 1975), esp. pp. 104–10; and Susan Crane, 'Alison's Incapacity and Poetic Instability in the *Wife of Bath's Tale*,' *PMLA* 102 (1987): 20–8.
7 Pratt, 'The Development of the Wife of Bath,' p. 45.
8 Robert B. Burlin, in his *Chaucerian Fiction* ([Princeton, NJ: Princeton University Press, 1977], pp. 217–27), provides an optimistic analysis of the Wife's ability to 'transcen[d] the limits of [her] own fictive universe': 'When the Wife of Bath attacks Jankyn's book, which is both her enemy and the source of her being, it is as if she were usurping the role of creator, destroying the "original" so that she might recast herself in her own image' (pp. 225, 227). But that 'as if' is crucial: Chaucer is, of course, still and ever her creator, and we must ask what purpose it serves him to create a woman who *seems* to usurp the role of creator.
9 I take 'trowe' here in its most common Middle English usage as denoting a speculation, a guess. See the *Oxford English Dictionary*, s.v. 'trow' 3.b: 'To believe or suppose (a thing or person) to be (so and so)'; and *A Chaucer Glossary*, ed. Norman Davis et al. (Oxford: Clarendon Press, 1979), s.v. 'trowe(n)' 1: 'Believe; think, judge.' C. David Benson comments:

> This word most commonly indicates speculation, but even if we take it in its less usual meaning of certainty, is this the assertion of the same narrator who agrees with the Monk's idea of cloistered duty and finds the murderous Shipman a good fellow? Certainly the phrase 'I trowe' qualifies what is to follow to some degree. ('Chaucer's Pardoner: His Sexuality and Modern Critics,' *Mediaevalia* 8 [1985 for 1982]: 339)

We can't read 'trowe' here too easily and ironically; Benson stresses the uncertainty of any knowledge of the Pardoner's sexual makeup. Moreover, he suggests that recent critical emphasis on the Pardoner's sexuality is a modern distortion: 'The real perversion of this pilgrim is not sexual but moral' (p. 346). While I agree with Benson that the Pardoner's portrait confounds any sure knowledge of his sexuality, I would argue that the issue of sexuality was in fact central to medieval audiences of this text: as James A. Brundage has recently stated, sexual practices, from the late twelfth century on, were 'taken as indicators of doctrinal orthodoxy,' so that sexual deviance implied spiritual deviance (*Law, Sex, and Christian Society in Medieval Europe* [Chicago: University of Chicago Press, 1987], pp. 256–324, esp. 313–14]). Indeed, the moral cannot be opposed to the sexual, but is deeply implicated in it.

The Canterbury Tales: Critical Extracts

10 For a discussion of the 'obligatory heterosexuality' in the exchange model of society (and the implied ban on homosexual relations, even though the society is 'homosocial' – i.e. constituted by bonds between men), see Gayle Rubin, 'The Traffic in Women: Notes on the "Political Economy" of Sex,' in *Toward an Anthropology of Women*, ed. R. R. Reiter (New York: Monthly Review Press, 1975), pp. 179–80; Eve Kosofsky Sedgwick, *Between Men: English Literature and Male Homosocial Desire* (New York: Columbia University Press, 1985); and Craig Owens, 'Outlaws: Gay Men in Feminism,' in *Men in Feminism*, ed. Alice Jardine and Paul Smith (New York: Methuen, 1987), pp. 219–32.

11 Robert B. Burlin, *Chaucerian Fiction* (Princeton, NJ: Princeton University Press, 1977), p. 170; Lee W. Patterson, 'Chaucerian Confession: Penitential Literature and the Pardoner,' *Medievalia et Humanistica*, n.s. 7 (1976): 153–73, esp. p. 163. H. Marshall Leicester, Jr., in *The Disenchanted Self: Representing the Subject in the 'Canterbury Tales'* (Berkeley: University of California Press, 1990), also stresses the Pardoner's hiding his intentions from others. Leicester's reading of the Pardoner as an embodiment of lack has much in common with mine; and his contrast of 'the feminine' in the Wife of Bath and in the Pardoner runs parallel to my contrast, below, of the Clerk (and Chaucer) and the Pardoner as they occupy the 'feminine' position.

12 For a discussion of the hermeneutic provocations of retaining such a veil, see D. A. Miller, 'The Administrator's Black Veil: A Response to J. Hillis Miller,' *ADE Bulletin* 88 (1987): 49–53.

13 For an account of the Pardoner's literary reception from medieval to modern times, see Betsy Bowden, *Chaucer Aloud: The Varieties of Textual Interpretation* (Philadelphia: University of Pennsylvania Press, 1987), pp. 77–173. 'About the Pardoner,' she writes, 'critics have almost always agreed to disagree' (p. 79).

14 R. Howard Bloch, in 'Silence and Holes: The *Roman de Silence* and the Art of the Trouvère' (in *Images of Power: Medieval History/Discourse/Literature*, ed. Stephen G. Nichols and Kevin Brownlee, YFS 70 [1986]: 81–99), reads Macrobius in precisely this way. Looking at Macrobius's commentary on the *Somnium Scipionis*, Bloch sees that Macrobius discusses the wont of Nature to wrap her truths in allegorical texts:

> sicut vulgaribus hominum sensibus intellectum sui vario rerum tegmine operimentoque subtraxit, ita a prudentibus arcana sua voluit per fabulosa tractari.

> [Just as she has withheld an understanding of herself from the uncouth senses of men by enveloping herself in variegated garments, [she] has also desired to have her secrets handled by more prudent individuals through fabulous narratives.]

Further on in this prefatory section, Macrobius describes the tradition of representing divinities, such as Nature or the Eleusinian goddesses:

adeo semper ita se et sciri et coli numina maluerunt qualiter in vulgus antiquitas fabulata est, quae et imagines et simulacra formarum talium prorsus alienis, et aetates tam incrementi quam diminutionis ignaris, et amictus ornatusque varios corpus non habentibus adsignavit.

[In truth, divinities have always preferred to be known and worshipped in the fashion assigned to them by ancient popular tradition, which made images of beings that had no physical form, represented them as of different ages, though they were subject neither to growth nor decay, and gave them clothes and ornaments, though they had no bodies.] (Macrobius, *Commentarii in Somnium Scipionis*, ed. J. Willis [Leipzig: Teubner, 1963], pp. 7–8; trans. William Harris Stahl [New York: Columbia University Press, 1952], pp. 86–7)

Macrobius's comment here may be taken to refer to the idea that the gods are transcendent entities – that deities have no real bodies and thus are transcendent signifieds. But Bloch uses the context of the preface to suggest that the nature of all representation is implicated:

The relation of truth, Nature, to its representation or image is thus that of the body to the clothes which are a potent paradigm of representation in Macrobius's terms – bodiless, empty, less capable of expressing a reality exterior to it than of covering up an absence that is also, finally, scandalous. ('Silence and Holes,' p. 95)

There are varieties of response to such an idea about representation: if, say, Ovid can gaily face such a possibility – in the *Remedia* he blithely remarks, 'Auferimur cultu; gemmis auroque teguntur / Omnia; pars minima est ipsa puella sui' ('We're dazzled by feminine adornment, by the surface; all is concealed by gold and jewels; a woman is the least part of herself') – others might find it terrifying, the possibility of a radical absence unbearable. I shall suggest that the Pardoner poignantly demonstrates the latter response. (For the Ovid, see the *Remedia amoris* 343–4, in *'The Art of Love' and Other Poems*, ed. and trans. J. H. Mozley, Loeb Classical Library [London: William Heinemann, 1929], p. 200; I combine Mozley's English translation with Peter Green's in *Ovid: The Erotic Poems* [Harmondsworth: Penguin, 1982], p. 249.)

15 The narrator's perception of lack is what Donald R. Howard stresses in his reading of the line, 'I trowe he were a geldyng or a mare'; see his *The Idea of the 'Canterbury Tales'* (Berkeley and Los Angeles: University of California Press, 1976), p. 343. Howard seeks to restore the sense of the Pardoner's inexplicably strange presence among the pilgrims but accepts, nonetheless, Curry's determination that the Pardoner is a eunuch (see n. 16 below and the excellent critical analysis of critical analyses of the Pardoner in Monica McAlpine's 'The Pardoner's Homosexuality and How It Matters,' *PMLA* 95 [1980]: 8–22).

16 The gloss of 'geldyng' as 'eunuch' is attested by both the *Middle English Dictionary* and the *Oxford English Dictionary*. The wide acceptance of eunuchry as the description of the Pardoner's condition derives ultimately from 'The Secret of Chaucer's Pardoner,' W. C. Curry's ground-breaking article (*JEGP* 18 [1919]: 593–606; later appearing in his *Chaucer and the Mediaeval Sciences*, revd edn [New York: Barnes and Noble, 1960], pp. 54–90). Curry was the first to bring the inference of eunuchry under critical scrutiny, attempting to provide evidence from classical and medieval scientific discourse. Curry's particular interpretation of this evidence – his conclusion that the Pardoner is a congenital eunuch, a *eunuchus ex nativitate*, rather than a castrated one – has come under attack: see Muriel Bowden, *A Commentary on the General Prologue to the 'Canterbury Tales'* (New York: Macmillan, 1957), pp. 274–6; Beryl Rowland, 'Chaucer's Idea of the Pardoner,' *ChauR* 14 (1979): 140–54; McAlpine, 'The Pardoner's Homosexuality and How It Matters'; and Benson, 'Chaucer's Pardoner: His Sexuality and Modern Critics.' Curry bases his diagnosis on his own interpretation of the Pardoner's character and not on the medieval physiognomists (according to whom all eunuchs look alike). And his medieval evidence is not, as Benson points out, as compelling or conclusive as is often assumed by modern critics. Still, the reading of the equine figure 'geldyng' as 'eunuch,' either congenital or castrated, is supported by physical details in the General Prologue; as McAlpine concedes, Chaucer does evoke the medieval stereotype of the eunuch in details of the Pardoner's portrait. Robert P. Miller has provided the scriptural background that supports the diagnosis *eunuchus* (see his classic article, 'Chaucer's Pardoner, the Scriptural Eunuch, and the Pardoner's Tale,' *Speculum* 30 [1955]: 180–99); Chaucer's detailing of the Pardoner's physical condition, Lee Patterson argues, renders it meaningful both in the realm of science and of religious symbol ('Chaucerian Confession: Penitential Literature and the Pardoner'). As I hope to demonstrate, eunuchry as a figure has a powerful psychological value in the *Prologue* and *Tale*.

'Mare' is defined in the *MED* (s.v. 'mere,' n.(1) 2.e) as figuratively denoting 'a bad woman, a slut'; attestations include *Handlyng Synne* and the *Castle of Perseverance*. Sexually wayward femininity can thus be evoked by this term. The gloss of 'mare' as 'effeminate male' is not attested by the *MED* or *OED* but is a likely reading of this equine figure in context of a description of a male; such a gloss was suggested by Curry ('The Secret of Chaucer's Pardoner,' p. 58) and has been reiterated by McAlpine:

> 'Mare' must be a term commonly used in Chaucer's day to designate a male person who, though not necessarily sterile or impotent, exhibits physical traits suggestive of femaleness, visible characteristics ... that were thought to have broad effects on the psyche and on character. ('The Pardoner's Homosexuality,' p. 11)

See also Benson, who seems to accept the reading of 'mare' as 'effeminate in some way' ('Chaucer's Pardoner,' p. 339).

Other analyses of the Pardoner's sexuality – that he is a 'testicular pseudo-hermaphrodite of the feminine type' (Beryl Rowland, 'Animal Imagery and the Pardoner's Abnormality,' *Neophilologus* 48 [1964]: 56–60), or a combination pervert, e.g. 'a manic depressive with traces of anal eroticism, and a pervert with a tendency toward alcoholism' (Eric W. Stockton, 'The Deadliest Sin in the *Pardoner's Tale*,' *Tennessee Studies in Literature* 6 [1961]: 47) – seem far more specific and certain than is warranted by the portrait and performance of the character.

17 McAlpine argues at length for the possibility of reading 'mare' as 'a possibly homosexual male,' suggesting that 'certain types of feminized behavior and appearance in males were sometimes interpreted as evidence of homosexuality' ('The Pardoner's Sexuality,' p. 12). Citing a variety of medieval examples, she bases her discussion on the apparent conflation of sexual categories – effeminacy, homosexuality, eunuchry, hermaphroditism, impotence – in common medieval understanding.... McAlpine mentions the anachronism of the term 'homosexual' in this context (p. 11), but she retains it nonetheless to refer not just to sexual acts but to sexual and moral identity. For a thorough and clear discussion of appropriate terminology for older literatures, see John Boswell, *Christianity, Social Tolerance, and Homosexuality: Gay People in Western Europe from the Beginning of the Christian Era to the Fourteenth Century* (Chicago: University of Chicago Press, 1980), pp. 43–6: Boswell distinguishes between 'homosexuality' (referring to the 'general phenomenon of same-sex eroticism') and 'gay' (referring to 'persons who are conscious of erotic inclination toward their own gender as a distinguishing characteristic'). I shall use the more general term; my point about the Pardoner's character is not as specific as that he is 'gay.'

18 I wish to acknowledge a general indebtedness in the development of my idea of eunuch hermeneutics to R. Howard Bloch, *The Scandal of the Fabliaux* (Chicago: University of Chicago Press, 1986).

19 See Robert P. Miller, 'Chaucer's Pardoner, the Scriptural Eunuch, and the Pardoner's Tale.' Augustine's analyses of spiritual conditions are powerful psychological analyses as well, as Donald R. Howard comments in his discussion of the Pardoner in his *Idea of the 'Canterbury Tales,'* pp. 355–6. Janet Adelman, in '"That We May Leere Som Wit"' (in *Twentieth-Century Interpretations of the Pardoner*, ed. Dewey R. Faulkner [Englewood Cliffs, NJ: Prentice-Hall, 1973], pp. 96–106), discusses *aesthetic* implications of *cupiditas*, seeing in the *Tale*'s use of parody and analogy a pattern of false substitution.

Epilogue

If the range of criticism in this book has been dazzling, perhaps this is only fitting to a writer of such versatility, such skill in poetic variation. Chaucer can seem remarkably chameleon-like: the sombre grandeur of the *Knight's Tale* and *Troilus and Criseyde* is a long way from the ribald comic brilliance of the *Miller's* or *Merchant's Tales*, or the frenetic dream landscape of the *House of Fame*. Yet there are overlaps too. In Troilus's laments, perhaps, we can hear echoes of the Man in Black's sorrowful lyrics in the *Book of the Duchess*, while the *Knight's Tale*, *Troilus and Criseyde* and the *Franklin's Tale* share a profound engagement with the existential, rooted in Boethius's *Consolation of Philosophy*. In the portrait of Dido in the *House of Fame* are the seeds of the *Legend of Good Women*, and of Criseyde's tragic voice, and in the opposition of Venus and Nature in the *Parliament of Fowls*, a hint of the multi-faceted treatment of love in the *Canterbury Tales*. In Chaucer's narrator-personae the comic attributes of deference, fear of experience and bookishness recur, while in the wife of Bath, the voice of experience, we hear the obverse. The comedy of the windy eagle in the *House of Fame* resonates in Pandarus and in the humour of the *Canterbury Tales*. Most of all, perhaps, it is the ability to ventriloquize, to perform voices of all kinds from elegiac to bawdy, from Wife of Bath to Parson, which distinguishes Chaucer's works.

It would be bizarre in this context of variation if there were not a myriad critical voices, each rewriting Chaucer just as each age has done. Yet, again, there are patterns and enduring concerns: Chaucer's rhetoric and poetic art, his irony, his humour, his creation of fictional voices, his authorities. To an extent the history of Chaucer criticism reflects the history of English literary criticism more generally, in its progress through linguistic and textual emphasis, humanism, new criticism, structuralism, new historicism, psychoanalytic theory, deconstruction and gender theory. Chaucer criticism stands too as a mirror of the development of medieval studies, to which the study of Chaucer

Epilogue

has been central. Exegetical, socio-political, intellectual historical and feminist approaches have all tended to begin with Chaucer and to move outwards into other areas of medieval literature. The stimulus of Chaucer's writing has shaped new scholarship and much provocative criticism that in turn has animated and reanimated medieval studies. To read Chaucer and those who write on him opens out the medieval thought world in ways that radiate both across the medieval period into other writings and discourses, and down to the present.

The critical 'boom' of twentieth-century Chaucer criticism may have been unique, a reflection of the institutionalization of the study of English literature and the questioning and various reforms of this over the last hundred years. Chaucer as 'father of English literature' was central to this process. Yet new Chaucers continue to emerge: queer Chaucer and postcolonial Chaucer are in the vanguard, but no doubt soon to be overtaken by the latest theoretical approach. Perhaps the way forward lies in the vast potential of electronic resources, demonstrated by the various excellent websites listed at the end of the bibliography. It is an odd irony that this futuristic mode of criticism is most compatible with the traditional focus of the medievalist on manuscripts and language, as the several enormous electronic editing projects currently under way testify: scholars such as Furnivall and Skeat would have been delighted. Now, more than ever, there is room for both the traditional and the avant-garde scholar. Imaginative electronic resources offer, too, new creative ways into the medieval thought world. The enduring power of that world is of course evident in the popularization of Chaucer and especially of the *Canterbury Tales* through the art, film and music of the twentieth century. It may be that the internet has something of the quality of popular art in increasing our familiarity with Chaucer. Yet wherever one begins and despite the appeal of these alternative approaches to Chaucer, it is, finally, words that comprise his art, and offer the most flexible, creative and resonant links to this great English writer.

Bibliography

This is by no means a comprehensive bibliography, but as well as listing works cited, it aims to offer a range of reading in different areas of Chaucer criticism, including studies and articles on Chaucer's main writings, and audio and electronic material. Categories necessarily overlap and are intended as a rough guide only; particularly useful items are marked with an asterisk. Readers coming for the first time to Chaucer may wish to begin with these and the introductory works listed below.

Editions of Chaucer

*Benson, Larry D., ed. *The Riverside Chaucer*, 3rd edn. Oxford: Oxford University Press, 1988[1987].
Brewer, D. S., ed. *Chaucer: 'The Parlement of Foulys'*. Manchester: Manchester University Press, 1972[1960].
Donaldson, E. T., ed. *Chaucer's Poetry: An Anthology for the Modern Reader*, 2nd edn. New York: Holt, Rinehart and Winsten, 1975.
Fisher, John H., ed. *The Complete Poetry and Prose of Geoffrey Chaucer*, 2nd edn. New York: Ronald Press, 1989.
Havely, N. R., ed. *Chaucer: 'The House of Fame'*. Durham Medieval Texts 11. Durham: Durham Medieval Texts, 1994.
Kane, George and Janet Cowen, eds. *Chaucer: 'The Legend of Good Women'*. Medieval Texts and Studies 14. East Lansing, MI: Colleagues Press, 1995.
Kolve, V. A. and Glending Olson, eds. *'The Canterbury Tales': Nine Tales and the 'General Prologue'*. New York: W. W. Norton, 1989.
Manly, John M. and Edith Rickert, eds. *The Text of the 'Canterbury Tales'*, 8 vols. Chicago: University of Chicago Press, 1940.
Phillips, Helen, ed. *Chaucer: 'The Book of the Duchess'*, 3rd edn. Durham Medieval Texts 3. Durham: Durham Medieval Texts, 1997.
*Phillips, Helen and Nick Havely, eds. *Chaucer's Dream Poetry*. London: Longman, 1997.

Bibliography

Robinson, F. N., ed. *The Works of Geoffrey Chaucer*, 2nd edn. Boston: Houghton Mifflin-Riverside Press; Oxford: Oxford University Press, 1957.
Root, Robert Kilburn, ed. *The Book of 'Troilus and Criseyde'*. Princeton, NJ: Princeton University Press, 1926.
Ruggiers, Paul G., ed. *A Variorum Edition of the Works of Geoffrey Chaucer*. Norman, OK: University of Oklahoma Press, 1979– (ongoing).
Shoaf, R. A., ed. *Geoffrey Chaucer: 'Troilus and Criseyde'*. East Lansing, MI: Colleagues Press, 1989.
Skeat, W. W., ed. *The Complete Works of Geoffrey Chaucer*, 2nd edn. 6 vols. Oxford: Clarendon Press, 1897–1900.
Thynne, William, ed. *The Works, 1532: with supplementary material from the editions of 1542, 1561, 1598 and 1602*. Intro. Derek Brewer. London: Scolar Press, 1969.
Windeatt, B. A., ed. *'Troilus and Criseyde': A New Edition of 'The Book of Troilus'*, 2nd edn. London: Longman, 1990.

Bibliographical and Reference Works

*Allen, Mark and John H. Fisher. *The Essential Chaucer: An Annotated Bibliography of Major Modern Studies*. Reference Publication in Literature. London: Mansell, 1987.
The Chaucer Bibliographies. Toronto: University of Toronto Press, 1983– (ongoing series).
Crow, Martin M. and Clair C. Olson. *Chaucer Life-Records*. Oxford: Clarendon Press, 1966.
Davis, Norman, Douglas Gray, Patricia Ingham and Anne Wallace-Hadrill. *A Chaucer Glossary*. Oxford: Clarendon Press, 1979.
*Leyerle, John and Anne Quick. *Chaucer: A Bibliographical Introduction*. Toronto Medieval Bibliographies 10. Toronto: University of Toronto Press, 1986.
Rooney, Anne. *Geoffrey Chaucer: A Guide Through the Critical Maze*. Bristol: Bristol University Press, 1989.
*Rudd, G. A. ed. *A Complete Critical Guide to Chaucer*. New York: Garland, 2001.
Tatlock, John S. P. and Arthur G. Kennedy. *A Concordance to the Complete Works of Geoffrey Chaucer and to the 'Romaunt of the Rose'*. Gloucester, MA: P. Smith, 1963 [1927].
*Further bibliographies may be found in the two journals devoted to Chaucer, *Chaucer Review* and *Studies in the Age of Chaucer*. The latter offers annotated bibliography on all relevant publications.

Introductory Works

Aers, David. *Chaucer*. Brighton: Harvester, 1986.
Ashton, Gail. *Chaucer: 'The Canterbury Tales'*. Basingstoke: Macmillan; New York: St Martin's Press, 1998.
*Blamires, Alcuin. *'The Canterbury Tales'*. Basingstoke: Macmillan, 1987.

*Boitani, Piero and Jill Mann, eds. *The Cambridge Chaucer Companion*. Cambridge: Cambridge University Press, 1986.
*Brewer, Derek. *A New Introduction to Chaucer*, 2nd edn. London: Longman, 1998.
Brown, Peter. *Chaucer at Work: The Making of the 'Canterbury Tales'*. London: Longman, 1994.
*Cooper, Helen. *The Canterbury Tales*. Oxford: Oxford University Press, 1989.
Dillon, Janette. *Geoffrey Chaucer*. Basingstoke: Macmillan, 1993.
Hussey, S. S. *Chaucer: An Introduction*, 2nd edn. London: Methuen, 1981.
Kane, George. *Chaucer*. Oxford: Oxford University Press, 1984.
Knight, Stephen. *Geoffrey Chaucer*. Oxford: Blackwell Publishers, 1986.
Lawlor, John. *Chaucer*. London: Hutchinson, 1968.
Mehl, Dieter. *Geoffrey Chaucer: An Introduction to his Narrative Poetry*. Cambridge: Cambridge University Press, 1986 [1973].
*Minnis, A. J. *The Shorter Poems*. Oxford: Clarendon Press, 1995.
Norton-Smith, John. *Geoffrey Chaucer*. London: Routledge, 1974.
Pearsall, Derek. *'The Canterbury Tales'*. London: George Allen and Unwin, 1985.
Phillips, Helen. *An Introduction to the 'Canterbury Tales': Reading, Fiction, Context*. Basingstoke: Macmillan; New York: St Martin's Press, 2000.
Preston, Raymond. *Chaucer*. London: Sheed and Ward, 1952.
*Rowland, Beryl, ed. *Companion to Chaucer Studies*, revd edn. New York: Oxford University Press, 1979.
Traversi, Derek. *'The Canterbury Tales': A Reading*. London: Bodley Head, 1983.
Whittock, Trevor. *A Reading of the 'Canterbury Tales'*. Cambridge: Cambridge University Press, 1968.
*Windeatt, Barry. *Troilus and Criseyde*. Clarendon Press, 1992.

Anthologies of Chaucer Criticism

*Allen, Valerie and Ares Axiotis, eds. *Chaucer*. Basingstoke: Macmillan; New York: St Martin's Press, 1997.
*Anderson, J. J., ed. *Chaucer: 'The Canterbury Tales'. A Casebook*. Basingstoke: Macmillan, 1974.
*Andrew, Malcolm, ed. *Critical Essays on Chaucer's 'Canterbury Tales'*. Milton Keynes: Open University Press, 1991.
Barney, Stephen A., ed. *Chaucer's 'Troilus': Essays in Criticism*. London: Scolar Press, 1980.
*Benson, C. David, ed. *Critical Essays on Chaucer's 'Troilus and Criseyde' and His Major Early Poems*. Milton Keynes: Open University Press, 1991.
Brewer, Derek, ed. *Geoffrey Chaucer*. London: Bell, 1974.
Brewer, Derek, ed. *Geoffrey Chaucer: The Critical Heritage*. London: Routledge, 1978.
Burrow, J. A., ed. *Geoffrey Chaucer: A Critical Anthology*. Harmondsworth: Penguin Books, 1969.

Bibliography

Cawley, A. C., ed. *Chaucer's Mind and Art*. Essays Old and New 3. Edinburgh: Oliver and Boyd, 1969.

Economou, George D., ed. *Geoffrey Chaucer: A Collection of Original Articles*. New York: McGraw-Hill, 1975.

Ellis, Steve, ed. *Chaucer: 'The Canterbury Tales'*. London: Longman, 1998.

Faulkner, Dewey R., ed. *Twentieth Century Interpretations of the 'Pardoner's Tale': A Collection of Critical Essays*. Spectrum Book; 5–885. Englewood Cliffs, NJ: Prentice-Hall, 1973.

Hahn, Thomas, ed. *Chaucer's Readership in the Twentieth Century*. Basic Readings in Chaucer and His Time 4. New York: Garland, 2000.

Hermann, John P. and John J. Burke, Jr, eds. *Signs and Symbols in Chaucer's Poetry*. Tuscaloosa: University of Alabama Press, 1981.

Jost, Jean E., ed. *Chaucer's Humor: Critical Essays*. Garland Studies in Humor 5. Garland Reference Library of the Humanities 1504. New York: Garland, 1994.

Pinti, Daniel J., ed. *Writing After Chaucer: Essential Readings in Chaucer and the Fifteenth Century*. Basic Readings in Chaucer and His Time 1. Garland Reference Library of the Humanities 2040. New York: Garland, 1998.

Quinn, William A., ed. *Chaucer's Dream Visions and Shorter Poems*. Basic Readings in Chaucer and His Time 2. Garland Reference Library of the Humanities 2105. New York: Garland, 1999.

Rose, Donald M., ed. *New Perspectives in Chaucer Criticism*. Norman, OK: Pilgrim Books, 1981.

*Salu, Mary, ed. *Essays on 'Troilus and Criseyde'*. Chaucer Studies 3. Cambridge: D. S. Brewer; Totowa, NJ: Rowman and Littlefield, 1979.

Schoeck, Richard and Jerome Taylor, eds. *Chaucer Criticism*, 2 vols. Notre Dame, IN: University of Notre Dame Press, 1960–1.

Spurgeon, Caroline, ed. *Five Hundred Years of Chaucer Criticism and Allusion, 1357–1900*. 3 vols. New York: Russell and Russell, 1960 [1914–22].

Vasta, Edward and Zacharias P. Thundy, eds. *Chaucerian Problems and Perspectives: Essays Presented to Paul E. Beichner C. S. B.* Notre Dame, IN: University of Notre Dame Press, 1979.

Wagenknecht, Edward, ed. *Chaucer: Modern Essays in Criticism*. Oxford: Oxford University Press, 1959.

Wasserman, Julian N. and Robert J. Blanch, eds. *Chaucer in the Eighties*. Syracuse, NY: Syracuse University Press, 1986.

Early Chaucer Studies and Criticism (to 1950)

Brusendorff, Aage. *The Chaucer Tradition*. Oxford: Oxford University Press; Copenhagen: V. Pio, 1925.

Chesterton, G. K. *Chaucer*, 2nd edn. London: Faber and Faber, 1948 [1932].

Child, F. J., A. J. Ellis, et al. *On Early English Pronunciation*. Part I. Early English Text Society, Extra Series 2. London: Kegan Paul, Trench and Trübner, 1869.

Bibliography

Coghill, Nevill. *The Poet Chaucer*. Oxford: Oxford University Press, 1949.

Coulton, G. G. *Chaucer and His English*, 8th edn. London: Methuen; New York: Barnes and Noble, 1950 [1908].

Crosby, Ruth. 'Chaucer and the Custom of Oral Delivery.' *Speculum* 13 (1938) 413–32.

Curry, Walter Clyde. *Chaucer and the Medieval Sciences*, revd edn. New York: Barnes and Noble, 1960 [1926].

Dodd, William George. *Courtly Love in Chaucer and Gower*. Oxford: Oxford University Press; Boston: Ginn, 1913.

French, Robert Dudley. *A Chaucer Handbook*, 2nd edn. New York: F. S. Crofts; London: G. Bell, 1947.

Gerould, Gordon Hall. *Chaucerian Essays*. Princeton, NJ: Princeton University Press, 1952.

Goddard, H. C. 'Chaucer's *Legend of Good Women*.' *Journal of English and Germanic Philology* 7 (1907–8) 87–129; 8 (1908–9), 47–111.

Hamilton, George L. *The Indebtedness of Chaucer to Guido delle Colonney's 'Historia Trojana'*. New York: Columbia University Press, 1903.

Hinckley, Henry Barrett. 'The Debate on Marriage in the *Canterbury Tales*.' *PMLA* 32 (1917) 292–305.

Housman, A. E. *The Name and Nature of Poetry*. The Leslie Stephen Lecture delivered at Cambridge, 9 May 1933. Cambridge: Cambridge University Press, 1940.

Jefferson, Bernard L. *Chaucer and the 'Consolation of Philosophy' of Boethius*. New York: Gordian Press, 1968 [1917].

Kittredge, George Lyman. *Chaucer and His Poetry*. Fifty-fifth anniversary edn. Cambridge, MA: Harvard University Press, 1970 [1915].

Lawrence, William Witherle. *Chaucer and the 'Canterbury Tales'*. New York: Columbia University Press, 1950.

Legouis, Emile. *Geoffrey Chaucer*, trans. L. Lailavoix. London: J. M. Dent; New York: E. P. Dutton, 1913.

Lewis, C. S. *The Allegory of Love: A Study in Medieval Tradition*. Oxford: Oxford University Press, 1936.

Lounsbury, Thomas R. *Studies in Chaucer: His Life and Writings*, 3 vols. London: James R. Osgood, McIlvaine, 1892 [1891].

Lowes, John Livingston. 'Is Chaucer's *Legend of Good Women* A Travesty?' *Journal of English and Germanic Philology* 8 (1908–9) 513–69.

Lowes, John Livingston. *Geoffrey Chaucer and the Development of His Genius: Lectures Delivered in 1932 in the William J. Cooper Foundation in Swarthmore College*. Boston: Houghton Mifflin; Oxford: Clarendon Press, 1934.

Manly, John Matthews. *Some New Light on Chaucer: Lectures Delivered at the Lowell Institute*. London: G. Bell, 1926.

Mersand, Joseph. *Chaucer's Romance Vocabulary*. New York: Comet Press, 1937.

Neilson, William Allan. *The Origins and Sources of the 'Court of Love'*. Harvard University Studies and Notes in Philology and Literature 6. Boston: Ginn, 1899.

Rickert, Edith. *Chaucer's World*, ed. Clair C. Olson and Martin M. Crow. Oxford: Oxford University Press, 1948.

Bibliography

Root, Robert Kilburn. *The Poetry of Chaucer: A Guide to Its Study and Appreciation*, revd edn. Gloucester, MA: Peter Smith, 1957 [1922].
Sandras, E. G. *Etude sur G. Chaucer: considéré comme imitateur des trouvères*. Paris: A. Durand, 1859.
Shannon, Edgar Finley. *Chaucer and the Roman Poets*. Harvard Studies in Comparative Literature 7. Cambridge, MA: Harvard University Press; Oxford: Oxford University Press, 1929.
Skeat, Walter W. *The Chaucer Canon*. Oxford: Clarendon Press, 1900.
Tatlock, J. S. P. *The Development and Chronology of Chaucer's Works*. Chaucer Society, Second Series 37. London: Kegan Paul, Trench and Trübner, 1907.
Tatlock, J. S. P. 'Chaucer's *Merchant's Tale*'. *Modern Philology* 33 (1935–6) 367–81.
Tatlock, J. S. P. *The Mind and Art of Chaucer*. Syracuse, NY: Syracuse University Press, 1950.
Ten Brink, Bernhard. *The Language and Metre of Chaucer*, 2nd edn, revd Friedrich Kluge, trans. M. Bentinck Smith. London: Macmillan, 1901.
Whiting, Bartlett Jere. *Chaucer's Use of Proverbs*. Harvard Studies in Comparative Literature 11. Cambridge, MA: Harvard University Press, 1934.

General Studies and Collections of Essays

Benson, Larry D. ed. *The Learned and the Lewed: Studies in Chaucer and Medieval Literature*. Harvard English Studies 5. Cambridge, MA: Harvard University Press, 1974.
Bloomfield, Morton W. *Essays and Explorations: Studies in Ideas, Language and Literature*. Cambridge, MA: Harvard University Press, 1970.
Boitani, Piero and Anna Torti, eds. *Interpretation: Medieval and Modern*. The J. A. W. Bennett Memorial Lectures, 8th Series, Perugia 1992. Cambridge: D. S. Brewer, 1993.
Brewer, D. S. *Chaucer and Chaucerians: Critical Studies in Middle English Literature*. London: Thomas Nelson and Sons, 1966.
Brewer, Derek. *Tradition and Innovation in Chaucer*. London: Macmillan, 1982.
Carruthers, Mary J. and Elizabeth D. Kirk, eds. *Acts of Interpretation: The Text in Its Contexts 700–1600. Essays on Medieval and Renaissance Literature in Honor of E. Talbot Donaldson*. Norman, OK: Pilgrim Books, 1982.
Dean, James M. and Christian K. Zacher. *The Idea of Medieval Literature: New Essays on Chaucer and Medieval Culture in Honor of Donald R. Howard*. Newark: University of Delaware Press; London: Associated University Presses, 1992.
*Donaldson, E. Talbot. 'Designing a Camel; Or, Generalizing the Middle Ages.' *Tennessee Studies in Literature* 22 (1977) 1–16.
Empson, William. *The Structure of Complex Words*. London: Chatto and Windus, 1951.
Everett, Dorothy. *Essays in Middle English Literature*, ed. Patricia Kean. Oxford: Clarendon Press, 1959.
Ganim, John M. *Style and Consciousness in Middle English Narrative*. Princeton, NJ: Princeton University Press, 1983.

Josipovici, Gabriel. *The World and the Book: A Study of Modern Fiction*, 2nd edn. London: Macmillan, 1979.
Lewis, C. S. *The Discarded Image: An Introduction to Medieval and Renaissance Literature*. Cambridge: Cambridge University Press, 1964.
Morse, Ruth and Barry Windeatt. *Chaucer Traditions: Studies in Honour of Derek Brewer*. Cambridge: Cambridge University Press, 1990.
Spearing, A. C. *Criticism and Medieval Poetry*, 2nd edn. London: Edward Arnold, 1972.
Spearing, A. C. *Medieval to Renaissance in English Poetry*. Cambridge: Cambridge University Press, 1985.
Spearing, A. C. *The Medieval Poet as Voyeur: Looking and Listening in Medieval Love-Narratives*. Cambridge: Cambridge University Press, 1993.
Wimsatt, W. K., Jr. *The Verbal Icon: Studies in the Meaning of Poetry*. Lexington: University of Kentucky Press, 1954.
Zacher, Christian K. *Curiosity and Pilgrimage: The Literature of Discovery in Fourteenth-century England*. Baltimore, MD: Johns Hopkins University Press, 1976.

Language and Textual Studies

Barney, Stephen A. *Studies in 'Troilus': Chaucer's Text, Meter, and Diction*. Medieval Texts and Studies 14. East Lansing, MI: Colleagues Press, 1993.
Baum, Paull F. *Chaucer's Verse*. Durham, NC: Duke University Press, 1961.
Blake, N. F. *The Textual Tradition of the 'Canterbury Tales'*. London: Edward Arnold, 1985.
Burnley, David. *The Language of Chaucer*. Basingstoke: Macmillan, 1989 [1983].
*Cannon, Christopher. *The Making of Chaucer's English: A Study of Words*. Cambridge Studies in Medieval Literature 39. Cambridge: Cambridge University Press, 1998.
Elliott, Ralph W. V. *Chaucer's English*. London: André Deutsch, 1974.
Hanawalt, Barbara, ed. *Chaucer's England: Literature in Historical Context*. Medieval Studies at Minnesota 4. Minneapolis: University of Minnesota Press, 1992.
Kerkhof, J. *Studies in the Language of Geoffrey Chaucer*, 2nd edn. Leids Germanistische en Anglistische Reeks van de Rijksuniversiteit te Leiden 5. Leiden: E. J. Brill, Leiden University Press, 1982.
Kökeritz, Helge. *A Guide to Chaucer's Pronunciation*. Medieval Reprints for Teaching 3. Toronto: University of Toronto Press; Medieval Academy of America, 1978 [1961].
*Owen, Charles A., Jr. *The Manuscripts of the 'Canterbury Tales'*. Chaucer Studies 17. Cambridge: D. S. Brewer, 1991.
Robinson, Ian. *Chaucer's Prosody: A Study of the Middle English Verse Tradition*. Cambridge: Cambridge University Press, 1971.
Robinson, Ian. *Chaucer and the English Tradition*. Cambridge: Cambridge University Press, 1972.
Roscow, G. H. *Syntax and Style in Chaucer's Poetry*. Chaucer Studies 6. Cambridge: D. S. Brewer; Totowa, NJ: Rowman and Littlefield, 1981.

Bibliography

Sandved, Arthur O. *Introduction to Chaucerian English*. Chaucer Studies 11. Cambridge: D. S. Brewer, 1985.

Social Contexts

Brewer, Derek. *Chaucer in His Time*, 2nd edn, 1978. Cambridge: D. S. Brewer, 1992.
*Brewer, Derek. *Chaucer and His World*. London: Eyre Methuen, 1978.
Gardner, John. *The Life and Times of Chaucer*. London: Cape, 1977 [1976].
Hahn, Thomas, ed. 'Reconceiving Chaucer: Literary Theory and Historical Interpretation' (special issue). *Exemplaria* 2 (1990).
*Howard, Donald R. *Chaucer and the Medieval World*. London: Weidenfeld and Nicolson, 1987.
Hussey, Maurice. *Chaucer's World: A Pictorial Companion*. Cambridge: Cambridge University Press, 1967.
Knight, Stephen. 'Chaucer and the Sociology of Literature.' *Studies in the Age of Chaucer* 2 (1980) 15–51.
Loomis, R. S. *A Mirror of Chaucer's World*. Princeton, NJ: Princeton University Press, 1965.
*Pearsall, Derek. *The Life of Geoffrey Chaucer: A Critical Biography*. Blackwell Critical Biographies 1. Oxford: Blackwell Publishers, 1992.
Rigby, S. H. *Chaucer in Context: Society, Allegory and Gender*. Manchester: Manchester University Press, 1996.
Robertson, D. W., Jr. *Chaucer's London*. New York: John Wiley and Sons, 1968.
Robertson, D. W., Jr. *Essays in Medieval Culture*. Princeton, NJ: Princeton University Press, 1980.
*Strohm, Paul. *Social Chaucer*. Cambridge, MA: Harvard University Press, 1989.
Wallace, David. *Chaucerian Polity: Absolutist Lineages and Associational Forms in England and Italy*. Stanford, CA: Stanford University Press, 1997.

Sources and Cultural Contexts

Astell, Ann W. *Chaucer and the Universe of Learning*. Ithaca, NY: Cornell University Press, 1996.
Bisson, Lillian M. *Chaucer and the Late Medieval World*. Basingstoke: Macmillan, 1998.
Boitani, Piero, ed. *Chaucer and the Italian Trecento*. Cambridge: Cambridge University Press, 1983.
*Boitani, Piero. *Chaucer and Boccaccio*. Medium Ævum Monographs NS 8. Oxford: Society for the Study of Medieval Languages and Literature, 1977.
Boitani, Piero. *Chaucer and the Imaginary World of Fame*. Chaucer Studies 10. Cambridge: D. S. Brewer; Totowa, NJ: Barnes and Noble, 1984.
Boitani, Piero, ed. *The European Tragedy of Troilus*. Oxford: Clarendon Press, 1989.

*Bryan, W. F. and Germaine Dempster. *Sources and Analogues of Chaucer's 'Canterbury Tales'*. London: Routledge and Kegan Paul, 1958.

Carruthers, Mary J. *The Book of Memory: A Study of Memory in Mediaeval Culture*, 2nd edn. Cambridge: Cambridge University Press, 1992.

Cartlidge, Neil. *Medieval Marriage: Literary Approaches, 1100–1300*. Cambridge: D. S. Brewer, 1997.

Copeland, Rita. *Rhetoric, Hermeneutics and Translation in the Middle Ages: Academic Traditions and Vernacular Texts*. Cambridge Studies in Medieval Literature 11. Cambridge: Cambridge University Press, 1991.

Eisner, Sigmund. *A Tale of Wonder: A Source Study of 'The Wife of Bath's Tale'*. Essays in Literature and Criticism 41. New York: Burt Franklin, 1969 [1957].

Fyler, John M. *Chaucer and Ovid*. New Haven, CT: Yale University Press, 1979.

*Gordon, R. K., trans. *The Story of Troilus*. London: J. M. Dent, 1934.

Green, Richard Firth. *Poets and Princepleasers: Literature and the English Court in the Late Middle Ages*. Toronto: University of Toronto Press, 1980.

Green, Richard Firth. *A Crisis of Truth: Literature and Law in Ricardian England*. Philadelphia: University of Pennsylvania Press, 1999.

Hanly, Michael G. *Boccaccio, Beauvau, Chaucer: 'Troilus' and Criseyde'. Four Perspectives on Influence*. Norman, OK: Pilgrim Books, 1990.

*Havely, N. R. *Chaucer's Boccaccio: Sources for 'Troilus' and the 'Knight's' and 'Franklin's Tales'; Translations from the 'Filostrato', 'Teseida' and 'Filocolo'*. Chaucer Studies 5. Cambridge: D. S. Brewer, 1980.

Hoffman, Richard L. *Ovid and the 'Canterbury Tales'*. Philadelphia: University of Pennsylvania Press, 1966.

Jeffrey, David Lyle. *Chaucer and Scriptural Tradition*. Ottawa: University of Ottawa Press, 1984.

Kruger, Steven. *Dreaming in the Middle Ages*. Cambridge Studies in Medieval Literature 14. Cambridge: Cambridge University Press, 1992.

Lerer, Seth. *Chaucer and His Readers: Imagining the Author in Late-Medieval England*. Princeton, NJ: Princeton University Press, 1993.

*Miller, Robert P. ed., *Chaucer: Sources and Backgrounds*. New York: Oxford University Press, 1977.

Minnis, A. J. *Chaucer's 'Boece' and the Medieval Tradition of Boethius*. Chaucer Studies 18. Cambridge: D. S. Brewer, 1993.

*Minnis, A. J. *Chaucer and Pagan Antiquity*. Chaucer Studies 8. Cambridge: D. S. Brewer; Totowa, NJ: Rowman and Littlefield, 1982.

Miskimin, Alice S. *The Renaissance Chaucer*. New Haven, CT: Yale University Press, 1975.

*Muscatine, Charles. *Chaucer and the French Tradition: A Study in Style and Meaning*. Berkeley: University of California Press, 1957.

Neuse, Richard. *Chaucer's Dante: Allegory and Epic Theater in 'The Canterbury Tales'*. Berkeley: University of California Press, 1991.

Nolan, Barbara. *Chaucer and the Tradition of the Roman Antique*. Cambridge: Cambridge University Press, 1992.

North, J. D. *Chaucer's Universe*, revd edn. Oxford: Clarendon Press, 1988.

Bibliography

Payne, F. Anne. *Chaucer and Menippean Satire.* Madison: University of Wisconsin Press, 1981.
Schless, Howard. *Chaucer and Dante: A Revaluation.* Norman, OK: Pilgrim Books, 1984.
Stevens, John E. *Music and Poetry in the Early Tudor Court,* revd edn. Cambridge: Cambridge University Press, 1979.
Taylor, Karla. *Chaucer Reads the 'Divine Comedy'.* Stanford, CA: Stanford University Press, 1989.
Thompson, N. S. *Chaucer, Boccaccio, and the Debate of Love: A Comparative Study of 'The Decameron' and 'The Canterbury Tales'.* Oxford: Oxford University Press, 1996.
Wallace, David. *Chaucer and the Early Writings of Boccaccio.* Chaucer Studies 12. Woodbridge: D. S. Brewer, 1985.
Wilkins, Nigel. *Music in the Age of Chaucer,* 2nd edn. Chaucer Studies 1. Cambridge: D. S. Brewer, 1995.
Wimsatt, James I. *Chaucer and the French Love Poets: The Literary Background of the 'Book of the Duchess'.* University of North Carolina Studies in Comparative Literature 43. Chapel Hill: University of North Carolina Press, 1968.
Wimsatt, James I. *Chaucer and His French Contemporaries: Natural Music in the Fourteenth Century.* Toronto: University of Toronto Press, 1991.
*Windeatt, B. A., ed. and trans. *Chaucer's Dream Poetry: Sources and Analogues.* Chaucer Studies 7. Cambridge: D. S. Brewer; Totowa, NJ: Rowman and Littlefield, 1982.
Wise, Boyd Ashby. *The Influence of Statius Upon Chaucer.* New York: Phaeton Press, 1967 [1911].
Wood, Chauncey. *Chaucer and the Country of the Stars: Poetic Uses of Astrological Imagery.* Princeton, NJ: Princeton University Press, 1970.

General Critical Studies

Birney, Earle. *Essays on Chaucerian Irony,* ed. Beryl Rowland. Toronto: University of Toronto Press, 1985.
Bronson, Bertrand H. *In Search of Chaucer.* Toronto: University of Toronto Press, 1960.
Burlin, Robert B. *Chaucerian Fiction.* Princeton, NJ: Princeton University Press, 1977.
Calabrese, Michael A. *Chaucer's Ovidian Arts of Love* Gainesville: University Press of Florida, 1994.
Chance, Jane. *The Mythographic Chaucer: The Fabulation of Sexual Politics.* Minneapolis: University of Minnesota Press, 1995.
Christianson, Paul. 'Chaucer's Literacy'. *Chaucer Review* 11 (1976–7) 112–27.
Corsa, Helen Storm. *Chaucer: Poet of Mirth and Morality.* Notre Dame, IN: University of Notre Dame Press, 1964.
Crampton, Georgia Ronan. *The Condition of Creatures: Suffering and Action in Chaucer and Spenser.* New Haven, CT: Yale University Press, 1974.
*Davenport, W. A. *Chaucer: Complaint and Narrative.* Chaucer Studies 14. Cambridge: D. S. Brewer, 1988.
*David, Alfred. *The Strumpet Muse: Art and Morals in Chaucer's Poetry.* Bloomington: Indiana University Press, 1976.
Dempster, Germaine. *Dramatic Irony in Chaucer.* New York: Humanities Press, 1959.

*Donaldson, E. Talbot. *Speaking of Chaucer*. London: Athlone Press, 1970.
*Ferster, Judith. *Chaucer on Interpretation*. Cambridge: Cambridge University Press, 1985.
Fichte, Joerg O. *Chaucer's 'Art Poetical': A Study in Chaucerian Poetics*. Studies and Texts in English 21. Tübingen: Gunter Narr, 1980.
Fisher, John H. *The Importance of Chaucer*. Carbondale: Southern Illinois University Press, 1992.
Ganim, John M. *Chaucerian Theatricality*. Princeton, NJ: Princeton University Press, 1990.
Gardner, John. *The Poetry of Chaucer*. Carbondale: Southern Illinois University Press; London: Feffer and Simons, 1977.
Grudin, Michaela Paasche. *Chaucer and the Politics of Discourse*. Columbia: University of South Carolina Press, 1996.
Hill, John M. *Chaucerian Belief: The Poetics of Reverence and Delight*. New Haven, CT: Yale University Press, 1991.
Huppé, Bernard F. and D. W. Robertson, Jr. *Fruyt and Chaf: Studies in Chaucer's Allegories*. Princeton, NJ: Princeton University Press, 1963.
*Jordan, Robert M. *Chaucer and the Shape of Creation: The Aesthetic Possibilities of Inorganic Structure*. Cambridge, MA.: Harvard University Press, 1967.
*Jordan, Robert M. *Chaucer's Poetics and the Modern Reader*. Berkeley: University of California Press, 1987.
Kean, P.M. *Chaucer and the Making of English Poetry*, 2 vols. London: Routledge and Kegan Paul, 1972.
Kelly, Henry Ansgar. *Chaucerian Tragedy*. Chaucer Studies 24. Cambridge: D. S. Brewer, 1997.
*Kiser, Lisa J. *Truth and Textuality in Chaucer's Poetry*. Hanover, NH: University Press of New England, 1991.
Klassen, Norman. *Chaucer on Love, Knowledge and Sight*. Chaucer Studies 21. Cambridge: D. S. Brewer, 1995.
*Knapp, Peggy. *Chaucer and the Social Contest*. New York: Routledge, 1990.
Knight, Stephen. *Rymymg Craftily: Meaning in Chaucer's Poetry*. Sydney: Angus and Robertson, 1973.
Koff, Leonard Michael. *Chaucer and the Art of Storytelling*. Berkeley: University of California Press, 1988.
*Lawton, David. *Chaucer's Narrators*. Chaucer Studies 13. Cambridge: D. S. Brewer, 1985.
McGerr, Rosemarie P. *Chaucer's Open Books: Resistance to Closure in Medieval Discourse*. Gainesville: University of Florida Press, 1998.
Malone, Kemp. *Chapters on Chaucer*. Westport, CT: Greenwood Press, 1979 [1951].
Mitchell, Jerome and William Provost, eds. *Chaucer the Love Poet*. Athens: University of Georgia Press, 1973.
Mogan, Joseph J., Jr. *Chaucer and the Theme of Mutability*. De Proprietatibus Litterarum, Series Practica 3. The Hague: Mouton, 1969.
Myles, Robert. *Chaucerian Realism*. Chaucer Studies 20. Cambridge: D. S. Brewer, 1994.

Bibliography

Patch, Howard Rollin. *On Rereading Chaucer*. Cambridge, MA: Harvard University Press, 1953.
*Patterson, Lee. *Chaucer and the Subject of History*. London: Routledge, 1991.
Payne, Robert O. *The Key of Remembrance: A Study of Chaucer's Poetics*. Westport, CT: Greenwood Press, for the University of Cincinnati, 1973 [1963].
Reiss, Edmund. 'Chaucer and Medieval Irony.' *Studies in the Age of Chaucer* 1 (1979) 67–82.
Reiss, Edmund. 'Chaucer and His Audience.' *Chaucer Review* 14 (1979–80) 390–402.
Ridley, Florence H. 'Questions Without Answers – Yet or Ever? New Critical Modes and Chaucer.' *Chaucer Review* 16 (1981–2) 101–6.
Robertson, D. W. *A Preface to Chaucer: Studies in Medieval Perspectives*. Princeton, NJ: Princeton University Press, 1969 [1962].
Rowland, Beryl. *Blind Beasts: Chaucer's Animal World*. Kent, OH: Kent State University Press, 1971.
Sklute, Larry. *Virtue of Necessity: Inconclusiveness and Narrative Form in Chaucer's Poetry*. Columbus: Ohio State University Press, 1984.
Speirs, John. *Chaucer the Maker*, 2nd edn. London: Faber and Faber, 1960.
Taylor, Paul Beekman. *Chaucer's Chain of Love*. Madison, NJ: Fairleigh Dickinson University Press; London: Associated University Presses, 1996.
Williams, George. *A New View of Chaucer*. Durham, NC: Duke University Press, 1965.

Gender Studies

*Aers, David. 'Criseyde: Woman in Medieval Society.' *Chaucer Review* 13 (1978–9), 177–200.
Aers, David. *Community, Gender, and Individual Identity: English Writing 1360–1430*. London: Routledge, 1988.
Carruthers, Mary. 'The Wife of Bath and the Painting of Lions.' *PMLA* 94 (1979) 209–22.
Crane, Susan. *Gender and Romance in Chaucer's 'Canterbury Tales'*. Princeton, NJ: Princeton University Press, 1994.
Diamond, Arlyn and Lee R. Edwards. *The Authority of Experience: Essays in Feminist Criticism*. Amherst: University of Massachusets Press, 1977.
Dinshaw, Carolyn. 'Eunuch Hermeneutics.' *English Literary History* 55 (1988) 27–51.
Dinshaw, Carolyn. *Chaucer's Sexual Poetics*. Madison: University of Wisconsin Press, 1989.
Dinshaw, Carolyn. *Getting Medieval: Sexualities and Communities, Pre- and Postmodern*. Durham, NC: Duke University Press, 1999.
Green, Richard Firth. 'Chaucer's Victimized Women.' *Studies in the Age of Chaucer* 9 (1988) 146–54.
Hallissy, Margaret. *Clean Maids, True Wives, Steadfast Widows: Chaucer's Women and Medieval Codes of Conduct*. Contributions in Women's Studies 130. Westport, CT: Greenwood Press, 1993.

*Hansen, Elaine Tuttle. *Chaucer and the Fictions of Gender*. Berkeley: University of California Press, 1992.
Laskaya, Anna. *Chaucer's Approach to Gender in the 'Canterbury Tales'*. Chaucer Studies 23. Cambridge: D. S. Brewer, 1995.
*Mann, Jill. *Geoffrey Chaucer*. New York: Harvester Wheatsheaf, 1991.
*Martin, Priscilla. *Chaucer's Women: Nuns, Wives, and Amazons*. Iowa City: University of Iowa Press, 1990.
Rigby, S. H. *Chaucer in Context: Society, Allegory and Gender*. Manchester: Manchester University Press, 1996.
Schibanoff, Susan. 'Taking the Gold Out of Egypt: The Art of Reading as a Woman.' In Elizabeth A. Flynn and Patrocinio P. Schweickart, eds, *Gender and Reading: Essays on Readers, Texts, and Contexts*. Baltimore, MD: Johns Hopkins University Press, 1986.
Weisl, Angela Jane. *Conquering the Reign of Femeny: Gender and Genre in Chaucer's Romance*. Chaucer Studies 22. Cambridge: D. S. Brewer, 1995.

Dream Vision Poetry: Studies

Bennett, J. A. W. *'The Parlement of Foules:' An Interpretation*. Oxford: Clarendon Press, 1957.
Bennett, J. A. W. *Chaucer's 'Book of Fame'. An Exposition of the House of Fame*. Oxford: Clarendon Press, 1984 [1968].
*Clemen, Wolfgang. *Chaucer's Early Poetry*, trans. C. A. M. Sym. London: Methuen, 1963.
*Delany, Sheila. *Chaucer's 'House of Fame': The Poetics of Skeptical Fideism*. Chicago: University of Chicago Press, 1972.
Delany, Sheila. *The Naked Text: Chaucer's 'Legend of Good Women'*. Berkeley: University of California Press, 1994.
*Edwards, Robert R. *The Dream of Chaucer: Representation and Reflection in the Early Narratives*. Durham, NC: Duke University Press, 1989.
Frank, Robert Worth, Jr. *Chaucer and the 'Legend of Good Women'*. Cambridge, MA: Harvard University Press, 1972.
Kelly, Henry Ansgar. *Chaucer and the Cult of Saint Valentine*. Davis Medieval Texts and Studies 5. Davis: University of California Press; Leiden: E. J. Brill, 1986.
*Kiser, Lisa. *Telling Classical Tales: Chaucer and the 'Legend of Good Women'*. Ithaca, NY: Cornell University Press, 1983.
Koonce, B. G. *Chaucer and the Tradition of Fame: Symbolism in the 'House of Fame'*. Princeton, NJ: Princeton University Press, 1966.
*Percival, Florence. *Chaucer's Legendary Good Women*. Cambridge Studies in Medieval Literature 38. Cambridge: Cambridge University Press, 1998.
Rowe, Donald W. *Through Nature to Eternity: Chaucer's 'Legend of Good Women'*. Lincoln: University of Nebraska Press, 1988.
*Spearing, A. C. *Medieval Dream-Poetry*. Cambridge: Cambridge University Press, 1976.

Bibliography

Dream Vision Poetry: Articles

Aers, David. *The 'Parliament of Fowls*: Authority, the Knower and the Known.' *Chaucer Review* 16 (1981–2) 1–17.
Allen, Peter L. 'Reading Chaucer's Good Women.' *Chaucer Review* 21 (1986–7) 419–34.
Anderson, J. J. 'The Narrators in the *Book of the Duchess and the Parlement of Foules.*' *Chaucer Review* 26 (1991–2) 219–35.
Blamires, Alcuin. 'A Chaucer Manifesto.' *Chaucer Review* 24 (1989–90) 29–44.
Butterfield, Ardis. 'Lyric and Elegy in the *Book of the Duchess.*' *Medium Ævum* 60 (1991) 33–60.
Cherniss, Michael D. 'Chaucer's Last Dream Vision: The *Prologue* to the *Legend of Good Women.*' *Chaucer Review* 20 (1985–6) 183–99.
Cowen, Janet M. 'Chaucer's *Legend of Good Women*: Structure and Tone.' *Studies in Philology* 82 (1985) 416–36.
Dean, James. 'Artistic Conclusiveness in Chaucer's *Parliament of Fowls.*' *Chaucer Review* 21 (1986–7) 16–25.
Dean, James. 'Chaucer's *Book of the Duchess: A Non-Boethian Interpretation.*' *Modern Language Quarterly* 46 (1985) 235–49.
Donnelly, Colleen. 'Challenging the Conventions of Dream Vision in *The Book of the Duchess.*' *Philological Quarterly* 66 (1987) 421–35.
Ferster, Judith. 'Intention and Interpretation in the *Book of the Duchess.*' *Criticism* 22 (1980) 1–24.
Frank, Robert Worth, Jr. 'Structure and Meaning in the *Parlement of Foules.*' *PMLA* 71 (1956) 530–9.
Grennen, Joseph E. '*Hert-huntyng* in the *Book of the Duchess.*' *Modern Language Quarterly* 25 (1964), 131–9.
Hardman, Phillipa. 'The *Book of the Duchess* as a Memorial Monument.' *Chaucer Review* 28 (1993–4) 205–15.
Kelley, Michael R. 'Antithesis as the Principle of Design in the *Parlement of Foules.*' *Chaucer Review* 14 (1979–80) 61–73.
Kruger, Steven F. 'Passion and Order in Chaucer's *Legend of Good Women.*' *Chaucer Review* 23 (1988–9) 219–35.
Kruger, Steven F. 'Imagination and the Complex Movement of Chaucer's *House of Fame.*' *Chaucer Review* 28 (1993–4) 117–34.
Lumiansky, R. M. 'The Bereaved Narrator in Chaucer's *The Book of the Duchess.*' *Tulane Studies in English* 9 (1959) 5–17.
Lynch, Kathryn M. 'The *Book of the Duchess* as a Philosophical Vision: The Argument of Form.' *Genre* 21 (1988) 279–305.
McDonald, Charles O. 'An Interpretation of Chaucer's *Parlement of Foules.*' *Speculum* 30 (1955) 444–57.
Miller, Jacqueline T. 'The Writing on the Wall: Authority and Authorship in Chaucer's *House of Fame.*' *Chaucer Review* 17 (1982–3) 95–115.
Morse, Ruth. 'Understanding the Man in Black.' *Chaucer Review* 15 (1980–1) 204–8.

Peck, Russell A. 'Love, Politics, and Plot in the *Parlement of Foules.*' *Chaucer Review* 24 (1989–90) 290–305.
Phillips, Helen. 'Structure and Consolation in the *Book of the Duchess.*' *Chaucer Review* 16 (1981–2) 107–18.
Prior, Sandra Pierson. '*Routhe* and *Hert-Huntying* in the *Book of the Duchess.*' *Journal of English and Germanic Philology* 85 (1986) 3–19.
Rambuss, Richard. '"Processe of tyme": History, Consolation and Apocalypse in the *Book of the Duchess.*' *Exemplaria* 2 (1990) 659–83.
Rooney, Anne. '*The Book of the Duchess*: Hunting and the "Ubi Sunt" Tradition.' *Review of English Studies* n.s. 38 (1987) 299–314.
Ross, Diane M. 'The Play of Genres in the *Book of the Duchess.*' *Chaucer Review* 19 (1984–5) 1–13.
Shoaf, A. A. 'Stalking the Sorrowful H(e)art: Penitential Lore and the Hunt Scene in Chaucer's *The Book of the Duchess.*' *Journal of English and Germanic Philology* 78 (1979) 313–24.
Wilhelm, James J. 'The Narrator and his Narrative in Chaucer's *Parlement.*' *Chaucer Review* 1 (1966–7) 201–6.
Wimsatt, James I. 'The *Book of the Duchess*: Secular Elegy or Religious Vision?' In John P. Hermann and John H. Burke, Jr., eds, *Signs and Symbols in Chaucer's Poetry.* Tuscaloosa: University of Alabama Press, 1981.

Troilus and Criseyde: Studies

Benson, C. David. *The History of Troy in Middle English Literature.* Woodbridge: D. S. Brewer; Totowa, NY: Rowman and Littlefield, 1980.
*Benson, C. David. *Chaucer's 'Troilus and Criseyde'.* London: Unwin Hyman, 1990.
*Bishop, Ian. *Chaucer's 'Troilus and Criseyde': A Critical Study.* Bristol: University of Bristol Press, 1981.
Fleming, John V. *Classical Imitation and Interpretation in Chaucer's 'Troilus'.* Lincoln: University of Nebraska Press, 1990.
*Frantzen, Allen J. *'Troilus and Criseyde': The Poem and the Frame.* New York: Twayne; Toronto: Maxwell Macmillan, 1993.
Gordon, Ida L. *The Double Sorrow of Troilus: A Study of Ambiguities in 'Troilus and Criseyde'.* Oxford: Clarendon Press, 1970.
Kaminsky, Alice R. *Chaucer's 'Troilus and Criseyde' and the Critics.* Athens: Ohio University Press, 1980.
McAlpine, Monica. *The Genre of 'Troilus and Criseyde'.* Ithaca, NY: Cornell University Press, 1978.
Martin, June Hall. *Love's Fools: Aucassin, Troilus, Calisto and the Parody of the Courtly Lover.* London: Tamesis Books, 1972.
Rowe, Donald W. *O Love O Charite! Contraries Harmonized in Chaucer's 'Troilus'.* Carbondale: Southern Illinois University Press; London: Feffer and Simons, 1976.

Shoaf, R. A., ed. *Chaucer's Troilus and Criseyde: 'subgit to alle poesye.'* Essays in Criticism. Medieval and Renaissance Texts and Studies 104. Pegasus paperbooks 10. Binghamton, NY: Medieval and Renaissance Texts and Studies, 1992.

Spearing, A. C. *Chaucer: 'Troilus and Criseyde'*. Studies in English Literature 59. London: Edward Arnold, 1976.

Steadman, John M. *Disembodied Laughter: 'Troilus' and the Apotheosis Tradition. A Reexamination of Narrative and Thematic Contexts*. Berkeley: University of California Press, 1972.

Wetherbee, Winthrop. *Chaucer and the Poets: An Essay on 'Troilus and Criseyde'*. Ithaca, NY: Cornell University Press, 1984.

Wood, Chauncey. *The Elements of Chaucer's Troilus*. Durham, NC: Duke University Press, 1984.

Troilus and Criseyde: Articles

Barney, Stephen A. 'Troilus Bound.' *Speculum* 47 (1972) 445–58.

Bestul, Thomas H. 'Chaucer's *Troilus and Criseyde*: The Passionate Epic and Its Narrator.' *Chaucer Review* 14 (1979–80) 366–78.

Fehrenbacher, Richard W. '"Al that which chargeth nought to seye": The Theme of Incest in *Troilus and Criseyde*.' *Exemplaria* 9 (1997) 341–69.

Fries, Maureen. '(Almost) Without a Song: Criseyde and Lyric in Chaucer's *Troilus*.' *Chaucer Yearbook* 1 (1992) 47–63.

Fyler, John M. 'The Fabrications of Pandarus.' *Modern Language Quarterly* 41 (1980) 115–30.

Knapp, Peggy A. 'The Nature of Nature: Criseyde's "Slydyng Corage"' *Chaucer Review* 13 (1978–9) 133–40.

Leyerle. John. 'The Heart and the Chain'. In Larry D. Benson, ed., *The Learned and the Lewed: Studies in Chaucer and Medieval Literature*. Harvard English Studies 5. Cambridge, MA: Harvard University Press, 1974.

Macey, Samuel L. 'Dramatic Elements in Chaucer's *Troilus*.' *Texas Studies in Literature and Language* 12 (1970–1) 307–23.

Morgan, Gerald. 'The Ending of *Troilus and Criseyde*.' *Modern Language Review* 77 (1982) 257–71.

Sadlek, Gregory M. 'Bakhtin, the Novel and Chaucer's *Troilus and Criseyde*.' *Chaucer Yearbook* 3 (1996) 87–102.

Salter, Elizabeth. '*Troilus and Criseyde*: A Reconsideration.' In John Lawlor, ed., *Patterns of Love and Courtesy: Essays in Memory of C. S. Lewis*. London: Edward Arnold, 1966.

Slocum, Sally K. 'Criseyde Among the Greeks.' *Neuphilologische Mitteilungen* 87 (1986) 365–74.

Stanley, E. G. 'About Troilus.' *Essays and Studies* n.s. 29 (1976) 84–106.

Wentersdorf, Karl P. 'Some Observations on the Concept of Clandestine Marriage in *Troilus and Criseyde*.' *Chaucer Review* 15 (1980–1) 101–26.

Windeatt, Barry. '"Love that oughte ben secree" in Chaucer's *Troilus.*' *Chaucer Review* 14 (1979–80) 116–31.

The Canterbury Tales: Studies

Allen, Judson Boyce and Theresa Anne Moritz. *A Distinction of Stories: The Medieval Unity of Chaucer's Fair Chain of Narratives for Canterbury.* Columbus: Ohio State University Press, 1981.
Baldwin, Ralph. *The Unity of the 'Canterbury Tales'.* Anglistica 5. Copenhangen: Rosenkilde and Bagger, 1955.
*Benson, C. David. *Chaucer's Drama of Style: Poetic Variety and Contrast in the 'Canterbury Tales'.* Chapel Hill: University of North Carolina Press, 1986.
Benson, C. David and Elizabeth Robertson. *Chaucer's Religious Tales.* Chaucer Studies 15. Cambridge: D. S. Brewer, 1990.
Bishop, Ian. *The Narrative Art of the Canterbury Tales: A Critical Study of the Major Poems.* London and Melbourne: Dent, 1988 [1987].
Bowden, Muriel. *A Commentary on the 'General Prologue' to the 'Canterbury Tales'*, 2nd edn. New York: Macmillan; London: Collier Macmillan, 1967.
*Brooks, Harold F. *Chaucer's Pilgrims: The Artistic Order of the Portraits in the 'Prologue'.* London: Methuen, 1962.
*Brown, Peter and Andrew Butcher. *The Age of Saturn: Literature and History in the 'Canterbury Tales'.* Oxford: Blackwell Publishers, 1991.
Condren, Edward I. *Chaucer and the Energy of Creation: The Design and the Organization of the 'Canterbury Tales'.* Gainesville: University Press of Florida, 1999.
*Cooper, Helen. *The Structure of the Canterbury Tales.* London: Duckworth, 1983.
Craik, T. W. *The Comic Tales of Chaucer.* University Paperbacks 202. London: Methuen, 1964.
*Davenport, W. A. *Chaucer and His English Contemporaries: Prologue and Tale in the 'Canterbury Tales'.* Basingstoke: Macmillan, 1988.
*Ellis, Roger. *Patterns of Religious Narrative in the 'Canterbury Tales'.* London: Croom Helm, 1986.
Fein, Susanna Greer, David Raybin and Peter C. Braeger. *Rebels and Rivals: The Contestive Spirit in the 'Canterbury Tales'.* SMC 29. Kalamazoo: Medieval Institute Publications, Western Michigan University, 1991.
Gittes, Katharine S. *Framing the 'Canterbury Tales': Chaucer and the Medieval Frame Narrative Tradition.* Contributions to the Study of World Literature 41. New York: Greenwood Press, 1991.
Hines, John. *The Fabliau in English.* London: Longman, 1993.
Howard, Donald R. *The Idea of the 'Canterbury Tales'.* Berkeley: University of California Press, 1976.
Huppé, Bernard F. *A Reading of the 'Canterbury Tales'.* Albany: State University of New York, 1967 [1964].
Jones, Terry. *Chaucer's Knight: The Portrait of a Medieval Mercenary.* London: Methuen, 1994 [1982].

Bibliography

Kendrick, Laura. *Chaucerian Play: Comedy and Control in the 'Canterbury Tales'*. Berkeley: University of California Press, 1988.

*Kolve, V. A. *Chaucer and the Imagery of Narrative: The First Five 'Canterbury Tales'*. London: Edward Arnold, 1984.

Lawler, Traugott. *The One and the Many in the 'Canterbury Tales'*. Hamden, CT: Archon Books, 1980.

Leicester, H. Marshall, Jr. *The Disenchanted Self: Representing the Subject in the 'Canterbury Tales'*. Berkeley: University of California Press, 1990.

Lindahl, Carl. *Earnest Games: Folkloric Patterns in the 'Canterbury Tales'*. Bloomington: Indiana University Press, 1987.

*Lumiansky, R. M. *Of Sondry Folk: The Dramatic Principle in the 'Canterbury Tales'*. Austin: University of Texas Press, 1955.

Mandel, Jerome. *Building the Fragments of the 'Canterbury Tales'*. Rutherford, NJ: Fairleigh Dickinson University Press; London: Associated University Presses, 1992.

*Mann, Jill. *Chaucer and Medieval Estates Satire: The Literature of Social Classes and the 'General Prologue' to the 'Canterbury Tales'*. Cambridge: Cambridge University Press, 1973.

Olson, Paul A. *'The Canterbury Tales' and the Good Society*. Princeton, NJ: Princeton University Press, 1986.

Owen, Charles A., Jr. *Pilgrimage and Storytelling in the 'Canterbury Tales': The Dialectic of 'Ernest' and 'Game'*. Norman: University of Oklahoma Press, 1977.

Richardson, Janette. *Blameth Nat Me: A Study of Imagery in Chaucer's Fabliaux*. Studies in English Literature 58. The Hague: Mouton, 1970.

Rogers, William E. *Upon the Ways: The Structure of 'The Canterbury Tales'*. English Literary Studies 36. Victoria: University of Victoria, 1986.

*Ruggiers, Paul G. *The Art of the 'Canterbury Tales'*. Madison: University of Wisconsin Press, 1965.

Salter, Elizabeth. *Chaucer: The Knight's Tale and the Clerk's Tale*. London: Edward Arnold, 1962.

Wetherbee, Winthrop. *Chaucer: 'The Canterbury Tales'*. Cambridge: Cambridge University Press, 1989.

The Canterbury Tales: Articles

General

Benson, C. David. 'Their Telling Difference: Chaucer the Pilgrim and His Two Contrasting Tales.' *Chaucer Review* 18 (1983–4) 61–76.

Delasanta, Rodney. 'Penance and Poetry in the *Canterbury Tales*.' *PMLA* 93 (1978) 240–7.

Howard, Donald R. 'Chaucer's Idea of an Idea.' *Essays and Studies* n.s. 29 (1976) 39–55.

Jacobs, Kathryn. 'Rewriting the Marital Contract: Adultery in the *Canterbury Tales*.' *Chaucer Review* 29 (1994–5) 337–47.

Leyerle, John. 'Thematic Interlace in *The Canterbury Tales*.' *Essays and Studies* n.s. 29 (1976) 107–21.
Lindahl, Carl. 'The Festive Form of the *Canterbury Tales*.' *English Literary History* 52 (1985) 531–74.
McIlhaney, Anne E. 'Sentence and Judgement: The Role of the Fiend in Chaucer's *Canterbury Tales*.' *Chaucer Review* 31 (1996–7) 173–83.
Mandel, Jerome. 'Courtly Love in the *Canterbury Tales*.' *Chaucer Review* 19 (1984–5) 277–89.
Owen, Charles A., Jr. 'Chaucer's *Canterbury Tales*: Aesthetic Design in Stories of the First Day.' *English Studies* 35 (1954) 49–56.
Patterson, Lee W. 'The *Parson's Tale* and the Quitting of the *Canterbury Tales*.' *Traditio* 34 (1978) 331–80.
Portnoy, Phyllis. 'Beyond the Gothic Cathedral: Post-Modern Reflections in the *Canterbury Tales*.' *Chaucer Review* 28 (1993–4) 279–92.
Richardson, Cynthia C. 'The Function of the Host in *The Canterbury Tales*.' *Texas Studies in Literature and Language* 12 (1970–1) 325–44.
Windeatt, B. A. 'The Scribes as Chaucer's Early Critics.' *Studies in the Age of Chaucer* 1 (1979) 119–41.

General Prologue

Andrew, Malcolm. 'Context and Judgement in the *General Prologue*.' *Chaucer Review* 23 (1988–9) 316–37.
Cooney, Helen. 'The Limits of Human Knowledge and the Structure of Chaucer's *General Prologue*.' *Studia Neophilologica* 63 (1991) 147–59.
Morgan, Gerald. 'The Design of the *General Prologue* to the *Canterbury Tales*.' *English Studies* 59 (1978) 481–98.
Woolf, Rosemary. 'Chaucer as a Satirist in the *General Prologue* to the *Canterbury Tales*.' *Critical Quarterly* 1 (1959) 150–7.

Comic Tales

Beidler, Peter G. '"Art and Scatology in the *Miller's Tale*."' *Chaucer Review* 12 (1977–8) 90–102.
Brody, Saul Nathaniel. 'Truth and Fiction in the *Nun's Priest's Tale*.' *Chaucer Review* 14 (1979–80) 33–47.
Brown, Emerson, Jr. 'Chaucer, the Merchant, and their Tale: Getting Beyond Old Controversies.' *Chaucer Review* 13 (1978–9) 141–56, 247–62.
Brown, Peter. 'The Containment of Symkyn: The Function of Space in the *Reeve's Tale*.' *Chaucer Review* 14 (1979–80) 225–36.
Copland, M. '*The Reeve's Tale*: Harlotrie or Sermonyng?' *Medium Ævum* 31 (1962) 14–32.
Dane, Joseph A. 'The Mechanics of Comedy in Chaucer's *Miller's Tale*.' *Chaucer Review* 14 (1979–80) 215–24.

Bibliography

Rowland, Beryl L. 'Chaucer's Blasphemous Churl: A New Interpretation of the *Miller's Tale*.' In Beryl L. Rowland, ed. *Chaucer and Middle English Studies in Honour of Rossell Hope Robbins*. London: George Allen and Unwin, 1974.

Scanlon, Larry. 'The Authority of Fable: Allegory and Irony in the *Nun's Priest's Tale*.' *Exemplaria* 1 (1989) 43–68.

Schneider, Paul Stephen. '"Taillynge Ynough": The Function of Money in the *Shipman's Tale*.' *Chaucer Review* 11 (1976–7) 201–9.

Silverman, Albert H. 'Sex and Money in Chaucer's *Shipman's Tale*.' *Philological Quarterly* 32 (1953) 329–36.

Woods, William F. 'Private and Public Space in the *Miller's Tale*.' *Chaucer Review* 29 (1994–5) 166–78.

Wurtele, Douglas. 'Ironical Resonances in the *Merchant's Tale*.' *Chaucer Review* 13 (1978–9) 66–79.

Religious and Moral Tales

Baker, Denisen. 'Chaucer and Moral Philosophy: The Virtuous Women of the *Canterbury Tales*.' *Medium Ævum* 60 (1991) 241–56.

Børdu, Marianne. 'Chaucer's *Second Nun's Tale*: Record of a Dying World.' *Chaucer Yearbook* 5 (1998) 19–40.

Carruthers, Mary J. 'The Lady, the Swineherd, and Chaucer's Clerk.' *Chaucer Review* 17 (1982–3) 221–34.

Clasby, Eugene. 'Chaucer's Constance: Womanly Virtue and the Heroic Life.' *Chaucer Review* 13 (1978–9) 221–33.

Collette, Carolyn P. 'Sense and Sensibility in the *Prioress's Tale*.' *Chaucer Review* 15 (1980–1) 138–50.

Collette, Carolyn P. '"Peyntyng with Greet Cost": Virginia as Image in the *Physician's Tale*.' *Chaucer Yearbook* 2 (1995) 49–62.

Fradenburg, Louise O. 'Criticism, Anti-semitism and the *Prioress's Tale*.' *Exemplaria* 1 (1989) 69–115.

Grennen, Joseph E. 'The Canon's Yeoman and the Cosmic Furnace: Language and Meaning in the *Canon's Yeoman's Tale*.' *Criticism* 4 (1962) 225–40.

Grennen, Joseph E. 'Saint Cecilia's "Chemical Wedding": The Unity of the *Canterbury Tales*, Fragment VIII.' *Journal of English and Germanic Philology* 65 (1966) 466–81.

Guerin, Dorothy. 'Chaucer's Pathos: Three Variations.' *Chaucer Review* 20 (1985–6) 90–112.

Hahn, Thomas. 'The Performance of Gender in the Prioress.' *Chaucer Yearbook* 1 (1992) 111–34.

Harding, Wendy. 'The Dynamics of Law in the *Clerk's Tale*.' *Chaucer Yearbook* 4 (1997) 45–59.

Hirsh, John C. 'Modern Times: The Discourse of the *Physician's Tale*.' *Chaucer Review* 27 (1992–3) 387–95.

Hirsh, John C. 'Chaucer's Roman Tales.' *Chaucer Review* 31 (1996–7) 45–57.

Lee, Brian S. 'Justice in the *Physician's Tale* and the *Pardoner's Tale*: A Dialogic Contrast.' *Chaucer Yearbook* 4 (1997) 21–31.

Bibliography

McAlpine, Monica E. 'The Pardoner's Homosexuality and How It Matters.' *PMLA* 95 (1980) 8–22.
McCall, John P. 'The *Clerk's Tale* and the Theme of Obedience.' *Modern Language Quarterly* 27 (1966) 260–9.
Maleski, Mary A. 'The Culpability of Chaucer's Prioress.' *Chaucer Yearbook* 5 (1998) 41–60.
Rowland, Beryl. 'Chaucer's Idea of the Pardoner.' *Chaucer Review* 14 (1979–80) 140–54.

Romances

Collette, Carolyn. 'Seeing and Believing in the *Franklin's Tale*.' *Chaucer Review* 26 (1991–2) 395–410.
Dane, Joseph. 'Double Truth in Chaucer's *Franklin Tale*.' *Studia Neophilologica* 63 (1991) 161–7.
Finlayson, John. 'The *Knight's Tale*: The Dialogue of Romance, Epic, and Philosophy.' *Chaucer Review* 27 (1992–3) 126–49.
Fyler, John M. 'Love and Degree in the *Franklin's Tale*.' *Chaucer Review* 21 (1986–7) 321–37.
Ganim, John M. 'Chaucerian Ritual and Patriarchal Romance.' *Chaucer Yearbook* I (1992) 65–86.
Gaylord, Alan T. 'The Promises in *The Franklin's Tale*.' *English Literary History* 31 (1964) 331–65.
Golding, M. R. 'The Importance of Keeping 'Trouthe' in the *Franklin's Tale*.' *Medium Ævum* 39 (1970) 306–12.
Morgan, Gerald. 'A Defence of Dorigen's Complaint.' *Medium Ævum* 46 (1977) 77–97.
Pratt, Robert A. '"Joye after Wo" in the *Knight's Tale*.' *Journal of English and Germanic Philology* 57 (1958) 416–23.
Rowe, Elizabeth Ashman. 'Structure and Pattern in Chaucer's *Knight's Tale*.' *Florilegium: Carleton University Annual Papers on Classical Antiquity and the Middle Ages* 8 (1986) 169–86.
Schmidt, A. V. C. 'The Tragedy of Arcite: A Reconsideration of the *Knight's Tale*.' *Essays in Criticism* 19 (1969) 107–17.
Scott, Anne. '"Considerynge the Beste on Every Syde": Ethics, Empathy, and Epistemology in the *Franklin's Tale*.' *Chaucer Review* 29 (1994–5) 390–415.
Westlund, Joseph. 'The *Knight's Tale* as an Impetus for Pilgrimage.' *Philological Quarterly* 43 (1964) 526–37.

Wife of Bath's Prologue and Tale

Dinshaw, Carolyn. 'The Law of Man and Its "Abhomynacions".' *Exemplaria* 1 (1989) 117–48.
Gottfried, Barbara. 'Conflict and Relationship, Sovereignty and Survival: Parables of Power in the *Wife of Bath's Prologue*.' *Chaucer Review* 19 (1984–5) 202–24.

Bibliography

Knapp, Peggy A. 'Alisoun of Bathe and the Reappropriation of Tradition.' *Chaucer Review* 24 (1989–90) 45–52.
Knapp, Peggy A. 'Alisoun Weaves a Text.' *Philological Quarterly* 65 (1986) 387–401.
Leicester, H. Marshall. 'Of a Fire in the Dark: Public and Private Feminism in the Wife of Bath's Tale.' *Women's Studies* 11 (1984) 157–78.
Malvern, Marjorie M. '"Who peynrede the leon, tel me who": Rhetorical and Didactic Roles Played By an Aesopic Fable in the *Wife of Bath's Prologue*.' *Studies in Philology* 80 (1983) 238–52.
Quinn, Esther C. 'Chaucer's Arthurian Romance.' *Chaucer Review* 18 (1983–4) 211–20.
Quinn, William A. 'The Rapes of Chaucer.' *Chaucer Yearbook* 5 (1998) 1–17.
Slade, Tony. 'Irony in the *Wife of Bath's Tale*.' *Modern Language Review* 64 (1969) 241–7.
Storm, Melvin. 'Alisoun's Ear.' *Modern Language Quarterly* 42 (1981) 219–26.
Szittya, Penn R. 'The Green Yeoman as Loathly Lady: The Friar's Parody of the *Wife of Bath's Tale*.' *PMLA* 90 (1975) 386–94.
Weissman, Hope Phyllis. 'Why Chaucer's Wife is From Bath.' *Chaucer Review* 15 (1980–1) 11–36.

Audio and Video Recordings

Chaucer, Geoffrey. *The Canterbury Tales: The Prologue*. The English Poets from Chaucer to Yeats. The British Council and Oxford University Press. Argo Record Company RG 401.
Chaucer, Geoffrey. *The Canterbury Tales: The Nun's Priest's Tale*. The English Poets from Chaucer to Yeats. The British Council and Oxford University Press. Argo Record Company RG 466.
Chaucer, Geoffrey. *Troilus and Criseyde* (extracts). The English Poets from Chaucer to Yeats. The British Council and Oxford University Press. Argo Record Company ZPL 1003–4.
Chaucer, Geoffrey. *The Canterbury Tales*. Read by Trevor Eaton. Wadhurst: Pavilion Records, 1986–93.
The Miller's Tale (1986) THE 595.
The General Prologue, The Reeve's Tale (1988) THE 606.
The General Prologue, The Pardoner's Prologue and Tale (1988) THE 607.
The Wife of Bath's Prologue and Tale (1989) THE 612.
The Franklin's Prologue and Tale (1989) THE 616.
The Merchant's Prologue and Tale (1990) THE 618.
The Nun's Priest Tale, The Shipman's Tale, The Prioress's Prologue and Tale (1990) THE 619.
The Friar's Prologue and Tale, The Summoner's Prologue and Tale, The Tale of Sir Thopas (1991) THE 620.
The Clerk's Tale, The Physician's Tale (1991) THE 621.
The Knight's Tale (1992) THES 625 (2 cassettes).
The Man of Law's Tale, The Cook's Tale, The Manciple's Tale (1992) THE 626.

Bibliography

The Second Nun's Prologue and Tale, The Canon's Yeoman's Prologue and Tale (1992) THE 629.
The Squire's Tale, The Monk's Tale (1993) THE 630.
The Tale of Melibee (1993) THE 632.
The Parson's Tale (1993) THE 633.
Chaucer, Geoffrey. *The Animated Epics: The Canterbury Tales*, 3 videos. Wetherby: BBC Educational Publishing. 474157; 474165; 542047.
The Chaucer Studio, an organization assisted by the English departments of the University of Adelaide and Brigham Young University, in conjunction with the New Chaucer Society, has recorded an almost complete *Canterbury Tales* and several other works, including the *Book of the Duchess*, the *Parliament of Fowls*, and *Troilus and Criseyde*. For full details, see http://humanities.byu.edu/chaucer/about.htm

Websites and CD-ROMs

Chaucer: Life and Times CD-ROM. Reading: Primary Source Media, 1995.
Chaucer: 'The Wife of Bath's Prologue' on CD-ROM, ed. Peter Robinson. Cambridge: Cambridge University Press on CD-ROM, 1996.
Chaucer: 'The General Prologue' on CD-ROM, ed. Elizabeth Solopova. Cambridge: Cambridge University Press on CD-ROM, 2000.
The Hengwrt Chaucer Digital Facsimile CD-ROM, ed. Estelle Stubbs. Leicester: Scholarly Digital Editions, 2000.
www.luminarium.org/medlit/chaucer.htm (beginner's guide to Chaucer)
http://icg.fas.harvard.edu/~chaucer (beginner's guide to Chaucer)
http://ncs.rutgers.edu (New Chaucer Society)
www.le.ac.uk/engassoc/linkchauc.html (links to Chaucer sites)
http://etext.lib.virginia.edu/mideng.browse.html (complete original text of *Canterbury Tales*)
http://academic.brooklyn.cuny.edu/webcore/murphy/canterbury/ (text of *Canterbury Tales* put into modern spelling and glossed by Michael Murphy)
http://www.canterburytales.org (ELF Edition of *Canterbury Tales*: original text and modern rhymed translation)
http://www.cta.dmu.ac.uk/projects/ctp/ (*Canterbury Tales* Project: transcriptions of all manuscripts and early printed versions into computer-readable form)
http://icg.fas.harvard.edu/~chaucer/vowels.html (guide to Chaucer's pronunciation with audio illustrations)
www.vmi.edu/english/audio/audio_index.html (guide to Chaucer's pronunciation with audio extracts)
www.ancestral.co.uk/gpipes2.htm (discussion of Miller's pipes)
http://cwolf.uaa.alaska.edu/~afdtk/ECT Main htm (The Electronic *Canterbury Tales* with extensive links to other sites)

Index

Addison, Joseph, 6
Aers, David, 136, 161–71, 287, 303
aesthetics, 210–17
Alain de Lille, 29, 84, 85, 95, 102, 221
Alceste, 116–20, 144
Alcyone, 52, 58, 69–70, 72–4
Alexander, 99
Allen, Judson B., 157, 194
Allen, Peter L., 65
Allen, Valerie, 17
amphitheatre, 240
Anderson, J. J., 17
Andrew, Malcolm, 193
Anne of Bohemia, 64, 109
anti-feminism, 65, 144, 283–98
anti-semitism, 270, 272, 280–2
Aquinas, Thomas, 221
Arnold, Matthew, 8
Ashton, Gail, 193
Athanasius, 123
Auchinleck MS, 24–5
audience, 43–56, 69–70
Augustine, 122, 126
authority, 32–43, 86–7, 116–20, 177–85
Axiotis, Ares, 17

Bakhtin, Mikhail, 44, 45 n. 1, 47–8, 196, 252 n. 1, 268
Baldwin, Ralph, 194, 206
Barney, Stephen A., 135

Barrett Browning, Elizabeth, 9
Beaumont, Francis, 6
Bennett, J. A. W., 13, 15, 61–2, 76, 95–101, 106
Benoît de Sainte-Maure, 180, 184, 185
Benson, C. David, 135, 171–6, 194
Benson, Larry D., 9
Bernard of Clairvaux, 37, 39
Bethurum, Dorothy, 134
Bible, 23, 32, 57, 283
bibliographical guides, 17
Birney, Earle, 197
Bishop, Ian, 269–83
Bisson, Lillian M., 16
Black Knight, 49–52, 69–70, 73–4
Blake, N. F., 194
Blake, William, 7
Blamires, Alcuin, 65, 193
Blanche, Duchess of Lancaster, 44, 49–52, 58, 73
Bloomfield, Morton, 134, 174
Boccaccio, 46, 85, 90, 93, 95, 98–100, 102, 109, 124, 129–30, 131, 134, 135, 140, 152, 156, 164, 171–2, 175, 179, 181, 191, 232, 240, 242–8
Boethius, 23, 29, 33, 84–5, 105, 173, 233, 240, 247, 251
Boitani, Piero, 17, 62, 83–96
Book of the Duchess, 3, 14, 23–5, 44, 49–52, 57–60, 68–76

350

Index

books *see* authority
Booth, Wayne, 175
Bowden, Muriel, 195, 205–6
Breton lay *see* Marie de France
Brewer, Derek, 15, 17, 22–32
Bronson, Bertrand, 173, 204
Brown, Peter, 16, 193, 196
Bryan, W. F., 10
Bukton, 49, 313
Burlin, Robert, 197, 315
Burnley, David, 16
Burrow, John, 17, 267
Butcher, Andrew, 16, 196

Cannon, Christopher, 16
canon, 9
Canterbury Tales, 3, 15, 31–2, 189–324
  General Prologue, 190–1, 203–4, 222–8, 293, 314
  Canon's Yeoman's Tale, 251, 262–5
  Clerk's Tale, 300–1, 316–17
  Cook's Tale, 264
  Franklin's Tale, 37–8, 262, 267, 299–306
  Knight's Tale, 150, 153, 155, 234–7, 239–48, 251, 262, 303
  Man of Law's Tale, 281, 310–11
  Merchant's Tale, 38–9, 236–7, 292–3, 297–8
  Miller's Tale, 26, 38, 150, 234–5, 239, 251, 254, 259–63
  Monk's Tale, 143, 147
  Nun's Priest's Tale, 37, 39–41, 102, 280–1
  Pardoner's Tale, 257, 264–7, 309, 314–17
  Parson's Tale, 251, 256–9, 261–3, 266–7
  Physician's Tale, 269–71, 273–8
  Prioress's Tale, 269–82
  Reeve's Tale, 251, 254, 259–60, 263
  Retractions, 251
  Second Nun's Tale, 121, 126, 269–71, 284
  Shipman's Tale, 265–6, 313
  Squire's Tale, 236–7
  Summoner's Tale, 267
  Tale of Melabee, 45–6
  Tale of Sir Thopas, 25
  Wife of Bath's Prologue and Tale, 26, 41–3, 251, 262, 265–6, 283–98, 300, 305–14, 317
Capellanus, Andreas, 12–13
Catherine of Siena, 151, 154
Cato, 38
Caxton, William, 5
chain of love, 150–8
Chartier, Alain, 100
chastity, 269–82, 284–8, 300–6
Chaucer, Geoffrey
  cultural influences on, 22–3
  life, 3–4
  literary influences on: classical, 31; English, 22–7; French, 27–30; Machaut, 23, 29–30; religious, 31–2; *Roman de la Rose*, 27–9
  marriage to Philippa de Roet, 3, 51
  see also titles of individual works
Chaucer, Lewis, 4
Chaumpaigne, Cecily, 4
Chesterton, G. K., 11
Child, F. J., 9
Chrétien de Troyes, 23, 82, 155
Cicero, 57, 59–60, 97, 102, 104–7, 109, 113
Clanvowe, Sir John, 110
class, 43–5, 48–52, 112
Claudian, 99
Clemen, Wolfgang, 76–82
Cleopatra, 118, 123
clerks, 283–98, 299–306
Coghill, Nevill, 11
Coleridge, 7
Complaint of Nature see Alain de Lille
Confessio Amantis see Gower, John
confession, 251, 254–69
Conrad, Joseph, 174, 206
Consolation of Philosophy see Boethius
Cooper, Helen, 17, 193–5, 218–39
court, 44, 48–9

351

Index

Cowen, Janet M., 64
Craik, T. W., 195
Crane, Susan, 195, 299, 301, 304–5
critical approaches
  bibliographical, 21 n. 45
  cultural, 15–16, 20 n. 38
  deconstructive, 68
  editing, 8–9
  exegetical, 14–15
  feminist, 16, 20 n. 41, 161–71, 197, 283–324
  hermeneutics, 68
  historicist, 20 n. 11
  linguistic, 9–10, 20 n. 39
  Marxist, 16
  New Critical, 13–14, 140, 197
  new historicist, 15–16, 20 n. 41, 43–4, 163–9, 195
  postmodern, 16, 20 n. 41, 68
  pre-1950, 10–13
  psychoanalytical, 196, 307–17
  rhetoric and poetics, 19 n. 36
  sources, 19–21 n. 37, 42
  speech act theory, 47–8
Crosby, Ruth, 10
Crow, Martin, 10
Curry, 134, 195
Curtius, Ernst Robert, 97

Dame Sirith, 254
Dante, 12, 33, 35–7, 39, 59–60, 62, 84–6, 88–9, 94–5, 97, 99, 104, 107, 134–5, 149, 154, 171, 174, 211, 221, 271
Dares, 99, 180
dating, 20 n. 18
Davenport, W. A., 63, 195, 250–69
David, Alfred, 50, 164, 194, 303
Decameron see Boccaccio
Delany, Sheila, 63, 95
Dempster, Germaine, 10
Deschamps, Eustache, 1, 23, 27, 30, 286, 288–91
di Nardo, Mariotto, 243
Diamond, Arlyn, 197
Dictys, 180

Dido, 33, 59, 76–82
Dinshaw, Carolyn, 136, 173, 197, 303, 307–24
Divine Comedy see Dante
Dodd, W. G., 12, 133
Donaldson, E. Talbot, 13, 15, 133, 135, 139–50, 171, 173, 176, 202, 204
Donnelly, Colleen, 63
Douglas, Gavin, 5, 197
drama, roadside, 10–11, 194, 196, 198, 201–10
Dream of Scipio see Cicero
dream theory, 33–7, 39–41, 70–1, 87–9, 102–8, 280
dream vision poetry, 57–128
Dryden, John, 6–7, 9
Dunbar, William, 1, 5

eagle, 34–5, 46, 84–9, 92, 95
Early English Text Society, 9
Economou, George, 17
editions, 20 n. 6
Edward I, 280
Edward III, 52, 270, 276
Elizabeth, Countess of Ulster, 3
Ellesmere MS, 194, 215, 217
Ellis, Roger, 197
Ellis, Steve, 193
Empson, William, 13
encyclopedia tradition, 28, 212, 218–39
Epistola Valerii, 286, 288–91
estates satire, 190–1, 225
eunuchs, 309, 314–17
Eve, 283–4
Everett, Dorothy, 10
exemplum, 116–17, 122–4

fabliau, 195, 228, 230–1, 250–1, 254, 259–63, 265–9
Fame, 59, 81, 83–96
Faulkner, William, 206
Ferster, Judith, 63, 68–76
films, 12
fin'amors see love, courtly
formalism, 47–8

Index

formulae, 235–7
Fortune, 95, 131, 240, 242
Foucault, Michel, 44, 45 n. 1, 46
Frank, Robert Worth, 64, 118
Froissart, Jean, 23–4, 27, 30, 52, 58
Frye, Northrop, 233
Furnivall, F. J., 9
Fyler, 119

Ganim, John, 196
gardens, 239, 242–8
Gardner, Helen, 158
Gawain-poet, 30, 255, 258, 273–4, 276
genre, 192, 239–50
gentillesse, 299–306
Geoffrey of Vinsauf, 156, 214, 217
glossing, 307–13
God of Love, 116–18
Goddard, H. C., 117
Gordon, Ida L., 134, 174–5
Gothic, 23, 26, 28–30, 63, 194, 201–2, 210–11, 214–15, 218
Gower, John, 1, 26, 30, 221, 251–3, 256, 266, 268
Green, Richard Firth, 65
Gregory the Great, 154
Guido delle Colonne, 180, 184
Guillaume de Lorris, 27–8, 30, 57, 98–100; *see also Roman de la Rose*
Guy of Warwick, 25

hagiography, 121–6, 229–30, 269
Hallissy, Margaret, 197
Hanning, Robert W., 195
Hansen, Elaine Tuttle, 64, 136, 197, 284
Harley lyrics, 25–6
Harvey, Gabriel, 6
Havely, N. R., 15
Hazlitt, William, 7
heart, 150–8
Heinrich von Veldecke, 82
Henryson, Robert, 1, 129
hermeneutics, 68, 69 n. 1, 70
Heroides see Ovid
Hill, John M., 197

Hines, John, 195
history, Trojan, 177–86
Hoccleve, 5, 30
Holy Innocents, 270, 274
Homer, 31, 144, 180, 182
homosexuality, 309, 315–16
House of Fame, 3, 33–5, 57–9, 76–82, 108, 223, 233, 317
Housman, A. E., 9
Howard, Donald R., 15, 194, 212–18, 241
Hunt, Leigh, 7, 9
Huppé, Bernard F., 15
Hurd, Richard, 7
hymns, 157, 279

iconography, 217, 239–50
imagery, 150–8, 239–48
introductory works, 17
Irigaray, Luce, 307, 309 n. 1, 311
Italy, 23

James, Henry, 201–3
Jankin, 293–8
Jean de la Mote, 58
Jean de Meun, 28–9, 57, 98–9, 114, 221; *see also Roman de la Rose*
Jerome, 283–93, 295, 310, 312
John of Gaunt, 3, 44, 49–52, 58, 69, 73
Johnson, Samuel, 7
Jones, Terry, 195–6, 226
Jordan, Robert M., 15, 63, 173–4, 194, 196, 201–12, 219
Joseph of Exeter, 99
Josipovici, Gabriel, 32–43
Jost, J. E., 197
Jovinian, 287
Judaism, 270, 272, 280–2
Jung, 102

Kaminsky, Alice R., 133
Kelly, H. A., 134
Kendrick, Laura, 196
Ker, W. P., 8
Kerkhof, J., 16

353

Index

Kiser, Lisa J., 63–4, 119, 121–8
Kittredge, G. L., 10–11, 14, 16, 134, 197, 202, 205, 250
Knapp, Peggy, 196
Knight, Stephen, 47–58, 63, 226–7
Koff, Leonard Michael, 197
Kolve, V. A., 195, 232, 239–50
Koonce, B. G., 95
Kruger, Stephen F., 63, 65

Lacan, Jacques, 307, 309 n. 1
Lactantius, 98
Langland, William, 30, 33, 36–7, 39, 91, 211, 217, 221, 225–6, 251, 255–7, 262–3, 268
Laskaya, Anna, 197
Lawton, David, 175, 196
Leavis, F. R., 13–14
Legend of Good Women, 3, 33, 36, 57, 59, 61, 77, 82, 115–28, 140, 144, 161, 236, 284–5, 302
   Prologue, 115–21, 123
Leicester, H. Marshall, 196
Lenaghan, R. T., 51
Lerer, Seth, 195
Lévi-Strauss, Claude, 109, 311
Lewis, C. S., 12–13, 15–16, 46, 61, 76, 93, 96, 98, 122, 133
Leyerle, John, 17, 150–60
Lindahl, Carl, 196
Livre du cueur d'amour épris, 155
Livy, 273
locus amoenus, 97–100
Lollius, 133, 172, 176
London, 23, 44, 48
Loomis, Roger Sherman, 10
Lounsbury, Thomas R., 10
love, courtly, 12–13, 132, 135, 150–1, 165, 169, 219, 246
Lowes, John Livingston, 117, 209
Lucan, 31
Lucrece, 122, 125–6
Lumiansky, R. M., 194, 206
Lydgate, John, 1, 5, 30
lyrics, 25–7

McAlpine, Monica, 134
McGerr, Rosemarie, 63
Machaut, Guillaume de, 23, 27, 29–30, 51–2, 58, 69, 74, 82
Macrobius, 33, 40, 87, 102, 106; *see also* dream theory
magic, 299, 301–2
Malone, Kemp, 13
Mandel, Jerome, 194
Mandeville, Sir John, 31
Manly, J. M., 9–11, 15, 195, 202, 205
Mann, Jill, 17, 64, 136, 195, 197, 283–99, 307, 309
Marie de France, 23, 299, 306
marriage group, 11, 17, 232, 299
marriage, 165–9, 283–98
Martianus Capella, 84, 89, 95
Martin, Priscilla, 136, 197
Master of René of Anjou, 243
Matheolus, 286
Matthew of Vendôme, 278
Medvedev, P. N., 47–8
memory, 212–14
Menippean satire, 233
Mersand, Joseph, 9
Metamorphoses see Ovid
Middleton, Thomas, 28
Miller, Jacqueline, 63
Miller, Robert P., 15, 316
Minnis, Alistair, 17
minstrels, 24
miracle tale, 269–82
Mizener, Arthur, 162
moral tale, 269–82
Moritz, T. A., 194
Morpheus, 52, 69, 72–3
Morse, Ruth, 63
Muscatine, Charles, 13–15, 61–2, 63, 162, 173
Myles, Robert, 197

narrator, 2–3, 30, 32–43, 49–52, 71–4, 104–6, 132–3, 139–49, 171–6
Nature, 97–101, 109–14, 164, 276–7

Index

nucleus, 150–8
Nykrog, Per, 267

Olson, Clair C., 10
Olsson, Paul, 305
Oton de Graunson, 58
Ovid, 6, 23, 29, 31, 52, 69, 73, 76–82, 85, 91, 108, 119, 191, 196, 241, 285
Owen, Charles, A., 194
Owl and the Nightingale, 111
Oxford English Dictionary, 9

paradise, earthly, 97–100
Pardoner, 228, 309, 314–17
Paris, Gaston, 12
parliament, 111–12
Parliament of Fowls, 3, 57, 59–60, 96–115, 150, 161
Parson, 225–6
Patch, Howard R., 134
Patterson, Lee, 134, 177–88, 293, 315
Paul, St, 89, 284
Payne, Robert O., 162, 174
Pearl see Gawain-poet
Pearsall, Derek, 15, 193
penitentials, 231
Percival, Florence, 64–5
Petrarch, 46, 85, 90, 93, 95, 240
Philippa de Roet, 3, 51
Phillips, Edward, 6
Phillips, Helen, 193
Piers Plowman see Langland, William
pilgrimage, 189–90, 222, 239–41
Ploughman, 225
Pope, Alexander, 7, 93, 95, 99
Pratt, Robert A., 313
Preston, Raymond, 13
prison, 151, 239, 242–8
prose, 32
Provost, William, 174
Puttenham, George, 6

Quick, Anne, 17

radio broadcasts, 12
reception theory, 45 n. 1, 47
Richard II, 69–70, 102, 109
Richards, I. A., 13
Rickert, Edith, 9–10
Ricks, Christopher, 295
Rigby, S. H., 195
rime royal, 96–7, 129
Robertson, D. W., 14–15, 17, 34, 41–2, 63, 134, 161, 163–4, 176, 193, 194
Robinson, F. N., 9, 117
Rogers, William E., 194
Roman de la Rose, 3, 23, 27–9, 57, 59, 61, 82, 98, 102, 107–9, 114, 116, 155–7, 265–6, 277–8, 285–6, 288–91, 293
romance, 24–5, 229–30, 253, 299–306
Romaunt of the Rose, 23, 27; *see also Roman de la Rose*
Rooney, Anne, 17
Root, R. K., 9, 134
Rowe, Donald W., 115–21, 134
Rowland, Beryl, 17
Ruggiers, Paul, 194
Rumour, 84, 86–7, 91–2, 95
Ruskin, 7

saints' lives *see* hagiography
Salter, Elizabeth, 48, 164, 174
Sandras, E. G., 9
satire, 251–69
Schoeck, Richard J., 17
Scogan, 49
sermon, 231, 251, 255–9, 261–3, 266–7
Servius, 183
sins, deadly, 255–69
Sir Degaré, 25
Sir Gawain and the Green Knight see Gawain-poet
Skeat, W. W., 9
Solomonic proverbs, 286
Somnium Scipionis see Cicero
South English Legendary, 280
Spearing, A. C., 63, 101–15, 135

355

Index

Speirs, John, 13
Spenser, Edmund, 6
Stanley, E. G., 135
Statius, 31, 97–9
Stevens, John, 135
story collections, 191, 218–39
Strohm, Paul, 43–56, 63
summa see encyclopedia tradition
Surrey, Henry Howard, Earl of, 6
Sypher, Wylie, 210–11
Sypherd, W. G., 95
Szarmach, Paul E., 17

Taylor, Jerome, 17
ten Brink, Bernard, 9
Theophrastus, 285, 288–9, 295
Thomas à Becket, St, 189, 270
Thynne, William, 5, 8
Tickhill Psalter, 215–17
Tolkien, J. R. R., 76, 96
Towneley plays, 258
tragedy, 230
Treatise of the Astrolabe, 4, 6
Troilus and Criseyde, 3, 12, 14–15, 61, 129–88
trouthe, 299–306
Troynovant, 177
Tschann, Judith, 197
Tuke, Sir Brian, 5
Tyrwhitt, Thomas, 8

Urry, John, 8
Usk, Thomas, 1, 3

Valentine, St, 60, 112, 114
Venus, 60, 76, 78, 84, 87, 90, 92, 95, 102, 108–9, 112–13
Villon, 100
Vincent of Beauvais, 221
Virgil, 31, 59, 76–82, 84–5, 87, 90, 92–3, 95, 98, 143–4, 177, 182–3
virginity *see* chastity
Voloshinov, V. N., 47–8

Wallace, David, 195
Warton, Joseph, 7
Warton, Thomas, 7
Weisl, Angela Jane, 299–307
Wetherbee, Winthrop, 173
widowhood, 165–9
Wife of Bath, 224, 228, 283–98, 307–14, 317
Wimsatt, James I., 61, 63
Wimsatt, W. K., 13, 15
Windeatt, B. A., 15, 135
Wölfflin, Heinrich, 210
Woolf, Virginia, 11
Wordsworth, William, 9, 272
Wyatt, Sir Thomas, 5–6

Zacher, Christian K., 17